Lecture Notes in Computer Science   1526
Edited by G. Goos, J. Hartmanis and J. van Leeuwen

Springer
*Berlin
Heidelberg
New York
Barcelona
Hong Kong
London
Milan
Paris
Singapore
Tokyo*

Manfred Broy Bernhard Rumpe (Eds.)

Requirements Targeting Software and Systems Engineering

International Workshop RTSE'97
Bernried, Germany, October 12-14, 1997
Proceedings

 Springer

Series Editors

Gerhard Goos, Karlsruhe University, Germany
Juris Hartmanis, Cornell University, NY, USA
Jan van Leeuwen, Utrecht University, The Netherlands

Volume Editors

Manfred Broy
Bernhard Rumpe
Institut für Informatik, Technische Universität München
Arcisstraße 21, D-80290 München, Germany
E-mail: {broy,rumpe}@in.tum.de

Cataloging-in-Publication data applied for

Die Deutsche Bibliothek - CIP-Einheitsaufnahme

Requirements targeting software and systems engineering : proceedings /
International Workshop RTSE'97, Bernried, Germany, October 12 - 14, 1997.
Manfred Broy ; Bernhard Rumpe (ed.). - Berlin ; Heidelberg ; New York ;
Barcelona ; Hong Kong ; London ; Milan ; Paris ; Singapore ; Tokyo : Springer, 1998
 (Lecture notes in computer science ; Vol. 1526)
ISBN 3-540-65309-0

CR Subject Classification (1998): D.2, F.3

ISSN 0302-9743
ISBN 3-540-65309-0 Springer-Verlag Berlin Heidelberg New York

This work is subject to copyright. All rights are reserved, whether the whole or part of the material is
concerned, specifically the rights of translation, reprinting, re-use of illustrations, recitation, broadcasting,
reproduction on microfilms or in any other way, and storage in data banks. Duplication of this publication
or parts thereof is permitted only under the provisions of the German Copyright Law of September 9, 1965,
in its current version, and permission for use must always be obtained from Springer-Verlag. Violations are
liable for prosecution under the German Copyright Law.

© Springer-Verlag Berlin Heidelberg 1998
Printed in Germany

Typesetting: Camera-ready by author
SPIN 10692867   06/3142 – 5 4 3 2 1 0   Printed on acid-free paper

Preface

Software engineering research has different profiles in Europe and North America. While in North America there is a lot of knowhow in the practical, technical, and organizational aspects of software engineering, in Europe the work concentrates more on foundations and formal modeling of software engineering issues. Both approaches have their individual strengths and weaknesses. Research driven solely by practice in software engineering runs the danger of developing into a shallow field that fails to find a solid scientific basis or to contribute substantially to the progress in software engineering. Work concentrating on formal aspects alone is in the danger of becoming too theoretical and isolated from practice, so that any transfer into practical application will fail.

Substantial progress in software engineering can be achieved, however, by bringing together pragmatic and foundational work in software engineering research. This can provide a step toward a common scientific basis for software engineering that allows us to integrate the various research results, leading to fruitful synergetic effects. It will also help to identify critical research paths and to develop an appropriate paradigm for the scientific discipline of software engineering.

In software and systems engineering it is necessary to distinguish the enormous difference between the dynamics in development we refer to and the limited scope assumed by many of today's software managers who still use outdated techniques. Many of the unsolved problems associated with the old techniques are symptoms of a lack of formalization and a lack of automation support.

It was the goal of this workshop to bring together experts from science and practice in software and systems engineering from North America and Europe. The workshop focused on unified sets of formal models and associated methods suitable for automation for many aspects of software development, in particular those that address change and those that apply on a large scale. Some of the aspects of software evolution are

- modifiable software architectures,
- resource changes,
- context changes,
- requirements changes,
- changes to decomposition structures, and
- changes in plans.

These issues are closely related to formal representations of the version history, and formal representations of the activities that produced existing versions or have been proposed to produce future versions. The essence of the software engineering product model is to establish and maintain consistency among various kinds of software artifacts throughout the development and evolution process, including consistency between requirements, architectures, and programs. Automated support is needed to determine dependencies and to use this dependency information to provide decision aid for software synthesis, analysis, and evolution. Many versions of each artifact are produced as the software evolves, and changes in the dependency structure must be recognized and reacted to. The challenge is to formalize the problems in this area better, and to develop some of the badly needed technical solutions.

If we as a community can succeed in doing this, the results will provide convincing evidence that formal methods can have strong practical value, and help reverse the trend of weakening support for the subject from both industry and governments. It seems that previous work on formal methods can be applied to problems related to these topics, but it may require non-traditional approaches. This challenge helped to trigger new ideas at the workshop, and perhaps opened new opportunities for progress.

It is well recognized nowadays that software and systems engineering is an important issue in technical systems that still lacks a proper scientific basis. Numerous initiatives in academia, especially under the heading of formal methods, toward such a scientific basis have produced many valuable and interesting scientific results; but still a lot of work lies ahead of us to actually integrate this with the practice of software engineering. Nevertheless, we can observe that a beginning has been made to bring together practical and scientific approaches. A good example for this is the Unified Modeling Language, which was designed only recently and will evolve further. The fact that a proper semantic basis is needed for proper methodological support is much more widely recognized than before. Further efforts are now needed to give scientific research the right focus on the questions that are important in practice and to stimulate a transfer of ideas between academia and application. It was the goal of the workshop to contribute to this process.

The workshop took place in early October 1997 in Bernried, Germany. It was a highly successful event and an encouraging step toward the unification of the various aspects and techniques of software and systems engineering. It is our pleasure to thank Luqi for excellent cooperation in preparing and implementing the workshop and Sascha Molterer for his distinguished help in organizing the workshop. We also thank the Army Research Office and in particular Dave Hislop for financial support.

August 1998   Manfred Broy, Bernhard Rumpe

Table of Contents

Foundations of Software Engineering

Domains as a Prerequisite for Requirements and Software Domain
Perspectives & Facets, Requirements Aspects and Software Views 1
  Dines Bjørner

Software and System Modeling Based on a Unified Formal Semantics 43
  *Manfred Broy, Franz Huber, Barbara Paech, Bernhard Rumpe,
  Katharina Spies*

Postmodern Software Design with NYAM: Not Yet Another Method 69
  Roel Wieringa

Methodology

A Discipline for Handling Feature Interaction 95
  Egidio Astesiano, Gianna Reggio

Merging Changes to Software Specifications 121
  Valdis Berzins

Combining and Distributing Hierarchical Systems 133
  Chris George, Đỗ Tiến Dũng

Software Engineering Issues for Network Computing 155
  Carlo Ghezzi, Giovanni Vigna

A Two-Layered Approach to Support Systematic Software Development . . 179
  Maritta Heisel, Stefan Jähnichen

Evaluation and Case Studies

A Framework for Evaluating System and Software Requirements
Specification Approaches 203
  Erik Kamsties, H. Dieter Rombach

Formal Methods and Industrial-Strength Computer Networks 223
  Joy Reed

Tool Support and Prototyping

Integration Tools Supporting Development Processes 235
   Stefan Gruner, Manfred Nagl, Andy Schürr

Formal Models and Prototyping 257
   Luqi

Abstraction and Modular Verification of Infinite-State Reactive Systems .. 273
   Zohar Manna, Michael A. Colón, Bernd Finkbeiner, Henny B. Sipma, Tomás E. Uribe

NSA's MISSI Reference Architecture - Moving from Prose to Precise
Specification 293
   Sigurd Meldal, David C. Luckham

Requirements Engineering Repositories: Formal Support for Informal
Teamwork Methods 331
   Hans W. Nissen, Matthias Jarke

Author Index 357

Domains as a Prerequisite for Requirements and Software
Domain Perspectives & Facets, Requirements Aspects and Software Views

Dines Bjørner

Department of Information Technology
Bldg. 344, Technical University of Denmark
DK–2800 Lyngby, Denmark
Fax: +45-45.88.45.30; E–Mail: db@it.dtu.dk; URL: http://www.it.dtu.dk/~db

Abstract. We take software [systems] engineering to consist of three major phases: domain engineering, requirements engineering and software [systems] design engineering. We outline these and emphasise domain perspectives andfacets, requirements aspects and software architecture and program organisation views.

This paper is the direct result of a US Office of Army Research October 12–14, 1997 workshop on *Requirements Targeting Software and Systems Engineering* held at Bernried am Staarnberger See, Bavaria, Germany. In consonance with the aims & objectives of that workshop we conclude some subsections with a set of meta–requirements (i.e. requirements to *software engineering, its research, education and practice*).

The paper is discursive and informal: we identify a number of methodological principles, techniques and tools. Not all such (hence discursive) and not all necessarily formalisable (hence informal). Wrt. the latter: one cannot formalise the principles that are needed in a systematic, well-guided process of selecting and applying techniques and tools in the analysis and synthesis of specifications — whether of domain, requirements or software. Instead we are left to conjecture the usefulness of certain such principles, techniques and tools. Sometimes such conjectures are refuted when better principles, techniques and tools are proposed.

Some sociological issues of 'formal methods' are summarised (in section 4.5).

Since this paper will appear in a workshop proceedings with a number of other papers from that workshop, the paper will not repeat the relevant points made by other workshop participants and supposedly published in their contributions. I refer, amongst several, to contributions made at the workshop by Carl Gunther, Anthony Finkelstein, Michael Jackson, Tom Maibaum and others.

On issues of requirements, I have, in particular, benefited much from [83, 82, 111]. The handy book [82] is simply a pearl: delightful and thought provoking!

1 Introduction

We present an interpretation of the state of affairs, i.e. level of professionalism, in software engineering, the thesis of this paper, and a first justification of the thesis.

1.1 The State of Affairs

In the US more than USD 180 billion was spent in 1996 on software development projects that were curtailed, given up and abandoned, because management did not believe they could conclude these projects. Most often cited reasons for this failure were: The requirements were insufficient, elusive or changed, and the domains were not properly understood. This is according to the article: *Formal Methods: Promises and Problems,* IEEE Software, Vol. 14, No. 1, Jan. 1997, pp. 73-85. USD 180 billion is a sizable amount.

To this we can add that even if and when developers get the domains and requirements right, they often get the implementation wrong — but this aspects apparently does not bother people who willingly buy MicroSoft software even when it is known that it definitely contains thousands upon thousands of (even known) bugs.

A survey, in Europe, by the industry 'Think Tank' ESI, the European Software Institute in Bilbao, Spain, records that most software industry managers express that their most urgent problems have to do with grossly insufficient methods, techniques and especially tools for coping with requirements definitions — and they are basically unaware of the pre-cursor to requirements development, namely domain modelling!

1.2 The Thesis — and the Contributions

The thesis of this paper is that the kind of domain, requirements, software architecture and program organisation principles and techniques expounded in this paper — and which have been rather thoroughly tried out over the last many years (to which later citations are given) — seems to offer workable solutions to the problems. At least they address the issues "head-on" and in a systematic manner not yet reported this extensively. Besides the 'triptych' decomposition of development into domain, requirements, software architecture and program organisation organisation, we also would offer the identification of domain perspectives and facets, the requirements aspects and the redefinition of software views as a contribution.

1.3 The 'Triptych'

Software (systems) engineering, to us:

- "Starts"[1] with domain engineering. Result: A formal theory $\mathcal{D}$.

---

[1] We often put double quotes around words when their meaning is only approximate. The actual sequence from 'start' to 'conclusion' is usually iterative and "spiral"!

- "Goes on" with requirements engineering. Result: A formal theory $\mathcal{R}$.
- "Concludes" with software (systems) design engineering. Result: A formal theory $\mathcal{S}$

Lest the point be missed: domain engineering is **not** requirements engineering. Many ideas of the current practice of requirements engineering more properly belong to domain engineering in the sense being defined here.

We expect the following kind of relationship[2] to hold between $\mathcal{D}, \mathcal{R}, \mathcal{S}$:

- $\mathcal{D}, \mathcal{S} \models \mathcal{R}$

A classical example is compiler development:

- **Domain:**
  We define the concrete (BNF) and the abstract syntaxes, the abstract mathematical semantics of the source and target languages (programming, resp. (e.g.) machine), and a proof system for the source language.
- **Requirements:**
  We define the specific compiler and run-time requirements: fast compilation, or fast execution, or extensive compilation diagnostics, or extensive run-time execution diagnostics, or some combination of these (+ many other facets).
- **Design:**
  We develop the compiler and run-time systems: possibly a single or a multi--pass compiler while using such design tools as lexical scanner generators, (possibly syntax error correcting) parser generators, (possibly a variety of) attribute grammar evaluators, etc.

We define:

- A **method** is a set of principles, techniques and tools for analysing problems and for selecting and applying techniques and tools in order efficiently to construct an efficient artifact — here software (a system).
- **Methodology** is the study and knowledge of methods.

Jackson [83, 82] has proposed a decomposition of the unending variety of problems for which software engineers are expected to develop software solutions, into a possibly in[de]finite set of problem frames. Our compiler development example above thus is archetypical of a 'translation problem frame'. Each frame is characterised by its distinct cluster of development principles, techniques and tools. Therefore we speak not of one method but of possibly an in[de]finite collection of methods.

Common to these, we argue [27], is that they all evolve along domain, requirements and design engineering axes.

---

[2] See Carl Gunther [65].

1.4 First Justifications

Software offers functions. Usually the client expresses expectations about the software to be delivered: that is, requirements that include characterisations of externally observable properties of these functions.

So before we develop software we ought know very precisely the externally observable, that is: the user expectations about the concepts & facilities to be offered by the software.

These requirements usually deal with components, actions and behaviours of the client domain, the application domain. And usually the requirements are expressed in terms of terms (nouns and verbs) that 'reside' in — are special, professional terms of — the domain.

So before we develop the requirements definition it seems a good idea to recognise, discover and capture the domain and to make precise the structure and meaning of all the special, professional domain terms otherwise used in informally expressing requirements.

The situation is not new. In other engineering branches we encounter the need for securing the domain understanding — and usually also formally — before requirements are expressed. In control engineering for aerospace the domain is typically that of Kepler's and Newton's laws. So there was Johannes and Isaac working on their laws only to get an understanding of celestial mechanics, or to prove the existence (or non-existence) of God, or at least to be able to calculate (predict) planetary movements. There was, in those days, little expectation of the laws being generally applicable, and certainly not to for example automotive engineering or satellite orbit determination. Usually a problem in these areas starts with the control engineer specialising the normative theories of Kepler and Newton to the specifics of the problem at hand. Requirements are then usually expressed as constraints on the mechanical behaviours specified (typically) by the differential equations that describe the instantiated problem domain (i.e. instantiated theory). Control design then finds controllers $(\mathcal{S})$ and show that they satisfy the requirements $(\mathcal{R})$ under the assumption of the domain model $(\mathcal{D})$. One would never dream of hiring a person to develop control for flight systems unless they were well-educated and professionally specialised in the appropriate control, respectively aerospace engineering disciplines.

Similarly for electrical and communications engineers, etcetera. They, or you, may not think that the laws of electronics (Ohm's, Kirschoff's, etc.), or Maxwell's equations, constitute domain models; but that is what they do! And so it goes. One would never dream of hiring a person to develop sensor electronics or space communications for flight systems unless they were well-educated and professionally specialised in the appropriate electronics and communications engineering disciplines.

It is high time that software engineers become as smart and mature, productive and responsible, professional and specialised as other engineers. On one hand most practising software engineers today are unaware of the advances wrt., and the broad applicability of formal techniques — available for many years now. On the other hand: how can they believe that they can develop software for

banking, railway or manufacturing industry applications without having studied
— or themselves developed — appropriate domain theories for these application
areas ?

1.5 Structure and Form of Paper

The rest of the paper essential contains three main sections: domain engineering, requirements engineering and software (and systems) design. An appendix suggests a terminology for software engineering in the light of this 'triptych'.

The paper summarises a rather comprehensive view of software engineering, trying to come to terms with many methodological issues that the author believes are not sufficiently treated in the literature, and at least not with the "slant" given here.

As such the paper could also be used in class! Objections that we do not properly treat the concept of design calculi are being "resolved" by numerous references to documents in which our collaborators over the past some 10 years covers calculation issues in a substantial manner.

2 Domain Engineering

The aim of domain engineering is to develop, together with stake-holders of, or in, the selected domain, a precise set of concordant descriptions of the domain, a set that the parties, developers and stake-holders, can agree upon.

Thus we foresee some set of loose contractual obligations binding the two parties.

From a formal point of view, domain engineering establishes the theory $\mathcal{D}$.

2.1 Example Domains — Infrastructures

Examples of domains, limited to infrastructure systems, are:

- **Transport Systems:** [101]
  - **Railways** [14, 28, 37, 49, 20, 21]
  - **Air: Trafic and Lines** [17, 11]
  - **Metropolitan Transport** (bus, train, taxi, ec.) [109, 46]
  - **Shipping**
- **Manufacturing Industry:** [61, 62, 6, 85, 7, 84, 86]
  Infrastructures 'connecting' software packages(across each of the individual (intra: (i)), respectively between these (inter: (ii)) spectra: (i) marketing, design, order processing, shop floor production, warehousing, sales, service, etc., and (ii) suppliers and consumers, producers and traders, etc.
- **Financial Service Industry:**
  With individual models, and with models that span across the entire industry:
  - **Banking:** Demand/deposit, savings & loan, investment, etc. [18, 90, 19]

- **Insurance Companies:** Health, life, accident, theft, risk, etc.
- **Securities:** Exchanges, brokers, traders, etc.
- Etcetera: credit card and bank cheque clearing; portfolio management, etc.

– **Ministry of Finance:** [44]
– **Health Care Systems**
– **Decision Support Systems for Sustainable Development:** [69, 15]
– **Resource Management:** [16, 102]
– *&c.*

We have affixed a number of citations to a rather limited selection of documents. They all relate to either work that we have done or to projects that we have lead. The purpose, therefore, of the citations is to act as a way of substantiating what could be, and by some early readers have been seen as mere claims.

2.2 First Aims of Domain Engineering

An aim of domain engineering is to provide partial and sufficient answers to questions like: *What is a railway company?, a transport industry?, a bank?, a financial service industry?, a manufacturing enterprise?*, respectively: *What is a manufacturing industry?* The question is expected answered without any reference to possible requirements to potential software, and (certainly) without any reference to implementations of such software — as the domain in question already exists, existed (or still exists) without any software for a long time. We expect the domain description to be both informal, but in the professional language of the domain (including its diagrammatic and other linguistic devices), and formal, in the form of a formal specification of the crucial terms (viz.: nouns and verbs) of the professional domain language(s). We will not in this paper analyse any perceived problem of extracting or communicating this domain knowledge.

A domain description is a model of the domain, that is: necessarily an abstraction. To conquer possible complexities of the domain we may focus on various **perspectives** of the domain — i.e. understandings as held by various groups of domain stake-holders.

2.3 Domain Models — An Example: Railway Systems

Let us try give an example. The problem of giving an example of a domain model of a sizable domain is that the example need be kept within limits, but the domain is usually perceived, by the reader, as being inordinately complex and "large".

First we give an informal description — which ideally consists of a triple: a **synopsis**, a **narrative** and a **terminology**. Then we present a formal specification (in the RAISE [64] Specification Language: RSL [63]).

Synopsis, Narrative & Terminology

- **Synopsis:**[3]
  A synopsis is a terse informal text which — by mentioning, in a reasonably structured and "softly" enumerative way, the names of a number of components, actions and behaviours — may lead the reader onto *'what the whole thing is all about'*.

  | **Example 1: Railways**

  The domain (and hence its description) is normative,[4] and is that of railway systems. Common to these we find that railway systems can be characterised in terms of the railway net with lines and stations, of timetables, of traffic (in terms of the movement of trains), of passenger and freight ticket and space reservation, ticketing, loading and unloading, of the shunting and marshaling of trains, of various concerns about rolling stock, of the management and human operation of the system, and of repair, maintenance and development of all of these resources.
  End of Example 1 |

- **Narrative:**[5] A narrative is a careful description of all the relevant notions of the described "thing":

  | **Example 2: Railways**

  * **Railway Nets**: A net consists of lines and stations. A line connects two distinct stations.
    Stations consists of tracks and other combinations of rail units. Lines and tracks consists of sequences of linear units.[6] Lines can be seen as a sequence of blocks which are then sequences of linear units.
    Units have connectors. A linear unit is a unit with exactly two connectors. A switch (unit) has three connectors. A cross-over (unit) has four connectors. Etc.[7]
    Connectors have identity. At most two units can share at most two connectors and do so if they have identical identity.[8]

---

[3] The synopsis shown may be claimed to be sufficient.
[4] By a normative description we mean a description of a class, rather than a particular member of the class.
[5] The narrative shown here is much too simplified — but the example shows what is meant by a narrative.
[6] Pragmatically: Example tracks are: passenger and freight train through tracks, passenger train platform tracks, freight train sidelines, load/unloading tracks and shunting and marshaling yard tracks.
[7] Pragmatically: Connectors seem to be an artificial "device" needed in order to easily define nets. Units are similarly pragmatically chosen atomic quantities.
[8] Pragmatically: the two units are connected at the "join" of those two identically identified connectors.

With a unit we can associate the set of its potential states. A state of a unit is the set of open paths through a unit. A path of a unit is a direction through the unit in which traffic (train movement) is possible. Over time a unit can undergo state changes.[9]

* Timetables:

Several notions of timetables may (co-)exist:

A timetable may be very basic and show, for example for each train number, the route of the train, that is: the sequence of station visits together with the train arrival and departure times at those stations. Or a timetable may additionally be train-dispatch oriented and may furthermore show train clearance and station routing information as well as approximately when (at which times) the train should be at which blocks along the lines. Or a timetable may be passenger-oriented and also show quantity and quality of seats and sleepers. Etcetera.

Stations have unique names.

* Traffic:

Traffic is the continuous movement — interspersed by temporary stops — of trains along the net. Trains have both train numbers and unique train identifiers.[10]

By movement we mean that if at two relatively close times (say separated by a few seconds, t, t'') a train is moving and is at, i.e. occupy, two distinct sequences of units, i.e. at positions (p, p''), then at any time (t') in-between, the train is at monotonic positions (p') in-between p and p''.[11]

Traffic can be observed, and ideally, as the above 'continuous' function, or traffic can be scheduled (planned). Scheduled traffic may be in the form of a prescription, as in the train-dispatch oriented timetable.

* &c.

End of Example 2

- **Terminology:**[12] A terminology is an alphabetically sorted list of concise, informal definitions.

---

[9] Pragmatics: The state of a unit may be effected by the setting of switches and signals — but so far we abstract that. The state of a unit serves to route trains properly. Trains are intended to only pass in the direction of an open unit: from one connector towards another. Whether trains obey the state setting is a matter outside the domain. In the domain we must also model human errors, technology failures and catastrophes.

[10] Pragmatics: Two or more trains on the net may have identical train numbers — since their journey may last longer than the time interval by means of which a timetable may be defined. In this case we may wish to use train identities in order to be able to distinguish any two trains.

[11] By monotonic movement we mean that the direction of the train does not change in the closed interval $[p, p'']$.

[12] Another term could be: 'Dictionary'. This one is very "sparse", but we hope sufficient for the reader to get the idea.

We only exemplify a few terms.
Capitalised terms used in definitions refer to separate entries. Defined terms are listed alphabetically.

Example 3: Railways

* **Connector**: A Connector has an Identity and is further undefined. At most two Units may share at most one identical Connector.
* **Hump**: A Hump is a Unit and is a notion of Marshalling.[13]
* **Incoming (Marshalling) Tracks**: A set of one or more Tracks form an Incoming (Marshalling) Track configuration if the Tracks at one end are 'fanned-in' (merged) into a Hump.[14]
* **Line**: A Line is a non–empty sequence of Linear Units. A Line 'connects' two Stations.
* **Marshalling**: Marshalling are the actions of decomposing a (potentially unending) series of sequences of freight cars, passenger waggons, etc., into a potentially unending series of set of (parallel) sequences of freight cars, passenger waggons, etc.
* **Marshalling Yard**: A Marshalling Yard consists of three main parts: a small set of one or more Incoming Tracks (otherwise connected, at an incoming end, to (other) units of a Station), a usually large set of Outgoing Tracks (otherwise connected, at an outgoing end, to (other) units of a Station), and a Hump. Usually routes through the Marshalling Yard are only possible from the Incoming to the Outgoing Tracks.
* **Net**: A Net consists of a set of one or more (known) Lines and a set of two or more (known) Stations. All known Lines must connect known Stations. Each known Station must be connected to at least one known Line.
* **Outgoing (Marshalling) Tracks**: A set of one or more Tracks form an Outgoing (Marshalling) Track configuration if from a Hump there is a 'fan-out' to the Tracks at one end which at the the other end are connected to other Station Units.[15]
* **Open Path**: An Open Path is a Path which is in the current Traffic State of a Unit.
* **Open Route**: An Open Route is a Route all of whose Paths are in the current Traffic State of the Net.
* **Path**: A Path is a way through (a direction along) a Unit.
* **Route**: A Route is an orderly connected sequence of Paths.

---

[13] Pragmatics: A Hump 'connects' Incoming and Outgoing Tracks and permit the orderly selection of cars, waggons, etc. from Incoming Tracks and their distribution to appropriate Outgoing Tracks.

[14] Pragmatics: A series of incoming sequences of cars and waggons may be routed onto the other end so that individual cars or waggons may be routed onto the Hump from either Incoming Track.

[15] Pragmatics: It may be better to say that a Hump is the root of a fan–out to a number of tracks, where the fan-out is a configuration of mainly switch units whose "leaves" are connected to one end of the Outgoing Tracks.

* Station: A Station consists of a set of one or more Tracks and a set of Units.[16]
* Traffic State of a Net: The totality of the Traffic States of the Units of a Net makes up the Traffic State of a Net.
* Traffic State of a Unit: A Unit can, at various times, "occupy" one or another Traffic State.[17]
* Track: A Track is a linear sequence of one or more Linear Units.[18]
* Unit: A Unit is — for the purposes of this description — a smallest 'unit' of rail. Units serve to compose Nets. Nets can be decomposed into Units. There are Linear Units, Switch Units, Crossover Units, Turntable Units, Track End Units, etc.[19]

End of Example 3

Formal Specification

Example 4: Railways

* **Nets:**

  type
    Net, Lin, Sta, Trk, Uni, Con
  value
    obs_Lins: Net → Lin-**set**
    obs_Stas: Net → Sta-**set**
    obs_Unis: (Net|Sta|Lin) → Uni-**set**
    obs−Cons: Uni → Con-**set**
    LinStas: Lin → Sta × Sta
  axiom
    ∀ n:Net •
      let stas = obs_Stas(n),
        lins = obs_Lins(n) **in**
      ∀ s,s' **in** stas s≠s' ⇒ ∃ l **in** lins • LinStas(l) = (s,s')
      end
    ...

---

[16] Pragmatics: The Tracks serve a main purpose of a Station: to Load and Unload Passengers and Freight, to temporarily 'park' trains, to Marshal a set of Trains into another set, and to let Through Trains pass the Station. The (other) Station Units serve to Route Trains between Lines and Tracks.

[17] Pragmatics: A Traffic State of a Unit indicates a number of Paths through that Unit as being open for Traffic.

[18] Pragmatics: Tracks can be classified to belong to one or more of either: Platform Tracks, Through Tracks, Shunting/Sideline Tracks, Freight Load/Unloading Tracks, Incoming and Outgoing Marshalling Tracks, etc.

[19] Pragmatics: You may wish to think of a linear Unit as a pair of rails, a large set of sleepers, each sleeper fastened to the rails by 'nails', etc.

* **Timetable:**

  type
    TT, T, Sn, Tn
    TimeTable = Tn $\overrightarrow{m}$ (Sn $\overrightarrow{m}$ (T × T))
  value
    obs_Sn: S → Sn
  axiom
    /* observed station visits are linearly ordered: trains */
    /* arrive at stations before they leave, and arrival times */
    /* at `later, subsequent' stations follow departure */
    /* times from `earlier, previous' stations. */

The times shown in one way (TimeTable) of observing (i.e. projecting) an abstract timetable (TT) are modulo some reasonable interval, say working days, week-ends, holidays.

* **Traffic:**

  type
    TF, Tid, Rou
    rTraffic = T $\overset{\sim}{\rightarrow}$ (Tid $\overrightarrow{m}$ Rou)
    sTraffic = T $\overrightarrow{m}$ (Tid $\overrightarrow{m}$ Uni)
  value
    obs_Tn: Tid → Tn
    obs_UniRou: Rou → Uni*
    obs_Traffic: TF → rTraffic

* **Managed Nets and Traffic:**

  type
    MN, MTF
    MgdNet = T → Net
    MgdTraffic = T → (Net × ((Tid $\overrightarrow{m}$ Rou)×(Tid $\overrightarrow{m}$ Uni)))
  axiom
    /* Routes and Units of train positions must be those of the */
    /* net. Unit positions of scheduled traffic must have */
    /* appropriately open paths. Etcetera. */

A managed net reflects the time changing set of unites and states of units. A managed traffic reflects the managed net, the real and the scheduled traffic.

End of Example 4

2.4 Domain Perspectives

The concept of perspective is a pragmatic one. It serves to decompose an otherwise large domain description into a more manageable, structured set of related descriptions — each corresponding, as closely as possible, to a stake-holder perspective. The pragmatics, at the domain level of perspectives is that each perspective, i.e. each sub-description covers a distinguishable set of closely related components, properties, actions and behaviours of the domain being described.

- **Domain Perspective:**
  We can (formally) define a **perspective** as a partial specification of a domain, consisting of a type space and a set of functions.

We continue the railway systems example from above.

Example 5: Railways

- **Base Perspectives:**
  It seems that railway nets and timetables form the main two base perspectives.
  As a minimum any stake-holder seems to agree that the railway net in terms just of lines and stations and a simple observation of timetables suffice to characterise many aspects of railway systems.
  The timetable and the net are related by stations and — implicitly — by lines.
- **Signalling Perspectives:**
  By signalling, at the intrinsic level (see domain facets, section 2.5) of domain descriptions, we mean just the state of the net (including its units). Signalling is a control perspective.
  For trains to actually journey across the net through stations and along lines signalling must be in effect: paths and routes must be opened and closed in order to ensure safe and speedy traffic.
  So we need to further detail the net into units and their states, open and closed. Managed nets and traffic may be a way to describe signalling.
- **Passenger Perspectives:**
  Passengers, in addition to the basic net and timetable descriptions, as well as railway system staff with whom they interact, have a perspective of the railway systems as somehow embodying ticket reservation, cancellation, etc. Passenger perspectives are user perspectives.

type
  B, Date, Tn
  Occ = Tid $\overrightarrow{m}$ ((Sn × Sn) $\overrightarrow{m}$ (Free × Bound))
value
  ide: Date × Tn $\stackrel{\sim}{\rightarrow}$ Tid
  res: Date × Tn × (Sn × Sn) × B $\stackrel{\sim}{\rightarrow}$ (B × Ticket)
  can: Ticket × B $\stackrel{\sim}{\rightarrow}$ B

axiom
/∗ Can only reserve if free seats. Accepted reservation∗/
/∗ leads to less free seats, more booked ones ∗/
/∗ Cancellation only if ticket is validly reserved. ∗/
/∗ Etcetera. ∗/

We should have stressed before, and will here stress, that domain descriptions of components, like B, and actions, like reservations and cancellations, and constraints, like the axioms stated, are abstractions of "real world"[20] phenomena which may not (or may already) be machine supported. That is: our descriptions are assumptions about the "real world", with or without computing support for what is being described. In other words, B, may or may not become the basis for a computerisation, etc.

End of Example 5

There are many other (rail net and rail service development (i.e. plant), statistics, timetable planning (i.e. management), etc.) perspectives. It is not the purpose of this paper to enumerate as many as possible, nor to further analyse the concept of perspectives.

2.5 Domain Facets

The 'domain perspective' concept was application-oriented. Each perspective portrayed a suitably and pragmatically chosen part of the domain.

The 'domain facet' concept is a somewhat technical one, but still is basically determined on pragmatic grounds.

Any domain has some intrinsic parts. These are parts which reflect 'stable' properties of the domain, that is: properties which remain properties also when the "hard" technologies that 'support' the domain change, or when the rules & regulations that 'govern' stake-holder domain actions and behaviours change, etc.

- **Domain Facet:**
  We can (formally) define a **facet** as a partial specification of a domain, consisting of a type space and a set of functions.

In the following we will illustrate 'clusters' of these facets in the context of the railways example:

- **Intrinsic Facets:**
  By an intrinsics of a domain we loosely (pragmatically) mean those facets which remain invariant under changing support technologies, changing enterprise system or infrastructure rules & regulations, changing stake-holder

---

[20] No-one knows what 'real traffic is. Therefore we put double (tongue-in-cheek) quotes around that concept.

behaviours, etc. That is: We define intrinsics as a core and relative to (modulo) other facets.
Therefore an improved characterisation of intrinsics should emerge as we next deal with supposedly non-intrinsic facets.
- **Support Technology Facets:**
Much of the technology that reside in any domain is changing regularly while its intrinsics remain stable.

Example 6: Railways

* Switch Technology:
One example is the switch technology. In the early years of railways switches were thrown manually, by railway staff, *one per switch!* Later mechanical gadgets, including momentum amplifiers, were connected by thick wires to a central cabin house which predominantly featured a row of 'throwers'. Now we find that combinations of switches are activated electronically and electrically through so-called solid-state switches. The same underlying, intrinsic concept, a switch, has its internal functioning determined by varieties of support technologies.

* Signal Technology:
Another example is, or was, the visible, mechanical signals consisting of a tall mast (or pole) to which are affixed, at the top, for example one or two 'flags'. These are hoisted or lowered through cabin-located 'throwers'. Later some such mechanical signals were replaced by signals consisting of not so tall poles on which are fixed red/yellow/green or just red/green lamps. In future we can foresee that all such signals are replaced by radio messages sent to each individual train informing it of whether to make a stop or not, including actually performing that control — the meaning of a signal.

* Sensor Technology:
Yet a third example is the following. It is based in how we observe traffic. In the intrinsics we claim that traffic is a continuous function from time (at least within a suitably chosen interval) to train positions. In "physical reality" we know that at whichever time we choose to observe the traffic there will indeed be trains. In the "observable reality" we cannot observe all the time all the positions. Instead we place observers at suitably chosen points (units). That is, wrt. **space**, we choose to sample, and this spatial sampling discretises our observations. Also: we do not observe all the **time**, but chooses to let the observers inform us only of changes: *now there is a train starting to pass by in that direction, now the trains ends passing by.* That is: rather than being subject to continuous evaluation we discretise in the form of observable events. The observers form a kind of 'support technology'. In the "old days" the observers were railway staff that might have used some form of telegraphic or telephonic equipment to inform a more-or-less central gathering of observations. Today optical sensors (optical gates) may be used as observers (and perhaps with extended functionality). The point is: the support technology changes.

– &c.

End of Example 6

(The point is also that) Support technology may fail. In the intrinsics observations, switch setting, unit openings and closing were "ideal". In the presence of possibly and probabilistically failing technology switches may fail to change state, signals may "get stuck", and sensors may register a 'train-passing-by' event when in "real reality" there is no such train, or vice-versa: may fail to register a passing train.

Modelling:
The intrinsics descriptions (models, whether informal or formal) must therefore be extended (enriched) to include the components, actions and behaviours of support technology.
Typically the models must incorporate real-time, safety criticality, (failure) probabilistic, etc. properties.
Formal specification languages that are able to cope with some of these facets are the Duration Calculi of Zhou Chaochen [35, 40, 39, 33, 34, 76, 38, 77].

– **Rules & Regulations Facets:**
Written procedural guidelines exists in most man-made domains. They are intended to regulate the actions and behaviours of staff in operating, i.e. interacting with the domain.

Examples, relating to the railways and to banks, are:

Example 7: Railways

* Trains at Stations:
In China, as we were told, due to some pretty disastrous train crashes at stations, there is a rule, concerning acceptance of incoming trains and dispatch of departing trains at stations. This rule states that in any n minute interval (where $n = 5$) there must at most be one train arriving or departing a station — even though some stations may have ample tracks and disjoint routes from and to lines: sufficient to actually receive or send several trains simultaneously.[21] But a rule is a rule!

* Trains along Lines:
Lines may be decomposed into blocks, with blocks delineated by for example signals. The purpose of blocks is usually to ensure that there is at most one train in each block, or that there is at least one block between any two trains on the same line. Again blocking may be introduced in order to make it simpler to monitor and "control"[22] traffic along lines in order to ensure safety (no crashes). Thus some support technology (e.g. signals) may be a means to ensure a rule.

---

[21] This kind of rule is similar to air traffic at airports: Pairwise adjacent landings on any given runway must be separated by, say, at least 2 minutes. Similar for take offs. And any adjacent pair of a landing and a take-off, or a take-off and a landing must be separated by, say, 5 minutes!

[22] What exactly is meant by 'control' is left undefined.

* Dispatch & Rescheduling Rules:
  Rules governing the dispatch and rescheduling priorities among train types (international vs. local passenger trains vs. similar grades of freight trains vs. military trains) abound.[23]
* &c.

End of Example 7

Example 8: Banks Customer deposit monies into savings accounts, for example as 'exchanged' with a bank teller, involve 'interpretation', by the teller, of *rules & regulations* for posting such deposits. Depending on the customer *account contract* (in which the *rules & regulations* concerning all transaction are 'defined'), the clerk performs one or another set of actions (a 'script') "against" the account (i.e. banking) system. The *account contract* (generally set up when the account is first established) 'binds' concepts (i.e. concept identifiers) such as for fees, interest rates, loan limits, etc. to actual values. (This binding is reminiscent of environments *ENV* when modelling block-structured programming languages.) The domain model of deposit and other transactions are therefore modelled as a Bank Programming Language script. A script could have two formal parameter lists, a transaction argument list and a contract identifier list. When performing a transaction, i.e. when invoking the script, transaction parameter values are bound to identifiers of the transaction argument list, while the (latest) contract environment is used to find the values of the contract parameter list.

Model:

type
  Pid, Cid, Cmd
  Bank = {accounts} $\overrightarrow{m}$ (C $\overrightarrow{m}$ Acc) ...
  ENV = Cid $\overrightarrow{m}$ VAL
  Script = (Pid* × Cid*) × Cmd
  Sn = {...,deposit,withdraw,save,borrow,...}
  Acc = ...
      ∪ {balance} $\overrightarrow{m}$ VAL
      ∪ {limit} $\overrightarrow{m}$ VAL
      ∪ {interest} $\overrightarrow{m}$ VAL
      ∪ {fee} $\overrightarrow{m}$ VAL
      ∪ {yield} $\overrightarrow{m}$ VAL
      ∪ {overdraw} $\overrightarrow{m}$ VAL
      ...
      ∪ {scripts} $\overrightarrow{m}$ (Sn $\overrightarrow{m}$ Script)

---

[23] Especially these rules are changing rapidly these years in the light of the "ownership" decomposition of of railway systems: base net & signalling infrastructure in terms of one operator vs. commercial passenger and freight traffic in terms of possibly several, competing operators. They are changing in order to further competition.

$$\begin{array}{l}\ldots\\ \bigcup \{\text{contract}\} \overrightarrow{m} \text{ Text}\\ \bigcup \{\text{env}\} \overrightarrow{m} (\text{ENV} \times \text{T})^*\\ \ldots\end{array}$$

Trans = Sn × VAL*

value
  int_Rou: C × Trans → Bank → Bank
  int_Rou(c,sn,vall)(b) ≡
    let a = (b(accounts))(c) **in**
    let ((pl,cl),cmd) = (a(scripts))(sn),
        env = a(env) **in**
    /∗ assert: ∗/ **len** vall = **len** pl /∗ end assert ∗/
    let ρ = [pl[i] ↦ vall[i] | i:**Nat** • i ∈ **inds**]
        ∪ [cl[i] ↦ env(cl[i])] **in**
    int_Cmd(cmd)ρ **end end end**

End of Example 8

Comments: Many other domains have rules & regulations that must be interpreted by humans, and the same rule & regulation may have to be interpreted according to some 'context'.

More generally on modelling we can say:

General Comments on Modelling:
The intrinsics and technology support descriptions (models, whether informal or formal) must therefore be extended (enriched) to include the components, actions and behaviours of *rules & regulations*.

Procedural (human ↔ domain) matters tend to express logical properties for which also "exotic" logics like [auto]epistemic, belief, defeasible, deontic, and modal logics in general, may well serve as a basis for formalisation [53, 52, 54, 55].

In general *rules & regulations* seem to be best modelled in terms of a special script language of commands. The command language is "tailored" to be able to access the domain state components. So: on one hand we do define major aspects of the intrinsics (basis), support technology, rules & regulations, human (stake-holder) behaviour, etc., using one (or another) specification language. But when it comes to typically the rules & regulations facet we defer further modelling to scripts written in a further defined domain specific (rules & regulations) script language. Now each such rule & regulation is then, in the domain model, associated with some script. Which script some rule & regulation is 'paired' with we do not model! But we should give example of sample interpretations of rules & regulations in terms of such rules!

We refer to the item on **Ground Staff Sub–facets** page 18, in particular the continued bank example (page 19), for further on how humans may interpret rules & regulations.

– **Stake-holder Facets:**
An important facet of the domain is the stake-holder concept: the staff of the system of interest within the domain (owners, managers, workers), the clients and customers, politicians, otherwise affected citizens, etc. Each have their own 'agenda' vis-a-vis the system, the domain in which it is embedded and more loosely connected issues which we may otherwise think of as "outside the domain".
They express opinions, they have goals and objectives (not to be confused with requirements [to computing]), they manage other staff and other resources of the system (i.e. the enterprise, viz. a specific railway system operator), they operate its resources, they use the services or acquire the products of the enterprise, and they are otherwise "interested" in the well-being of the domain and its surroundings.
Again some examples may serve to illustrate the points being made here:
- Owner Sub–facets:
  Owners of a system — an enterprise — residing within the system or domain may think of that system (or enterprise) in terms of goals and objectives that do not (later) easily translate into software requirements. Their facet is that of profitability, of growth, and of market share. Further subsidiary goals may then have to do with customer and staff satisfaction, with environmental (bio-sphere) concerns, etc. A model facet may try to cover this — but formalisation is probably difficult. It is impossible if there is no other formalisation of the domain, that is: formalisation of owner sub-facets may be enhanced in the presence of formal models of the domain. The system (state) 'variables' or 'indicators' in terms of which their sub-facets are to be formulated need be rather directly relatable to the domain model notion of state (and other) components.
- Manager Sub–facets:
  Managers acquire and dispose (i), allocate and schedule (ii), and deploy (iii) resources in order to meet goals and objectives at various levels: strategic (i), tactical (ii) and operational (iii) — respectively. At the higher, the strategic to tactical levels, one may be able to identify the kinds of components — including clients — involved and the kind (i.e. the type) of predicates that express satisfaction of goals and objectives — where the type of components are the type of the various resources being managed: time, people, equipment, monies, etc. Similar the decisions taken by management can be characterised, if neither algorithmically nor logically, then at least through their (algebraic) signatures. Report [16] shows that one can formally capture the domain sub-facets of the strategic, tactical and operational management of resources.
- Staff Sub–facets:
  The staff are the persons, "on the ground", being managed, and most directly exposed to the daily operations of the domain. They are the ones who directly handle the actual, tangible (manifest) mechanical and other like resources — as well as customers. In the case of the railways this staff is comprised from train staff: engineers, sleeper attendants, etc., station

staff: train dispatchers, shunting staff, etc., passenger service staff: seat reservation and ticketing staff, etc. As do the managers, the ground staff must carry out actions according also to Rules & Regulations. And they may fail or succeed, more-or-less 'punctually & precisely'. Also this may be describable, informally, and perhaps also formally. Experiments and experience will show!

To illustrate an issue we take up the thread from the bank example above.

Example 9: Bank

A clerk may perform the transaction correctly (and many different sequences of actions may be involved and applicable), or the clerk may make a mistake, or the clerk — or some already installed software support — maliciously diverts sums to "other" accounts! The contract therefore, in the domain, denotes a set of named *rule & regulation* designations. Each such named *rule & regulation*, since it may be potentially interpreted in any number of ways, is now modelled as a set of scripts. Transaction processing, say be a human clerk, then involves a non-deterministic choice among the possibly infinite ways of interpreting a client request.

type
  Acc = ...
    ...
    $\bigcup$ {scripts} $\overrightarrow{m}$ (Sn $\overrightarrow{m}$ Script-**infset**)
    ...

value
  int_Script: C × Trans → Bank → Bank
  int_Script(c,sn,vall)(b) ≡
    let a = (b(**accounts**))(c) **in**
    let ((pl,cl),cmd) = select((a(**scripts**))(sn)),
        env = a(**env**) **in**
    /∗ assert: ∗/ **len** vall = **len** pl /∗ end assert ∗/
    let ρ = [pl[i] $\mapsto$ vall[i] | i:**Nat** • i ∈ **inds**]
        ∪ [cl[i] $\mapsto$ env(cl[i])] **in**
    int_Cmd(cmd)ρ **end end end**

  select: Script-**infset** $\xrightarrow{\sim}$ Script
  select(ss) **as** s **post** s ∈ ss

End of Example 9

- User Sub–facets:
  Users (clients) interact with ground staff and with equipments (products) and service offerings of the domain system. They may interact according to expectations, or they may fail. They may be satisfied, or disgruntled.

They may be loyal customers, or they may search for other 'vendors' of services and products in a competitive manner.
- &c.

Our list of facets have "moved" from the seemingly more easily formalisable, the "hard" facets, to "softer" facets that are increasingly more difficult to formalise.

Modelling:
The intrinsics, support technology and rules & regulations descriptions (models, whether informal or formal) must therefore be extended (enriched) to include the components, actions and behaviours of *humans*.
To model, informally and formally, stake-holder facets may be difficult — but that is no reason for not trying. It seems that more research is needed, especially in the area of formalisation and in the concordance of informal and formal descriptions. That research may result in altogether different syntactical (visual) forms of descriptions.

There are many other (customer, economics, etc.) facets. It is not the purpose of this paper to enumerate as many as possible, nor to further analyse the concept of facets.

The list of facets given above is illustrative. The developers may be guided by this list, or may have to analyse the problem domain in order to determine for themselves the nature of other, not exemplified, facets.

2.6 Domain Elicitation & Validation

The terms elicitation and acquisition are used interchangeably.

There is an emerging, "rich" literature on techniques and tools that might help domain developers in extracting domain knowledge from stake-holders of the domain.

"Classical" software engineering tends to have focused on requirements elicitation and to have bundled occasional domain elicitation with requirements elicitation.

We would have liked, at this place, to give a reasonably thorough survey of contributions made by researchers and practitioners in the area — but refrain! We hope, at a later date, to review some of the very many diverse requirements engineering publications in the context of this papers seemingly sharp secularisation of domain engineering from that of current requirements engineering.

2.7 FAQ: Domains

- [24] *Can stake-holders understand the domain descriptions?*
  Appropriate stake-holders should understand corresponding perspectives of the informal descriptions. In fact it is desirable — in future, after computing

---
[24] FAQ: Frequently Asked Questions

scientists have identified basic methods — that they be able to write informal domain descriptions.

Whether these stake-holders also can read the formal descriptions is another matter. We do not think that it is — at the moment — necessary that all classes of stake-holders meet this criterion.

For certain developments the client may make use of independent software engineering consultants (who can indeed both read and write formal descriptions) to inspect the developers documents — much like Norwegian Veritas and Lloyd's Register of Shipping act on behalf of future large scale system clients (nuclear power plants, ship-owners, etc.) when such systems (ships, etc.) are built.

- *What should be the languages of informal descriptions?*

We believe they should be the languages spoken by the staff and users (customers) of the domain.

In the example of railways this means that a variety of informal, yet sufficiently precise, professional languages should be used in a "cleaned-up" manner. The clean-up should only affect the non-professional, usually, national and natural language parts and consists in improving the narrative and terminological precision.

The informal, professional languages often deploy various diagrammatic parts (pictures, figures, tables) as well as sometimes even mathematical formulas. Such parts should be 'ported' to the narratives, etc.

- *What should be the languages of formal descriptions?*

In this paper we show only the formal specification language of RSL [63], the RAISE [64] Specification Language. RAISE (*RSL*) is not the only possibility: we could probably as well have used B, VDM-SL, Z, or some other sufficiently endowed language. We do find, however, that RSL's concurrency constructs (not found in for example VDM-SL and Z) as well as its clear and simple methodology [64], currently bias us in the direction of RAISE.

Where the domain exhibit temporal notions then RSL, VDM-SL and Z cannot be used — for those, temporal parts. Instead we might decide on using a suitable Duration Calculus.

Many formal specification languages exists:

- **B** [5, 3, 75, 4],
- **Duration Calculi** [36, 40, 39, 33, 34, 76, 38, 77],
- **Larch** [66, 67],
- **RAISE/RSL** [63, 64]
- **STeP** [97, 98],
- **VDM** [22, 23, 87, 43, 92, 45, 91, 51],
- **Z** [70, 107, 106],
- etc.

- *When have we specified enough — minimum/maximum?*

Recall that a domain description aims not primarily, but only also to serve as a basis for requirements description. That is: if we were only to describe the instantiated domain that very explicitly relates to requirements — we may call this kind of domain description 'minimal', then it is not so difficult to know when we have specified enough: We have specified a minimal domain when all the professional domain (system) terms that "pop-up" in requirements have been defined in the domain. But usually that "minimum" is insufficient for a number of reasons. 'Minimum' terms may need clarifications which refer to undefined domain terms. Any one domain may give rise to several requirements, each covering (supporting) more-or-less "disjoint" areas of domain activity. Eventually emerging (i.e. resulting) software packages that implement these different requirements are desired to share facilities and concepts, i.e. to exchange data and 'call' each other! Any "gap" between the software packages usually is a reflection on some similar gap in their counterpart "minimal" domain descriptions. 'Domain-describing' these gaps — perhaps already before the software package interactions might have been conceived — amount to "non-minimal" domain descriptions. The process of securing a suitably comprehensive domain description is an uncertain one.

We take the position wrt. to the above "minimality/maximality" problem, that it is an issue of normative versus instantiated domain descriptions: minimal when instantiated, maximal when normative!

– *Normative and/or Instantiated Domain Descriptions?*

  • **Normative Domain Descriptions:**
    A normative domain description is a description which is intended to describe a class of usually two or preferably more "closely resembling domains". A normative railway domain description should thus cover for example the railways of Denmark, Norway, Sweden, perhaps even Russia and China — in fact: should desirably describe any national or private railway system! Whether such a normative description is possible is another matter!

    So a normative description may ideally cover the class of all instances of a domain, but will probably do so in a way that makes their use for any particular, any specifically instantiated domain a less than trivial, but not an altogether unreasonable task.

    Research into and the development of such normative domain descriptions may typically not be a concern of any one particularly instantiatable domain (system): why should they develop more than they think they need? Why, in competitive situations, should they develop something that might as well benefit competition? Etcetera. So we may conclude that if it is reasonable to develop normative domain descriptions, then the needed precursor research as well as the development ought take place in peer-reviewed contexts, in an open fashion, that is: typically at a public research centre or at a university.

    One can therefore imagine a potentially many year university project, with internationally collaborating "schools" — with varying participation over the years. To develop a reasonably comprehensive, normative model of a typical infrastructure domain may take 10–20 years. As in nuclear physics, the domain model emerges through partial contributions, slowly, but steadily.

We suggest such a possibility for a number of domains: railways (residing in transport departments or institutes at technical universities), financial service industry (residing at schools of economics, finance and business management), etc. There is already loose collaboration between individuals of such schools, but perhaps 'human genome'-like 'domain projects' could be justified.

- **Instantiated Domain Descriptions:**
  Since there can be little if any doubt that any specific domain (or system within such) needs domain descriptions that are particularly "geared" to its "peculiarities", there can also be little doubt that it would be nice if there were already available a normative, and appropriate domain description from which a rewrite, editing or parameterisation into an instantiated domain description was a reasonably straightforward development step.

We foresee a day when the description methods, techniques and tools of computing science and software engineering have matured to such a degree and relative to a number of domains such that continued methodology research and tool development takes place, not in computing science and software engineering departments, but in the more domain specific institutes. This predicated situation is akin to that of numerics, in fact of classical mathematics: many branches of natural sciences and engineering are today themselves capable of conducting necessary and sufficient mathematical work on modelling their own domains.

– *Why Domain Engineering by Computing Scientists & Software Engineers?*
If we examine the basic development issue across the spectrum of domain, requirements and software design engineering (especially for man-made domain systems, in particular infrastructure systems), then we find that the overwhelmingly largest construction tasks all have to do with structuring very large descriptions: securing proper syntax, semantics and pragmatics. These descriptions shall primarily satisfy laws of mathematics, in particular of mathematical logic.

No other engineering focuses so intensely on textual structures. No other engineering discipline speaks of syntax, semantics and pragmatics. In all other engineering branches there is sooner or later a quantum jump: from some diagrammatic, computable description to the (assembly line or refractory tower or other) construction of tangible, manifest products satisfying laws of nature.

A major contribution of computing science and software engineering is exactly that of devising precise techniques and tools for handling large descriptions.

That is the reason why computing science must study and software engineering must practice domain engineering — for years to come.

2.8 Domain Research, Education and Development Issues

The Bernried workshop, sponsored by the US Department of Defence (DoD) Office of Naval Research (ONR), had as a main objective of the ONR to evaluate, on the background of workshop presentations and discussions, which were and are the research, education and development issues. In this section, and in sections 3.5 on page 29 and 4.6 on page 33, we therefore relate our own contribution to that of needed research, education and development.

- **Domain Research Issues:**
  We need do more research on the linguistic and formal domain recognition and capture issues that may govern both informal and formal descriptions of domains [81].
  Specialisation in software engineering is one way of achieving the level of other engineering disciplines' professionalism and methodology. We may most likely be well-advised in moving firmly in that direction by following Jackson's notion of Problem Frames [81, 82, 27].
  To do this research we envisage a number of desirably parallel executed experimental research projects. The number and kind of these should preferably be chosen so as to span a suitable spectrum of problem frames, and within the specifically chosen (problem frame specific) examples also span a suitable variety of perspectives and facets.
  We need sharper, more methodology-oriented, perhaps formally founded and explored, ways of characterising the perspective and facet concepts, as well as individual such perspectives and facets. For a beginning we may follow the software view notion of Daniel Jackson [79].
- **Domain Education Issues:**
  There are currently no appropriate text books and monographs in the area of domain knowledge engineering, but there are papers on knowledge engineering, ontology and enterprise modelling.
  The current author is issuing a series of reports covering the spectrum from domain engineering via requirements engineering to software design. These are intended to also be part of a monograph on formal aspects of software engineering.
- **Domain Development Issues:**
  Much experimental and exploratory development is needed in order to ensure that the researched and evolving domain modelling techniques and the concepts of perspectives and facets are appropriate. Over the years 1994–1997 we explored domain models for railways [24, 28, 37, 49, 26], manufacturing industry [61, 62, 6, 85, 7, 84, 86], ministry of finance [44], etc. while we established, built up and directed UNU/IIST, the UN University's International Institute for Software Technology. We are currently, 1998, at our current address, with colleagues and students, further exploring domain methodologies in the areas of railways, metropolitan transports, banking, full scale finance accounting [25, 90, 19], etc.

3 Requirements

The aim of requirements engineering is to develop, together with stake-holders of the selected domain, a precise set of concordant descriptions of the requirements, a set that the parties, developers and stake-holders, can agree upon.

We will not give a detailed account, such as in the previous section on domain engineering, but only touch upon some issues.

Thus we expect a set of precise contractual obligations binding the two parties.

From a formal point of view, requirements engineering establishes the theory $\mathcal{R}$.

Grossly we may speak of two kinds of requirements:

- **Functional Requirements:** a functional requirements specification, i.e. a requirements model, basically builds upon the domain model, possibly a subset. *Functional requirements reside in the domain* [112].
- **Non–functional Requirements:** non-functional requirements are basically such which can be stated independent of the domain and hence relate more to the computing platform for the desired software, the techniques and tools required in the software developments and the computer-human interfaces.

3.1 Requirements Models

A requirements model is a concordant (coherent, consistent) set of models of requirements aspects.

3.2 Requirements Aspects

* **Requirements Aspect:**
  We can (formally) define an **aspect** as a partial specification of a requirements, consisting of a type space and a set of functions.

A number of aspects seems to govern the composition of requirements:

- **Domain Aspects — 'Functional' Requirements:**
  o **Domain Projections:**
    Some of the domain type (i.e. state) space is usually projected onto the requirements.

Example 10: Railways

From the railway domain model we have:

type
  rTraffic = T $\overset{\sim}{\rightarrow}$ (Tid $\overrightarrow{m}$ Rou)
  oTraffic = T $\overrightarrow{m}$ (Tid $\overrightarrow{m}$ Uni)

That is: "real traffic" is a partial function (total over a closed time interval) from time to the discrete routes of the railway net occupied by identified trains. Observable traffic discretises (through 'sampling') the partial function.

This was in the domain. Now, if the requirements have to do with monitoring the air traffic, then we must decide upon (i) what, more precisely, of the air traffic is being observed, (ii) how often (i.e. more precisely about the 'sampling'), and (iii) by whom (i.e. how).

From an underlying reality of support technology of sensors one could imagine that what we are observing is more like:

type
  Interval = T × T
  Sensing = Interval $\overrightarrow{m}$ (Uni $\overrightarrow{m}$ Tid)

hence

value
  Convert: Sensing $\overset{\sim}{\rightarrow}$ oTraffic

The requirements have to deal with domain component (here state) projection issues related to this.

Similarly with the functions that may need be computed by the software:

value
  TooClose: oTraffic $\overset{\sim}{\rightarrow}$ (Tid $\overrightarrow{m}$ Uni)
  Crashes: oTraffic $\overset{\sim}{\rightarrow}$ (Tid $\overrightarrow{m}$ Uni)

End of Example 10

- **Domain Instantiation:**
  Usually the domain description is normative. For the particular client for which some software is to be developed, and for which functional requirements need be expressed with respect to the particularities of the client's problems, an instantiation $\mathcal{D}$ of the normative (for example projected) domain need therefore be made — one that accurately portrays all those perspectives and facets which are special to that client and which have a bearing on the requirements, including those that are needed in order to prove that any subsequent design $\mathcal{S}$ is a correct implementation of the requirements $\mathcal{R}$.
- **Domain 'Dichotomies':**
  Here we take a dichotomy as a potential conflict between what is expressed in one part of the domain model and what is expressed in another part of that domain model. Dichotomies only need be resolved by a requirements if the general requirements otherwise relate to the concerned parts of the domain model.
  An example is that of "ghost trains". If the requirements is about monitoring (and 'controlling') traffic, then the Law of N 'Ghost' Trains of the

intrinsics somehow conflicts with the possibility of failing support technology to create the illusion, through misleading samplings, that there are indeed 'ghost' trains. On one hand we know that the intrinsics expresses that there can not be 'ghost' trains, while on the other hand we might indeed register such!

A requirements to a traffic monitoring system may be to resolve such conflicts through re-sampling, and — if such fails — to correct the illusion, for example by stopping appropriate trains.

○ **Domain 'Extensions':**
Functional requirements usually focus on some domain concepts and facilities and direct the support of some of these. Once the whole apparatus of for example extensive and expensive, net-wide train sensing is being demanded, it may be little extra to demand that a number of traffic prediction and rescheduling functions also be required: functions that were not in the domain because they were impractical or inordinately expensive to realise without computing.

In other words: the software + hardware machine, once inserted into the domain, becomes a part of it, and its concepts and facilities becomes a part of the domain for the next round of development.

○ **State Internalisation:**
Some type space of the projected and instantiated domain reflects observable (and controllable) variables — i.e. some external state.

This state must initially be input. This input action must be requirements specified.

The frequency with which this external state is being sampled for possible state update must likewise be requirements specified.

Upon any such input and update the sampled data must be validated (wrt. constraints etc.). and such validation must likewise be requirements specified.

– **Machine Aspects:**
Among so-called "non-functional"[25] requirements we have those that relate to the machine itself, where by the machine we mean the computing systems made up by the required software and its execution platform, both soft and hard. Aspects include:

○ **Execution Platforms:**
Requirements may dictate the use of specific hardware as well as run-time system software such as operating system, database management system, data (network) communication software etc. Among "etc." we include OMG packages (CORBA), etc.

○ **Dependability & Performance Issues:**
For the specific combination: (i) provision of functional aspects (concepts and facilities), and (ii) computing platform, the client usually expects a certain quality of dependability & performance:

---

[25] The functional requirements are those (formalisable) ones that derive directly from (i.e. 'reside' in) the domain.

* **Availability**: minimum down–time
* **Reliability**: mean time between and to next failures, etc.,
* **Safety**: machine response in case of equipment failures,
* **Security**: hierarchies of authorised access to the use of facilities, and:
* **Performance**: execution times needed in order to provide timely computations of certain functions; and: response times expected wrt. domain interactions.

Some of these aspects may be formalisable, others not (yet).

o **Maintenance Issues:**
Perfective, corrective and adaptive maintenance is unavoidable. Requirements (actually they are a kind of meta-linguistic requirements) may make statements as to the "ease" with which such maintenance can be performed.
Perfective maintenance aims at improving performance. Corrective maintenance aims at removing bugs. Adaptive maintenance aims at fitting existing software to new hardware and/or new software extensions to previously required software.
As in our response to user-friendliness requirements below, we argue now that carefully developed and sufficiently broad domain models help us to "anticipate software sockets" for next generation software packages within the domain. And thus to help improve adaptability.

- **Domain ↔ Machine Interface Aspects:**
Among further, so-called "non-functional" requirements we have those that relate specifically to the man/machine interface.

  o **Graphical & other User Interfaces**
  Our view is here: Visualising clear, well-described domain concepts determine basic concepts of graphical interfaces.,

  o **Dialogue Monitoring & Control**
  Again our view is: clear, well-described domain concepts, including events and behaviour, determine basic concepts of dialogue management.

  o **User Friendliness: Psychology, Physiology, etc. of Interface:**
  Often a broad sweeping statement is made: *"the software, when the basis of executions, should lead to a user-friendly system"*.
  As in our response to adaptability requirements above, we repeat the argument that carefully developed and sufficiently broad domain models where the eventually developed software is expected (required) to primarily reflect only the concepts and facilities of the domain, in some isomorphic or homomorphic manner[26], is an indispensable basis for securing user friendliness.

---

[26] A step of development from one, abstract step to a concrete step can be said to be homomorphic if individual concepts of the abstract step are likewise individually identifiable in the concrete step.

3.3 Requirements Elicitation & Validation

The terms elicitation and acquisition are used interchangeably.

I have little to say on this subject — and, although I have indeed followed the literature on requirements [108, 47, 50, 88, 41, 103, 99, 13, 104, 96, 94, 72, 42, 110, 78, 71, 89, 48] I have much to do as I find that most of the literature need be re-conceptualised, re-worked and re-worded substantially to relate meaningfully in a formal and domain-based setting.

Fine insight need be rather substantially revised when requirements, as here suggested, are separated, but derived from domains.

Immediate, fine candidates, in my rather personal view, are: [60, 100, 12, 80, 93, 30, 112, 95].

3.4 FAQ: Requirements

- *Where do requirements come from?*
  From the domain, and basically only from the domain. The functional requirements are expressed by stake-holders in the domain and in terms of their professional language.
- *What about platform and interface requirements?*
  Well they are usually domain-independent. An example are software correctness. If computers etc. already exist in the domain, platform requirements and interface usually relate to these.
- *Should clients read formal requirements document?*
  The answer is along the same line as given above — FAQ: Domains — first item.
- *Requirements always change, so why formalise?*
  Well, requirements do change, but the domain from which they emerge change much less rapidly. Therefore it is additionally useful (i) to try "complete" a domain specification, (ii) to formulate requirements using terms only from the domain, and (iii) to base a software architecture on the core concepts of the domain, and hence the requirements. For situations where the application problem "occupies" but a tiny fraction of the domain it is usually still useful, in anticipation of future requirements changes, to 'relate', in the requirements and in the software architecture, "back" to the larger concepts of the domain. By mandating that the requirements 'homomorphically' reflect the domain, and that the software design 'homomorphically' reflects the requirements, some considerable robustness is achieved — and one can calmly await and handle requirements changes.

3.5 Requirements: Research, Education and Development Issues

For the issues listed below answers in line with those of section 2.8 on page 24 can be given here.

– **Requirements Research Issues:**
We need better understand the relations between domains and requirements and between requirements and software architecture. The issues of projection, of the input, vetting and update of domain (data value) projections need also be studied. Finally the issue of relations between functional and non-functional requirements need skeptic clarification. In particular we need to better understand whether non-functional requirements can be formalised. To this end one may need to investigate entirely new (formal) specification paradigms.
– **Requirements Education Issues**
Current textbooks in requirements engineering are full of many very good, mostly pragmatic observations, but I believe that we need textbooks on requirements engineering (etc.) that use formal specification and design calculation techniques [113, 105].
– **Requirements Development Issues:**
We refer to the domain item on this issue page 24.

4 Software/Systems Design

An aim of design engineering is to develop, for the client, a software package or system (i.e. a set of "connected" packages) that satisfies the requirements.

Usually, given a requirements specification we can normally design both the hardware configuration and the software system — so we may take the term 'systems engineering' to include both hardware and software (sub–)system design.

A legally binding contract between the developer and the client describes mutual obligations wrt. delivery of ("more-or-less") correct software.

From a formal point of view, design engineering establishes the software design theory $\mathcal{S}$.

4.1 Software Architecture

By a software architecture we understand a specification which primarily specifies the external interface behaviour of the software (to be, or already designed).[27] Software architecture, typically, implements functional requirements

---

[27] David Garlan et al. ([8, 58, 1, 59, 9, 2, 56, 57]) define the concept of Software Architecture much more broadly than we do. We do not mind, but find it a little disturbing. In the 1960s computer (ie. hardware) architecture was agreed, and was defined, seminally, by Amdahl, Blaauw and Brooks [10], to be the interface as seen by programmers: the computer data structures (byte, halfword, word, double word and variable length character strings), the addressing forms, the instruction repertoire, the channel commands, etc. That is: All things that were visible at the assembler code level. In 1964 the one IBM/360 architecture gave rise to a variety of machine organisations: from the IBM 360 Model 20, via Models 30, 40, 44, 50, 60, 65 and

whereas, program organisation typically, implements non-functional requirements.

The important aspect of software architectures that we need to focus on here is that they are basically derived from the requirements.

Indeed, it can sometimes be a bit difficult to see any deeper difference between a requirements specification and a software architecture specification. We have found, however, that the following characterises the step from requirements to software architecture:

- **Requirements as a Set of Partial Specifications:**
  — in contrast to a software architecture specification which collects all the "bits and pieces" of the various, aspect-oriented partial specifications.
  The software architecture specification therefore formulates a consistent and complete whole.
- **Requirements as a Under-specified Specification:**
  — in contrast to a software architecture specification which completes the requirements: fills in "wholes" that were deliberately left under-specified.
  It is often useful to let some requirements facet specifications be completed during software design.
- **Functional vs. Non-functional Requirements:**
  Functional requirements usually can be rather explicitly "carried" into software architectures — as they were usually also formally specified.
  Non-functional requirements are usually not (yet) formalisable. A software architecture — or, at the "latest", a program organisation — proposal therefore has to come up with initial answers as how to satisfy these non-functional requirements (such as performance, security, user-friendliness, maintainability, etc.).

4.2 Program Organisation (Software Structure)

By a program organisation (or [internal] software structure) we understand a specification which, in addition to the externally observable interface behaviour also specifies the internal structuring of the software (to be, or already designed).

70; that is: from byte via halfword, and word to double word machine data busses, from strictly sequential machines to highly overlapped (pipelined) flows. So: when it came to hardware there was a clear distinction between the architecture and the organisation — just as we have seen with the Intel (etc.) series from eight bit byte organisations (8086) via halfword, and word to double word machine data busses. But with basically the same architecture. We also refer to Hennesey and Pattersons two tomes: [74, 73]

Instead it seems that Garlan et al. defines an architecture to be anything you would like to say about the structure of either soft- or hardware and such that you say this diagrammatically.

We do not mind their definition, only — in relation to our software related definitions — theirs mean: any form of software architecture, program organisation or more refined structure.

A determining factor in choosing one organisation design over another is whether non-functional requirements can thereby be satisfied.

A program organisation thus settles many issues that might have been left 'abstract' even by the software architecture. Examples are: A software architecture may specify a data type abstractly. A concretisation of this seemingly 'monolithic' abstract data type may be in the form of a set of data types. The program organisation specification further commits each member of the set to be implemented as a state variable (i.e. as an assignable variable) — and these may then be [geographically] distributed.

And a program organisation, in line with the above, introduces and specifies internal processes, committed (concrete) data structures — including the use of for example database management system support, data communication system support — etc.

One person's program organisation is another person's software architecture: Where non-functional requirements, for example about performance, imply that facilities management staff may wish to inspect internal interface behaviours for purposes of performance tuning, etc., we see that such staff consider a certain level of program organisation as "their" software architecture.

4.3 Refinement

Although an element of software development we need not treat this methodology concept in this paper — since we primarily wishes to relate domains to requirements, requirements to software, and since we also primarily wish to enunciate the concepts of domain perspectives, domain facets, requirements aspects and software views.

4.4 Software Views

[79] defines a:

- **Software View:**
  as a partial specification of a program, consisting of a state space and a set of operations.

We have "re-used" this definition, slightly paraphrased, in our characterisations of domain perspectives and facets and requirements aspects.[28]

Since Daniel Jackson has basically set the agenda for the study of software views we shall refer to his paper [79].

4.5 FAQ: Formal Software Design

Instead of listing frequently asked questions wrt. software design we list a number of myths and commandments more generally related to the larger concept of 'formal methods':

---

[28] Pages 12, 13 and 25 respectively.

- In [68] Anthony Hall lists and dispels the following seven "Myths":
  1. *Formal Methods can Guarantee that Software is Perfect*
  2. *Formal Methods are all about Program Proving*
  3. *Formal Methods are only Useful for Safety-Critical Systems*
  4. *Formal Methods Require highly trained Mathematicians*
  5. *Formal Methods Increase the Cost of Development*
  6. *Formal Methods are Unacceptable to Users*
  7. *Formal Methods are Not Used on Real, Large-Scale Software*
- In [31] Jonathan P. Bowen and Michael G. Hinchey continue dispelling myths:
  8. *Formal Methods Delay the Development Process*
  9. *Formal Methods are Not Supported by Tools*
  10. *Formal Methods mean Forsaking Traditional Engineering Design Methods*
  11. *Formal Methods only Apply to Software*
  12. *Formal Methods are Not Required*
  13. *Formal Methods are Not Supported*
  14. *Formal Methods People always use Formal Methods*
- And in [32] Jonathan P. Bowen and Michael G. Hinchey suggests ten rules of software engineering conduct:
  I. *Thou shalt choose an appropriate notation*
  II. *Thou shalt formalise but not over-formalise*
  III. *Thou shalt estimate costs*
  IV. *Thou shalt shall have a formal methods guru on call*
  V. *Thou shalt not abandon thy traditional development methods*
  VI. *Thou shalt document sufficiently*
  VII. *Thou shalt not compromise thy quality standards*
  VIII. *Thou shalt not be dogmatic*
  IX. *Thou shalt test, test, and test again*
  X. *Thou shalt reuse*

4.6 Software Design: Research, Education and Development Issues

The:

- **Software Design Research**
- **Software Design Education**
- **Software Design Development**
  issues seem reasonably well taken care of in at least Europe. The European, so-called 'formal methods' awareness "movement" (as exemplified through the more than a decade-long efforts of first VDM Europe, later Formal Methods Europe (FME)) These propagation efforts are based primarily on European research.
  The US attitude is basically that formal methods are anchored in, yes some (John Rushby) even state: only have to do with tools. The European attitude, in contrast, take formal methods are mostly specification (i.e. formal specification and design calculi).

It will be interesting to see how these two schools may eventually merge. The US school on 'software architecture', notably that part which we call: 'program organisation', is very strong [8, 58, 1, 59, 9, 2, 56, 57]. We should like to see a clearer separation between what we define as separate concepts: software architecture and program organisation. Some research is needed to clarify this issue and to develop principles and techniques for the 'derivation' of (families of) architectures from requirements specifications and of (families of) program organisations from these architectures.

5 Conclusion

A proposal for a triptych decomposition of software engineering has been presented. Some of the subsidiary, methodology principle concepts has been likewise presented: domain principles and facets, requirements aspects and software design views. A development methodology assumption is that all descriptions being presented (both informally and formally), and that relations between triptych phase documents and between stages and steps within these, be also formally characterised.

The paper has suggested a number of software engineering practices be currently dispensed by software engineers rather than domain professions. We argue so since the disciplines of computing science and software engineering has carefully developed and honed attendant description principles, techniques and tools. The paper has likewise suggested that a number of subsidiary areas be subject either to research, and/or to support by more or less mechanised tools, and/or to more specialised education: teaching and training.

What has been described is essentially the authors current research, university education and technology transfer interests. With colleagues we are trying out ideas of this paper in student project work, in exploratory & experimental demo & prototyping work — some with one or another of the kind of infrastructure enterprises or industries mentioned in section 2.1 — and hence also in more or less applied research. It is therefore to be expected that future publications will report on this as well as on more foundational work.

We refer to our home page for references to documents reporting on many practical applications and examples of the ideas expressed in this document. Several such URL-accessible documents report on software architecture and program organisation design techniques only covered cursorily in this document.

References

1. G. Abowd, R. Allen, and D. Garlan. Using style to understand descriptions of software architecture. *SIGSOFT Software Engineering Notes*, 18(5):9–20, December 1993.
2. G.D. Abowd, R. Allen, and D. Garlan. Formalizing style to understand descriptions of software architecture. *ACM Transactions on Software Engineering and Methodology*, 4(4):319–364, Oct 1995.

3. J.-R. Abrial, M.K.O. Lee, D.S. D.S. Neilson, P.N. Scharbach, and I.H. Sorensen. The B-method (software development). In S. Prehn and W.J.Toetenel, editors, *VDM '91. Formal Software Development Methods. 4th International Symposium of VDM Europe Proceedings. Vol.2: Tutorials; Springer-Verlag, LNCS.* VDM Europe, 1991.
4. Jean-Raymond Abrial. *The B Book.* Cambridge University Press, The Edinburgh Building, Cambridge CB2 1RU, England, 1996.
5. J.R. Abrial. The B Tool (Abstract). In *[29]*, pages 86–87, September 1988.
6. Cleta Milagros Acebedo. An Informal Domain Analysis for Manufacturing Enterprises. Research Report 62, UNU/IIST, P.O.Box 3058, Macau, March 1996.
7. Cleta Milagros Acebedo and Erwin Paguio. Manufacturing Enterprise Simulation: A Business Game. Research Report 64, UNU/IIST, P.O.Box 3058, Macau, March 1996.
8. R. Allen and D. Garlan. A formal approach to software architectures. In *IFIP Transactions A (Computer Science and Technology); IFIP Wordl Congress; Madrid, Spain*, volume vol.A-12, pages 134–141, Amsterdam, Netherlands, 1992. IFIP, North Holland.
9. R. Allen and D. Garlan. Formalizing architectural connection. In *16th International Conference on Software Engineering (Cat. No.94CH3409-0); Sorrento, Italy*, pages 71–80, Los Alamitos, CA, USA, 1994. IEEE Comput. Soc. Press. .
10. Gene Amdahl, Gerrit Blaauw, and Frederik Brooks. The IBM System/360 Architecture. *IBM Systems Journal*, 1964.
11. Dao Nam Anh and Richard Moore. Formal Modelling of Large Domains — with an Application to Airline Business. Technical Report 74, UNU/IIST, P.O.Box 3058, Macau, June 1996. Revised: September 1996.
12. D. M. Berry. The importance of ignorance in requirements engineering. *Journal of Systems and Software*, 28(2):179–184, February 1995.
13. B. Biebow and S. Szulman. Acquisition and validation of software requirements. *Knowledge Acquisition*, 6(4):343–367, December 1994.
14. D. Bjørner. Prospects for a Viable Software Industry — Enterprise Models, Design Calculi, and Reusable Modules. Technical Report 12, UNU/IIST, P.O.Box 3058, Macau, 7 November 1993. ppendix — on a railway domain model — by Søren Prehn and Dong Yulin,
    Published in *Proceedings from first ACM Japan Chapter Conference*, March 7–9, 1994: World Scientific Publ., Singapore, 1994.
15. D. Bjørner. Federated GIS+DIS–based Decision Support Systems for Sustainable Development — a Conceptual Architecture. Research Report 61, UNU/IIST, P.O.Box 3058, Macau, March 1996. Draft.
16. D. Bjørner. Models of Enterprise Management: Strategy, Tactics & Operations — Case Study Applied to Airlines and Manufacturing. Technical Report 60, UNU/IIST, P.O.Box 3058, Macau, January – April 1996.
17. D. Bjørner. A Software Engineering Paradigm: From Domains via Requirements to Software. Research report, Dept. of Information Technology, Technical University of Denmark, Bldg.345/167–169, DK–2800 Lyngby, Denmark, July 1997.
18. D. Bjørner. Models of Financial Services & Industries. Research Report 96, UNU/IIST, P.O.Box 3058, Macau, January 1997. ncomplete Draft Report.
19. D. Bjørner. Towards a Domain Theory of The Financial Sevice Industry. Research report, Dept. of Information Technology, Technical University of Denmark, Bldg.345/167–169, DK–2800 Lyngby, Denmark, July 1997.

20. D. Bjørner, C.W. George, B.Stig Hansen, H. Laustrup, and S. Prehn. A Railway System, Coordination'97, Case Study Workshop Example. Research Report 93, UNU/IIST, P.O.Box 3058, Macau, January 1997.
21. D. Bjørner, C.W. George, and S. Prehn. *Scheduling and rescheduling of trains*, page 24 pages. Prentice Hall (?), 1997.
22. D. Bjørner and C.B. Jones, editors. *The Vienna Development Method: The Meta-Language*, volume 61 of *Lecture Notes in Computer Science*. Springer-Verlag, 1978.
23. D. Bjørner and C.B. Jones, editors. *Formal Specification and Software Development*. Prentice-Hall, 1982.
24. Dines Bjørner. Prospects for a Viable Software Industry — Enterprise Models, Design Calculi, and Reusable Modules. Technical Report 12, UNU/IIST, P.O.Box 3058, Macau, 7 November 1993. ppendix — on a railway domain model — by Søren Prehn and Dong Yulin,
Published in *Proceedings from first ACM Japan Chapter Conference*, March 7–9, 1994: World Scientific Publ., Singapore, 1994.
25. Dines Bjørner. Models of Financial Services & Industries. Research Report 96, UNU/IIST, P.O.Box 3058, Macau, January 1997. ncomplete Draft Report.
26. Dines Bjørner, Chris W. George, Bo Stig Hansen, Hans Laustrup, and Søren Prehn. A Railway System, Coordination'97, Case Study Workshop Example. Research Report 93, UNU/IIST, P.O.Box 3058, Macau, January 1997.
27. Dines Bjørner, Souleimane Koussobe, Roger Noussi, and Georgui Satchok. Michael Jackson's Problem Frames: . In Li ShaoQi and Michael Hinchley, editors, *ICFEM'97: Intl. Conf. on Formal Engineering Mehtods*, Los Alamitos, CA, USA, 12–14 November 1997. IEEE Computer Society Press.
28. Dines Bjørner, Dong Yu Lin, and Søren Prehn. Domain Analyses: A Case Study of Station Management. Research Report 23, UNU/IIST, P.O.Box 3058, Macau, 9 November 1994. resented at the *1994 Kunming International CASE Symposium*: KICS'94, Yunnan Province, P.R.of China, 16–20 November 1994. .
29. R. Bloomfield, L. Marshall, and R. Jones, editors. *VDM – The Way Ahead*. Proc. 2nd VDM-Europe Symposium 1988, Dublin, Ireland, Springer-Verlag, Lecture Notes in Computer Science, Vol. 328, September 1988.
30. B. Boehm and H. In. Identifying quality-requirement conflicts. In *Second International Conference on Requirements Engineering (Cat. No.96TB100037); Colorado Springs, CO, USA*, page 218, Los Alamitos, CA, USA, 1996. IEEE Comput. Soc. Press.
31. J.P. Bowen and M. Hinchey. Seven More Myths of Formal Methods. Technical Report PRG–TR–7–94, Oxford Univ., Programming Research Group, Wolfson Bldg., Parks Road, Oxford OX1 3QD, UK, June 1994. Shorter version published in LNCS Springer Verlag FME'94 Symposium Proceedings.
32. J.P. Bowen and M. Hinchey. Ten Commandments of Formal Methods. Technical report, Oxford Univ., Programming Research Group, Wolfson Bldg., Parks Road, Oxford OX1 3QD, UK, 1995.
33. Zhou Chaochen. Duration Calculi: An Overview. Research Report 10, UNU/IIST, P.O.Box 3058, Macau, June 1993. Published in: *Formal Methods in Programming and Their Applications*, Conference Proceedings, June 28 – July 2, 1993, Novosibirsk, Russia; (Eds.: D. Bjørner, M. Broy and I. Pottosin) LNCS 736, Springer-Verlag, 1993, pp 36–59.
34. Zhou Chaochen and Michael R. Hansen. Lecture Notes on Logical Foundations for the Duration Calculus. Lecture Notes, 13, UNU/IIST, P.O.Box 3058, Macau, August 1993.

35. Zhou Chaochen, C. A. R. Hoare, and A. P. Ravn. A Calculus of Durations. *Information Proc. Letters*, 40(5), 1992.
36. Zhou Chaochen, C.A.R. Hoare, and A.P. Ravn. A Calculus of Durations. *Information Processing Letters*, 40(5):269–276, 1991.
37. Zhou Chaochen and Yu Huiqun. A duration Model for Railway scheduling. Technical Report 24b, UNU/IIST, P.O.Box 3058, Macau, May 1994.
38. Zhou Chaochen, Dang Van Hung, and Li Xiaoshan. A Duration Calculus with Infinite Intervals. Research Report 40, UNU/IIST, P.O.Box 3058, Macau, February 1995. ublished in: *Fundamentals of Computation Theory*, Horst Reichel (ed.), pp 16-41, LNCS 965, Springer-Verlag, 1995.
39. Zhou Chaochen, Anders P. Ravn, and Michael R. Hansen. An Extended Duration Calculus for Real-time Systems. Research Report 9, UNU/IIST, P.O.Box 3058, Macau, January 1993. Published in: *Hybrid Systems*, LNCS 736, 1993.
40. Zhou Chaochen and Li Xiaoshan. A Mean Value Duration Calculus. Research Report 5, UNU/IIST, P.O.Box 3058, Macau, March 1993. Published as Chapter 25 in *A Classical Mind*, Festschrift for C.A.R. Hoare, Prentice-Hall International, 1994, pp 432–451.
41. A. Cucchiarelli, M. Panti, and S. Valenti. Supporting user-analyst interaction in functional requirements elicitation. In *First Asia-Pacific Software Engineering Conference; Tokyo, Japan*, pages 114–23, Los Alamitos, CA, USA, 1994. IEEE Comput. Soc. Press.
42. P. Darke and G. Shanks. Stakeholder viewpoints in requirements definition: a framework for understanding viewpoint development approaches. *Requirements Engineering*, 1(2):88–105, 1996.
43. John Dawes. *The VDM-SL Reference Guide*. Pitman Publishing, 1991.
44. Do Tien Dung, Le Linh Chi, Nguyen Le Thu, Phung Phuong Nam, Tran Mai Lien, and Chris George. Developing a Financial Information System. Technical Report 81, UNU/IIST, P.O.Box 3058, Macau, September 1996.
45. Rene Elmstrøm, Peter Gorm Larsen, and Poul Bøgh Lassen. The IFAD VDM-SL Toolbox: A Practical Approach to Formal Specifications. *ACM SIGPAN Notoces*, 29(9):77–80, September 1994.
46. Myatav Erdenechimeg, Richard Moore, and Yumbayar Namsrai. MultiScript I: The Basic Model of Multi-lingual Documents. Technical Report 105, UNU/IIST, P.O.Box 3058, Macau, June 1997.
47. J.A. Hess et al. Feature-oriented domain analysis (FODA) feasibility study. Technical Report CMU-SEI-90-TR-21, Carnegie Mellon University. SEI Software Engineering Institute, DoD, Pittsburgh, Penn., USA, 1990.
48. R. Thayer et al., editor. *Software Requirements Engineering*. IEEE Computer Society Press, Los Alamitos, California, USA.
49. Yu Xinyiao et al. Stability of Railway Systems. Technical Report 28, UNU/IIST, P.O.Box 3058, Macau, May 1994.
50. A. Finkelstein. Tracing back from requirements. In *IEE Colloquium on 'Tools and Techniques for Maintaining Traceability During Design' (Digest No.180)*, London, UK, 1991. IEE.
51. John Fitzgerald and Peter Gorm Larsen. *Developing Software using VDM-SL*. Cambridge University Press, The Edinburgh Building, Cambridge CB2 1RU, England, 1997.
52. Dov M. Gabbay, C.J. Hogger, J.A. Robinson, and D. Nute, editors. *Deduction Methodologies*, volume 2 of *Handbook of Logic in Artificial Intelligence and Logic Programming*. Oxford Science Publications, Clarendon Press, Oxford, England, 1993.

53. Dov M. Gabbay, C.J. Hogger, J.A. Robinson, and D. Nute, editors. *Logical Foundations*, volume 1 of *Handbook of Logic in Artificial Intelligence and Logic Programming*. Oxford Science Publications, Clarendon Press, Oxford, England, 1993.
54. Dov M. Gabbay, C.J. Hogger, J.A. Robinson, and D. Nute, editors. *Nonmonotonic Reasoning and Uncertain Reasoning*, volume 3 of *Handbook of Logic in Artificial Intelligence and Logic Programming*. Oxford Science Publications, Clarendon Press, Oxford, England, 1994.
55. Dov M. Gabbay, C.J. Hogger, J.A. Robinson, and D. Nute, editors. *Epistemic and Tempral Reasoning*, volume 4 of *Handbook of Logic in Artificial Intelligence and Logic Programming*. Oxford Science Publications, Clarendon Press, Oxford, England, 1995.
56. D. Garlan. Research directions in software architecture. *ACM Computing Surveys*, 27(2):257–261, June 1995.
57. D. Garlan. Formal approaches to software architecture. In *Studies of Software Design. ICSE '93 Workshop. Selected Papers*, pages 64–76, Berlin, Germany, 1996. Springer-Verlag.
58. D. Garlan and M. Shaw. Experience with a course on architectures for software systems. In *Software Engineering Education. SEI Conference 1992; San Diego, CA, USA*, pages 23–43, Berlin, Germany, 199. Springer-Verlag.
59. D. Garlan and M. Shaw. *An introduction to software architecture*, pages 1–39. World Scientific, Singapore, 1993.
60. J.A. Goguen and LuQi. Formal methods and social context in software development. In P.D. Mosses, M. Nielsen, and M.I. Schwartzbach, editors, *TAPSOFT '95: Theory and Practice of Software Development. 6th International Joint Conference CAA/FASE*, pages 62–81, Aarhus, Denmark, 1995.
61. Jan Goossenaerts and Dines Bjørner. An Information Technology Framework for Lean/Agile Supply-based Industries in Developing Countries. Technical Report 30, UNU/IIST, P.O.Box 3058, Macau, 1994. ublished in *Proceedings of the International Dedicated Conference on Lean/Agile Manufacturing in the Automotive Industries*, ISATA, London, UK.
62. Jan Goossenaerts and Dines Bjørner. Interflow Systems for Manufacturing: Concepts and a Construction. Technical Report 31, UNU/IIST, P.O.Box 3058, Macau, 1994. ublished in *Proceedings of the European Workshop on Integrated Manufacturing Systems Engineering*.
63. The RAISE Language Group. *The RAISE Specification Language*. The BCS Practitioner Series. Prentice-Hall, Hemel Hampstead, England, 1995.
64. The RAISE Method Group. *The RAISE Method*. The BCS Practitioner Series. Prentice-Hall, Hemel Hampstead, England, 1992.
65. Carl Gunther. Higher Order Logics in Requirements Engineering. In Manfred Broay, editor, *Requirements Targeting Software (Systems) Engineering*, 1997.
66. J. Guttag, J.J. Horning, and J.M. Wing. Larch in Five Easy Pieces. Technical Report 5, DEC SRC, Dig. Equipm. Corp. Syst. Res. Ctr., Palo Alto, California, USA, 1985.
67. John V. Guttag, James J. Horning, S.J. Garland, K.D. Jones, A. Modet, , and J.M. Wing. *Larch: Languages and Tools for Formal Specification*. Texts and Monographs in Computer Science. Springer-Verlag, Springer-Verlag New York, Inc., Attn: J. Jeng, 175 Fifth Avenue, New York, NY 10010-7858, USA, 1993.
68. Anthony Hall. Seven Myths of Formal Methods. *IEEE Software*, 7(5):11–19, 1990.

69. P.A.V. Hall, D. Bjørner, and Z. Mikolajuk. Decision Support Systems for Sustainable Development: Experience and Potential — a Position Paper. Administrative Report 80, UNU/IIST, P.O.Box 3058, Macau, August 1996.
70. Ian J. Hayes, editor. *Specification Case Studies*. International Series in Computer Science. Prentice Hall, Hemel Hempstead, Hertfordshire HP2 4RG, UK, 1987.
71. E. Haywood and P. Dart. Analysis of software system requirements models. In *Australian Software Engineering Conference*, pages 131–138. IEEE Comput. Soc. Press, 1996.
72. C.L. Heitmeyer, R.D. Jeffords, and B.G. Labaw. Automated Consistency Checking of Requirements Specifications. *TOSEM: ACM Transactions on Software Engineering and Methodology*, 5(3):231–261, July, 1996.
73. Hennesy and Patterson. *Computer Architectures*. Addison Wesley, 199?
74. Hennesy and Patterson. *Computer Organisations*. Addison Wesley, 199?
75. J. Hoare, J. Dick, D. Neilson, and I.H. Sorensen. Applying the B technologies to CICS. In C. Gaudel M and J. Woodcock, editors, *FME '96: Industrial Benefit and Advances in Formal Methods. Third International Symposium of Formal Methods Europe. Proceedings; Springer-Verlag, LNCS*. Formal Methods Europe, 1996.
76. Dang Van Hung and Zhou Chaochen. Probabilistic Duration Calculus for Continuous Time. Research Report 25, UNU/IIST, P.O.Box 3058, Macau, May 1994. resented at *NSL'94 (Workshop on Non-standard Logics and Logical Aspects of Computer Science, Kanazawa, Japan, December 5–8, 1994)*, submitted to *Formal Aspects of Computing*.
77. Dang Van Hung and Phan Hong Giang. A Sampling Semantics of Duration Calculus. Research Report 50, UNU/IIST, P.O.Box 3058, Macau, November 1995. ublished in: *Formal Techniques for Real-Time and Fault Tolerant Systems*, Bengt Jonsson and Joachim Parrow (Eds), LNCS 1135, Spriger-Verlag, pp. 188–207, 1996.
78. IEEE. *Proceedings of the Second International Conference on Requirements Engineering;C olorado Springs, CO, USA*, Los Alamitos, CA, USA, 1996. IEEE Comput. Soc. Press.
79. Daniel Jackson. Structuring Z Specifications with Views. *ACM Transactions on Software Engineering and Methodology*, 4(4):365–389, October 1995.
80. M. Jackson. Problems and requirements (software development). In *Second IEEE International Symposium on Requirements Engineering (Cat. No.95TH8040)*, pages 2–8. IEEE Comput. Soc. Press, 1995.
81. Michael Jackson. Problems, methods and specialisation. *Software Engineering Journal*, pages 249–255, November 1994.
82. Michael Jackson. *Software Requirements & Specifications: a lexicon of practice, principles and prejudices*. ACM Press. Addison-Wesley Publishing Company, Wokingham, nr. Reading, England; E-mail: ipc@awpub.add-wes.co.uk, 1995. ISBN 0-201-87712-0; xiv + 228 pages.
83. Michael A. Jackson. *Software Development Method*, chapter 13, pages 215–234. Prentice Hall Intl., 1994. Festschrift for C. A. R. Hoare: *A Classical Mind*, Ed. W. Roscoe.
84. T. Janowski and C.M. Acebedo. Virtual Enterprise: On Refinement Towards an ODP Architecture. Research Report 69, UNU/IIST, P.O.Box 3058, Macau, May 1996.
85. Tomasz Janowski. Domain Analysis for Manufacturing: Formalization of the Market. Research Report 63, UNU/IIST, P.O.Box 3058, Macau, March 1996.

86. Tomasz Janowski and Rumel V. Atienza. A Formal Model For Competing Enterprises, Applied to Marketing Decision-Making. Research Report 92, UNU/IIST, P.O.Box 3058, Macau, January 1997.
87. C.B. Jones. *Systematic Software Development using VDM*. Prentice Hall International, second edition, 1990.
88. M. Kirikova and J.A. Bubenko Jr. Software requirements acquisition through enterprise modelling. In *SEKE '94. The 6th International Conference on Software Engineering and Knowledge Engineering*, pages 20–27, Skokie, IL, USA, 1994. Knowledge Syst. Inst.
89. G. Kosters, H.-W. Six, and J. Voss. Combined analysis of user interface and domain requirements. In *Second International Conference on Requirements Engineering (Cat. No.96TB100037); Colorado Springs, CO, USA*, pages 199–207. IEEE Comput. Soc. Press, 1996.
90. Souleymane Koussoubé. Knowledge-Based Systems: Formalisation and Applications to Insurance. Research Report 108, UNU/IIST, P.O.Box 3058, Macau, May 1997.
91. P. G. Larsen, B. S. Hansen, H. Brunn N. Plat, H. Toetenel, D. J. Andrews, J. Dawes, G. Parkin, et al. Information technology — Programming languages, their environments and system software interfaces — Vienna Development Method — Specification Language — Part 1: Base language, December 1996.
92. Peter Gorm Larsen. The IFAD VDM-SL Toolbox Brochures. Technical report, Institute for Applied Datalogy, Forskerparken 10, DK-5230 Odense M, Denmark, 1994.
93. Nancy G. Leveson, M.P.E. Heimdahl, H H. Hildreth, and J.D. Reese. Requirements Specification for Process-Control Systems. *IEEE Transactions on Software Engineering*, 20(9):684–707, September 1994.
94. P. Loucopoulos and E. Kavakli. Enterprise modelling and the teleological approach to requirements engineering. *International Journal of Intelligent & Cooperative Information Systems*, 4(1):45–79, March 1995.
95. M et al. M. Jarke. Requirements engineering: an integrated view of representation, process, and domain. In I. Sommerville and M. Paul, editors, *Software Engineering - ESEC '93. 4th European Software Engineering Conference Proceedings; Garmisch-Partenkirchen, Germany*, pages 100–114, Berlin, Germany, 1993. Springer-Verlag.
96. N.A.M. Maiden and A.G. Sutcliffe. Requirements critiquing using domain abstractions. In *First International Conference on Requirements Engineering (Cat. No.94TH0613-0); Colorado Springs, CO, USA*, pages 184–193, Los Alamitos, CA, USA, 1994. IEEE Comput. Soc. Press.
97. Zohar Manna and Amir Pnueli. *The Temporal Logic of Reactive Systems: Specifications*. Addison Wesley, 1991.
98. Zohar Manna and Amir Pnueli. *The Temporal Logic of Reactive Systems: Safety*. Addison Wesley, 1995.
99. T.L. McCluskey, J.M. Porteous, Y. Naik, C.N. Taylor, and S. Jones. A requirements capture method and its use in an air traffic control application. *Software - Practice and Experience*, 25(1):47–71, January 1995.
100. M. Moulding and L.Smith. Combining formal specification and CORE: an experimental investigation. *Software Engineering Journal*, 10(2):31–42, March 1995.
101. Nikolaj Nikitchenko. Towards Foundations of the General Theory of Transport Domains. Research Report 88, UNU/IIST, P.O.Box 3058, Macau, December 1996.

102. Roger Noussi. An Efficient Construction of a Domain Theory for Resources Management: A Case Study. Research Report 107, UNU/IIST, P.O.Box 3058, Macau, May 1997.
103. B. Nuseibeh, J. Kramer, and A. Finkelstein. Expressing the relationships between multiple views in requirements specification. In *15th International Conference on Software Engineering (Cat. No.93CH3270-6)*, pages 187-96, Los Alamitos, CA, USA, 1993. EEE Comput. Soc. Press.
104. C. Shekaran, D. Garlan, and et al. The role of software architecture in requirements engineering. In *First International Conference on Requirements Engineering (Cat. No.94TH0613-0); Colorado Springs, CO, USA*, pages 239-245, Los Alamitos, CA, USA, 1994. IEEE Comput. Soc. Press.
105. E.V. Sørensen, J. Nordahl, and N.H. Hansen. From CSP Models to Markov Models: A Case Study. *To be published in IEEE Transactions on Software Engineering*, Dept. of Computer Science, Technical University of Denmark, August 15 1991.
106. J. Michael Spivey. An Introduction to Z and Formal Specifications. *Software Engineering Journal*, 4(1), January 1989.
107. J. Michael Spivey. *The Z Notation: A Reference Manual.* International Series in Computer Science. Prentice Hall, Hemel Hempstead, Hertfordshire HP2 4RG, UK, 1989.
108. J.J.P. Tsai, T. Weigert, and H.C. Jang. A hybrid knowledge representation as a basis of requirement specification and reasoning. In *2nd International IEEE Conference on Tools for Artificial Intelligence (Cat. No.90CH2915-7)*, pages 70-76. IEEE Comput. Soc. Press, 1990.
109. Tan Xinming. Enquiring about Bus Transport-Formal Development using RAISE. Technical Report 83, UNU/IIST, P.O.Box 3058, Macau, September 1996.
110. S. Yamamoto, H. Tadaumi, and M. Ueno. DREM: domain-based requirements engineering methodology. *NTT R & D*, 45(8):711-718, 1996. n Japanese.
111. P. Zave and M. Jackson. Four dark corners of requirements engineering. *ACM Transactions on Software Engineering and Methodology*, 6(1):1-30, January 1997.
112. P. Zave and M. Jackson. Requirements for telecommunications services: an attack on complexity. In *Proceedings of the Third IEEE International Symposium on Requirements Engineering (Cat. No.97TB100086)*, pages 106-117. IEEE Comput. Soc. Press, 1997.
113. Liu ZhiMing, A.P. Ravn, E.V. Sørensen, and Zhou ChaoChen. A Probabilistic Duration Calculus. Technical report, Dept. of Computer Science, Technical University of Denmark, February 1992. Submitted for: 2nd Intl. Workshop on Responsive Systems, Japan, 1992.

Software and System Modeling Based on a Unified Formal Semantics

Manfred Broy, Franz Huber, Barbara Paech,
Bernhard Rumpe, and Katharina Spies

Fakultät für Informatik, Technische Universität München
{broy,huberf,paech,rumpe,spiesk}@in.tum.de

Abstract. Modeling and documentation are two essential ingredients for the engineering discipline of software development. During the last twenty years a wide variety of description and modeling techniques as well as document formats has been proposed. However, often these are not integrated into a coherent methodology with well-defined dependencies between the models and documentations. This hampers focused software development as well as the provision of powerful tool-support. In this paper we present the main issues and outline solutions in the direction of a unified, formal basis for software and system modeling.

1 Introduction

Computer technology for commercial applications has evolved rapidly from mainframes through personal computers to distributed systems. Software engineering could not keep pace with the resulting demand for powerful application development methods. This is exemplified by an ever growing number of software projects running behind schedule, delivering faulty software, not meeting users' needs, or even failing completely. There is a number of reasons for that, ranging from inadequate project management, over communication problems between domain experts and software developers to poorly documented and designed software. A recent inquiry on industrial software developers [DHP+98] has shown that despite the great variety of CASE-tools, development methods, and modeling techniques, software development still largely produces informal, incomplete and inconsistent requirements and design descriptions and poorly documented code. Modeling techniques are used selectively, but not integrated with each other or the coding. The large variety of proprietary modeling techniques and tools makes it difficult to choose an adequate selection for a project. As exemplified by the newly evolving standard *Unified Modeling Language* [BRJ97], the techniques provide a rich collection of complex notations without the corresponding semantic foundation. Since only static models are linked to code, behavioural models can only serve as illustrations not worthwhile the big effort of building the model.

This situation will only change if modeling techniques come with a set of development steps and tools for incremental model development, consistency checks, reasoning support and code generation. Mathematical description techniques like Z [Wor92] or LOTOS [Tur93] provide such development steps, but their uptake by industry is hampered by their cumbersome notation, lack of tools and lack of integration to established specification and assurance techniques [CGR93]. Recently, a number of approaches for the combination of mathematical and graphical modeling techniques has evolved (e.g. [Huß97,BHH+97]) proving the viability of the integration of selected modeling techniques and formalisms. However, the integration of mathematical and graphical modeling techniques covering the whole process of system and software development is still an open problem.

The paper describes coherently the major issues in providing such an integrating basis. Experience on this subject has been gained mainly in the projects FOCUS [BDD+93], SYSLAB [BGH+97b] and AUTOFOCUS [HSS96]. The project FOCUS is devoted to developing a mathematical development method for distributed systems. SYSLAB concentrates on graphical description techniques, their formal semantics based on FOCUS and their methodical use, in particular for object-oriented systems. AUTOFOCUS is building a tool aimed at the development of distributed/embedded systems allowing the combined use of mathematical and graphical description techniques and providing powerful development steps based on the formal semantics. Its main application areas are components of embedded systems. None of the projects covers the whole development process, but taken together they provide a clear picture of the road to follow.

The paper is structured as follows. In the first section we introduce FOCUS, the theory of stream processing functions, as the mathematical basis of our work. First, we present FOCUS independent of a particular application area. Then we show how to adapt it to object-oriented systems. FOCUS comes with a set of notations and a methodology for developing formal specifications that can only be touched on in this paper. Refinement and compositionality provide the foundation for the formal development steps. We close this section with a discussion on the enhancement of formal notations to be useful for practitioners.

We then go on to describe the *indirect* use of FOCUS as the common formal semantics for graphical modeling techniques used in software development. We describe a set of graphical description techniques covering the main system aspects. These modeling techniques are similar to the ones used by structured or object-oriented methods. However, they differ in detail, because they were developed with a particular focus on a common formal semantics. The aim of that section is to make explicit the most important issues in providing this semantics.

The indirect use of formal methods is very valuable to the method developer. However, it is only useful to the system developer if the modeling techniques are accompanied by powerful development steps that allow to check and enforce the formal dependencies between the models. In the third section we discuss consistency checking, model validation and transformation as the most important development steps, together with possible tool support.

The modeling techniques and development steps must be integrated into a process of system development, covering requirements definition, analysis, design and implementation. In the fourth section we present a framework making explicit the different modeling areas to be covered, namely the application domain, the system usage, and the software system, as well as the interplay between different system views and their corresponding modeling techniques.

We close with an outlook on future work. Related work is dicussed along the way.

2 Semantic Framework

In this section we describe the formal semantics as the basis for the description techniques and methodological aspects presented later. First we sketch the mathematics of system descriptions treating object-oriented systems as a special case. Then we present refinement as a major constituent of formal system development. After a short description of the formal system development process, we close with an evaluation of the direct use of FOCUS, our general framework for formal handling of distributed reactive systems.

2.1 Mathematical Basics

FOCUS incorporates a general semantics basis with some variants and a variety of techniques and specification formalisms based on this semantics. Here, we only give a short and informal description of the main concepts and some simple formulas. For further details, the interested reader is referred to [BS97,BDD+93] for an introduction and more formalization, and [BBSS97] for an overview of case studies. Besides FOCUS there are many other formal development methods and description techniques like TLA, UNITY or PROCOS. For further reading and a comparison between these and many other formal methods like algebraic or temporal logic approaches in combination with an uniform example we refer to [BMS96a,BMS96b].

According to the concepts of FOCUS, a distributed system consists of a number of components that are partially connected with each other or with the environment via one-way communication channels. Because our model is based on a discrete global time and on channels comparable with unbounded FIFO-buffers, the communication is time-synchronous and message-asynchronous. With the behaviour of each component and the topology of the network – the connection of components via the communication channels – the system is completely described: The behaviour of a system can be deduced from the behaviour of its constituents because the formal basis of FOCUS allows *modular* systems specification by *compositional* semantics.

Timed Streams

The basic data structure needed for the definition of component behaviour are *timed streams*. Assuming global and discrete time we model time flow by a special time signal $\sqrt{}$ (pronounced *tick*), indicating the end of a time interval. A timed stream is a sequence of $\sqrt{}$ and messages that contains an infinite number of time ticks. Apart from the time ticks a stream contains a finite or infinite number of messages. Let M be a set of messages that does not contain the time signal $\sqrt{}$. By M^ω we denote streams of messages and by $M^{\overline{\omega}}$ the set of infinite timed streams containing an infinite number of ticks. To illustrate the concept of a timed stream we show a simple example. The timed stream

$$a \sqrt{} \ ab \sqrt{} \sqrt{} \ bca \sqrt{} \ b \sqrt{} \ldots$$

contains the sequence of small letters $aabbcab$. In the first time interval a is communicated, in the third interval there is no communication, and in the fourth interval first b then c and last a is communicated.

The special time signal $\sqrt{}$ should not be understood as a message that is transmitted, but as a semantic concept to represent the global time progress. Timed streams model complete communication histories: A specific stream associated with a channel between two components contains all information about *what* message is sent *when* between these components. Semantic variants of FOCUS abstract from time into the *untimed model* or describe, in the *synchronous model*, streams in which in each time interval at most one message can be transmitted between two components.

Component Definition

A (system) component is an active information processing unit that communicates with its environment through a set of input and output channels. To define a component, the *interface* must be declared at first. This contains a description of its input and output channels as well as the types of messages that can be received or sent via these channels. The *behaviour* of a component is described by a relation between its input and output streams fixing the set of communication histories that are valid for this component. One way to describe this relation is to define a *stream-processing function* that maps input streams to sets of output streams. Such a function reads an input stream message by message, and - as a reaction - writes output messages onto the output channels. Stream-processing functions must fulfill semantic properties like continuity, realizability, time-guardedness, as explained in the FOCUS-literature. Additionally it is possible to use state parameters to store control states or additional data and thus ease the modeling.

Let I be the set of input channels and O be the set of output channels. Then by (I, O) the *syntactic interface* of a component is given. With every channel in $I \cup O$ we associate a data type indicating the type of messages sent on that channel.

To describe and to design the topology and the behaviour of distributed systems and their components, FOCUS offers different graphical and diagrammatical notations. All these description formalisms are well founded in the mathematical framework described in this section. A graphical representation of a component with its syntactic interface $I = \{i_1, \ldots, i_n\}$ and $O = \{o_1, \ldots, o_m\}$, and the individual channel types $S_1, \ldots, S_n$ and $R_1, \ldots, R_m$ is shown in Figure 1.

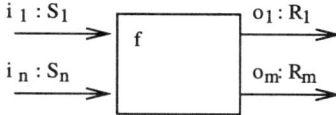

Fig. 1. Graphical Representation of a Component as Dataflow Node

Given a set of channels C we denote the set of all channel valuations by $\boldsymbol{C}$. It is defined by:

$$\boldsymbol{C} = (C \to M^{\bar{\omega}})$$

Channel valuations are the assignments of timed streams to all channels in C. We assume that the streams for the channels carry only messages of the correct type specified by the interface declaration.

We describe the behaviour of a component by a stream-processing function. It defines the relation between the input streams and output streams of a component that fulfills certain conditions with respect to their timing. A stream-processing function is represented by a set-valued function on valuations of the input channels by timed streams that yields the set of histories for the output channels

$$f : \boldsymbol{I} \to \mathcal{P}(\boldsymbol{O})$$

and fulfills the timing property of *time-guardedness*. This property ensures that output histories for the first $i+1$ time intervals only depend on the input histories for the first i time intervals. In other words, the processing of messages in a component takes at least one tick of time. Thus, time-guardedness axiomatizes the time flow and supports the modeling of realistic applications, since the processing of messages or the execution of computing steps always consumes time. For a precise formal definition of this property see [BS97].

2.2 Foundations of Object Orientation

Based on the theory given above, we have defined a set of concepts to enrich FOCUS with an object-oriented flavor. This allows us to give a formal semantics to object-oriented modeling techniques, like UML [BRJ97], as we have done in [BHH+97].

For that purpose, we have defined a *system model* in [KRB96] that characterizes our notion of object-oriented systems. Objects can be naturally viewed as components, as defined in the last section. Based on that, communication paths are defined using identifiers, where each object is associated with exactly one identifier (its identity).

In the system model, objects interact by means of *asynchronous message passing*. Asynchronous exchange of messages between the components of a system means that a message can be sent independently of the actual state of the receiver, as, e.g., in C++ or Java. To model communication between objects we use the FOCUS basic data structure of streams and stream-processing functions.

Objects encapsulate data as well as processes. *Encapsulation of a process* means that the exchange of a message does not (necessarily) imply the exchange of control: Each object is regarded as a separate process. *Encapsulation of data* means that the state of an object is not directly visible to the environment but can be accessed using explicit communication. The data part of the object defines its state. It is given in terms of typed attributes.

Objects are grouped into classes, that define the set of attributes of an object and its method interface (message interface). This allows to model the behavior of the objects of each class c as stream-processing functions f_c mapping input histories to sets of output histories. As usual, classes are structured by an inheritance relation $\sqsubseteq$. We thus get a natural definition of inheritance of behavior: We postulate if a class inherits from another, its possible behaviors are a subset:

$$\forall c, d : Class.\ c \sqsubseteq d \;\Rightarrow\; f_c \subseteq f_d$$

In case of method extension, this constraint is adapted to an interface refinement constraint.

Dynamic and mobile features, such as creation of new instances and change of communication structures, are also characterized as extension of Focus.

2.3 Refinement and Compositionality

Based on a first formal specification, the development of software and also of distributed systems goes through several development phases (or levels of abstraction). Through these phases the envisaged system or system component is described in an increasing amount of detail until a sufficiently detailed description or even an implementation of the system is obtained. The individual steps of such a process can be captured by appropriate notions of refinement. In a refinement step, parts or aspects of a system description are specified more completely or more detailed. For this purpose, FOCUS offers a powerful compositional refinement concept as well as refinement calculi. On the semantic level, refinement is modeled by logical implication. The important refinement concepts are:

Behavioural Refinement: The aim of this refinement is the elimination of underspecification as needed, e.g., for the specification of fault-tolerant behavior.

Interface Refinement: Here, the interface of a specification is refined by changing the number or types of the channels as needed, e.g., for concretization of messages or splitting communication connections between components.

Structural Refinement: This concept allows the development of the structure of the distributed system by refining components by networks of components.

2.4 A Formal System Development Process

FOCUS provides a general framework and a *methodology in the large* for formal specification and stepwise top-down development of distributed reactive systems.

The formal system development process consists of several phases of abstraction and three main development phases:

During the *Requirements Phase*, a first formalization of a given informal problem description is developed. Since the informal description is often not detailed enough, this first step of a system specification is hard to develop. It is, however, essential for the formal system development because it will be used as the basis for further development of specifications with a growing degree of accuracy in the following phases. In this step, specifications can be formalized either as trace or as functional specifications. The transition between these paradigms is formally sound and preserving correctness.

During the *Design Phase*, the essential part of the system development, the structure of a distributed system is developed by refining it up to the intended level of granularity. These formal development steps are based on the specification determined in the requirement phase and their correctness will be shown relative to the first formalization. Because the formal development of a more detailed specification possibly uncovers mistakes or unprecise properties in earlier formalizations, the top-down development is not linear but rather leads to respecifications of some parts of earlier formalizations. Only the description of system properties in a mathematical and precise manner gives a system developer the possibility to formally prove and refine system properties and descriptions. During this phase, specifications in FOCUS are based on the denotational semantics which models component behaviour by stream-processing functions. For the development of the specifications during the design phase, paradigms like relational and functional specifications as well as several specification styles like Assumption/Commitment[1] or equational specifications are defined. To increase its usability FOCUS is adapted to support various engineering oriented and practically used techniques and formalisms like tables or diagrams, see section 3. Due to the specific natures of these variants they can be used tailor-made for the solution of specific problems.

During the *Implementation Phase* the design specification is transformed into an implementation. This phase is subject of future work.

2.5 Further Work

Since the semantic foundation of FOCUS, including its development techniques, have already been explored in depth, the emphasis of further work lies in better applicability of the methodology, especially for system developers less experienced in formal methods. For that purpose, additional wide-spread description techniques, (semi-)automatic and schematic proof support have to be offered. Several techniques for describing and specifying systems (like tables, state or system diagrams, MSC-like event traces (cf. Section 3.5), the "Assumption/Commitment" style) were successfully integrated in the methodology. With

---

[1] a special relational specification style where the "Assumption" formalizes the constraints about the input histories that have to be fulfilled in order to guarantee the behaviour of a component formalized by the "Commitment". For further reading see e.g. [Bro94] and [SDW95])

AutoFocus, tool support for system development is already available, giving future case studies a new quality by offering appropriate editors, consistency checks, code generation and even simulation. Current research activities concern the enhancement of Focus with methodical guidelines to ease the use of the mathematical formalism, the description techniques and the development methodology for non-specialists and to support solutions for specific application fields, like the modeling of operating systems concepts in [Spi98].

Case studies are an important and stimulating work for testing Focus in different application areas. Focus will be further improved, using the experience gained from the great number of case studies collected in [BFG$^+$94,BBSS97] and future studies to come.

2.6 On the Direct Use of Formal Description Techniques

In the last sections we have sketched a mathematical framework and the semantic basis for system specification. This allows developers to precisely describe structural and behavioural properties of the components and the composed system. As will be argued in section 3, one can hide the mathematics from developers through the use of graphical description techniques whose semantics are based on the formal framework. However not everything can be adequately expressed in diagrams. Especially behavioural properties are difficult to express. Thus for example, object-oriented specification methods typically use state transition diagrams to describe method acceptance in classes or collaboration diagrams to describe method calls between classes, but only programming language code to define the method bodies. Mathematical specification languages like Focus allow complete behaviour description in a much more declarative style. To be useful for practitioners, however, the notation must be simple and the specification language must be enhanced with guidelines for a systematic development of specifications. These guidelines are useful for developers formulating properties of individual systems and application areas, as well as for method developers who need to state and verify properties of the (diagrammatic) description techniques on the basis of the formal semantics.

In the following we present an example of some guidelines to write down formal specifications in Focus. To make formal specification techniques and methods more acceptable it is essential that the developer is in the position to concentrate on the problem and not on the correctness of the formalization. In Focus, equations on stream-processing functions describe the mapping of patterns of input messages to patterns of output messages. [Spi98] proposes a special strategy to formulate the required behaviour as structured text. The translation of this text into a functional equation is supported by special schemes. In the following we show such a scheme regarding a component C with one input channel In and one output channel Out, where messages of type $Integer$ flow on these channels. We require that C computes the square of each input message and sends it on the output channel. For this input/output behaviour we give the following textual description:

If the component C receives a message $X \in Integer$ on input channel In, then C sends as reaction the square X^2 as output message on output channel Out.

This structured text, which includes all information needed to specify the required behaviour, can be translated with the available schemes in the following functional equation (here f_C denotes the stream-processing function modeling the behaviour of the component C):

$$f_C(\{In \to X\} \circ s) = \{Out \to X^2\} \circ f_C(s)$$

3 Description Techniques

A description technique can be best characterized as a specialized language to describe a particular view of the systems to be developed. With the FOCUS method, we can precisely define our notion of a system. It is an important task to define an appropriate set of description techniques which allow developers to describe properties of systems.

In the first subsection, we will describe the notion of description techniques in general, how we treat them, and what the benefits of this treatment are.

3.1 Description Techniques, Notations and Semantics

A description technique serves the purpose of describing particular aspects (views) of a system. There exists a variety of graphical and textual description techniques that allow to describe different aspects.

A description technique comes along with

- a concrete syntax (this is the concrete layout of all documents),
- an abstract syntax (without "syntactic sugar"),
- context conditions for wellformedness, and
- a semantics definition.

For a precisely defined description technique all four parts must be present. In case of textual notations, concrete and abstract grammars are common for the syntax, attributes on this grammar can be used for wellformedness conditions, and the semantics is usually defined as a mapping from the syntax into an appropriate semantic domain.

Similar techniques can be used for graphical notations. Each graphical notation basically defines a *language* of wellformed documents, which serves as the syntactic domain. In order to use several description techniques to describe different aspects of the same systems, semantics definitions are necessary that map the different syntactic domains onto the same semantic domain. This is the basis needed to integrate the different description techniques during development. If we map different notations onto the same semantic domain, we (meaning the *notation developer*) can compute context conditions between different notations, which ensure consistency of several views onto a system. Moreover, we can justify the correctness of translations from one notation into another one, e.g., translating Message Sequence Charts into State Machines, or generating code. Last but not least, we can justify the correctnes of refinement calculi for the given descriptions.

There are other benefits of defining a precise semantics, e.g., the developer of the semantics gains a deeper understanding of the used notations. However, usually this formal semantics definition cannot be communicated to method users, but only the (informal) interpretation of the insights [FB97]. Thus, the most important bargain of precise semantics is the possibility to automate development steps.

Since graphical techniques usually are not powerful enough to describe (or prove) every property of a system, it is often essential to translate the documents from a graphical notation into their "semantics" and use the power of the semantic formalism to specify further aspects or verify required properties. In our case, different kinds of diagrams, such as SSDs (see Section 3.2), can be translated into formulas only using concepts of FOCUS.

In the following, we sketch the most important notations we have dealt with. We sketch the purpose of the notation in a methodological context and the results we have achieved on that notation, such as, semantics definitions or refinement calculi that have been developed.

We emphasize that it is important to also use explanations or other informal kinds of diagrams and text during development. A good method does not only deal with formal notations but also allows the systematic treatment of informal documents.

The AUTOFOCUS tool uses a subset of the description techniques introduced below in variations that are tailored for the development of embedded systems (see Figure 2). Graphical and textual editors are available to create and edit specifications using different views on an embedded system. Consistency between these views can be ensured, controlled by the developer any time during the development process (see Section 4.1). From sufficiently detailed specifications, executable prototypes can be generated (see Section 4.2). Implementation work on mapping graphical specifications into semantic domains, based on our theoretical work, e.g., to conduct proofs of correctness on specifications, is currently in progress (see Section 4.3).

3.2 System Structure Diagrams (SSD)

System Structure Diagrams as used in AUTOFOCUS (Figure 2, upper middle) focus on the static structure of a system. They graphically exhibit the components of a system and their interconnections. They describe the glass box view of a FOCUS component and are therefore similar to ROOM charts [SGW94]. These diagrams focus more on the static part of a system and are not used in UML [BRJ97], where everything is assumed to be highly dynamic.

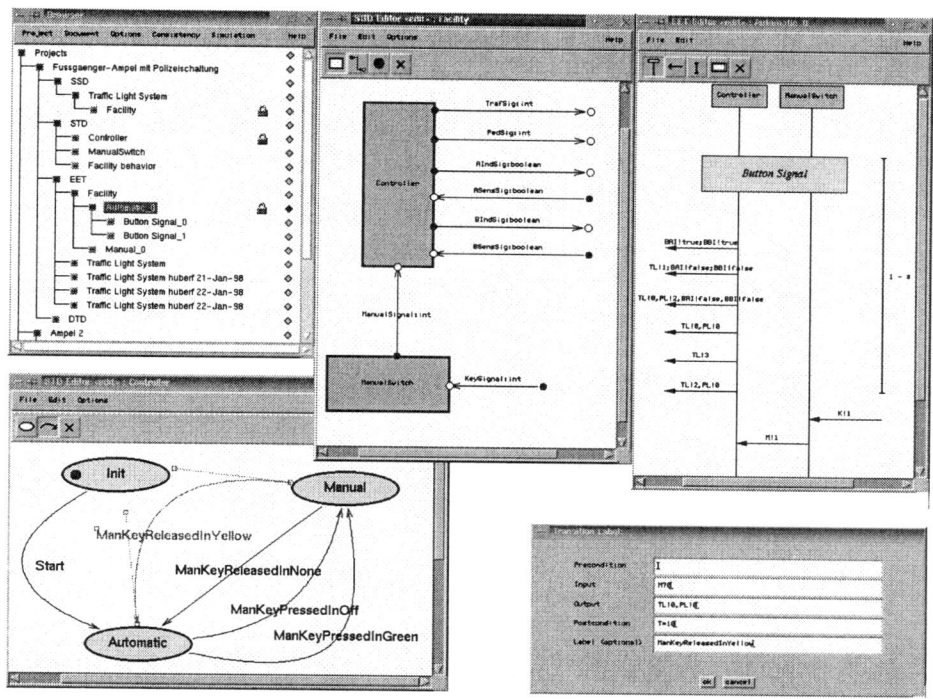

Fig. 2. AUTOFOCUS Description Techniques: SSD, EET, and STD

Components may be hierachically decomposed. Therefore, for each non-elementary component an SSD can be defined, leading to a hierachy of SSD documents describing a hierachical system structure.

If a system (or system component) exhibits dynamic properties, like changing the communication structure or creating/deleting components, the SSD can be used to describe structural snapshots or the static part of the structure. In an object-oriented flavor, an SSD defines a snapshot of data and communication paths between a set of objects.

As SSDs describe the architectural part of a system, there exists a refinement calculus for architectures that allows to transform the internal structure of a component by adding new components or changing communication paths, e.g., without affecting the external behavior of the component [PR97b,PR97c].

3.3 Class Diagrams (CD)

Class Diagrams are the most important object-oriented notation, and are therefore part of UML [BRJ97]. They are used to describe data aspects of a system as well as possible structure layouts. In contrast to System Structure Diagrams, which focus on the "instance level", Class Diagrams focus on the "type level".

Each class may have several objects as instances, each association represents links between corresponding objects.

Class Diagrams define a large class of possible structures. To further detail these structures, different kinds of invariants are added. E.g., associations have multiplicities and additionally, it is possible to add predicates defined in our Specification Language SL (see below).

Class Diagrams are also used to define the signature of a class and their state space. The signature consists of a set of method definitions that also define the set of possible messages. The attributes define the state space.

In [BHH+97] we have argued about the semantics of Class Diagrams. Although Class Diagrams are a rather well understood technique, there are still open questions how to treat aggregates.

3.4 Specification Languages (SL)

Not every aspect of a system can or should be described using graphic techniques. For example datatype definitions or additional constraints are best described using a textual notation. In UML, e.g., OCL has been introduced for describing a certain type of constraints. However, since OCL does not allow to define data types or auxilary functions, and based on our experiences with algebraic specification techniques [BBB+85,BFG+93a], we decided to define an own language for that purpose.

SL is an axiomatic specification language based on predicate logic, resembling Spectrum [BFG+93a,BFG+93b]. SL allows declarative definitions of properties. Particularly, SL is used for the definition of pre- and post-conditions of transitions and for the definition of state invariants not only in single objects but also between several objects in the Class Diagrams. In order to enable automatic testing of verification conditions, SL also incorporates concepts of functional programming, especially from Gofer [Jon93]. The step from high-level descriptions towards executable code is facilitated, which in turn facilitates prototyping.

With the restriction to the executable sublanguage and furthermore to the datatype definitions, an automatic translation into simulation code is possible.

We also have experimented with the higher order logic **HOLCF** [Reg94] as a property definition language, in particular as a front end for the theorem prover Isabelle [Pau94].

3.5 Message Sequence Charts (MSC) and Extended Event Traces (EET)

Message Sequence Charts and Extended Event Traces are both used to describe the flow of communication within exemplary runs of a part of a system. Constituting a high level of abstraction, MSC are well suited to capture system requirements. Moreover, MSC can be used for and generated by simulation, respectively. We have developed different flavors of this technique. One focuses on synchronous message passing between different components [BHS96,BHKS97] and its semantics is primarily a set of traces. These are called Extended Event Traces and are used in AutoFocus (Figure 2, top right).

The other variant focuses on object-oriented systems and is more similar to MSC'96 [Int96]. Both variants are compared and argued about their semantics in [BGH+97a]. For EETs a set of operators was defined to combine them sequentially, in parallel and iterated. This allows not only to define exemplary behavior, but also complete sets of behaviors.

Currently, work is in progress to map EETs into State Transition Diagrams.

3.6 State Transition Diagrams (STDs)

Basically State Transition Diagrams (STDs) describe the behavior of a component using the state of this component. But different abstractions and therefore flavors are possible. Thus STDs can be used early in the development (analysis) and also in the design phase, when some kind of "lifecycle" of a component is modeled. During detailed design and also prototyping, pre- and postconditions of a certain form (executable) can be used to generate code.

We have explored and developed several versions of State Transition Diagrams that allow to capture more than just one input or one output element on a transition. Usually a transition is attributed with a set of messages (sometimes restricted to one message) to be processed during the transition and a set of messages to be produced. There are timed and untimed variants, and there are variants incorporating pre- and postconditions on transitions [RK96,PR94,GKR96,GKRB96,GR95,Rum96,PR97a].

In the object-oriented flavor, State Transition Diagrams describe the lifecycle of objects. In STDs, descriptions of state and behavior are combined. STDs can be used at different levels of abstraction that allow both the specification of an object interface as well as the specification of individual methods. Refinement techniques support not only inheritance of behaviour but also stepwise refinement of abstract STDs [Rum96], resulting in an implementation.

A textual representation of State Transition Diagrams can be given using appropriate tables [Spi94,Bre97]. Hierachical variants of State Transition Diagrams are examined in [NRS96] and also used in AutoFocus (Figure 2, bottom left).

State Transition Diagrams are an extremely promising notation, as they on one hand allow to describe behavior, while on the other relate it to the state of a component. They allow to think in rather abstract terms of interaction sequences, but can also be used to describe a strategy of implementation (and therefore code generators). It is therefore worthwhile to explore more precise variants of STDs than the ones given in nowadays methods such as UML.

3.7 Programming Language (PL)

The ultimate description technique is the target programming language. For object-oriented systems, Java [GJS96] is a rather interesting choice for an implementation language, as it exhibits a lot of desirable properties. It is not only a language with a set of consolidated and clear concepts, it also exhibits some notion of concurrency, which allows to implement the concurrency concepts of FOCUS. Hence, we have had a closer look on Java, e.g., selecting a suitable sublanguage which will be the target for our code generation from STD and MSC.

To include the programming language in a proper way into the formal development process, a step has been taken in [PR97a] towards a FOCUS-based transitional semantics of conventional languages like Java.

3.8 Further Work

For some of the above described notations, we already have prototype tools—like AUTOFOCUS—that allow to edit and manipulate documents of that notation. Several others still need consolidation, as the process of finding not only a precise semantics for given notations, but adapting the notation in such a way that it is convenient to use and allows to express the desired properties, needs to do examples.

Currently refinement calculi on Class Diagrams and State Transition Diagrams are implemented.

4 Methodical Ingredients

A software or system development method (see Section 5) covers a variety of different aspects. Supplying description techniques, as introduced in Section 3, is only one of these aspects, yet probably the most "visible" one. However, a development method also contains a notion of a development *process*, a model, how developers proceed during the development of a system in order to produce the results (the documents, the specifications etc.) necessary for a complete and consistent system description that fulfills the requirements and ultimately results in the desired software product.

Such a process model usually operates on different levels of granularity, ranging from a coarse view down to very detailed, even atomic operations on specification elements or documents. The former will be treated in more detail in Section 5, while the latter are covered in this section.

Methodical steps can basically be partitioned in two disjoint sets of operations on specifications, operations that modify the *contents* of specifications, thus effectively yielding a different (possibly refined) description, and operations that change the (possibly informal) *status* of specifications, for instance from a draft status to a status "validated", indicating that certain properties of the specification are fulfilled in an informal process.

In the following sections, we give a set of examples for both kinds of steps that have been treated in our work.

4.1 Completeness and Consistency

Generally, a system specification, just like a program that is being written, is neither complete nor consistent most of the time within a development process.

This is particularly the case in view-based systems development, which specifically aims at separating different aspects of a system description in different specification units (specifiation documents, for instance) that use appropriate description techniques. From a methodical point of view, allowing inconsistency and incompleteness during a development process is reasonable because enforcing them at any time restricts developers way too much in their freedom to specify systems. For instance, instead of concentrating on a certain aspect of a specification, developers, when changing parts thereof, would immediately have to update all other specification units that are possibly affected by such a change in order to maintain a consistent specification. Apart from diverting the developers' attention from their current task, this is virtually impossible in practical development, especially with respect to completeness of specifications. Note that the notion of consistency used here refers to the properties of the abstract syntax (the "meta-model") of the description techniques used to specify a system. Semantic aspects, such as consistency of behavior with certain requirements, are not treated in this context. This approach is quite similar to compilers for programming languages, which can ensure the "consistency" of a program, but not the correctness of the algorithm encoded in the program.

The AUTOFOCUS tool, which uses a view-based approach to specify distributed systems, offers such a mechanism to test specifications for completeness and consistency. System specification is based on a subset of the description techniques introduced in Section 3, namely, system structure diagrams, datatype definitions, state transition diagrams, and extended event traces. The view specifications covered by these techniques can be developed separately to a large extent. Only at specific points in the development process, for instance, when generating a prototype from a specification (see Section 4.2), some global conditions of consistency have to be fulfilled. Consequently, the consistency mechanism available in AUTOFOCUS is user-controlled and can be invoked at any time during development, allowing to select both an appropriate set of specifications to be checked and the (sub-)set of consistency conditions to be applied.

4.2 Validation of Specifications

Today in practical systems development, validation techniques, in contrast to formal verification techniques, are widely used [BCR94] to gain more confidence in specifications and implementations fulfilling their requirements. However, only verification techniques can *prove* correctness. They will be treated in the next section. Validation techniques are the focus of this section. They cover a broad range of diverse techniques, such as

- review of specifications,
- systematic specification inspection,
- (usability) test of software, or
- prototype generation and execution.

These techniques show different facets of validation. For instance, testing is usually applied to ensure that program code (the ultimate target of a development process) fulfills certain required properties. Reviews and inspections techniques, in contrast to that, are applicable in virtually any stage in the development process to ensure consistency and certain correctness aspects on an informal level. Reviews, for instance, can be held about requirements documents in the very early stages of a devlopment process as well on program code implemented by developers. Prototype generation for a system or parts thereof can be used once a specification has been developed that is sufficiently consistent and complete to validate the desired properties. Since a prototype, especially an executable prototype in the form of a program, virtually brings a system specification "into life", this kind of validation technique is relevant in communicating development results to customers. Prototyping has been successfully applied particularly in areas like graphical user interfaces (GUI).

In software engineering, the usage of graphical formalisms that describe systems from a point of view rather close to an implementation is widespread. Examples for such techniques are statecharts [HPSS87] used in the STATEMATE tool [Ilo90], or state transition diagrams as used in the AUTOFOCUS tool, both of which can basically be regarded as a kind of graphical programming language. In such cases generating executable prototypes (or as well final implementation code) is possible.

In the remainder of this section, we will take a brief look at such a prototyping environment, the AUTOFOCUS component SIMCENTER [HS97]. It is based on generating program code from a set of sufficiently detailed and consistent system specifications and on observing the behavior of that prototype program in its environment.

SIMCENTER works by generating Java program code from a specification of a distributed system, given in the AUTOFOCUS description techniques briefly outlined in Section 4.1. The generated program code, executed in SIMCENTER's runtime environment, is linked to a visualization component where the progress of the prototype execution can be monitored at the same level of description techniques as used to specify the system. An obvious prerequisite for generating such an executable prototype is that the specification is sufficiently complete and consistent in the sense outlined in Section 4.1. Nondeterminism, however, may be present in the behavioral aspects of the specification. It is currently resolved by selecting *one* possible behavior in the code generation process. This approach can be made more flexible for developers, for instance, by allowing them to select one of several nondeterministic behaviors during prototype execution.

As the primary application domain of AUTOFOCUS are embedded systems, SIMCENTER allows to monitor the interactions of such a gerated prototype with its environment. In particular, developers are able to inject stimuli into the system and observe its reactions, both from its environment interface in a black box manner and from the internal perspective, as outlined above. Additionally, black box behavior of an embedded system prototype can be optionally observed and influenced from a user-definable, application domain-oriented environment view that can be attached to SIMCENTER via a standard communication interface. This allows developers to build a very customer-oriented presentation of the behavior of such a prototype and thus supports communication between system developers and application domain experts.

For technical details about the process and the basics of code generation in SIMCENTER we refer the reader to [HS97], for an AUTOFOCUS development case study using SIMCENTER to validate certain correctness aspects of a specification of a simple embedded system, we refer to [HMS+98].

4.3 Verification Techniques

In contrast to informal validation, formal techniques allow developers to mathematically prove that a system specification fulfills certain requirements. As a prerequisite, both the requirements and the specifications need to be formalized using a common mathematical basis, thus allowing formal proofs to be conducted.

Our goal is to integrate formal techniques as seamless as possible with some of the description techniques introduced in Section 3. Within the AUTOFOCUS project two categories of verification tools are currently under consideration for an integration with graphical formalisms. First, verification systems such as PVS [ORS92], STeP [BBC+96], or interactive theorem provers like *Isabelle* [Pau94] in conjunction with HOLCF [Reg94] could be used to interactively prove properties of a specification. For that purpose, graphical specifications have to be transformed into the specification laguage used in the verification system, and developers have to conduct their proofs on this notational level. Obviously, this approach is not very intuitive because it forces developers used to graphical notations to use a more or less complex mathematical formalism to conduct proofs.

Thus, the second category of tools, automated verification tools like model checkers seem to be more suitable for a seamless integration. Currently, a prototype for the integration of the μ-cke model checker [Bie97] into AUTOFOCUS is implemented. It will check whether a concrete system specification, given by a component network and the corresponding behavioral descriptions, exposes a refinement of the behavior of a given, more abstract specification.

4.4 Transformations

Transformations are methodical steps that effectively change a system description. Thus, each action that adds or changes specification elements results in a different system description. Whether such modifications to specifications preserve certain properties of a specification that have been established before, is not clear *a priori* and has thus again to be validated (or verified, in case of a formal development process). For that reason, it is desirable as well as feasible to have a class of methodical steps that allow developers to change specifications in a way that previously established properties will still hold after the modifications [BHS96]. Providing such property-preserving modification steps for a set of object-oriented description techniques is one of the main goals of the SYSLAB project. Such property-preserving transformations are defined on the level of the description techniques and provided for developers in the form of a syntactical refinement calculus that will be integrated in the toolset currently being developed within SYSLAB. These transformation rules are formally proven to be property-preserving by the method developers and thus enable system developers to perform transformations on specifications on the syntactical level without having to re-establish the validity of previously valid properties. Currently, such transformation calculi exist for state transition diagrams [Rum96] and for system structure diagrams [PR97b,PR97c], and are being integrated into the SYSLAB toolset. If developers choose not to use transformations provided by the refinement calculus, but to modify their specifications in an arbitrary way, they have to explicitly re-establish the necessary properties again.

4.5 Further Work

In the context of methodical development steps, tool-based active developer support is a major area of work in the near future. One aspect consists of guiding developers through the development process, offering them possible development steps that can be or must be performed in order to develop a system.

Another important aspect consists of tracing the development steps applied to specifications and their effects on other specifications. This pertains both to syntactic consistency and completeness of the specifications and to possibly invalidated semantic properties that need to be re-established after development steps.

5 A Model-Based Software Development Process

Up to now we have looked at formal modeling techniques, tool-support for model development and analysis based on an integrating formal basis, and a formal development process. The modeling techniques mentioned above aim at the description of the software system on various levels of granularity. In the following we show that they can naturally be complemented with a set of description techniques for the software system context and the informal problem description. We will sketch a framework for a model-based development process. This framework is made up of three main ingredients:

– the distinction between the world, the machine, and their interface [Jac95] and the explicit system models of all three of them,
– the distinction between the external view, the internal analysis view, and the (distributed) design view of each system, and
– a careful deployment of formality.

The last issue has been discussed in the preceding sections, the first two will be discussed in the following subsections. Depending on the application domain and the project context this framework needs to be instantiated. We sketch an example process for information system development at the end of this section.

5.1 The World, the Machine and their Interface

The distinction between *the world and the machine* is due to Jackson [Jac95]. The problem to be solved by a software system is in the world, the machine constitutes the solution we construct. Phenomena shared by the world and the machine make up the *interface*. Descriptions produced during software development must be clearly associated to one of the these three domains. This is especially difficult for requirement documents, which typically contain references to the world, namely the effects to be achieved by the software system, to the interface, namely the system services, and to the machine. In particular, it is not possible to describe the system services precisely without a clear understanding of the relevant phenomena of the world. Therefore software engineering methods - formal or pragmatic - typically start with informal descriptions of the issues in the world relevant to the software system. These are then transformed into so-called analysis models. The modeling techniques used for these models are the same as the ones used for the description of the machine. Object-oriented methods like OMT [RBP+91] or OOSE [Jac92] use object models, structured methods like SSADM [DCC92] use dataflow models. This is reasonable, because the world and the machine can both be viewed as systems, thus allowing the use of the same modeling techniques. However, there are semantical differences: in object models of the software systems associations represent references directly implementable in the programming language. Associations between objects in the world represent invariant relationships which typically manifest themselves as natural phenomena (e.g., a person has a mother and a father) or as social or legal processes (e.g., a book has an author). Also, the purpose of the models of the world and the machine is quite distinct. Models of the world capture the understanding of important phenomena while models of the software system capture requirements to be realized by the software system or document the running system.

To make these distinctions explicit, we therefore distinguish three categories of models:

Models of the world: They model the context of the software system, e.g., a railway system or a lift to be controlled by the software system, or a production company whose engineers are supported by software systems. In particular, it is important to model the processes that the software system is involved in.

Models of the interface: They model the phenomena shared between the world and the machine. In particular, it is important to model the interaction between the software system and its external partners. The latter may be humans or machines.

Models of the machine: They model the internals of the software system, namely the internal components (e.g., objects, subsystems) and how they render the system services.

5.2 The External View, the Internal View and the Design View

The world, the interface, and the machine constitute systems. They all consist of actors, communicating with each other and executing activities making use of their (data) ressources. Figure 3 collects elements of the three different systems in case of a railway control system.

	actors	data	activities
world	trains, passengers, conductor	timetable, position	passengers enter and get off the train, train stops
interface	train personnel, software system	signals	signaling, to switch the points
machine	objects, operating system processes	attributes	assignment, method call

Fig. 3. The world, the interface and the machine as systems

Software development methods traditionally either focus on the activities and their data flow (structured methods) or on the actors and their communication (object-oriented methods). We claim that both views are important during system development, and that a third view has made to be explicit: the *external* view. The external view describes the services to be delivered by the system. The activities describe steps to achieve the required services. We call activities and their data the *internal analysis view* because at this level one experiments with different ways of achieving the services without regard for the actors. The actors constitute the *distributed design view*. Activities and data are encapsulated within actors such that data flow between activities has to be realized through communication. As exemplified by object-oriented designs, an actor-oriented structure allows better reusability and extensibility of designs than activity-structured designs.

Each of these views can be applied to the world, the interface, and the machine. To understand the purpose of the context of the software system, it is usually helpful to describe the services of this context. In the case of the railway control the services are the transport services offered by trains at particular locations and at particular times. In order to adequately understand the services, the activities and data of the world have to be modelled quite extensively. The actor structure of the world is frequently changed by introduction of the software system since often human labour is replaced. Furthermore, it is very often subject to a lot of political decisions.

The services of the interface are the work processes or technical processes to be supported by the software system. Jacobsen [Jac92] has coined the term *use case* for this. Very often there is a close correspondence between machine and interface services, the latter being a high-level view of the former. The internal analysis and the design view of the interface are heavily intertwined. In the interface the actors are mostly given (humans and technical systems), but there is a choice of how to distribute the activities between the machine and the external partners.

The services of the machine are determined by the design of the interface. Typically, the external view and the internal analysis view of the machine is heavily intertwined, because the services cannot be described without resorting to the data of the software system. Often, also some parts of the design view are fixed because the machine has to fit into an already existing landscape of software systems. Thus, for example, one actor may be a particular database, other actors may be given by a library of classes for a particular application domain.

5.3 An Example Process

The discussions above can be captured in the following proposal for the deliverables of an informations systems development process. In this short overview we do not go into detail into the dependencies between the deliverables and the possible timing of their production. The deliverables cover the external, internal, and design views for the world, the interface, and the machine. The formal system descriptions and development steps discussed in the previous sections are typically only used for the machine view. Only if the effects of the software system in the world are critical (e.g., chemical processes), formalization of the world and interface models will be worthwhile.

Figure 4 lists the deliverables for developing a software system design.

View	World	Interface	Machine
service specification	(textual) description of the enterprise services	use case model listing the user tasks	system services (specified in terms of their input/output and/or the data changes)
data and activity analysis	glossary, application domain processes	work processes or technical processes	data model described as ERD or CD, data changes described by STD
actor and communication design	(textual) description of the responsibility (in terms of data and activities) of the departments	(textual) description of user roles and technical system partners, allocation of data, and activities to software system	description of the component-oriented design by SSD, CD, STD, EET

Fig. 4. Products of a model-based software development process

The choice of the deliverables is influenced by SSADM [DCC92], especially regarding the the machine service and analysis view. It has similarities to OOSE in the use of use cases for the external view of the interface. The use of exemplary communication flow descriptions like EETs in the machine design view is borrowed from FUSION [CAB+94].

Of course, these deliverables constitute only a framework to be instantiated for different application domains and projects. The interface models have to be quite detailed in case of human-computer interaction with a new technology [Suc95]. The world models have to be quite detailed in case of a new or critical application domain. Models of the software system should support a systematic transition to code using the development steps described in Section 4.

6 Conclusion

The paper has discussed the issues of using formally founded description techniques for system and software engineering. We have shown that formal methods like FOCUS provide a rich basis for textual and graphical system descriptions as well as the basic methodical steps for system development. This formal basis allows an integrated view on the wealth of description techniques found in the literature. Equally important for the system developer are the methodical elements based on the formal semantics, like consistency checks and transformations. For real-world applications, this formal development process must be embedded into a process of application domain (world) and usage (interface) understanding and description. From our experience, each of these issues is worth its own project. Our projects have demonstrated that it is possible to resolve each of these issues on its own, restricted to a particular application domain. The challenge is now to connect all of this together and to transfer it to new application domains. This can only be achieved by a widespread use of these techniques in university and industry.

Acknowledgments

We like to thank all the people who have contributed to the work presented in this paper, especially those involved in the projects FOCUS, AUTOFOCUS, FORSOFT and SYSLAB. Furthermore, we like to thank Bernhard Schätz for his careful proof reading of the whole paper.

The authors of this paper were funded by the DFG-Sonderforschungsbereich 342, the project SYSLAB supported by DFG-Leibnitz and Siemens Nixdorf, and the Forschungsverbund FORSOFT supported by the Bayerische Forschungsstiftung.

References

[BBB+85]   F.L. Bauer, R. Berghammer, M. Broy, W. Dosch, F. Geiselbrechtinger, R. Gnatz, E. Hangel, W. Hesse, B. Krieg-Brückner, A. Laut, T. Matzner,

B. Möller, F. Nickl, H. Partsch, P. Pepper, K. Samelson, M. Wirsing, and H. Wössner. *The Munich Project CIP, Vol 1: The Wide Spectrum Language CIP-L*. LNCS 183. Springer-Verlag, 1985.

[BBC+96] N. Bjørner, A. Browne, E. Chang, M. Colón, A. Kapur, Z. Manna, H. B. Sipma, and T. E. Uribe. STeP: Deductive Algorithmic Verification of Reactive and Real-Time Systems. In R. Alur and T. A. Henzinger, editors, *Computer Aided Verification: 8th International Conference*, volume 1102 of *Lecture Notes in Computer Science*. Springer, 1996.

[BBSS97] M. Broy, M. Breitling, B. Schätz, and K. Spies. Summary of Case Studies in FOCUS – Part II. SFB-Bericht 342/24/97 A, Technische Universität München, September 1997.

[BCR94] V.R. Basili, G. Caldiera, and H.-D. Rombach. Goal Question Metric Paradigm. In J.J. Marciniak, editor, *Encyclopedia of Software Engineering*, pages 528–532. John Wiley & Sons, 1994.

[BDD+93] M. Broy, F. Dederichs, C. Dendorfer, M. Fuchs, T. F. Gritzner, and R. Weber. The Design of Distributed Systems – An Introduction to FOCUS. SFB-Bericht Nr. 342/2-2/92 A, Technische Universität München, January 1993.

[BFG+93a] M. Broy, C. Facchi, R. Grosu, R. Hettler, H. Hußmann, D. Nazareth, F. Regensburger, O. Slotosch, and K. Stølen. The Requirement and Design Specification Language SPECTRUM, An Informal Introduction, Version 1.0, Part 1. Technical Report TUM-I9312, Technische Universität München, 1993.

[BFG+93b] M. Broy, C. Facchi, R. Grosu, R. Hettler, H. Hußmann, D. Nazareth, F. Regensburger, O. Slotosch, and K. Stølen. The Requirement and Design Specification Language SPECTRUM, An Informal Introduction, Version 1.0, Part 2. Technical Report TUM-I9312, Technische Universität München, 1993.

[BFG+94] M. Broy, M. Fuchs, T. F. Gritzner, B. Schätz, K. Spies, and K. Stølen. Summary of Case Studies in FOCUS — a Design Method for Distributed Systems. SFB-Bericht 342/13/94 A, Technische Universität München, June 1994.

[BGH+97a] R. Breu, R. Grosu, Ch. Hofmann, F. Huber, I. Krüger, B. Rumpe, M. Schmidt, and W. Schwerin. Exemplary and Complete Object Interaction Descriptions. In H. Kilov, B. Rumpe, and I. Simmonds, editors, *Proceedings OOPSLA'97 Workshop on Object-oriented Behavioral Semantics*. TUM-I9737, 1997.

[BGH+97b] R. Breu, R. Grosu, F. Huber, B. Rumpe, and W. Schwerin. Towards a Precise Semantics for Object-Oriented Modeling Techniques. In J. Bosch and S. Mitchell, editors, *Object-Oriented Technology, ECOOP'97 Workshop Reader*. Springer Verlag, LNCS 1357, 1997.

[BHH+97] R. Breu, U. Hinkel, C. Hofmann, C. Klein, B. Paech, B. Rumpe, and V. Thurner. Towards a Formalization of the Unified Modeling Language. In *ECOOP, LNCS 1241*, pages 344–366, 1997.

[BHKS97] M. Broy, C. Hofmann, I. Krueger, and M. Schmidt. Using Extended Event Traces to Describe Communication in Software Architectures. In *Proceedings APSEC'97 and ICSC'97,*. IEEE Computer Society, 1997.

[BHS96] M. Broy, H. Hußmann, and B. Schätz. Formal Development of Consistent System Specifications. In M.-C. Gaudel and J. Woodcock, editors, *FME'96: Industrial Benefit and Advances in Formal Methods, LNCS 1051*, pages 248–267. Springer, 1996.

[Bie97]   A. Biere. *Effiziente Modellprüfung des μ-Kalküls mit binären Entscheidungsdiagrammen.* PhD thesis, Universität Karlsruhe, 1997.
[BMS96a]   M. Broy, S. Merz, and K. Spies, editors. *Formal Systems Specification – The RPC-Memory Specification Case Study*, LNCS 1169. Springer, 1996.
[BMS96b]   M. Broy, S. Merz, and K. Spies. The RPC-Memory Specification Problem: A Synopsis. In *[BMS96a]*, pages 5–20, 1996.
[Bre97]   M. Breitling. Formalizing and Verifying TIMEWARP with FOCUS. SFB-Bericht 342/27/97 A, Technische Universität München, 1997.
[BRJ97]   G. Booch, J. Rumbaugh, and I. Jacobson. The Unified Modeling Language for Object-Oriented Development, Version 1.1, 1997.
[Bro94]   M. Broy. A Functional Rephrasing of the Assumption/Commitment Specification Style. Technical Report TUM-I9417, Technische Universität München, 1994.
[BS97]   M. Broy and K. Stølen. FOCUS on System Development – A Method for the Development of Interactive Systems, 1997. Manuskript.
[CAB+94]   D. Coleman, P. Arnold, S. Bodoff, C. Dollin, H. Gilchrist, F. Hayes, and P. Jeremaes. *Object-Oriented Development - The FUSION Method.* Prentice Hall, 1994.
[CGR93]   D. Craigen, S. Gerhart, and T. Ralston. Formal Methods Reality Check: Industrial Usage. In *FME, LNCS 670*, pages 250–267. Springer, 1993.
[DCC92]   E. Downs, P. Clare, and I. Coe. *Structured Systems Analysis and Design Method: Application and Context.* Prentice-Hall, 1992.
[DHP+98]   B. Deifel, U. Hinkel, B. Paech, P. Scholz, and V. Thurner. Die Praxis der Softwareentwicklung: Eine Erhebung. Submitted to publication, 1998.
[FB97]   R. B. France and J.-M. Bruel. Integrated Informal Object-Oriented and Formal Modeling Techniques. In H. Kilov and B. Rumpe, editors, *Proceedings ECOOP'97 Workshop on Precise Semantics for Object-Oriented Modeling Techniques.* Technische Universität München, TUM-I9725, 1997.
[GJS96]   J. Gosling, B. Joy, and G. Steele. *The Java Language Specification.* Addison-Wesley, 1996.
[GKR96]   R. Grosu, C. Klein, and B. Rumpe. Enhancing the SysLab System Model with State. TUM-I 9631, Technische Universität München, 1996.
[GKRB96]   R. Grosu, C. Klein, B. Rumpe, and M. Broy. State Transition Diagrams. TUM-I 9630, Technische Universität München, 1996.
[GR95]   R. Grosu and B. Rumpe. Concurrent Timed Port Automata. TUM-I 9533, Technische Universität München, 1995.
[HMS+98]   F. Huber, S. Molterer, B. Schätz, O. Slotosch, and A. Vilbig. Traffic Lights – An AutoFocus Case Study. In *International Conference on Application of Concurrency to System Design.* IEEE CS Press, 1998.
[HPSS87]   D. Harel, A. Pnueli, J.P. Schmidt, and R. Sherman. On the Formal Semantics of Statecharts. Proceedings on the Symposium on Logic in Computer Science, pages 54 – 64, 1987.
[HS97]   F. Huber and B. Schätz. Rapid Prototyping with AutoFocus. In A. Wolisz, I. Schieferdecker, and A. Rennoch, editors, *Formale Beschreibungstechniken für verteilte Systeme, GI/ITG Fachgespräch 1997, pp. 343-352.* GMD Verlag (St. Augustin), 1997.
[HSS96]   F. Huber, B. Schätz, and K. Spies. AutoFocus - Ein Werkzeugkonzept zur Beschreibung verteilter Systeme. In U. Herzog and H. Hermanns, editors, *Formale Beschreibungstechniken für verteilte Systeme*, pages 165–174. Universität Erlangen-Nürnberg, 1996. Arbeitsberichte des Insituts für mathematische Maschinen und Datenverarbeitung, Bd.29, Nr. 9.

[Huß97]   H. Hußmann. *Formal Foundations for Software Engineering Methods, LNCS 1322.* Springer, 1997.
[Ilo90]   i-Logix Inc., 22 Third Avenue, Burlington, Mass. 01803, U.S.A. *Languages of Statemate,* 1990.
[Int96]   International Telecommunication Union, Geneva. *Message Sequence Charts,* 1996. ITU-T Recommendation Z.120.
[Jac92]   I. Jacobson. *Object-Oriented Software Engineering.* Addison-Wesley, 1992.
[Jac95]   M. Jackson. The World and the Machine. In *ICSE-17,* pages 283–294, 1995.
[Jon93]   M. P. Jones. *An Introduction to Gofer,* Manual, 1993.
[KRB96]   C. Klein, B. Rumpe, and M. Broy. A Stream-based Mathematical Model for Distributed Information Processing Systems - SysLab system model - . In E. Naijm and J.-B. Stefani, editors, *FMOODS'96 Formal Methods for Open Object-based Distributed Systems,* pages 323–338. ENST France Telecom, 1996.
[NRS96]   D. Nazareth, F. Regensburger, and P. Scholz. Mini-Statecharts: A Lean Version of Statecharts. Technical Report TUM-I9610, Technische Universität München, 1996.
[ORS92]   S. Owre, J. M. Rushby, and N. Shankar. PVS: A Prototype Verification System. In D. Kapur, editor, *Proceedings International Conference on Automated Deduction (CADE) '92.* Springer, 1992.
[Pau94]   Lawrence C. Paulson. *Isabelle: A Generic Theorem Prover, LNCS 828.* Springer-Verlag, 1994.
[PR94]   B. Paech and B. Rumpe. A New Concept of Refinement Used or Behaviour Modelling with Automata. In *FME'94, Formal Methods Europe, Symposium '94,* LNCS 873. Springer-Verlag, Berlin, October 1994.
[PR97a]   B. Paech and B. Rumpe. State Based Service Description. In J. Derrick, editor, *Formal Methods for Open Object-based Distributed Systems.* Chapman-Hall, 1997.
[PR97b]   J. Philipps and B. Rumpe. Refinement of Information Flow Architectures. In M. Hinchey, editor, *ICFEM'97 Proceedings, Hiroshima. Japan.* IEEE CS Press, 1997.
[PR97c]   J. Philipps and B. Rumpe. Stepwise Refinement of Data Flow Architectures. In M. Broy, E. Denert, K. Renzel, and M. Schmidt, editors, *Software Architectures and Design Patterns in Business Applications.* Technische Universität München, TUM-I9746, 1997.
[RBP+91]   J. Rumbaugh, M. Blaha, W. Premerlani, F. Eddy, and W. Lorensen. *Object-oriented Modeling and Design.* Prentice-Hall, 1991.
[Reg94]   F. Regensburger. *HOLCF: Eine konservative Erweiterung von HOL um LCF.* PhD thesis, Technische Universität München, 1994.
[RK96]   B. Rumpe and C. Klein. *Automata Describing Object Behavior,* pages 265–287. Kluwer Academic Publishers, Norwell, Massachusetts, 1996.
[Rum96]   B. Rumpe. *Formal Method for the Development of Distributed Object-Oriented Systems (in German).* Herbert Utz Verlag Wissenschaft, 1996. PhD thesis, Technische Universität München.
[SDW95]   K. Stølen, F. Dederichs, and R. Weber. Specification and Refinement of Networks of Asynchronously Communicating Agents using the Assumption/Commitment Paradigm. *Formal Aspects of Computing,* 1995.
[SGW94]   B. Selic, G. Gulkeson, and P. Ward. *Real-Time Object-Oriented Modeling.* John Wiley and Sons, 1994.

[Spi94]   K. Spies. Funktionale Spezifikation eines Kommunikationsprotokolls. SFB-Bericht 342/08/94 A, Technische Universität München, May 1994.

[Spi98]   K. Spies. *Eine Methode zur formalen Modellierung von Betriebssystemkonzepten.* PhD thesis, Technische Universität München, 1998.

[Suc95]   L. Suchman(ed.). Special Issue on Representations of Work. *CACM*, 38(9), 1995.

[Tur93]   K.J. Turner(ed.). *Using Formal Description Techniques - An Introduction to ESTELLE, LOTOS and SDL.* John Wiley & Sons, 1993.

[Wor92]   J.B. Wordsworth. *Software Development with Z.* Addison-Wesley, 1992.

Postmodern Software Design with NYAM: Not Yet Another Method

Roel Wieringa

Department of Computer Science
University of Twente
the Netherlands
roelw@cs.utwente.nl*

Abstract. This paper presents a conceptual toolbox for software specification and design that contains techniques from structured and object-oriented specification and design methods. The toolbox is called TRADE (Toolkit for Requirements and Design Engineering). The TRADE tools are used in teaching informatics students structured and object-oriented specification and design techniques, but the toolkit may be of use to practicing software engineers as well. The conceptual framework of TRADE distinguishes external system interactions from internal components. External interactions in turns are divided into external functions, behavior and communication. The paper shows that structured and OO analysis offer a small number of specification techniques for these aspects, most of which can be combined in a coherent software design specification. It is also shown that the essential difference between structured and object-oriented software design approaches lies in the separation of data storage, data processing and control in data flow diagrams, versus the encapsulation of these into objects by OO analysis. Functional and subject-domain-oriented decomposition, on the other hand, are shown to be compatible with both approaches.

1 Introduction

In this paper, we view design as uncertainty reduction about the future of an artifact. In this broad view, design decisions may concern external properties as well as the internal structure of new artifacts, and may concern changes to existing artifacts or may concern new artifacts. The result of design is a documentation of the decisions made about the artifact, called a **specification**. Specifications always consist of a combination of text and graphics, both of which may vary in degree of formality. Software design specification methods are grouped into two camps. Structured methods emphasize data flows and functional decomposition. Object-oriented methods emphasize the encapsulation of operations and data and recommend something that we refer to as subject-domain-oriented decomposition.

---
* Work done while at the Faculty of Mathematics and Computer Science, *Vrije Universiteit*, Amsterdam.

The need for integration of structured and object-oriented software specification methods has been long recognized [1, 3, 32, 48, 53]. One of the advantages of such an integration is that it allows practitioners raised in the world of data flow modeling and functional decomposition to incorporate useful elements of object-oriented specification in a stepwise, evolutionary manner. Another advantage is that it allows us to pick the best elements of both groups of methods in an eclectic way, which should allow us to advance the state of the art beyond each of the contributing groups of methods. For example, we show that structured analysis offers useful techniques for the specification of external functionality but is a bit muddled in its specification of internal decomposition. Object-oriented analysis, on the other hand, offers useful techniques for the specification of decompositions but tends to ignore the specification of external functionality.

Early integration proposals incorporate object-oriented ideas in structured analysis without fundamentally changing structured analysis [53], or incorporate structured analysis in object-oriented analysis [3], or simply use structured analysis as a front-end to object-oriented design [1, 32, 48]. None of these proposals is based upon a thorough analysis of the underlying principles of structured and OO analysis. Without such an analysis, it is not possible to see which elements of structured and OO methods can or cannot be combined and why this is so. The integration proposed in this paper is based upon a thorough survey and analysis of six structured and 19 object-oriented specification methods, recently completed [58].

The results of the analysis are used to define the Toolkit for Requirements and Design Engineering (TRADE). This is a kit of *conceptual* tools, not software tools. TRADE contains techniques and heuristics taken from many different methods and allows combination of these tools in a coherent way. There is a software tool called TCM that can be used to use some of the techniques in TRADE, but TCM is not described in this paper, because the essential design tools are made not from software but from the experience and understanding of the designer. The essential tools are conceptual and consist of design techniques and heuristics and the tacit knowledge needed to apply them. This approach is postmodern in the sense that TRADE contains only elements borrowed from existing methods. It adds nothing except a framework in which these elements are put, and set of rules for using these elements in a coherent way. I hope that TRADE will not be viewed as yet another method but as a toolkit that, as any other toolkit, should be used flexibly and in a context-sensitive way.

The TRADE toolkit has been designed for use in teaching informatics students about structured and object-oriented methods in a non-partisan way. When given complex specification tools, students tend to produce unnecessarily complex specifications The TRADE tools have therefore been defined with clarity and simplicity in mind, while at the same time attempting to show the full range of techniques present in structured and object-oriented methods.

I start in section 2 with setting out a framework for software design methods that allows us to analyze structured and object-oriented methods and their techniques in a coherent manner. This framework is explained and motivated at length elsewhere [57]. In addition to allowing us to understand and analyze the use that can be made of specification techniques, the framework also allows us to define the relationships that must hold between the different techniques in a coherent multi-perspective specification. In section 3, a catalog is given of techniques taken from structured and object-oriented methods, and I show how they fit into this framework. In section 4, it is shown which techniques are adopted in TRADE, and how these are connected. Section 5 concludes the paper with a discussion.

2 A Framework for Software Systems

The TRADE framework classifies the kinds of properties of software systems that a designer might want to specify. It ignores the design process but focuses on the system; we return briefly to this below. The framework is derived from frameworks for systems engineering [17, 18] and product development [46] and from an analysis of software design methods [58]. The two basic dimensions of the framework are those of external interactions and internal (de)composition (figure 1).[1] Each system interacts with its external environment and is viewed

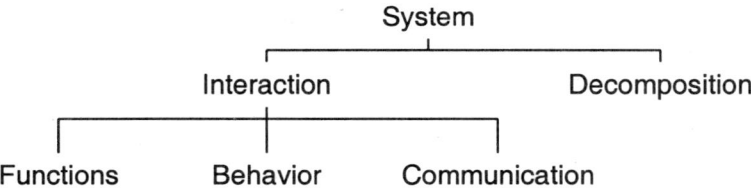

Fig. 1. A framework for systems.

as part of an aggregation hierarchy, in which higher-level systems are composed of lower-level systems. External interactions and internal decomposition are orthogonal in the sense that design decisions about these two dimensions of a system can be separated.

The external interactions of a system should be useful for at least some other systems in its external environment (people, hardware or software). This means that we should always be able to partition external interactions into chunks of useful interactions that we call **external functions**. These chunks may be atomic from an external point of view (i.e. they are external *transactions*), or

---

[1] The terms "composition" and "decomposition" used in the paper do not refer to bottom-up or top-down design processes but are used to refer to the internal structure of a system.

they may be complicated dialogs between the system and some external entities. They are not to be confused with mathematical functions or with functions written in a programming language. They are similar to Jacobson's [31, 40] *use cases*: pieces of external behavior that have some use for an external agent. Of the many properties that external functions can have, we single out two kinds: the ordering of functions in time, called **behavior**, and their ordering in "space", called **communication**. An external function is an external interaction, and each external interaction involves communication with one or more external entities. Moreover, external interactions are usually governed by rules of temporal precedence, which leads to the concept of behavior. The distinction between behavior and communication is the same as the classification of process operators in CCS into dynamic and static ones [38].

There should be a safety valve in our framework in the form of a category "all other properties". This includes the famous "ilities" such as usability, portability, interoperability, reliability etc. Many of these can be construed as properties of interactions or as properties of the decomposition. However, structured and object-oriented methods provide no techniques or heuristics for specifying these properties and TRADE contains no tools for this, so we ignore this category in this paper.

This completes the sketch of our framework for techniques. We will classify the techniques used in structured and object-oriented methods as techniques for specifying external functions, behavior or communication, or internal decomposition of a system. Before we do that, we point out a number of special features of the framework and show how it can be applied to software systems.

First, observe that each component of a system is itself a system, that has an internal decomposition and interacts with other components and external entities of the system. In fact, each interaction of the entire system is realized by interactions of its components. In terms of specification techniques, this means that we can use the same technique to specify interaction of systems at different levels in the aggregation hierarchy.

Next, we can specify a system's external external interactions at several levels of refinement, where higher levels of refinement correspond to more detail and less abstraction. We can also specify a system's components, components of those components, etc., leading to an aggregation hierarchy. The orthogonality of external interaction and decomposition implies that interaction refinement and system decomposition are orthogonal. This is visualized in figure 2, called the **magic square** by Harel and Pnueli [24]. Orthogonality means that decisions about interactions can be intertwined with decisions about decompositions in any way [50].

To explain this further, we return briefly to the process dimension. It is useful to distinguish logical design tasks from the way these tasks are ordered in time. Very generally, for any design task, the logical tasks are

– analysis of problem situation,
– synthesis of proposed solutions,
– simulation of solutions, and
– **evaluation of simulations [46, 57]**.

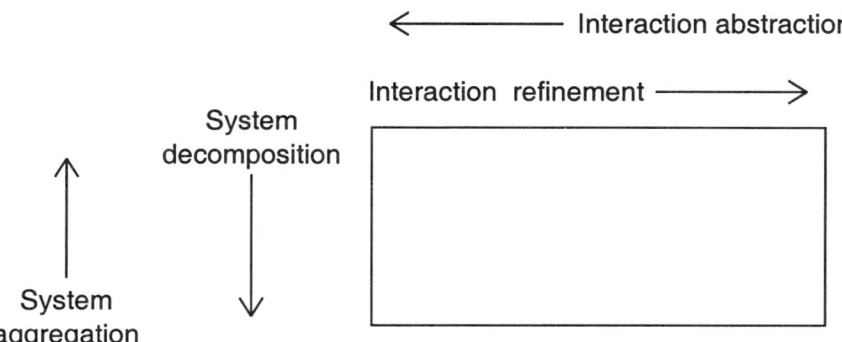

Fig. 2. The magic square.

For example, we may refine an interaction specification by analyzing the needs of the external environment, proposing a refinement, simulating the specified interactions, and evaluating this simulation. Or again, we may design a decomposition by analyzing the desired interactions of the system, proposing a decomposition, simulating its behavior, and evaluating this simulation. During an actual project, these tasks may be ordered in time in various ways. For example, in waterfall development, the entire set of external interactions is specified before the system is decomposed in a top-down way. This is characterized by a path through the magic square that starts at the upper left corner and then proceeeds in a top-down way by alternately moving right (refining) and down (decomposing). In incremental development, only the most important external interactions are specified before a system architecture is determined. The corresponding path through the magic square starts at the upper left corner and moves sufficiently right and down to determine the overall functionality and architecture of the system. It then performs a linear process for each increment of the system. Other strategies are possible too [24, 57, 61]. In each strategy, decisions about interactions and architectures are intertwined in a particular way. In whatever way this is done, the result of these decisions must be justifiable as if they were taken by means of a rational design process [41]. This is the design analogy to the way in which the historical progress of scientific knowledge can be rationally reconstructed as if a rational, empirical discovery procedure were followed [33, 57].

So far, the framework does not refer to special properties of software systems and is therefore applicable to all kinds of design. In the case of software systems, we add two features to our framework that will turn out to be useful to understand the use that is made of specification techniques. First, each software system interacts with its environment by exchanging symbol occurrences with its external entities. Now, a symbol occurrence is a physical item to which people have assigned a meaning. So for these people, it refers to part of the external world. I call the part of the world referred to by the external interactions of a software system the **subject domain** of the system. (Another term often used is *Universe of Discourse*.) The subject domain is itself a system and may itself be under development by another design team. So the framework of figure 1 is applicable to it. To understand how techniques are used in methods, it is important to understand what they are used for: to specify the subject domain or to specify the software system.

The second feature to be added to our framework is the identification of the essential level of aggregation in the specification of software systems. Given a specification of external functions, behavior and communications of a software system, we can design a decomposition of this system that would be optimal for this specification of external properties, and that ignores the properties of underlying implementation layers. I call this an **essential decomposition** of the software system. The only decomposition criteria that can be used for the essential decomposition are derived from the external environment of the system, such as its external functionality, external behavior, external communications, or its subject domain. The concept of essential decomposition arose with McMenamin and Palmer [37] and also occurs in the object-oriented method Syntropy under the guise of the specification model [10]. I return to this when we discuss structured and object-oriented decomposition criteria in section 3.2. All other decomposition levels of a software system are designed by taking aspects of the underlying implementation environment into account. For example, in a distributed system, the essential decomposition must be allocated to processors in the network, and at each processor, essential components must be mapped to schedulable sequential processes. I call these decomposition levels **implementation-oriented**.

3 A Catalog of Techniques

3.1 External interaction specification

External functions In our framework, external interactions are partitioned into useful portions called functions. Functions can be organized in a refinement hierarchy such that the root of the hierarchy is the overall system function, called the **mission** of the system, and the leaves are **elementary functions**. I regard a function elementary if it is triggered by an event and includes all desired responses to the event. Borrowing from structured analysis, we distinguish **external events**, which arise from an external entity, from **temporal events**, which consist of a significant moment in time [52]. For example, pushing an elevator button is an external event. If the elevator doors have been open for a certain amount of time, a timeout occurs, which is a temporal event.

Techniques for specifying external functions come mainly from structured analysis.

- Often forgotten but extremely important is the **mission statement** of the system. In the Yourdon Systems Method (YSM) this is called the statement

of purpose [67]. It consists of a general description of one or two sentences, the major responsibilities of the system and a list of things the system is agreed *not* to do.
- The external function hierarchy can be represented by a **function refinement tree** whose root represents the mission and the leaves represent the elementary functions. This is a well-known technique from Information Engineering [34]. The tree is merely an organization of external functions and does not say anything about the internal decomposition of the system.
- Elementary functions, which are at the leaves of the tree, can be represented as a list of **event-response pairs**, another technique from YSM, in which the source of the event, its meaning, the desired response of the system, timing requirements and other relevant externally observable properties are described [66, 67].
- If the data interface of events and responses is important, their **pre- and postconditions** in terms of input and output data can be specified. This technique is used in structured and object-oriented analysis alike [9, 66, 67].

There are several techniques to specify behavioral and communication properties in structured and object-oriented analysis, discussed next. Many of these techniques are too detailed to be used for a specification of external system behavior at the higher levels of aggregation but as we specify the requirements of lower-level components, they become increasingly useful. These lower-level components are systems in their own right and we continue to refer to them as such.

Behavior Two groups of behavior representation techniques are used in structured and object-oriented analysis, state transition diagrams (STDs) and process dependency diagrams.

- State transition diagrams come in several flavors. In all flavors, an STD is a directed graph in which the nodes represent states and the edges state transitions. In the **Mealy convention**, an edge can be labeled by the *event* that triggers the transition and the *action* generated by the transition. The triggering event is an external event received from the environment of the system being specified and the generated action is the response sent to the environment. For example, in the Mealy STD of figure 3, if the system receives event e when it resides in state S1, it will generate a and move to state S2. Most structured analysis methods of the Yourdon school use Mealy STDs.
- In the **Moore convention**, actions must be associated with states rather than transitions. In the Moore STD of figure 3, if the system receives event e when it resides in state S1, it will move to state S2 and upon arrival in this state, generate a. The Shlaer-Mellor method for object-oriented analysis uses Moore STDs [49]. Formally, the Mealy and Moore representations have the same expressive power [26, page 42], because they can recognize the same language.

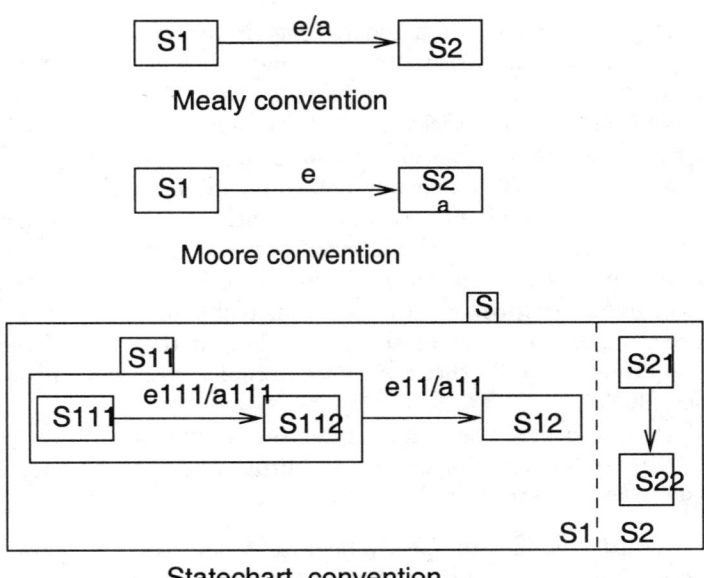

Fig. 3. The Mealy, Moore and statechart conventions.

- In the **Statechart convention**, both the Mealy and Moore conventions are allowed [19, 27]. More importantly, statecharts allow the representation of state hierarchies and parallelism. For example, in the statechart of figure 3, the system is represented by state S, which is partitioned into two parallel substates S1 and S2, each of which are further divided into substates. When the system is in state S111, it is also in state S11, in state S1 and in state S. If it receives event e11 when it is in state S111, it will leave S11 and S11, generate a11 and move to state S12. The generated action a11 may be sent to the external environment but may also be broadcast to all parallel components (such as S2). The execution semantics of statecharts is complex and has been studied in detail [4, 25]. Depending upon the execution semantics, a statechart can be replaced by a set of Mealy (or Moore) STDs that communicate via broadcasting. Most object-oriented methods use statecharts to represent behavior. This may give the impression that the use of statecharts is the hallmark of object-oriented specification. This is a false impression, because Statemate, which is a structured approach, also uses statecharts [22, 27]. The Statemate execution semantics of statecharts is precisely defined [23], but the statechart versions used in object-oriented methods do not have a formally defined semantics. The exception is the UML, for which a formally defined execution semantics is currently being defined [45, 20, 21]. The reader should be warned that this semantics is totally different from the Statemate semantics.

- In order to be able to draw an STD, the number of represented states in an STD must be finite and small. The number of representable states can be increased if we introduce **local variables**. This requires an extension of the graphical technique with the ability to define data types and declare variables. Furthermore, edge labels must be extended with the possibility to specify **guards** that test the value of these variables, and with the possibility to specify additional actions that consist of assignments to these variables. If a guard evaluates to false when an event occurs, then the event e will not trigger the transition. An STD with local variables is called an **extended STD**. Mealy STDs, Moore STDs and statecharts can all be extended this way. Yourdon-style structured analysis do not use extended STDs, but other structured methods such as JSD [29] and SDL [5] and all object-oriented methods use extended STDs.[2] I argue below that this lies at the heart of the difference between these approaches.
- A small number of methods use **process dependency diagrams** to represent behavior. These are directed graphs in which the nodes represent processes and the edges represent process dependencies. The process at the tail of an arrow must have terminated in order for the process at the head to begin. Process dependency diagrams are typically used to represent the flow of control through a number of processes, each of which may be executed by a different system. They are used for example in workflow modeling. Process dependency diagrams were introduced in Information Engineering [35]. Martin and Odell use an expanded form of the notation in their object-oriented specification method [36] and yet another form of the notation is adopted in the UML [44]. There is as yet no formal semantics for these notations in their complete forms.

Of the STD techniques, Mealy and Moore representations are alternatives with the same expressive power and statecharts are a more powerful variation. Extended versions of these techniques are more expressive than nonextended ones. Clearly, the STD techniques are not mutually incompatible but in a particular modeling effort, one of them should be chosen. Whatever STD convention is used, it assumes that external functions of the system have been specified as event-response pairs. The STD can then be used to represent temporal orderings of the event-response pairs.

Process dependency graphs do not require that functions have been specified as event-response pairs. Viewing each function as a process, the process dependency graph can then be used to represent temporal precedence relationships between these. Most varieties of process dependency graphs have no formal semantics. France [16] defines a formal semantics for data flow diagrams extended

---

[2] I regard JSD as a hybrid method that combines elements of structured and OO analysis. JSD uses process structure diagrams with accompanying text, that are equivalent to STDs. SDL is a description technique used for telecommunication systems based upon extended finite state machines. The design philosophy of SDL is functional decomposition but recently, object-oriented features have been added [7, 39].

with control constructs, but to the best of my knowledge, this has not been used in the reviewed methods. Because in the UML, process dependency diagrams (called activity diagrams) are based upon statecharts, there is hope that a formal statechart semantics can be used to define a formal semantics for activity diagrams. Until such a formal semantics is defined to decide the matter, an integrated approach should use STDs and not process dependency diagrams.

Communication The following communication specification techniques are used in structured and object-oriented analysis at the system level.

- Very useful to represent the system boundary is the **context diagram**, which represents the system and the external entities which it communicates with (and which are sources of external events or destinations of responses). This is an important technique from structured analysis [14], recently reinstated by Jackson [30].
- A variant of the context diagram, introduced in Objectory and since adopted by many object-oriented methods, is the **use case diagram** [8, 31, 44]. A use case is an interaction between the system and its environment that is useful for its environment — in other words, it is an external function. A use case diagram shows, for one or more system functions, which external entities may communicate with the system during an occurrence of each of these functions.
- The Shlaer/Mellor method uses a **communication diagram** to represent possible object communications [49]. This is a directed graph in which the nodes represent object classes or external entities and the edges represent possible communications. In the Shlaer/Mellor method, these are asynchronous, but in general there are many more options concerning the kinds of communication protocols that can be followed, to be discussed in a moment.

This exhausts the techniques used for the specification of communication. With the rising importance of high-level communication between possibly distributed components of software systems, there is clearly a need for richer high-level communication specification techniques. Polman et al. [42, 43] classify communication according to a number of dimensions, such as the capacity of the channel and the blocking behavior of the sender (which may be willing to wait for n time units for the communication attempt to succeed, with $n \geq 0$). For example, in asynchronous communication, the channel has a non-zero capacity and the sender will not wait for the communication to succeed. In synchronous communication, the channel has zero capacity and the sender will wait for the communication to succeed. Polman et al. list other relevant dimensions too. More work needs to be done on ways to represent properties like these at the specification level.

There are two other techniques offered by structured and object-oriented methods, that can be used to *illustrate* the communication and behavior of a system.

- A **sequence diagram** consists of a set of vertical lines, each representing a communicating entity. The downwards direction represents the advance of time. Arrows between these lines represent communications. Sequence diagrams have been used for a long time in telecommunication systems, where they are standardized as message sequence charts [28]. Variations of the technique are used in object-oriented analysis [31, 47] to represent the communication between objects or between the system and its environment. In an attempt to standardize on an object-oriented version of the technique it is adopted by the UML [44]. A sequence diagram represents behavior as well as communication. However, it does not represent all possible behaviors and communications, but only those that can occur in a particular scenario.
- **Collaboration diagrams** are directed graphs in which the nodes represent communicating entities and the edges communications. The edges are numbered to represent the order in which communications take place. Collaboration diagrams can be used as alternative to sequence diagrams. Like sequence diagrams, there are many versions, that differ in the elaborations and adornments that they allow. The technique plays a central role in responsibility-driven design [65] and in a number of object-oriented methods such as Booch [6], Fusion [9], and Syntropy [10]. It has been adopted in the UML as alternative to sequence charts [44].

The communication specification techniques are clearly compatible and can be integrated in an obvious way. For example, a context diagram can show where the events come from and where the responses of the system go to. If we add an STD to specify the behavior of external event-response pairs, a sequence or collaboration diagram can be used to illustrate possible communication sequences of the system generated by this behavior. In the specification of external interactions, therefore, there is no incompatibility between structured and object-oriented analysis. To find the difference, we must look at decomposition specification techniques.

3.2 Decomposition

	function 1	....	function n
component 1			
......			
component m			

Fig. 4. Format of a function decomposition table.

Taking a systems engineering view, we can represent the allocation and flowdown of external functions to components by means of a **function decomposition table**, also called a traceability table in systems engineering [11, page 192], [12]. In figure 4, the top row lists all external functions of the system (at a certain level of refinement) and the leftmost column represents all components of the system (at a certain level of aggregation). An entry of the table represents the functions that a component must have to in order to realize an external function. A column of the table represents all functions that act together to realize an external function. The table relates all perspectives that we identified: functions, decomposition, behavior (ordering of functions in a row) and communication (columns). Note that each such table corresponds to one point in the magic square of figure 2, i.e. a refinement level and an aggregation level.

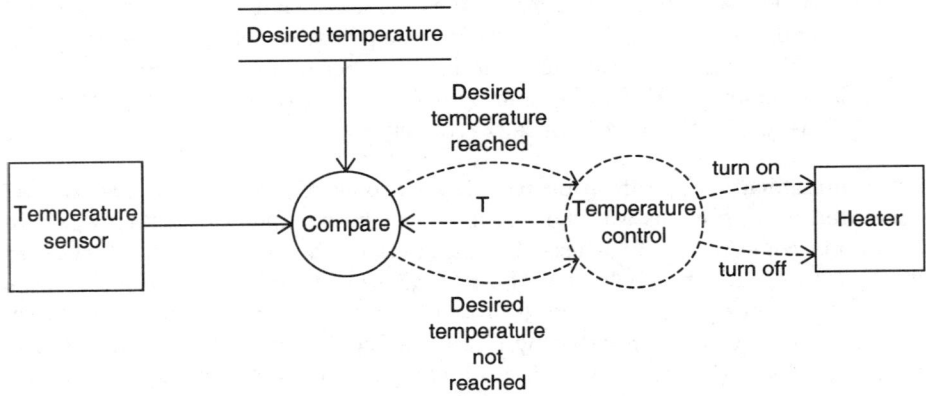

Fig. 5. A simple data flow diagram.

Decomposition specification Yourdon-style structured analysis uses **entity-relationship diagrams** (ERDs) and **data flow diagrams** (DFDs) to represent software decomposition. Figure 5 contains a simple DFD that represents three components and the way they communicate with each other and with external entities. Temperature sensor and Heater are external entities used to control the temperature of a fluid in a cooking tank. These are not components of the system but part of the environment. The rest of the diagram illustrates that DFDs recognize three different kinds of system components:

– The **data store** Desired temperature represents the desired temperature of the fluid. A data store is a place where part of the state of the system can be stored.
– The **data process** Compare compares the value stored in Desired temperature with the value measured by Temperature sensor and sends the result to

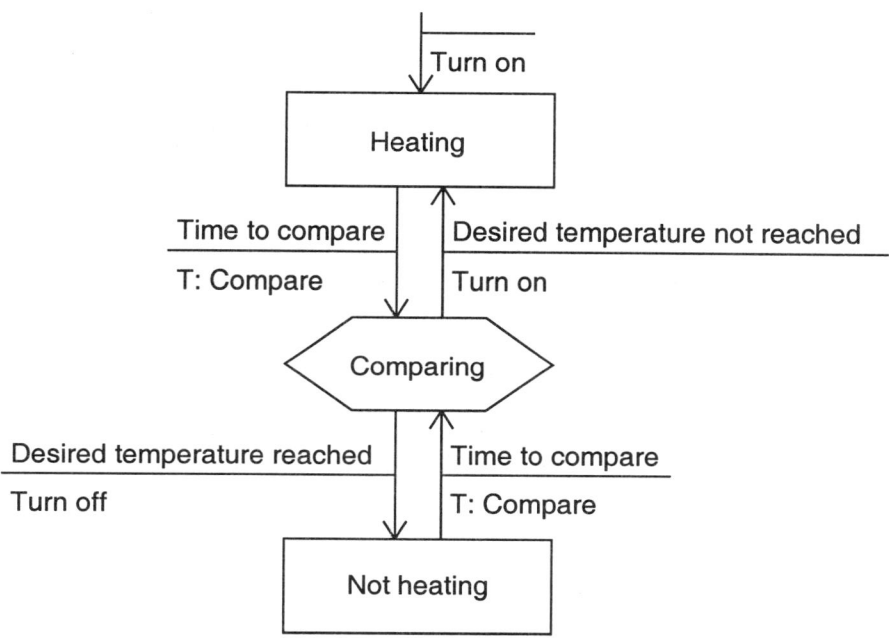

Fig. 6. A Mealy STD for the Temperature control process with a decision state.

Fig. 7. A simple entity-relationship diagram.

Temperature control. A data process is a function that transforms input data into output data.
- The **control process** Temperature control is a finite state machine that periodically triggers the data process Compare and, depending upon the answer, turns the Heater on or off.

Dashed arrows represent signals, solid arrows represent data flows. The Mealy STD for Temperature control is shown in figure 6. It shows that Temperature control triggers an external data process by the action T: Compare and then waits for the answer in the state Comparing. It moves to the Heating or Not heating state depending upon the answer, turning the heater on or off accordingly. Comparing is called a **decision state**.

The structure of all data in the system, stored or manipulated, can be represented by an ERD. Figure 7 shows a fragment of an ERD that describes the structure of some relevant data. It shows that the system must contain data about the Batch of juice to be heated, the Recipe according to which the batch must be heated, and the Cooking tank in which the batch must be heated. The arrow from Batch to Recipe means that there is exactly one Recipe for each Batch. The line between Batch and Cooking tank means that there is a many-many relationship between these. The Yourdon method does not prescribe the relationship between ERD and DFD other than that at least the structure of all stored data must be represented by the ERD.

Yourdon structured analysis thus recognizes three kinds of components to be listed in the leftmost column of the function decomposition table:

- data stores,
- data processes, and
- control processes.

Object-oriented methods recognize only one kind of component:

- objects, that encapsulate all these three aspects.

Each object contains data, can perform computations with these data, and has a behavior over time. This mans that object behavior can be specified by extended STDs. What this means can best be illustrated by an example.

Figure 8 shows a possible **class-relationship diagram** (CRD) of an object-oriented decomposition of the control software. Each rectangle represents an object class. Temperature_control_S has two attributes, Desired_temp and Actual_temp. To simplify the diagram, we omitted the attributes of other objects. The diagram is an extension of the ERD with object classes that correspond to external entities and to a control process in the DFD. Bidirectional arrows in the diagram represent one-one relationships, single arrows represent many-one relationships. To emphasize that all objects represented by the CRD are software components, we added -S to their names. We did not need to do this in the ERD of figure 7, because in structured analysis, ERDs always represent data structures of software systems.

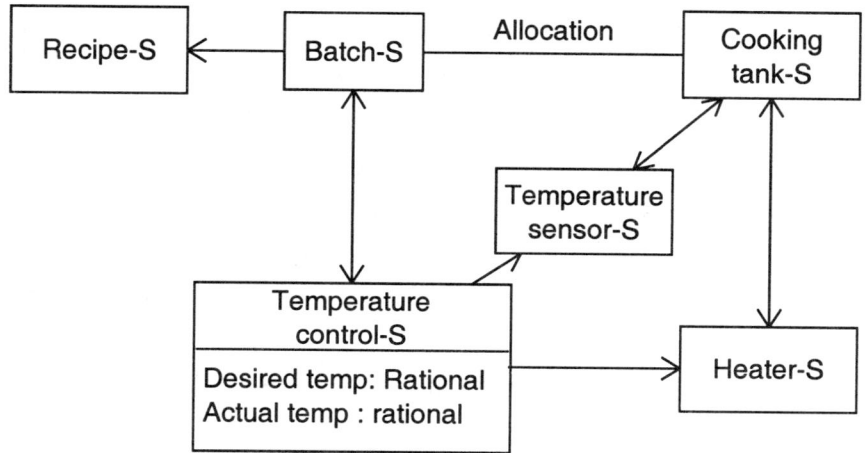

Fig. 8. A simple class-relationship diagram.

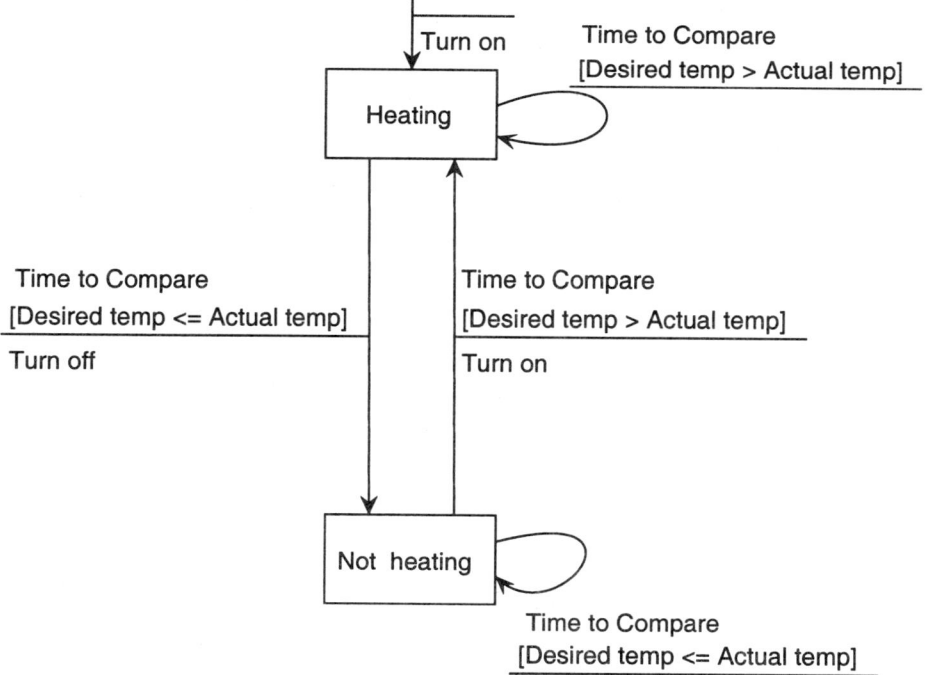

Fig. 9. An extended Mealy STD for the Temperature control object.

The behavior of the **Temperature control** object can be specified by an extended STD such as shown in figure 9. The STD uses the two attributes of **Temperature control** as local variables. They receive values from the environment of the **Temperature control**, in this case the **Temperature sensor** and **Recipe** software objects. This is not shown in the CRD: the lines in that diagram represent relationships between the software objects, which tells us which software objects know the identity of which other software objects. They do not tell us which communications between objects take place. The variables are tested in guards, which are denoted by Boolean expressions written between square brackets. Thus, if the event **Time to compare** occurs when the temperature control is in state **Not heating**, then the transition to **Heating** occurs if **Desired temp** > **Actual temp**, and the heater is turned on.

Now, compare this with the Mealy STD in figure 6. It is clear that separating data and control, as is done in DFD models, makes for more complex models because this forces us to introduce decision states in the Mealy machine to await the outcome of decisions, and it forces us to introduce data processes that compute the decisions, and that communicate with the Mealy machine. The communication typically has the following structure: The Mealy machine triggers a data process that must compute a decision, and the data process sends its output as an event to the Mealy machine. Further complexity is introduced because DFDs separate data processing from data storage. This means that the data process does not have the data to compute the decision. It must get this from an input data flow and/or a data store. Data that survives a single external system transaction must be stored in data store, whereas in OO models this data persists in the state of objects. The consequence of separating data processing, data storage and control is that DFD-based models are considerably harder to understand than object-oriented models. Also, these separations are incompatible with the encapsulation principle of object-oriented decomposition. I conclude that DFDs are incompatible with object-oriented decomposition.

Decomposition heuristics There are several criteria that can be used to find a decomposition. **Functional decomposition** uses external functionality as criterion. In its simplest form, every external elementary function corresponds to a component that implements that function. This would lead to a diagonal in the function decomposition table, mapping external functionality to internal structure. This is alright if it leads to small interfaces between components and if the external functionality never changes. If either of these conditions is false it is a bad decomposition. It is often claimed that functional decomposition is incompatible with object-orientation. However, there is nothing in the concept of an object that prevents us from using a functional decomposition criterion for an object-oriented decomposition. For example, in figure 8, **Temperature control** corresponds to a function of the system.[3]

---

[3] In JSD, such objects are called long-running functions [29] and in Objectory, they are called control objects [31].

A second decomposition criterion that can be used is **subject domain-oriented decomposition**. In section 2 it was noted that software systems interact with their environment by exchanging symbol occurrences with the environment. The subject domain of a software system was then defined as the part of the world referred to by these symbols. For example, the subject domain of a database system is the part of the world represented by the database, and the subject domain of a control system is the part of the world controlled by the system. In **subject domain-oriented partitioning**, there is a correspondence between the software system decomposition and a subject domain decomposition. For example, figure 8 contains software objects that correspond to a batch, a recipe and a cooking tank.

This decomposition principle has been adopted by many object-oriented methods but contrary to what is often thought, it is not characteristic of object-oriented methods. For example, the principle is central in JSD [29], which is not purely object-oriented. Furthermore, as I show elsewhere [56], the principle can easily be applied to data flow modeling. Finally, we find improper use of the principle of subject-domain partitioning in object-oriented methods. For example, the Fusion method recommends making an ER-like domain model first and then drawing a boundary around the object classes that will constitute the system [9]. By the act of drawing this boundary, objects in the domain (outside the system) become objects inside the system. Objects outside the boundary remain subject domain entities. This confuses the subject domain with the internal decomposition of the system. The resulting diagram combines features of a CRD showing the essential decomposition of the system with features of a context diagram showing the communications with the environment. Published examples show models of the domain (outside the system) that already contain system functions and other essential system components [2]. In some cases, the domain model contains two copies of an entity, one for the external entity and one for a essential system component. Use of the method in teaching shows difficulties precisely at this point [15].

In addition to functional decomposition and subject-domain-oriented decomposition, there are two intermediary decomposition heuristics. **Event partitioning** recommends defining one system component for every elementary event-response pair [37] and **device partitioning** recommends defining one system component for every external [67, pages 355, 509]. In practice, a combination of these heuristics will be used. For example, figure 8 contains components that correspond to external devices (**Heater-S** and **Temperature sensor-S**) and we have seen that it also contains components that correspond to subject domain objects and to a system function.

4 The Techniques in TRADE

Table 1 lists the techniques that have been adopted in TRADE. The reason for adopting these techniques is that together, they cover the kinds of properties that can be specified in a wide variety of structured and object-oriented methods [58].

Table 1. The techniques in TRADE.

	Function specification technique	Behavior specification technique	Communication specification technique	Decomposition specification technique
Mission statement	X			
Function refinement tree	X			
Event-response specification	X			
Pre-postcondition specification	X			
Extended Mealy machine diagram		X		
Communication diagram			X	
Sequence diagram		X	X	
Class diagram				X
Function decomposition table				X

For each dimension of our framework, we chose simple and useful techniques that can be used to represent system properties along that dimension. Because the primary aim of TRADE is to teach informatics students about software specification techniques, ease of understanding is preferred above expressive power. This is the reason why extended Mealy machines rather than extended statecharts are chosen to represent behavior. Experience has taught that students tend to produce unnecessarily complex models when using statecharts to represent behavior. Also, local variables gives us all the added expressive power that we need: state nesting and parallelism can be expressed by a set of communicating Mealy machines. And as argued earlier, the introduction of local variables in any STD technique allows us to avoid the complexities of data flow diagrams.

Simplicity of techniques also makes it feasible to define the connections that must hold between different parts of a coherent specifications in an understandable manner. Without going to details, if the techniques are used as indicated in table 2, the links shown in table 3 must hold.

Table 2. Use of the techniques in TRADE.

	Subject domain	External system interactions	System decomposition	Component interactions
Mission statement		Mission		
Function refinement tree		Mission refinement		
Event-response specification		Elementary external functions		Component functions
Pre-postcondition specification		Elementary external functions		Component functions
Extended Mealy machine diagram	Subject domain entity behavior			Component behavior
Communication diagram		Context diagram Use case diagram		Component interaction
Sequence diagram		External interaction sequences		Component interaction sequences
Class diagram	Subject domain decomposition		Essential decomposition	
Function decomposition table			Allocation and flowdown of functions	

The entries of the table indicate the techniques between which there exist links. The table is symmetric around the diagonal, which is why only half of it is shown. A brief explanation of the entries of the table follows, where the entries are identified by a pair (row.column).

(2.1) The root of the function refinement tree is labeled by the mission statement.
(3.2) Each leaf of the function refinement tree represents an external function, specified by means of an event-response specification and/or a pre-postcondition specification. Each external function specification corresponds to a node in the function refinement tree.
(4.2) See (3.2).

Table 3. Links between parts of a coherent specification.

	1.	2.	3.	4.	5.	6.	7.	8.	9.	10.	11.	12.	13.	14.
1. Mission statement														
2. Function refinement tree	X													
3. Event/response specification of external function		X												
4. Pre-postcondition specification of external function		X												
5. Context diagram			X											
6. Use case diagram		X			X									
7. Sequence diagram of external interactions					X	X								
8. Class diagram of essential decomposition														
9. Function decomposition table		X					X							
10. Event/response specification of function of component									X					
11. Pre-postcondition specification of function of component									X					
12. Extended Mealy diagram of behavior of component									X					
13. Communication diagram of interactions of components									X			X	X	
14. Sequence diagram of interactions of components													X	X

(5.3) The event sources and response destinations of an event-response specification of an external function are external entities represented by the context diagram, that interact with the system.

(6.2) Each use case corresponds to a node in the function refinement tree.

(6.5) The interactions between a use case and an external entity, represented in a use case diagram, also occur in the context diagram between the system and an external entity.

(7.5) The external communications in a sequence diagram of external interactions correspond to the external communications in the context and in use case diagrams.

(7.6) See (7.5).

(9.2) The top row of the function decomposition table corresponds one-one to the leaves of the function refinement tree (they represent external functions).

(9.8) The leftmost column of the function decomposition table corresponds one-one with the set of classes in the class diagram. In addition, the entries of the table must be consistent with the interface of the components declared in the class diagram.

(10.8) The events and responses in a event-response specification of a component must be consistent with the events and responses of the component declared in the class diagram.

(11.8) The terms in a pre-postcondition specification of an interaction of a component must be consistent with the attributes of the component declared in the class diagram.

(12.8) The events and responses of the transitions in the Mealy diagram of a class must correspond with the events and responses of the class declared in the class diagram. In addition, the local variables used in the Mealy diagram correspond to the attributes declared for the class in the class diagram.

(13.8) The communications represented in a communication diagram of component interactions correspond with the events and responses declared in the class diagram. (Each of these is part of the interface of the object and consists of a communication with another object or with an external entity.)

(13.10) See (13.8).

(13.12) See (13.8).

(14.12) The sequence of communications in a sequence diagram of component communications is consistent with the Mealy diagram of the communicating components.

(14.13) The communications in a sequence diagram of component communications are consistent with the communications represented by the communication diagram.

This list suffices to give an impression of the connection rules. There are two ways to make this more precise, by means of formalization and by means of a metamodel. To formalize the diagrams and their links, a formalization based upon order-sorted dynamic logic and process algebra will be used [54, 64, 63]. This is particularly important for the rules in the above list that contain the word "consistent". Definition of a metamodel is ongoing work, which is part of the specification and implementation of the TCM software tool [60].

Table 3 does not define links for the subject domain model (a class diagram with extended Mealy machines). These parallel the links between the class diagram and Mealy machines for the system decomposition. If subject-domain-oriented decomposition for the system is used, then there will be links between the class diagram of the subject domain and the class diagram of the system. These are however a result of design decisions and are not a consequence of the semantics of the notations. Table 3 only lists the links that must hold in all cases.

Observe that we can define the links only because we presuppose our framework for software design techniques. It is this framework that gives us the concepts of subject domain, functions, behavior, communication and decomposition, which give the links meaning.

Comparing the techniques in TRADE with the UML [44], we observe that the structure of TRADE models corresponds with that of UML models in that a software system is viewed as a collection of interacting objects, whose structure is represented by a class diagram and whose behavior is represented by state transition diagrams. In addition, a TRADE model represents external functionality by a mission statement and a function refinement tree, and adds traceability by defining a function decomposition table. TRADE only uses the simplest possible state machine notation (Mealy machines) rather than the complex statechart notation, and omits collaboration diagrams, which have roughly the same expressive power as sequence diagrams.

Just like the Yourdon Systems Method [67], TRADE models contain an elaborate specification of external functionality, using roughly the same techniques as used in YSM. Unlike YSM, the essential decomposition is not represented by means of data flow models but by means of a class diagram.

Another interesting comparison to make is with SDL [5], used for modeling telecommunication systems. An SDL model represents a system as a hierarchy of subsystems, called *blocks*, that may communicate via channels. Each block at the bottom of the hierarchy consists of one or more communicating processes, each of which is specified by means of an extended finite state machine. The major difference with TRADE models is that TRADE contains more techniques for specifying external functionality but contains no technique for representing subsystems. Addition of a subsystem representation technique, and heuristics for partitioning a system into subsystems, is a topic of current research.

Turning to the heuristics that can be used to apply the techniques in TRADE, these have already been described in section 3.2. These heuristics have their source in structured and object-oriented methods and can all be used in combination with the techniques in TRADE.

5 Discussion and Conclusions

TRADE techniques can be used in different design strategies, ranging from waterfall to incremental or evolutionary. They look familiar to developers with a structured background as well as those with an object-oriented background and therefore should help in combining the best elements of both practices. The essential element in this is to institute a systems engineering way of working, in which specification of external interactions is separated from a specification of internal decomposition, and explicit traceability from external interactions to internal components is maintained. Structured techniques for external interaction specification can then be seamlessly combined with object-oriented techniques for essential decomposition. DFDs cannot be integrated this way and should be dropped. However, I argued that functional decomposition is compatible with object-oriented decomposition. It can also be combined with other decomposition criteria, such as device partitioning and subject-domain-oriented partitioning.

To validate the TRADE framework, it has been applied to the industrial production cell case [55] and in the Esprit project 2RARE to the specification of a system for video on demand [62]. Two other case studies are available on the web [51, 59], and several others are in preparation. Further validation will take place in teaching, where it will be used to teach techniques in a method-independent way. Use of the TRADE framework in teaching is supported by a graphical editor called TCM (Toolkit for Conceptual Modeling), freely available for teaching and research purposes [13]. It supports most of the techniques discussed in this paper. Validation of another kind takes place by providing a formal semantics to the techniques in TRADE. A formal semantics of a combination of objects with behavior and communication, based on order-sorted dynamic logic and process algebra, has been given earlier [54, 64, 63]. Current work concentrates on declarative and operational semantics of behavior specifications so as to provide an execution semantics for STDs in TCM [60]. The methodological role of this is to strengthen the tools in TRADE by making their meaning and interconnections explicit. Our hope is that this makes the tools easier to use without burdening the tool user with the formal foundations.

References

1. B. Alabiso. Transformation of data flow analysis models to object oriented design. In N. Meyrowitz, editor, *Object-Oriented Programming Systems, Languages and Applications, Conference Proceedings*, pages 335–353. ACM Press, 1988. SIGPLAN Notices, volume 23.
2. M. Awad, J. Kuusela, and J. Ziegler. *Object-Oriented Technology for Real-Time Systems: A Practical Approach Using OMT and Fusion*. Prentice-Hall, 1996.
3. S.C. Bailin. An object-oriented requirements specification method. *Communications of the ACM*, 32:608–623, 1989.
4. M. von der Beeck. A comparison of Statecharts variants. In H. Langmaack, W.P. de Roever, and J. Vytopil, editors, *Formal Techniques in Real-Time and Fault-Tolerant Systems*, pages 128–148. Springer, 1994. Lecture Notes in Computer Science 863.
5. F. Belina, D. Hogrefe, and A. Sarma. *SDL with Applications from protocol Specification*. Prentice-Hall, 1991.
6. G. Booch. *Object-Oriented Design with Applications, Second edition*. Benjamin/Cummings, 1994.
7. R. Bræk and Ø. Haugen. *Engineering Real-Time Systems*. Prentice-Hall, 1993.
8. D. Coleman. Fusion with use cases: Extending Fusion for requirements modeling. Available through URL: http://www.hpl.hp.com/fusion/index.html, 1996.
9. D. Coleman, P. Arnold, S. Bodoff, C. Dollin, H. Gilchrist, F. Hayes, and P. Jeremaes. *Object-Oriented Development: The FUSION Method*. Prentice-Hall, 1994.
10. S. Cook and J. Daniels. *Designing Object Systems: Object-Oriented Modelling with Syntropy*. Prentice-Hall, 1994.
11. A. M. Davis. *Software Requirements: Objects, Functions, States*. Prentice-Hall, 1993.
12. Defense Systems Management College. Systems engineering management guide. Technical report, Technical Managament Department, January 1990.
13. F. Dehne and R.J. Wieringa. Toolkit for Conceptual Modeling (TCM): User's Guide. Technical Report IR-401, Faculty of Mathematics and Computer Science, *Vrije Universiteit*, De Boelelaan 1081a, 1081 HV Amsterdam, 1996. http://www.cs.vu.nl/~tcm.

14. T. DeMarco. *Structured Analysis and System Specification.* Yourdon Press/Prentice-Hall, 1978.
15. G. Eckert. *Improving the analysis stage of the Fusion method*, pages 276–313. 1996.
16. R. B. France. Semantically extended data flow diagrams: a formal specification tool. *IEEE Transactions on Software Engineering*, 18(4):329–346, April 1992.
17. A.D. Hall. *A Methodology for Systems Engineering.* Van Nostrand, 1962.
18. A.D. Hall. Three-dimensional morphology of systems engineering. *IEEE Transactions on System Science and Cybernetics*, SSC-5(2):156–160, 1969.
19. D. Harel. Statecharts: a visual formalism for complex systems. *Science of Computer Programming*, 8:231–274, 1987. Preliminary version appeared as Technical Report CS 84-05, The Weizmann Institute of Science, Rehovot, Israel, February 1984.
20. D. Harel and E. Gery. Executable object modeling with statecharts. In *Proceedings of the 18th International Conference on Software Engineering*, pages 246–257. IEEE Press, 1996.
21. D. Harel and E. Gery. Executable object modeling with statecharts. *Computer*, 30(7):31–42, July 1997.
22. D. Harel, H. Lachover, A. Naamad, A. Pnueli, M. Politi, R. Sherman, A. Shtull-Trauring, and M. Trakhtenbrot. STATEMATE: a working environment for the development of complex reactive systems. *IEEE Transactions on Software Engineering*, 16:403–414, April 1990.
23. D. Harel and A. Naamad. The STATEMATE semantics of statecharts. *ACM Transactions on Software Engineering and Methodology*, 5(4):293–333, October 1996.
24. D. Harel and A. Pnueli. On the development of reactive systems. In K. Apt, editor, *Logics and Models of Concurrent Systems*, pages 477–498. Springer, 1985. NATO ASI Series.
25. D. Harel, A. Pnueli, J. P. Schmidt, and R. Sherman. On the formal semantics of statecharts. In *Proceedings, Symposium on Logic in Computer Science*, pages 54–64. Computer Science Press, June 22–25 1987.
26. J.E. Hopcroft and J.D. Ullman. *Introduction to Automata Theory, Languages and Computation.* Addison-Wesley, 1979.
27. i-Logix. The Languages of STATEMATE. Technical report, i-Logix Inc., 22 Third Avenue, Burlington, Mass. 01803, U.S.A., January 1991. To be published as D. Harel and M. Politi, *Modeling Reactive Systems with Statecharts: The STATEMATE Approach.*
28. ITU. *Criteria for the Use and Applicability of Formal Description Techniques: Message Sequence Charts (MSC).* International Telecommunication Union, 1994. Z.120 (03/93).
29. M. Jackson. *System Development.* Prentice-Hall, 1983.
30. M. Jackson. *Software Requirements and Specifications: A lexicon of practice, principles and prejudices.* Addison-Wesley, 1995.
31. I. Jacobson, M. Christerson, P. Johnsson, and G. Övergaard. *Object-Oriented Software Engineering: A Use Case Driven Approach.* Prentice-Hall, 1992.
32. P. Jalote. Functional refinement and nested objects for object–oriented design. *IEEE Transactions on Software Engineering*, 15(3):264–270, March 1989.
33. I. Lakatos. *Proofs and Refutations.* Cambridge University Press, 1976. Edited by J. Worall and E. Zahar.
34. J. Martin. *Information Engineering, Book I: Introduction.* Prentice-Hall, 1989.
35. J. Martin. *Information Engineering, Book II: Planning and analysis.* Prentice-Hall, 1989.

36. J. Martin and J. Odell. *Object-Oriented Methods: A Foundation.* Prentice-Hall, 1995.
37. S. M. McMenamin and J. F. Palmer. *Essential Systems Analysis.* Yourdon Press/Prentice Hall, 1984.
38. R. Milner. *A Calculus of Communicating Systems.* Springer, 1980. Lecture Notes in Computer Science 92.
39. B. Møller-Pedersen, D. Belsnes, and H.P. Dahle. Rationale and tutorial on OSDL: an object-oriented extension of SDL. *Computer Networks and ISDN Systems*, 13:97–117, 1987.
40. Objectory AB. *Objectory: Requirements Analysis, Version 3.6*, 1995.
41. D.L. Parnas and P.C. Clements. A rational design process: How and why to fake it. *IEEE Transactions on Software Engineering*, SE-12:251–257, 1986.
42. M. Polman, M. van Steen, and A. de Bruin. Formalizing a design technique for distributed systems. In *Proceedings Second International Workshop on Software Engineering for Parallel and Distributed Systems*, pages pages 150–159, Boston, May 1997.
43. M. Polman, M. van Steen, and A. de Bruin. A structured design technique for distributed programs. In *Proceedings 22nd International Computer Software and Applications Conference (CompSac)*, Vienna, August 1998.
44. Rational. *Unified Modeling Language: Notation Guide, Version 1.1.* Rational Software Corporation, 2800 San Tomas Expressway, Santa Clara, CA 95051-0951, 1 September 1997. URL http://www.rational.com/uml/1.1/.
45. Rational. *Unified Modeling Language: Semantics, Version 1.1.* Rational Software Corporation, 1 September 1997. URL http://www.rational.com/uml/1.1/.
46. N.F.M. Roozenburg and J. Eekels. *Product design: Fundamentals and Methods.* Wiley, 1995.
47. J. Rumbaugh, M. Blaha, W. Premerlani, F. Eddy, and W. Lorensen. *Object-oriented modeling and design.* Prentice-Hall, 1991.
48. E. Seidewitz and M. Stark. Toward a general object-oriented software development methodology. *ADA Letters*, 7(4):54–67, july/august 1987.
49. S. Shlaer and S. J. Mellor. *Object Lifecycles: Modeling the World in States.* Prentice-Hall, 1992.
50. W. Swartout and R. Balzer. On the inevitable intertwining of specification and implementation. *Communications of the ACM*, 25:438–440, 1982.
51. B. van Vlijmen and R.J. Wieringa. Using the Tools in TRADE, I: A Decision Support System for Traffic Light maintenance. Technical Report IR-435, Faculty of Mathematics and Computer Science, *Vrije Universiteit*, November 1997. ftp://ftp.cs.vu.nl/pub/roelw/97-TRADE01.ps.Z.
52. P. T. Ward and S. J. Mellor. *Structured Development for Real-Time Systems.* Prentice-Hall/Yourdon Press, 1985. Three volumes.
53. P.T. Ward. How to integrate object orientation with structured analysis and design. *Computer*, pages 74–82, March 1989.
54. R.J. Wieringa. A formalization of objects using equational dynamic logic. In C. Delobel, M. Kifer, and Y. Masunaga, editors, *2nd International Conference on Deductive and Object-Oriented Databases (DOOD'91)*, pages 431–452. Springer, 1991. Lecture Notes in Computer Science 566. ftp://ftp.cs.vu.nl/pub/roelw/91-DynamicObjects.ps.Z..
55. R.J. Wieringa. LCM 3.0: Specification of a control system using dynamic logic and process algebra. In C. Lewerentz and T. Lindner, editors, *Formal Development of Reactive Systems — Case Study Production Cell*, pages 333–355. Springer,

1994. Lecture Notes in Computer Science 891. ftp://ftp.cs.vu.nl/pub/roelw/94-ProductionCell.ps.Z..
56. R.J. Wieringa. Combining static and dynamic modeling methods: a comparison of four methods. *The Computer Journal*, 38(1):17–30, 1995. ftp://ftp.cs.vu.nl/pub/roelw/95-MethodIntegration.ps.Z..
57. R.J. Wieringa. *Requirements Engineering: Frameworks for Understanding*. Wiley, 1996. http://www.cs.vu.nl/~roelw/RE1.ps..
58. R.J. Wieringa. A survey of structured and object-oriented software specification methods and techniques. Technical report, Faculty of Mathematics and Computer Science, *Vrije Universiteit*, De Boelelaan 1081a, 1081 HV Amsterdam, 1997. To be published, *ACM Computing Surveys*.
59. R.J. Wieringa. Using the tools in TRADE, II: Specification and design of a meeting scheduler system. Technical Report IR-436, Faculty of Mathematics and Computer Science, *Vrije Universiteit*, November 1997. ftp://ftp.cs.vu.nl/pub/roelw/97-TRADE02.ps.Z.
60. R.J. Wieringa and J. Broersen. A minimal transition system semantics for lightweight class- and behavior diagrams. In *Workshop on Precise Semantics for Software Modeling techniques*, 1998. To be published.
61. R.J. Wieringa and E. Dubois. Integrating semi-formal and formal software specification techniques. *Information Systems*, 23(3/4), 1998.
62. R.J. Wieringa, E. Dubois, and S. Huyts. Integrating semi-formal and formal requirements. In A. Olivé and J.A. Pastor, editors, *Advanced Information Systems Engineering*, pages 19–32. Springer, 1997. Lecture Notes in Computer Science 1250. ftp://ftp.cs.vu.nl/pub/roelw/97-TradeAlbert.ps.Z.ps.Z..
63. R.J. Wieringa, W. de Jonge, and P.A. Spruit. Using dynamic classes and role classes to model object migration. *Theory and Practice of Object Systems*, 1(1):61–83, 1995. ftp://ftp.cs.vu.nl/pub/roelw/95-DynamicClassesAndRoles.ps.Z..
64. R.J. Wieringa and J.-J.Ch. Meyer. Actors, actions, and initiative in normative system specification. *Annals of Mathematics and Artificial Intelligence*, 7:289–346, 1993. ftp://ftp.cs.vu.nl/pub/roelw/93-DeonticActors.ps.Z..
65. R. Wirfs-Brock, B. Wilkerson, and L. Wiener. *Designing Object-Oriented Software*. Prentice-Hall, 1990.
66. E. Yourdon. *Modern Structured Analysis*. Prentice-Hall, 1989.
67. Yourdon Inc. *Yourdon^{TM} Systems Method: Model-Driven Systems Development*. Prentice-Hall, 1993.

A Discipline for Handling Feature Interaction

Egidio Astesiano and Gianna Reggio

DISI
Dipartimento di Informatica e Scienze dell'Informazione
Università di Genova
Via Dodecaneso, 35 – Genova 16146 – Italy
{astes,reggio} @ disi.unige.it
http://www.disi.unige.it

Abstract. A challenging problem within the wider software evolution problem is the development of systems by features. While most of the recent work centered around the detection of feature interactions, we present an approach based on modular specification, separation of concerns and prevention of unwanted interactions. We illustrate our approach extending a formalism for the specification of reactive systems and showing its application to some aspects of the well-known case of telephone systems (POTS and variations).
The paper concentrates more on the methodological aspects, which are, at large extent, independent of the formalism. Indeed, this seems to be the case of some rather novel concepts like the distinction between pre-features (features in isolation) and features, closed and open semantics, feature composition and discipline of feature interaction, and finally the pervading role of a kind of anti-frame assumption.

1 Introduction

Evolution in software development has many facets. One which emerged in the last five years, especially in the area of telecommunications and networking, is the continual expansion of services. Recognizing that objected-oriented incrementality is not adequate to cope with this new problem in full generality, the concept of "feature" as unit of update has been introduced, see e.g., [11], and taken as a pivotal unit for even new paradigms, like feature-oriented programming, feature-oriented specification and so on [9].

In spite of the considerable effort (see some pointers to recent work at the end), still many issues deserve further attention and investigation, as it is admitted by the specialists of the subject, also taking into account the growing complexity of the applications concerned. Among the issues, feature composition and interaction is definitely the one attracting most attention. This is also witnessed by the success of an International Workshop on Feature Interaction, now reaching in '98 its fifth edition. In particular a lot of work is reported on the so-called feature interaction detection, possibly done automatically. According to this viewpoint, feature interaction is synonym with unexpected/unwanted results.

We are among those sharing the view that the problem of feature-interaction should be tackled within a wider methodological approach. This view is best expressed by Pamela Zave in [11], who calls for "an approach based on modular specifications and separation of concerns ... (aimed) to organize the specification so that it is easy to add without destroying its structure or desiderable properties". This is indeed the underlying challenging problem; again in P. Zave's words "the goal of extendible specifications is as difficult to achieve as it is easy to state". For example, in the realm of reactive and concurrent systems, the classical approach to incrementality has been based on the notion of process/ agent as unit of change; feature-driven incrementality deals instead with incrementality within a process and refers/affects the behaviour of the pre-existing processes.

Here we want to outline a specification framework supporting a feature-driven software development method with rigorous semantics, offering conceptual tools for expressing requirements on unwanted interactions. The framework intends to be adaptable to a variety of different application fields, like telecommunications, information systems; clearly, depending on the application, sensible domain specific methods should be derived.

This paper is devoted to a semiformal introductory illustration of our approach by means of a significant running example. A more formal and detailed presentation of the technicalities can be found in other papers [2].

At the end of the paper we discuss the relationship with the existing work.

Running example As running examples we consider various telephone systems modularly built by composing features. We start with POTS (Plain Old Telephone System) schematically presented in the following picture.

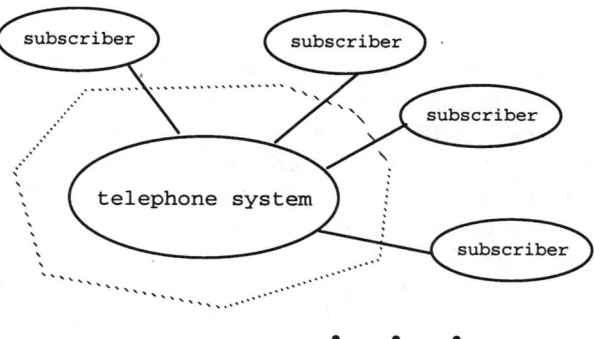

Each subscriber may

- hear the phone ringing,
- lift/put down the receiver,
- dial the number of another subscriber,
- hear a busy/free tone/the voice of another subscriber on the receiver,
- and speak on the microphone.

In this paper, following [3] and others, in order to illustrate our approach, we consider the telephone system as a simple reactive system consisting of the part enclosed by the dotted line in the above picture; and we consider as its interchanges with the external world (the subscribers) only those underlined in the above list. However, in the real life application it would be better to see POTS as a concurrent system, whose components are the phones and the telephone net.

We then extend the functionalities of POTS by adding the possibility of *automatic-call back* (ACB) in the case of a call to a busy subscriber and of *three-parts service* (TP), i.e., telephone communications involving three subscribers. Using a telecommunication terminology, we can extend the system by adding two "features"; in our setting also the starting system (POTS) is considered a feature.

Outline Let us now outline the main steps of our approach.

- First, a feature is treated almost in isolation and considered just a simple reactive system; thus POTS, ACB and TP are specified (Sect. 2) as generalized transition systems, whose states are sets of attribute values (as in many O-O approaches) and whose transitions, defined by a set of *activity rules*, denote action capabilities, with the labels indicating the interface with the external environment. Still a basic new concept is introduced for taking care of the possible addition of other features: transitions are grouped under *types*, essentially indicating the kind of performed activity; when composing two features only transitions with the same type will have the possibility of being merged into a more complex transition.
  We call *pre-feature specifications* those concerning features as reactive systems in isolation. With a pre-feature specification a *closed semantics* is associated, consisting of the generalized labelled transition system logically derived from the specification. This semantics is based on an underlying closed world/frame assumption: the attribute updates and transitions which are not explicitly asserted cannot happen.
- Then we consider the possibility of adding features (Sect. 3.1). We take a compositional style and speak of *composition* of pre-features; composition will be a partial, associative and commutative operation.
  As an example, POTS and ACB can be composed, resulting in another pre-feature specification POTS $\oplus$ ACB; analogously we can get POTS $\oplus$ TP. Analyzing the examples we show how in the composition the transitions can be combined, under an underlying anti-frame assumption: the fact that a rule of a pre-feature does not update an attribute does not mean that when we compose such rule with another one that attribute cannot be updated.
- The composition of pre-features provides the technical setting for analysing *interaction of features* (Sect. 3.2): roughly, PF_2 interacts with PF_1 iff in $PF_1 \oplus PF_2$ some parts of PF_1 are modified. We emphasize that, differently than in many other approaches, "interaction" is for us a neutral concept, namely it is not in itself good nor bad, as we show in the cases of POTS$\oplus$ACB and POTS $\oplus$ TP.

- One of the methodological keypoint of our approach, following P. Zave's quoted principle, is trying to prevent the occurrence of bad interactions qualifying the kind of interaction we admit as much as we can.

  Hence the full concept of *feature specification* comes out naturally as a pair (Sect. 4): a pre-feature specification and a set of *interaction requirements*, which are formulae in some logical formalism constraining the possibility of adding other features. As we show, interactions can be grouped in families of some kind, e.g., those concerning the atomic transitions, the overall behaviour, etc. Roughly speaking, a logic can *discipline* the interactions of some kind whenever it is powerful enough to express requirements preventing them. Thus, methodologically, we suggest to prevent bad interactions first of all by an appropriate specification, in some respect like in the specification phase of any system development. It may well happen that some bad interactions escape our qualification; but that means we need some feedback process, via testing, for adjusting our specification, not differently than in the usual development process.

- The technical, rather novel, concept supporting that aspect of the method is the *open semantics* of a feature specification. While the closed semantics of the pre-feature specification part gives just one generalized labelled transition system, the one logically deducible adopting the usual "frame-assumption", the open semantics consists of all the generalized labelled transition systems satisfying not only the interaction requirements, but also the activity rules under an *anti-frame assumption*. We have indeed to take into account that adding features can induce w.r.t. the closed semantics a variety of changes, like updates of the attributes and new transitions, as long as they are not explicitly forbidden; moreover all models have to be in a sense "logic extensions" of the closed semantics, intending that the activity rules producing the closed semantics have to be satisfied, though in a generalized sense; this last point is formalized as an inplicit *default requirement*, one for each rule. Verifying, with the help of available verification tools, that the closed semantics satisfies the interaction requirements, is a standard way of checking consistency. Technically speaking, the open semantics is a kind of ultra-loose semantics, since it consists of models over signatures extending the one of the pre-feature specification.

  What is then the relationship between the open and the closed semantics? Unless the feature specification is inconsistent (no models), the closed semantics is one of the possible models.

  Then the *complete semantics* of a consistent feature specification is the pair formed by the closed and the open semantics.

  Now the concept of composition carries over feature specifications; but two features are *compatible* only if their pre-feature parts are composable and the requirements, including the default ones, are not in conflict; this implies that the resulting composed feature is consistent, i.e., it admits some model.

2 Pre-Features

2.1 Pre-feature Specifications

First we consider a feature in isolation, i.e., without any concern about adding other features; we will use the name "pre-feature" for such an entity, to mark the difference with the complete concept of feature that we will introduce later.

We start illustrating what is for us the description of a pre-feature; then we discuss its semantics.

In our approach a pre-feature is a partial description of a reactive system, possibly intended as a description of only some "parts" of the system.

We distinguish reactive systems in *simple* and *structured or concurrent*; the latter are those having cooperating components, which are in turn reactive systems (simple or structured). Our specification technique considers differently the two cases; and in this paper we show how to handle the simple ones; the concurrent ones will be considered in some future work.

We formally model a reactive system R with a generalized labelled transition system (see [7]), shortly *glts*, which is a 4-uple

$$(STATE, LABEL, TT, \rightarrow),$$

where $STATE$, $LABEL$ and TT are sets, the *states*, the *labels* and the *transition types* of the system, and $\rightarrow \subseteq TT \times STATE \times LABEL \times STATE$ is the *transition relation*.

The states represent the intermediate (interesting) situations of the life of R and the arcs between them the possibilities of R of passing from a state to another one. It is important to note that here an arc (a transition) $tt\colon s \xrightarrow{l} s'$ has the following meaning: R in the state s has the *capability* of passing into the state s' by performing a transition, where the label l represents the interaction with the external (to R) world during such move. Thus l contains information on the conditions on the external world for the capability to become effective, and on the transformation of such world induced by the execution of the action; so transitions correspond to *action capabilities*. The transition type tt allows to classify transitions by putting together those corresponding to execute "conceptually" related activities. The reasons of the introduction of transition types will be clear later. We only anticipate that while labels, as usual, are a tool for supporting process composition, transition types will play an essential role when defining feature composition and hence handling feature interaction.

Our specification technique is described below, and exemplified with its application to POTS, whose specification as a pre-feature (simple reactive system) is given in Fig. 1.

- The POTS data part (keyword **data**) uses the specifications SET(IDENT) for the sets of subscriber identifiers and REL for binary relations on identifiers (just sets of identifier pairs). Here we neglect the part of the data specification; it is only important to recall that its semantics should result in a many-sorted first-order structure.

pre-feature POTS[s] =
data SET(IDENT), REL
attributes
    ACT: $set(ident)$
- - the set of the active subscribers, i.e., those which have lifted the receiver
    $BUSY$: $set(ident)$ - - the set of the subscribers hearing a busy tone
    $TRYING$: rel
- - the set of the pairs of subscribers (id, id') s.t. id is trying to connect with id'
    $CONN$: rel - - the set of the pairs of connected subscribers
interface
    $LIFT, DOWN(ident)$
- - a subscriber lifts/puts down the receiver
    $DIAL(ident, ident)$ - - a subscriber dials another one
auxiliary
    $Allowed, Available$: $ident$
- - a subscriber is allowed to dial iff he has lifted the receiver, is not hearing a busy
- - tone, and is neither trying to connect nor connected with another subscriber
    $Allowed(id) =_{def}$
        $id \in ACT$ **and** $id \notin BUSY$ **and**
        not exists id_1 s.t.
        $(id, id_1) \in TRYING$ **or** $(id, id_1) \in CONN$ **or** $(id_1, id) \in CONN$
- - a subscriber is available to be connected iff
- - he has not lifted the receiver and his telephone is not ringing
    $Available(id) =_{def} id \notin ACT$ **and not exists** id_1 s.t. $(id_1, id) \in TRYING$
activity
- **if** $Available(id)$ **then**
    START: $s \xrightarrow{LIFT(id)} s[ACT \cup \{id\}/ACT]$
- **if** $id \notin ACT$ **and** $(id', id) \in TRYING$ **then**
    ANSW: $s \xrightarrow{LIFT(id)} s[ACT \cup \{id\}/ACT]$
            $[TRYING - \{(id', id)\}/TRYING]$
            $[CONN \cup \{(id, id')\}/CONN]$
- **if** $id \in ACT$ **then**
    DWN: $s \xrightarrow{DOWN(id)} s[ACT - \{id\}/ACT]$
            $[BUSY - \{id\}/BUSY]$
            $[id \triangleleft TRYING/TRYING]$
            $[id \triangleleft CONN \triangleright id/CONN]$
- - $r \triangleright id$ ($r \triangleleft id$) is r minus all pairs whose right (left) component is id
- **if** $Allowed(id)$ **and not** $Available(id')$ **then**
    D: $s \xrightarrow{DIAL(id, id')} s[BUSY \cup \{id\}/BUSY]$
- **if** $Allowed(id)$ **and** $Available(id')$ **then**
    D: $s \xrightarrow{DIAL(id, id')} s[TRYING \cup \{(id, id')\}/TRYING]$

Fig. 1. The plain old telephone system pre-feature

- We characterize an intermediate state of a glts by means of attributes (keyword **attributes**) with values in the data part; in the case of POTS we must know which are the active subscribers, those hearing a busy tone, those trying to connect to another one and those connected each other.
  An attribute, say A, is a function from the states space into the corresponding value set; as usual in the O-O style, we write A for $A(s)$.
- We describe the various kinds of interactions of the system with the external world by means of label "constructors" possibly parameterized by values in the data part; we use the keyword **interface** since they really give the interface of the system. The label kinds of POTS (and so the label constructors) are: a subscriber lifts/puts down the receiver and dials another one.
- In the auxiliary definitions part (keyword **auxiliary**) we introduce some parametric shortcuts (macro definitions) which can be used in the activity; e.g., each occurrence of $Available(id)$ in a rule stands for

$$id \notin ACT \text{ and not exists } id_1 \text{ s.t. } (id_1, id) \in TRYING.$$

- The activity of POTS, i.e., the transitions of the glts modelling it, are given in the part after the keyword **activity** by means of conditional rules having the general form

$$\text{if } cond \text{ then } \mathsf{TT}\colon s \xrightarrow{L(y_1,\ldots,y_m)} s[x_1/A_1]\ldots[x_k/A_k],$$

where TT is the type of the transitions defined by the rule; s is the variable appearing on the first line of the specification denoting a generic state of the system; $y_1, \ldots, y_m, x_1, \ldots, x_k$ are variables; L is one of the label constructors; for $j = 1, \ldots, k$ $\_[\_/A_j]$ is the state update operation for the attribute A_j; and $cond$ is a formula built on the signatures of the used data extended with the attributes.
Usually the rules are written in a more friendly way, not only by substituting an attribute name A for each occurrence of $A(s)$, but also by dropping in the premise of a rule the atoms of the form $x_i = t$ ($y_j = t$) and by replacing then in such rule each occurrence of x_i (y_j) with t.
For example, the expanded version of the first rule of POTS is

$$\text{if } id \notin ACT(s) \text{ and (not exists } id' \text{ s.t. } (id', id) \in TRYING(s)) \text{ and}$$
$$a = ACT(s) \cup \{id\} \text{ then}$$
$$\mathsf{START}\colon s \xrightarrow{LIFT(id)} s[a/ACT].$$

The first two rules of POTS give the action capabilities corresponding to the interactions with the external world informally described by "a subscriber lifts the receiver"; notice that they have two different transition types, the first corresponding to the cases when the receiver is lifted for starting a call and the second for answering to a ringing phone. This distinction will be extremely useful when composing features together to avoid merging transitions corresponding to different activities.
The third rule describes the effect of putting down the receiver.

The last two rules with the same label and transition type describe the effect of dialling a number (we assume that in this case at a conceptual level there is just a kind of activity: to dial).

In our formalism transitions using the same label constructor may have different transition types, but it cannot happen the contrary; thus transitions with the same transition type must use the same label constructor.

Let us give two other examples of pre-feature specifications corresponding to add to a telephone system the automatic call back and communications involving three subscribers respectively.

ACB (Automatic Call Back) This pre-feature introduces in the telephone system the call-back possibility; precisely, a subscriber, say S, after calling another subscriber, say S1, non-available for the communication, can ask the telephone system by pressing a special button to automatically call S1 again when he and S1 will be both available; then, if S1 will lift the receiver, then the phone of S will start ringing.

The full specification is reported in Fig. 2.

TP (Three Parts service) This pre-feature introduces in the telephone system the possibility of having communications involving three subscribers. Precisely, once two subscribers, say S1 and S2, have established a connection, S1 (or S2) may put such connection on hold and start another connection with a third subscriber, say S3; now S1 can switch between the connection with S2 and that with S3; moreover he can also start a three-way connection among he, S2 and S3.

TP uses as data also REL3 the specification of the ternary relations over subscriber identifiers (sets of triples of identifiers).

The full specification is reported in Fig. 3.

2.2 Closed Semantics

In our setting the *closed semantics* of a pre-feature PF, denoted by $[\![PF]\!]_C$, is just the semantics associated with PF considered as a simple system specification, with no concern for the possible addition and interference with other features; thus it is essentially given by the glts determined by the rules; "essentially" because it includes also the used data structures, just a many-sorted first-order structure. In this paper, for simplicity, we call glts also these richer structures. By "glts determined by the rules" we mean the glts whose transitions are all and only those that can be logically deduced by the rules. Because of the very simple form of our rules, that means to consider just the transitions obtained by instantiating the given activity rules (of course interpreting syntactic terms within the given data structure). Notice that the closed semantics is implicitly using a "frame assumption": any update or transition which is not asserted to happen cannot happen.

pre-feature ACB[s] =
data SET(IDENT), REL
attributes
    ACT: $set(ident)$
-- the set of the active subscribers, i.e., those who have lifted the receiver
    $BUSY$: $set(ident)$ -- the set of the subscribers hearing a busy tone
    TO_CALL: rel
-- the set of the pairs of subscribers (id, id') s.t. id has required the call back of id'
    $DIALLED$: rel
-- the set of pairs of subscribers (id, id') s.t. id' has been automatically dialled by id
interface
    $CALL\_BACK(ident, ident)$
-- a subscriber requires the automatic call-back of another one
    INT -- internal activity
    $LIFT(ident)$ -- a subscriber lifts the receiver
auxiliary
    $Available$: $ident$
-- a subscriber is available to be connected iff
-- he has not lifted the receiver and his telephone is not ringing
    $Available(id) =_{\text{def}} id \notin ACT$ **and not exists** id_1 s.t. $(id_1, id) \in TRYING$
activity
- **if** $id \in BUSY$ **and not** $Available(id')$ **then**
      CB: $s \xrightarrow{CALL\_BACK(id, id')} s[TO\_CALL \cup \{(id, id')\}/TO\_CALL]$
- **if** $(id, id') \in TO\_CALL$ **and** $Available(id)$ **and** $Available(id')$ **then**
      ACB: $s \xrightarrow{INT} s[DIALLED \cup \{(id, id')\}/DIALLED]$
          $[TO\_CALL - \{(id, id')\}/TO\_CALL]$
- **if** $id \notin ACT$ **and** $Available(id')$ **and** $(id, id') \in DIALLED$ **then**
      ANSW_CB: $s \xrightarrow{LIFT(id)} s[ACT \cup \{id\}/ACT]$
          $[DIALLED - \{(id, id')\}/DIALLED]$
          $[TRYING \cup \{(id, id')\}/TRYING]$
- **if** $id \notin ACT$ **and (not** $Available(id')$**) and** $(id, id') \in DIALLED$ **then**
      ANSW_CB: $s \xrightarrow{LIFT(id)} s[ACT \cup \{id\}/ACT]$
          $[DIALLED - \{(id, id')\}/DIALLED]$
          $[BUSY \cup \{id\}/BUSY]$

Fig. 2. The automatic call back pre-feature

pre-feature $TP[s] =$
data $REL, REL3$
attributes
    $HOLD\_CONN: rel$
-- the set of pairs of connected subscribers, whose connection is hold-on
    $3\_CONN: rel3$ -- the set of the triples of subscribers connected together
    $CONN: rel$ -- the set of the pairs of connected subscribers
interface
    $ON\_HOLD(ident, ident)$
-- a subscriber puts on hold an established connection with another subscriber
    $SWITCH(ident)$
-- a subscriber switches the current connection to the hold-on one
    $THREE\_WAY(ident)$
-- a subscriber starts a three-way connection with the connected subscriber
-- and with the one whose connection was hold-on
    $DOWN(ident)$ -- a subscriber puts down the receiver
    $DIAL(ident, ident)$ -- a subscriber dials another one
auxiliary
    $Not\_Connected: ident$
-- a subscriber is not connected iff he is neither participating in a two-way
-- nor in a three-way connection, nor in a hold-on connection
    $Not\_Connected(id)$ **iff** (**not exists** id_1, id_2 s.t.
    $(id, id_1, id_2) \in 3\_CONN$ **or** $(id_1, id, id_2) \in 3\_CONN$ **or** $(id_1, id_2, id) \in 3\_CONN$
    or $(id, id_1) \in CONN$ **or** $(id_1, id) \in CONN$) **or** $(id_1, id) \in HOLD\_CONN$
activity
- **if** $(id, id') \in CONN$ **or** $(id', id) \in CONN$ **then**
  $$H: s \xrightarrow{ON\_HOLD(id, id')} s[HOLD\_CONN \cup \{(id, id')\}/HOLD\_CONN]$$
  $$[CONN - \{(id, id'), (id', id)\}/CONN]$$
- **if** $((id, id') \in CONN$ **or** $(id', id) \in CONN)$ **and** $(id, id'') \in HOLD\_CONN$ **then**
  $$SW: s \xrightarrow{SWITCH(id)} s[(CONN - \{(id, id'), (id', id)\}) \cup \{(id, id'')\}/CONN]$$
  $$[(HOLD\_CONN - \{(id, id'')\}) \cup \{(id, id')\}/HOLD\_CONN]$$
- **if** $((id, id') \in CONN$ **or** $(id', id) \in CONN)$ **and** $(id, id'') \in HOLD\_CONN$ **then**
  $$T: s \xrightarrow{THREE\_WAY(id)} s[CONN - \{(id, id'), (id', id)\}/CONN]$$
  $$[HOLD\_CONN - \{(id, id'')\}/HOLD\_CONN]$$
  $$[3\_CONN \cup \{(id, id', id'')\}/3\_CONN]$$
- $DWN: s \xrightarrow{DOWN(id)} s[id \triangleleft CONN \triangleright id/CONN]$
  $$[id \triangleleft HOLD\_CONN \triangleright id/HOLD\_CONN]$$
  $$[3\_CONN \boxminus id/3\_CONN]$$
  -- $r \boxminus id$ is r minus all triples having id as a component
- **if** $Not\_Connected(id)$ **then** $D: s \xrightarrow{DIAL(id, id')} s$

Fig. 3. The three-parts pre-feature

In Fig. 4 we depict a fragment (i.e., just few transitions) of the glts that together with a model for the data (sets of identifiers and binary relations over identifiers) gives the closed semantics of POTS; it shows the execution of a standard call between a subscriber *id* and another subscriber *id'*. In this paper, to keep the drawings small enough, we report the transition types only when they are really relevant, and we depict the states by reporting the values of the relevant attributes.

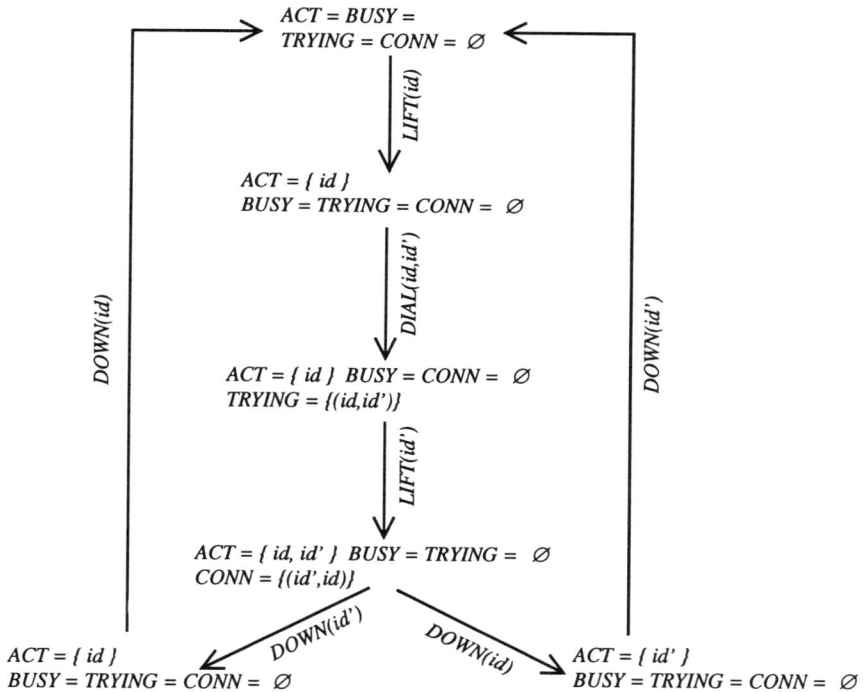

Fig. 4. A fragment of [POTS]$_C$

The closed semantics is already useful to analyse a pre-feature. For example, if we try to analyse TP by examining [TP]$_C$ we can see that a subscriber can put many connections on hold simultaneously; just look at the fragment of [TP]$_C$ reported in Fig. 5. For this reason the effect of a switch action is nondeterministic. Indeed the pre-feature TP has been designed by implicitly assuming that

not exists id_1, id_2, id_3 **s.t.**

$id_1 \neq id_2 \neq id_3$ **and** $(id_1, id_2), (id_1, id_3) \in HOLD\_CONN$

We can guarantee that the above formula holds if we change the rule about putting on hold a call as follows

if $((id, id') \in CONN$ **or** $(id', id) \in CONN)$ **and**
   not exists id_1 s.t. $((id_1, id) \in HOLD\_CONN$ **or** $(id, id_1) \in HOLD\_CONN)$ **then**

H: $s \xrightarrow{ON\_HOLD(id, id')} s[HOLD\_CONN \cup \{(id, id')\}/HOLD\_CONN]$
$[CONN - \{(id, id'), (id', id)\}/CONN]$

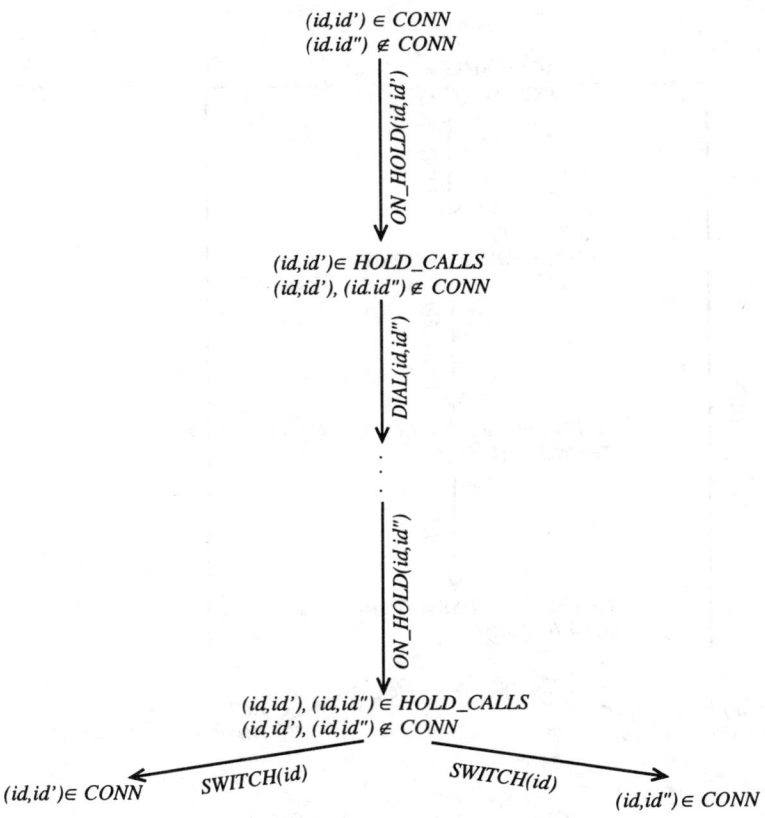

Fig. 5. A fragment of $[\![TP]\!]_C$

3 Pre-feature Composition and Interaction

3.1 Pre-feature Composition

In our approach adding pre-features is modelled by *composition*, which has nothing to do with parallel composition of processes (here is where the difference w.r.t.

a process-oriented approach comes to light). Indeed in a composition each pre-feature is seen as a part of a system roughly resulting from the union of the two parts following the principle "same name – same thing". We can compose two pre-features (they are composable) only if common names are used coherently in both.

Precisely, two pre-features PF_1 and PF_2 are *composable* iff

- any shared data type is defined in the same way;
- they use the same variables to denote the generic state of the system, the new values of shared attributes and the arguments of the shared label constructors;
- the attributes with the same name have the same result type;
- the label constructors with the same name have the same number of arguments, of the same type and in the same order;
- the auxiliary definitions with the same name coincide;
- for each rule r_1 of PF_1 and r_2 of PF_2 defining transitions with the same type
  * r_1 and r_2 define transitions using the same label constructor;
  * r_1 and r_2 do not share free variables except those denoting the new values of the attributes and the arguments of the label constructors.

It is easy to see that the three pre-features POTS, ACB and TP introduced in the previous section are pairwise composable.

Pre-features correspond to partial descriptions of simple systems; thus composing them means to put together the parts given by both to get a new simple system specification. That is easy for the data part, the attributes, the label constructors and the auxiliary definitions (just the union of the two parts); while since rules correspond to partial descriptions of action capabilities we need in the a mechanism for deciding which rules r_1 of PF_1 and r_2 of PF_2 describe parts of the same action capability, and thus have to be composed. We assume that rules defining transitions with the same type (shortly *rules with the same type*) describe parts of the same action capabilities.

Then the activity part of the composition of the two pre-features contains the rules of PF_1 with a type not present in PF_2, those of PF_2 with a type not present in PF_1 and the *pairwise compositions* of the rules of PF_1 and of PF_2 with a common type. The pairwise composition of two rules with the same type just means to make the conjuction of the premises and the union of the attribute updates (since the two pre-features are composable, the two rules use the same label constructor, the same variables for the state, for the arguments of the label constructor and for the new values of the attributes). Note that the composition of two rules may be a null rule (i.e., a rule which does not generate any transition, since its premises cannot be satisfied). Later on, when extending the composition of pre-features to the composition of pre-features, we will see that in such case the features are considered incompatible and so cannot be composed.

Most importantly we note that in some sense an *anti-frame assumption* underlies our concept of pre-feature composition; indeed the fact that a rule of a pre-feature does not update an attribute does not mean that when we compose such rule with another one that attribute cannot be updated. For example, a rule as

if $A > B$ then TT: $s \xrightarrow{L(y)} s[y - A/A]$

where the attribute B is not updated, can be composed with the rule

if $A > B$ then TT: $s \xrightarrow{L(y)} s[B - 1/B]$

where A is not updated, resulting in

if $A > B$ then TT: $s \xrightarrow{L(y)} s[y - A/A][B - 1/B]$

where both A and B are updated.

Notice also that the composition of two pre-features returns another pre-feature, which can then be further composed with other pre-features.

In the following, we use $\oplus$ to denote the composition operation for pre-features.

Let us illustrate the concepts introduced so far by means of the compositions of the pre-feature POTS with ACB and with TP respectively; we skip the composition of ACB with TP since it is not interesting and that of the three pre-features together for lack of room.

Composing POTS and ACB In this case the two pre-features do not share any transition type, and so we do not compose any pair of rules. That is exactly what we want; and it is worthwhile to note that this is due to the use of transition types; for example, if instead we compose rules sharing the same label constructor, then we would get inappropriate results, e.g., a subscriber may lift the receiver only if someone has called him back.

Hence POTS $\oplus$ ACB is obtained just by adding the respective parts, keyword by keyword.

Composing POTS and TP Much more interesting is the composition of POTS and of TP, which is in Fig. 6, where we have omitted the attribute, interface and auxiliary part, which are obtained just gluing together those of the respective single specifications.

In this case there are some interesting rule compositions, since the two pre-features share the transition types DWN and D. Notice how the composition of the two rules of type DWN puts together the attribute updates; while that of the rules of type D puts together the premises. In both cases the updates and the premises are not disjoint but they agree on the common part and so the compositions are not null rules (both rules update the attribute $CONN$, and both rules ask for the subscriber not to be in a binary connection).

Due to the anti-frame assumption the rule of type D of TP can avoid to repeat the attribute updates (clearly also the conditions) already given in POTS.

The anti-frame assumption allows us also to simplify the rule of type DWN of TP, by dropping the update of the attribute $CONN$ from it; the result of the composition will be exactly the same as in Fig. 6. Indeed, the simplified rule

DWN: $s \xrightarrow{DOWN(id)} s[id \triangleleft HOLD\_CONN \triangleright id/HOLD\_CONN]$
$[3\_CONN \boxminus id/3\_CONN]$

pre-feature POTS ⊕ TP[s] =
data SET(IDENT), REL, REL3
attributes ... ...
interface ... ...
auxiliary ... ...
activity
- **if** $Available(id)$ **then**
  START: $s \xrightarrow{LIFT(id)} s[ACT \cup \{id\}/ACT]$
- **if** $id \notin ACT$ **and** $(id', id) \in TRYING$ **then**
  ANSW: $s \xrightarrow{LIFT(id)} s[ACT \cup \{id\}/ACT]$
  $[TRYING - \{(id', id)\}/TRYING]$
  $[CONN \cup \{(id, id')\}/CONN]$
- **if** $id \in ACT$ **then**
  DWN: $s \xrightarrow{DOWN(id)} s[ACT - \{id\}/ACT]$
  $[BUSY - \{id\}/BUSY]$
  $[id \triangleleft TRYING/TRYING]$
  $[id \triangleleft CONN \triangleright id/CONN]$
  $[id \triangleleft HOLD\_CONN \triangleright id/HOLD\_CONN]$
  $[3\_CONN \boxminus id/3\_CONN]$
- **if** $Allowed(id)$ **and** (**not** $Available(id')$) **and** $Not\_Connected(id)$ **then**
  D: $s \xrightarrow{DIAL(id,id')} s[BUSY \cup \{id\}/BUSY]$
- **if** $Allowed(id)$ **and** $Available(id')$ **and** $Not\_Connected(id)$ **then**
  D: $s \xrightarrow{DIAL(id,id')} s[TRYING \cup \{(id, id')\}/TRYING]$
- **if** $(id, id') \in CONN$ **or** $(id', id) \in CONN$ **then**
  H: $s \xrightarrow{ON\_HOLD(id,id')} s[HOLD\_CONN \cup \{(id, id')\}/HOLD\_CONN]$
  $[CONN - \{(id, id'), (id', id)\}/CONN]$
- **if** $((id, id') \in CONN$ **or** $(id', id) \in CONN)$ **and** $(id, id'') \in HOLD\_CONN$ **then**
  SW: $s \xrightarrow{SWITCH(id)} s[(CONN - \{(id, id'), (id', id)\}) \cup \{(id, id'')\}/CONN]$
  $[(HOLD\_CONN - \{(id, id'')\}) \cup \{(id, id')\}/HOLD\_CONN]$
- **if** $((id, id') \in CONN$ **or** $(id', id) \in CONN)$ **and** $(id, id'') \in HOLD\_CONN$ **then**
  T: $s \xrightarrow{THREE\_WAY(id)} s[CONN - \{(id, id'), (id', id)\}/CONN]$
  $[HOLD\_CONN - \{(id, id'')\}/HOLD\_CONN]$
  $[3\_CONN \cup \{(id, id', id'')\}/3\_CONN]$

Fig. 6. The composition of POTS and TP

does not assert that $CONN$ cannot modify its value during a transition partly built by this rule (i.e., by a rule obtained by composing it with another one).

3.2 Pre-Feature Interaction

As already suggested, when organizing a system by features, it is of paramount importance to have a clear picture of the variations which may occur when adding features. On the basis of the concepts introduced before, we are able to single out some basic criteria for reasoning about feature interactions.

Together with many other (but not all) authors by "interaction of pre-feature PF_2 on PF_1" (or "PF_2 interacts with PF_1") we mean that the "part of $PF_1 \oplus PF_2$ due to PF_1 is not as specified by PF_1". We assume that "part of $PF_1 \oplus PF_2$ due to PF_1" is the projection on the signature of PF_1.

We may have different concepts of interaction between pre-features depending on how we compare $[\![PF_1]\!]_C$ with $[\![PF_1 \oplus PF_2]\!]_C$ projected on PF_1; for example we may consider:

atomic interaction: we compare the set of transitions (corresponding to atomic activities) of the system described by $[\![PF_1]\!]_C$ and of the one described by $[\![PF_1 \oplus PF_2]\!]_C$ projected onto the signature of PF_1;

behavioural interaction: we compare the behaviour of the system described by $[\![PF_1]\!]_C$, i.e., the labelled transition tree defined by the associated glts, and of the one described by $[\![PF_1 \oplus PF_2]\!]_C$ projected onto the signature of PF_1.

Moreover when comparing the transitions/behaviours of two systems we can look at

- transition types, attributes and labels (**TAL**);
- only attributes and labels (**AL**);
- or only labels (**L**).

It is not interesting to look only at the attributes, since we are considering reactive (open) systems in a formal framework where the interface of a system towards the outside world is represented by the labels.

There are various reasons for the transitions/behaviours of $[\![PF_1 \oplus PF_2]\!]_C$ projectd onto the signature of PF_1 to be different from those of $[\![PF_1]\!]_C$; e.g.

- the premises of a rule of PF_1 become more restrictive (conditions on the new attributes) when it is composed with a rule of PF_2;
- a rule of PF_1 when it is composed with one of PF_2 may update attributes of PF_1 previously not modified (anti-frame assumption);
- new rules about PF_1 transition types/labels modifying the PF_1 attributes are added by PF_2.
- new rules about new transition types are added by PF_2 with PF_1 labels and modifying the PF_1 attributes.

Here we do not formally define what is an "interaction", but we just try to illustrate these different views of interactions using the telephonic features introduced before.

Interactions between POTS and ACB

POTS and ACB do not atomically **TAL** interact, since they have disjoint sets of transition types.

[**Int 1**] ACB atomically **AL** interacts with POTS; indeed it is sufficient to consider the transitions of $[\![POTS \oplus ACB]\!]_C$ with label constructor $LIFT$ obtained by instantiating the following rule of POTS⊕ACB (originated from ACB).

if $id \notin ACT$ and $Available(id')$ and $(id, id') \in DIALLED$ then
$\quad$ ANSW_CB: $s \xrightarrow{LIFT(id)} s[ACT \cup \{id\}/ACT]$
$\qquad\qquad\qquad\qquad\qquad [DIALLED - \{(id, id')\}/DIALLED]$
$\qquad\qquad\qquad\qquad\qquad [TRYING \cup \{(id, id')\}/TRYING]$

while no transition of POTS with label $LIFT(id)$ adds more pairs to the attribute $TRYING$.

[**Int 2**] Consider now the fragment of $[\![POTS \oplus ACB]\!]_C$ reported in Fig. 7.

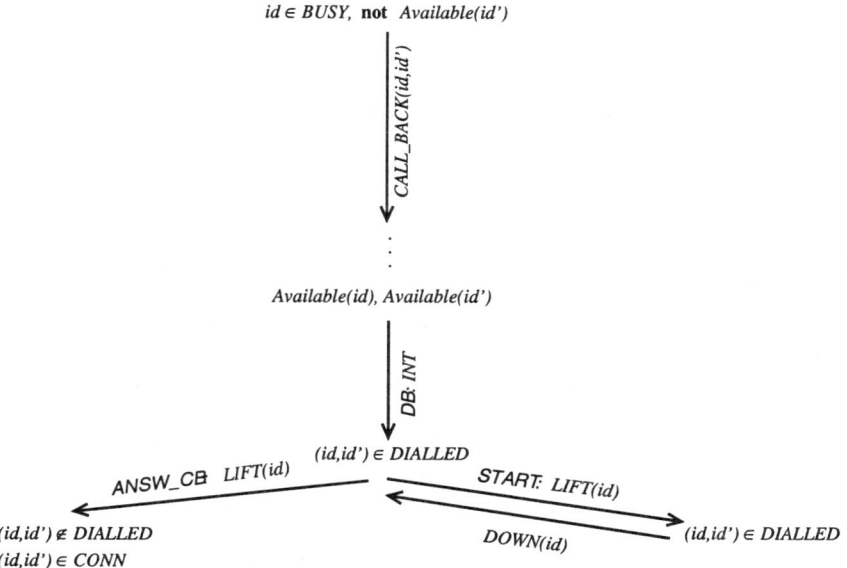

Fig. 7. A fragment of $[\![POTS \oplus ACB]\!]_C$

If the system chooses forever the right branch of the behaviour represented in the picture, then we have that forever the phone of id will ring (in this specification the telephone of a subscriber id is ringing whenever $(id, id') \in DIALLED$); and this is a typical example of interaction in a telephone system.

Technically POTS behaviourally **AL** interacts with ACB; indeed we have in
[POTS ⊕ ACB]$_C$ an infinite behaviour where forever $(id, id') \in DIALLED$ and where infinitely many times there is a transition labelled by $LIFT(id)$.

[**Int 3**] If instead the system takes the left branch in the picture, then we have in [POTS ⊕ ACB]$_C$ a behaviour not present in [POTS]$_C$, where between a state where id is busy and a state where id and id' are connected, there is always a transition labelled with $DIAL(id, id')$.

Technically ACB behaviourally **AL** interacts with POTS.

Interactions between POTS and TP

[**Int 4**] POTS atomically **AL** interacts with TP; indeed it is sufficient to consider the transitions labelled by $DOWN$, which in [TP]$_C$ are present in any state, while in the composition a subscriber may put down the receiver only if he is active.

[**Int 5**] POTS and TP do not behaviourally **L** interact; indeed TP just adds new parts of behaviours but using mainly its private labels.

4 Features

4.1 Interaction requirements

It is not true that any case of interaction is negative and must be prohibited. Consider, for example:

- a feature for a telephone system which offers a discount whenever some particular toll-free numbers are called (transition types/transitions which did not change the debt of a user, now decrease it) (**TAL** and **AL** atomic interaction);
- a feature cutting the telephone service for a subscriber when the debt exceeds some amount;
- a feature adding to a lift an external security block mechanism stopping the cabin to the nearest floor and opening the doors; in some case the lift has a new possibility of behaviour made by old labels and using old attributes (**AL** and **L** behavioural interaction);
- a feature adding the possibility of randomly winning a free recharge of a phonecard; now there are behaviours where the action of recharge is not preceded by the action pay (**TAL** behavioural interaction).

Let us consider again the telephone examples at the end of the previous section.

[**Int 1**] Good interaction (good means wanted, useful); indeed it is essential to have these new action capabilities acting differently also on the old attributes and label constructors.

[**Int 2**] This is really a bad unwanted interaction.

[**Int 3**] Good interaction.

[**Int 4**] Luckily the POTS interaction corrects a kind of error in TP, where not lifted receivers may be put down.

Thus we are naturally led to add to a pre-feature specification a set of constraints describing explicitly which interactions are good and which are not. We call those constraints *interaction requirements*.

How to express the interaction requirements ?

We choose to use logic formulae expressing the wanted properties of the transitions/behaviours of the composition of the feature with any other one. Now the problem is to choose an "appropriate" logic. We suggest to find a logic able to *discipline* the interaction (of some kind): for all pre-features PF_1, PF_2 s.t. PF_2 interacts with PF_1 there exists a formula of the logic ϕ s.t. $[\![PF_1]\!]_C$ satisfies ϕ and $[\![PF_1 \oplus PF_2]\!]_C$ does not satisfy ϕ.

For example, atomic **TAL** interaction can be disciplined by the following subset of first-order formulae.

atomic safety formulae
 if $tt\colon s \xrightarrow{l} s'$ then *cond*
 where tt, s, l, s' are variables of the appropriate types, *cond* is a first-order formula on tt, s, l and s', built using only the signature of the basic data structures, the operations extracting the value of the attributes from the states and the label constructors.

atomic liveness formulae
 if *cond* then $(\exists tt\,.\,)(\exists l\,.\,)(\exists s'\,.\,)tt\colon s \xrightarrow{l} s'$
 where tt, s, s', l and *cond* as above, and any of the existential quantifications may be omitted.

Also in these formulae we abbreviate $A(s)$, where A is an attribute name, to A and $A(s')$ to A'.

Instead, atomic **AL** interaction may be disciplined by the subset of the safety and liveness atomic formulae, where tt does not occur in *cond* and is always existentially quantified.

The most used interaction requirements just impose that a part of a pre-feature is protected in some way by the interactions of the other features; in the telephone examples we just need to require that a transition type/an attribute/a label constructor of a feature cannot be modified by any added feature, shortly it is "stable". Such particular requirements may be expressed by using atomic safety formulae, see below; but for sake of clarity we will simply write "... is stable.

A **is stable** requires that any added feature cannot change the way the attribute A is updated. If the rules of the feature in which the attribute A is updated are
$$\text{if } cond_j \text{ then } \mathsf{TT}_j\colon s \xrightarrow{l_j} s[v_j/A]\ldots \qquad (j = 1, \ldots, k)$$
A **is stable** stands for
$$\text{if } tt\colon s \xrightarrow{l} s' \text{ and } A \neq A' \text{ then } case_1 \text{ or } \ldots \text{ or } case_k$$

where $case_j$ is the existential closure w.r.t. all variables different from l, v_j, s of

$$cond_j \text{ and } tt = \mathsf{TT}_j \text{ and } l = l_j \text{ and } A' = v_j.$$

L is stable requires that any added feature cannot change the effects/the blocking conditions on the feature attributes of transitions labelled by L and the possibility of transitions labelled by L to have some type of that feature. If the rules of the feature in which the label constructor L appears are

$$\text{if } cond_j \text{ then } \mathsf{TT}_j \colon s \xrightarrow{L(y_1,\ldots,y_n)} s[v_1^j/A_1]\ldots \qquad (j = 1, \ldots, k)$$

L is stable stands for

$$\text{if } tt \colon s \xrightarrow{L(y_1,\ldots,y_n)} s' \text{ then } case_1 \text{ or } \ldots \text{ or } case_k$$

where $case_j$ is the existential closure w.r.t. all variables different from y_1, $\ldots$, y_n, v_1^j, $\ldots$, s of

$$cond_j \text{ and } tt = \mathsf{TT}_j \text{ and } A_1' = v_1^j \text{ and } \ldots.$$

TT is stable requires that any added feature cannot change how the transitions with type TT use the feature attributes and label constructors. If the rules of the feature in which TT appears are

$$\text{if } cond_j \text{ then } \mathsf{TT} \colon s \xrightarrow{L(y_1,\ldots,y_n)} s[v_1^j/A_1]\ldots \qquad (j = 1, \ldots, k)$$

TT is stable stands for

$$\text{if } \mathsf{TT} \colon s \xrightarrow{L(y_1,\ldots,y_n)} s' \text{ then } case_1 \text{ or } \ldots \text{ or } case_k$$

where $case_j$ is the existential closure w.r.t. all variables different from y_1, $\ldots$, y_n, v_1^j, $\ldots$, s of

$$cond_j \text{ and } A_1' = v_1^j \text{ and } \ldots.$$

As examples, we report below the expanded version of the stability interaction requirement **TO_CALL is stable** for the pre-feature ACB of Fig. 2.

if $tt \colon s \xrightarrow{l} s'$ and $TO\_CALL \neq TO\_CALL'$ then
(exists id, id' s.t. $id \in BUSY$ and (not $Available(id')$) and $tt = \mathsf{CB}$ and $l = CALL\_BACK(id, id')$ and $TO\_CALL' = TO\_CALL \cup \{(id, id')\}$)
or
(exists id, id' s.t. $(id, id') \in TO\_CALL$ and $Available(id)$ and $Available(id')$ and $tt = \mathsf{ANSW\_CB}$ and $l = INT$ and $TO\_CALL' = TO\_CALL - \{(id, id')\}$ and $DIALLED' = DIALLED \cup \{(id, id')\}$))

4.2 Feature Specifications

According to the preliminary discussion, a *feature specification* is a pair consisting of a pre-feature specification and a set of interaction requirements. If F is a feature, then PF will denote its pre-feature part.

Now we have to provide a semantics not only taking into account the interaction requirements, but also supporting the composition operation, where what we call "anti-frame assumption" is playing a major role. Indeed we have to express the fact that F is a "partial description" of a system, which will result in the end, possibly after the addition of other features. To this end we introduce the rather novel concept of *open semantics*, which is the class of all simple systems (glts's modelling them) having at least all parts specified by F. These systems may have more data, attributes, label constructors and transition types than those of F, and different transitions; technically, their signature is an *extension* of the signature of F. Thus the *open semantics* of F, denoted by $[\![F]\!]_O$, is the class of all glts over some extension of the signature of PF, satisfying the interaction requirements plus some *default requirements* enforcing that the basic activity defined by the rules is respected modulo an anti-frame assumption concerning the possible update of the attributes.

The default constraint corresponding to an activity rule of the form

if $cond$ **then** TT: $s \xrightarrow{L(y_1,\ldots,y_m)} s[x_1/A_1]\ldots[x_k/A_k]$

is

if $cond$ **then exists** s' s.t.
$A_1(s') = x_1$ **and** ... **and** $A_k(s') = x_k$ **and** TT: $s \xrightarrow{L(y_1,\ldots,y_m)} s'$.

Notice that, because of the default requirements, either a feature specification F is inconsistent (no models, i.e., $[\![F]\!]_O = \emptyset$) or $[\![PF]\!]_C \in [\![F]\!]_O$.

Neither the closed nor the open semantics are sufficient, each one, to qualify the semantics of a feature specification. The *complete semantics* of a consistent feature specification F, denoted by $[\![F]\!]$, is the pair formed by the closed and the open semantics; all inconsistent specifications are obviously considered semantically equivalent (meaningless).

The notion of composition is easily carried over to feature specifications. Two consistent feature specifications, say F_1 and F_2, with composable pre-feature parts PF_1 and PF_2, are *compatible* iff $[\![PF_1 \oplus PF_2]\!]_C \in [\![F_1]\!]_O \cap [\![F_2]\!]_O$. Intuitively this means that not only both interaction requirements parts are satisfied (and thus they are not inconsistent), but also that the activity rules of the two were not conflicting (both default requirements are satisfied). Then the composition $F_1 \oplus F_2$ is consistent and thus also $[\![PF_1 \oplus PF_2]\!]_C \in [\![F_1 \oplus F_2]\!]_O$. It is not difficult to see that the composition is well-defined w.r.t. the semantics: if $[\![F_1]\!] = [\![F_1']\!]$ then $[\![F_1 \oplus F_2]\!] = [\![F_1' \oplus F_2]\!]$.

Now we show how to transform the pre-features for the telephone systems introduced before into features, by adding appropriate interaction requirements.

POTS as a feature A telephone system is intended to have the following basic properties

- if a subscriber lifts the receiver, then he must become active,
- a subscriber can put down the receiver only if he is active, and then becomes inactive

and is designed assuming that they hold; so we impose that any added feature preserves them, by the following two safety formulae.

if $tt\colon s \xrightarrow{LIFT(id)} s'$ then $id \in ACT'$

if $tt\colon s \xrightarrow{DOWN(id)} s'$ then $id \in ACT$ and not $id \in ACT'$

As an example, we give in Fig. 8 a fragment of an element ALARM of $[\![POTS]\!]_O$ different from $[\![POTS]\!]_C$, corresponding to extend POTS with a telephone alarm clock service.

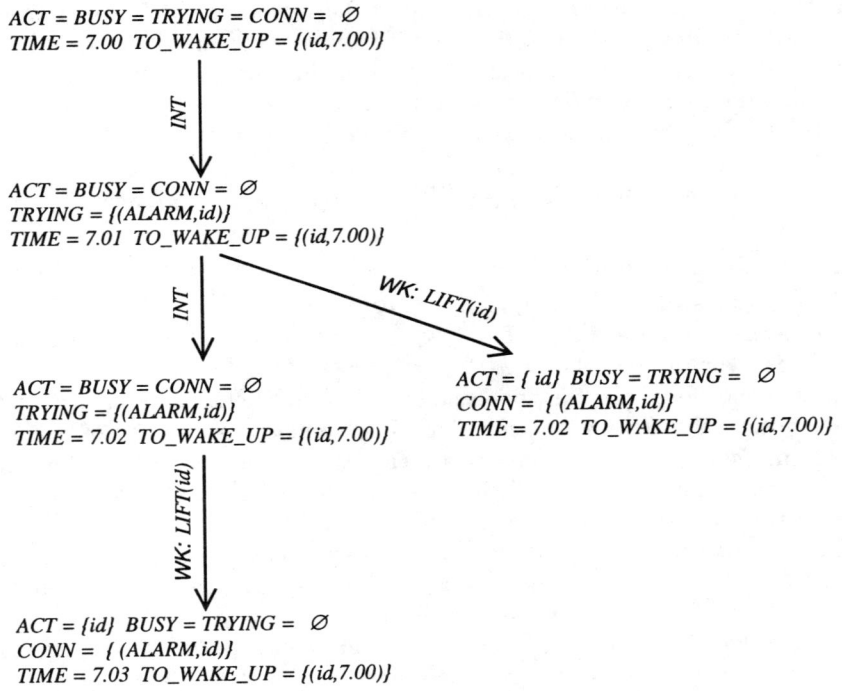

Fig. 8. A fragment of ALARM

ALARM has new attributes (the time and the list of the subscribers to be waken up with the corresponding time), new label constructors (*INT* corresponding to internal activity, i.e., null interaction with the external world) and new transitions (those labelled by *INT* and those of type WK).

ACB as a feature We first impose on ACB a set of rather standard interaction requirements, listed below, saying that in some sense the use of the attributes, label constructors and transition types for handling of the automatic call back cannot be redefined by a compatible feature. Clearly compatible features may extend the stable labels and transition types to act on new attributes; e.g., if we consider a billing feature, then an automatic call back may increase the bill.

TO_CALL is stable
$CALL\_BACK$ is stable
CB is stable
$DIALLED$ is stable
$ANSW\_CB$ is stable
ACB is stable

If instead we want to discipline the interaction with POTS [Int 2] (see Sect. 3.2), then we introduce also the interaction requirement

if $tt\colon s \xrightarrow{LIFT(id)} s'$ and $(id, id') \in DIALLED$ then $tt = \mathsf{ANSW\_CB}$.

But now POTS and ACB considered as features are not compatible anymore, due to the last interaction requirement. If we need to compose them, then we have to modify one of the two; in this case it seems sensible to add to ACB some rules expressing that transition of type START and ANSW can be done only by subscribers that have not automatically called some other one, as

if not exists id' s.t. $(id, id') \in DIALLED$ **then**
$\quad \mathsf{START}\colon s \xrightarrow{LIFT(id)} s'$
if not exists id' s.t. $(id, id') \in DIALLED$ **then**
$\quad \mathsf{ANSW}\colon s \xrightarrow{LIFT(id)} s'$

TP as a feature To get a feature we add to TP the following interaction requirements:

$SWITCH$ is stable
$THREE\_WAY$ is stable
ON_HOLD is stable

We do not make stable the attributes $HOLD\_CONN$ and 3_CONN, since it is sensible that can be used by other features, e.g., to handle urgent calls which automatically make a running call put on hold.

It is easy to see that the feature TP is compatible with POTS.

5 Conclusion and Related Work

We have illustrated a rather general framework for feature-oriented development. Somewhat differently than in other approaches, our aim is to provide a flexible discipline for handling features, more than just checking the interactions. The flexibility is provided by factorizing the specification development: features in isolation as pre-features with closed semantics, composition of pre-features and analysis of the variety of interactions, interaction requirements, and finally full feature specifications with open and complete semantics. We have also introduced some novel concepts like open semantics with the underlying anti-frame assumption, which we believe is a key issue in combining features.

In another paper [2] we provide the technical details (formal definitions, properties).

The approach we have presented can be used at two levels: one, methodological, which can be reified also using other technical formalisms, and another which adopts and exploits some specific technique [1]. We plan to turn the second level into a formalism for handling interactions within the COFI initiative (see [8] and http://www.brics.dk/Projects/CoFI).

In our opinion the general framework should be adapted to the particular domain-specific application, as it is supported by the work of P. Zave on telephone systems [12].

It is worthwhile mentioning that the useful graphical representations are really possible not only for the simple examples considered in the paper; indeed there is a way of presenting graphically design specifications for reactive and concurrent systems (see [10]), which is adjustable to the case of features, as we plan to do in some further work. As for the automatic generation of the graphical representations, it does not seem out of the state-of-the-art, though not yet explored by us.

Together with improving the graphical representation, our ongoing work aims first of all at dealing with features for structured systems, i.e. systems made of subsystems; in other words we want to have at hand both component and feature modularity.

Recently some papers trying to study features and their interactions on a formal ground have started to appear, but none of them presents something similar to our "interaction requirements"; moreover it seems that the role of concepts like anti-frame assumption and open semantics, not even in an implicit form, has not been noted.

Among them we recall [3], presenting feature specifications based on logical formulae conceptually similar to our rules, but their idea of "feature composition" and of "interaction" is really less flexible than our (e.g., using our terminology transitions are composed only when have the same label, and interaction is just atomic). In e.g., [4] Bredereke, trying to give a formal view of features and interactions, considers the importance of the behavioural aspects. Also [5] presents a formal based treatment of features for telecommunication systems, but at a more concrete level (i.e. more oriented towards the implementation) and so it is difficult it to fully relate to our work.

Prehofer considers both methodological aspects as in [9] and formal aspects, as in [6], where he presents an approach based on transition systems (diagrams); but differently from our work, for him to add a feature to a system means to refine graphically a part of the diagram specifying it. It is interesting to note that our framework may offer a formal counterpart to part of his work in [9] including the "lifters", i.e. feature modifiers for helping to resolve feature interactions.

References

1. E. Astesiano and G. Reggio. Labelled Transition Logic: An Outline. Technical Report DISI–TR–96–20, DISI – Università di Genova, Italy, 1996.
2. E. Astesiano and G. Reggio. Feature Interaction: Prevention Is Better than Detection: A Formal Modular Support for Feature Specification and Interaction Handling. Technical Report DISI–TR–98–14, DISI – Università di Genova, Italy, 1998.
3. J. Blom, R. Bol, and L. Kempe. Automatic Detection of Feature Interactions in Temporal Logic. Technical Report 95/61, Department of Computer Systems, Uppsala University, 1995.
4. J. Bredereke. Formal Criteria for Feature Interactions in Telecommunications Systems. In J. Norgaard and V. B. Iversen, editors, *Intelligent Networks and New Technologies*. Chapman & Hall, 1996.
5. M. Faci and L. Logrippo. Specifying Features and Analyzing their Interactions in a LOTOS Environment. In L.G. Bouma and H. Velthuijsen, editors, *Feature Interactions in Telecommunications Systems (Proc. of the 2nd International Workshop on Feature Interactions in Telecommunications Systems, Amsterdam)*, pages 136–151. IOS Press, 1994.
6. C. Klein, C. Prehofer, and B. Rumpe. Feature Specification and Refinement with State Transition Diagrams. In P. Dini, editor, *Fourth IEEE Workshop on Feature Interactions in Telecommunications Networks and Distributed Systems*. IOS-Press, 1997.
7. R. Milner. *Communication and Concurrency*. Prentice Hall, London, 1989.
8. P.D. Mosses. CoFI: The Common Framework Initiative for Algebraic Specification and Development. In M. Bidoit and M. Dauchet, editors, *Proc. TAPSOFT '97*, number 1214 in Lecture Notes in Computer Science, pages 115–137, Berlin, 1997. Springer Verlag.
9. C. Prehofer. Feature-Oriented Programming: A Fresh Look at Objects. In *Proceedings of ECOOP'97*, number 1241 in Lecture Notes in Computer Science. Springer Verlag, Berlin, 1997.
10. G. Reggio and M. Larosa. A Graphic Notation for Formal Specifications of Dynamic Systems. In J. Fitzgerald and C.B. Jones, editors, *Proc. FME 97 - Industrial Applications and Strengthened Foundations of Formal Methods*, number 1313 in Lecture Notes in Computer Science. Springer Verlag, Berlin, 1997.
11. P. Zave. Feature interactions and formal specifications in telecommunications. *Computer*, 26(8):20–29, 1993.
12. P. Zave. Calls considered harmful and other observations: A tutorial on telephony. In T. Margaria, editor, *Second International Workshop on Advanced Intelligent Networks '97*, 1997.

Merging Changes to Software Specifications*

Valdis Berzins

Computer Science Department, Naval Postgraduate School
Monterey, CA 93943, USA

Abstract. We propose a model of software changes and a method for combining changes to a software specification. This work was motivated by the desire to provide automated decision support for the evolution of software prototypes. We define a behavioral refinement ordering on software specifications and indicate how this structure can be used to automatically combine several changes to a specification. A set of examples illustrates the ideas.

1 Introduction

Changing software without damaging it is difficult and accounts for the bulk of software-related costs. This issue is particularly prominent in the context of software prototyping, where requirements, specifications, and designs are undergoing radical and repeated change, under constraints of low cost and rapid response. In this context teams often explore changes to different aspects of a system concurrently, and may develop prototypes of several competing formulations simultaneously, to obtain user guidance about the benefits and drawbacks of different alternatives. When the preferred alternatives are clear, we must consistently combine the changes to the system specification corresponding to the preferred alternative for each aspect of the system that has been explored.

This paper presents a formal model and a method for addressing this problem in the context of black-box specifications for systems. We address specifications expressed in logic, using a notation for system specification that has been designed to support development of large and complex systems [5]. We explore the problem in the context of prototyping because it is a promising way to address the main source of system faults, namely requirements errors [23]. Evolutionary prototyping provides an efficient approach to formulating accurate software requirements [20].

The focus of the current work is the evolution of proposed specifications and prototype designs. Much of the previous work on changes to software has focused on meaning-preserving transformations [2, 15, 17, 27]. However, it has been recognized that in realistic contexts, many changes do *not* preserve the observable behavior of the system [28]. Most of the work on the area of meaning-changing

---

* This research was supported in part by the National Science Foundation under grant number CCR-9058453, by the Army Research Office under grant number 30989-MA, and by the Army AI Center under grant number 6GNPG00072.

transformations has been concerned with classifying the types of semantic modifications that are used in practice [13, 12, 16]. We investigate the relationships between different versions of the specifications and propose an abstract model of the design history to provide a more formal model for understanding the details of this subject.

Modeling the design history can enhance the prototyping process by capturing the conceptual dependencies in a design. A properly structured derivation of a specification can highlight the structure of the design decisions leading to the proposed system, which can be used to record and guide systematic exploration of the design space. Such a representation is necessary if we are to develop software tools for managing this process and extracting useful information from the design history. These tools should help coordinate the efforts of analysts and designers faced with a changing set of requirements, to avoid repeated effort and inconsistent parallel refinements, and to aid the designers in combining design choices from different branches of a parallel exploration of the design space.

In larger prototyping efforts, several explorations of the requirements that are focused on distinct aspects of the system may proceed in parallel. In such cases, the lessons learned from different branches of the effort must be combined and integrated. This is a specification-level instance of the software change-merging problem [8]. Solutions to this problem can also be used to propagate improvements to all affected versions.

The rest of the paper is organized as follows. Section 2 defines a model of software changes and a behavioral refinement ordering for software specifications. Section 3 discusses change merging for specifications and indicates how merged versions can be constructed. Section 4 presents some examples. Section 5 contains conclusions.

2 Software Changes

To formalize changes to black-box descriptions of systems, we must consider what are the externally observable attributes of a system and how the attributes of different versions are related.

2.1 Attributes of System Behavior

We characterize changes to a system specification in terms of three orthogonal attributes of a system: its vocabulary, its behavior, and its granularity [22]. These concepts are reviewed below.

- The *vocabulary* of a system is the set of all external stimuli recognized by the system.
- The *granularity* of a system is the set of all internal stimuli recognized by the system.
- The *behavior* of a system is the set of all possible traces for the system relative to a given vocabulary and granularity.

	Effect of Change	
Attribute A	$A_S \subset A_{S'}$	$A_S \supset A_{S'}$
Vocabulary	extending	contracting
Granularity	refining	abstracting
Behavior	relaxing	constraining

Fig. 1. Types of Changes

Each of these three attributes is a set, and is subject to an ordering induced by the subset relation. The resulting partially ordered set becomes a Boolean algebra under the set union, set intersection, and set complement operations. As explained in Section 3, this structure can support a formal model of software change merging.

If we restrict primitive changes to be monotonic and to affect just one of the three attributes listed above, we get the classification of primitive changes shown in Figure 1, which is repeated from [22].

The symbol A_S represents the attribute A of the original system S, and $A_{S'}$ represents the attribute A of the modified system S'.

A decomposition of the chronological evolution history into primitive substeps conforming to these restrictions enables the rearrangement of a sequential derivation containing meaning-modifying changes into a tree-like rooted directed acyclic graph whose paths consist solely of meaning-preserving changes that add information via compatible vocabulary extensions, granularity refinements, or behavior constraints [11]. We propose this mechanism as a concrete means to document software as if it had been developed using a rational process [24], and conjecture that such structures will be useful for choosing demonstration scenarios, guiding requirements reviews, and summarizing past history for analysts formulating the next version.

A conceptual derivation history is a simplified version of the chronological history of an evolving system that includes only the decisions that were not undone in later steps. We model conceptual derivation histories as graphs whose nodes represent versions and whose arcs represent monotonic changes that add new capabilities or constraints. An idealized prototype evolution process should steadily strengthen the requirements in this sense, until they become acceptable to the users. In practice the path is often less direct. However, a reconstructed direct path in which each step strictly strengthens the requirements should provide a useful summary of the relevant parts of the evolution of the requirements. An example can be found in [11].

2.2 The Behavioral Refinement Ordering

Change merging depends on an ordering with a specialized algebraic structure, usually either a Boolean or Brouwerian algebra [8]. We propose a behavioral refinement ordering $\sqsubseteq$ on software specifications, defined as follows:

$p \sqsubseteq q \Leftrightarrow vocabulary(p) \subseteq vocabulary(q)$ &

$$granularity(p) \subseteq granularity(q) \ \&$$
$$behavior(p) \supseteq projection(behavior(q), vocabulary(p) \cup granularity(p))$$

The vocabulary, granularity, and behavior of a specification are defined in Section 2.1. The projection is needed to ensure that we are comparing just the corresponding parts of the two behaviors; it removes all events in traces of q that are outside the vocabulary and granularity of p. The ordering $p \sqsubseteq q$ means that q satisfies the specification of p. ¿From the point of view of a user q is just as good as p, and it may be strictly better if it provides some services that p does not. Enhancements can occur if q responds to additional external stimuli, its behavior is specified at a more detailed level of abstraction, or its behavior is subject to stricter constraints.

We would like to separate the effects of changes to orthogonal attributes of the system as much as possible, so that these independent changes can be automatically re-combined in different combinations. The problem of automatically combining different versions of programs has been formally studied in several different contexts [9, 10, 7, 8, 6, 25, 3], and has been informally discussed in terms of the development of requirements in [14], where the independence of elaborations was assessed manually. However, the problem has not yet been solved completely, particularly for requirements.

We make a step towards automating the detection of independent elaborations by proposing a formal model for refinement structures. There is potential for parallel elaboration whenever the software model has a function space or cross product structure with a componentwise refinement ordering, because different components of the structure can be refined independently. For example, this is the case for both the type signatures and the behaviors of different messages in a system.

A subtlety arises with respect to the behavior of types and machines, regarding invariants associated with state models of machines and instance models of types. These invariants express shared constraints that apply to all messages of the system. In a formal sense, the behavior (i.e. postconditions) of different messages can be refined and changed independently even in this case, although we must recognize that a change to an invariant constitutes a change to the behavior of *all* the messages in the system. If a modification to a message makes it unsatisfiable, one plausible strategy is to make a compensating invariant change. Such a situation can give the appearance of an interaction between changes to behaviors of different messages, although it is more precisely described as a system-wide change.

Previous methods for software change merging have assumed that the vocabulary is fixed and common to all versions to be merged. The model proposed here is a possible basis for extending some previous work on merging [7, 3] to cases where the vocabulary changes. Such an extension adopts an open and extensible view of the vocabulary: the behavior of a system whose vocabulary does not contain a given stimulus is considered equivalent to the behavior of a modified system that extends its vocabulary with the extra stimulus and leaves its response to that stimulus undefined and unconstrained. This is appropriate for requirements exploration and prototyping, although it is not consistent with the closed-world view typically adopted in software products, where requests outside the vocabulary are expected to produce error messages and have no other effect. Section 3 sketches some of the main ideas for this extension.

3 Combining Changes

The Boolean algebra structure of the vocabulary, granularity, and behavior of a specification identified in Section 2 implies that the usual formulation of the change merging operation can be applied in the context of changes to software specifications. If A, B, and C are specifications, the result of combining the change from B to A with the change from B to C is denoted by $A[B]C$, which is defined as follows.

$$A[B]C = (A - B) \sqcup (A \sqcap C) \sqcup (C - B)$$

Here $\sqcup$ denotes the least upper bound and $\sqcap$ denotes the greatest lower bound with respect to the ordering defined in Section 2.2. The difference is defined by

$$A - B = A \sqcap \overline{B}$$

where the bar denotes the complement operation. This operation is well defined for any Boolean algebra; in the special case of sets ordered by $\subseteq$, it is the set difference operation.

The definition of the change merging operator $\cdot[\cdot]\cdot$ is motivated by the desire to achieve the following properties:

1. the information added and removed by a change should not depend on what version the change is applied to,
2. the information added and removed by a change should be the minimum necessary to change the given base version (B above) into the given modified versions (A and C above), and
3. the combined change should incorporate the effects of both changes.

These properties are formalized and the minimal change property (2) is proved for the change merging operator in [8]. The change merging operator satisfies property (3) because it is derived from the composition of the two change transformations. As can be seen from the symmetry of the definition, the result of combining two changes does not depend on the order in which the transformations are composed.

The interpretations of the above Boolean operations for different aspects of software specifications are summarized in Figure 2. Since it is common to represent sets of behaviors by logical assertions representing postconditions, we include the postcondition representation as well.

The set inclusions in the definition of the specification refinement ordering (see section 2.2) go in the opposite direction for the system behavior than for the vocabulary and the granularity. This is reflected in the interpretations of the

	Operation			
Aspect	$X \sqsubseteq Y$	$X \sqcup Y$	$X \sqcap Y$	$X - Y$
Vocabulary	$X \subseteq Y$	$X \cup Y$	$X \cap Y$	$X - Y$
Granularity	$X \subseteq Y$	$X \cup Y$	$X \cap Y$	$X - Y$
Behavior	$X \supseteq Y$	$X \cap Y$	$X \cup Y$	$Y - X$
Postcondition	$X \Leftarrow Y$	$X \wedge Y$	$X \vee Y$	$X \vee \neg Y$

Fig. 2. Concrete Interpretations of Abstract Operations

Boolean operations for those aspects. Since the specification refinement ordering is derived from the orderings of the three different aspects according to the usual ordering construction for a cross product domain, all of the operations extend componentwise. This implies that we can compute change merges for the three aspects independently, according to the interpretations summarized in Figure 2.

4 Examples of Combining Changes to Specifications

Some examples illustrate the effects of the definitions presented in the previous section. Suppose we represent vocabularies as sets of messages. Then the combination of the change that removes the message m_2 from the starting vocabulary $\{m_1, m_2\}$ and the changes that adds m_3 to the same starting vocabulary is calculated as follows:

$\{m_1\}[\{m_1, m_2\}]\{m_1, m_2, m_3\}$
$= (\{m_1\} - \{m_1, m_2\}) \cup (\{m_1\} \cap \{m_1, m_2, m_3\}) \cup (\{m_1, m_2, m_3\} - \{m_1, m_2\})$
$= \{m_1, m_3\}$

The corresponding calculations on postconditions representing behaviors may be bit less intuitive. If P, Q, and R are assertions representing postconditions, we can apply the general definition and simplify to give the following rule:

$$P[Q]R = (P \vee \neg Q) \wedge (P \vee R) \wedge (R \vee \neg Q) = (P \vee R) \wedge (Q \Rightarrow P) \wedge (Q \Rightarrow R)$$

We illustrate the consequences of this rule for some common change patterns. Suppose that a, b, and c are three assertions representing postconditions in the specification of the behavior of a system in response to a given stimulus.

The combination of two different constraining changes to a behavior includes both constraints:

$$(a \wedge b)[b](b \wedge c) = (a \wedge b \wedge c)$$

The first changes adds the constraint a to the postcondition b of the base version and the second change adds a different constraint c. The original constraint and both of the new ones are present in the combination.

The combination of two relaxing changes loosens both of the affected constraints:

$$a[a \wedge b]b = a \vee b$$

```
FUNCTION spell_1
  MESSAGE spell(report: sequence{word} )
    REPLY(errors: sequence{word})
    WHERE ALL(w: word :: w IN errors <=>
              w IN report & ~(w IN dictionary))

  CONCEPT dictionary: set{word}
    -- The words in the Oxford English Dictionary.
END

INSTANCE word IMPORT Subtype FROM type
  WHERE Subtype(word, string),
    ALL(c: character, w: word ::
        c IN w => c IN ({a .. z} U {A .. Z}))
END
```

Fig. 3. Specification of Initial Spelling Checker

Note that the combination of removing each of two constraints separately does not result in a vacuous requirement: either of the two relaxed versions of the requirements is acceptable, but the system must satisfy at least one of them.

The combination of a relaxing change and a constraining change selectively loosens and also tightens the requirements:

$$b[a \wedge b](a \wedge b \wedge c) = b \wedge (a \Rightarrow c)$$

The constraint b is common to all three versions, and it appears in the combination as well. The first change drops the constraint a, while the second change adds the constraint c. In the combination, the new constraint c must hold only in the cases where the original constraint a is satisfied. This moderation of the constraining change is due to the presence of the relaxing change; if we do not remove the constraint a then the new constraint c is added unconditionally:

$$(a \wedge b)[a \wedge b](a \wedge b \wedge c) = a \wedge b \wedge c$$

To illustrate the effects of these rules in a more realistic context, consider the specification of a simple spelling checker whose base version is shown in Figure 3. We focus on the spell command. Figure 4 shows two changes to the behavior of this command, and the result of combining the changes using the method outlined in section 3.

All of the change merges in the examples follow directly from the definition, after simplification using the laws of ordinary propositional logic. These simplifications were performed manually and then checked via an automatic simplifier for propositional logic that is implemented using term rewriting with respect to a canonical set of rewrite rules.

```
-- base version:
MESSAGE spell(report: sequence{word} )
  REPLY(errors: sequence{word})
  WHERE ALL(w: word :: w IN errors <=>
            w IN report & ~(w IN dictionary) )

-- first modification:
MESSAGE spell(report: sequence{word} )
  REPLY(errors: sequence{word})
  WHERE ALL(w: word :: w IN errors <=>
            w IN report & ~(w IN dictionary) & ~acronym(w) )

-- second modification:
MESSAGE spell(report: sequence{word} )
  REPLY(errors: sequence{word})
  WHERE ALL(w: word :: w IN errors <=>
            w IN report & ~(w IN dictionary) ),
        sorted{less_or_equal@word}(errors)

-- result of change merging:
MESSAGE spell(report: sequence{word} )
  REPLY(errors: sequence{word})
  WHERE ALL(w: word :: w IN errors <=>
            w IN report & ~(w IN dictionary) & ~acronym(w) ),
        sorted{less_or_equal@word}(errors) |
          ALL(w: word :: w IN report & ~(w IN dictionary) &
              acronym(w) & ~(w IN errors))
```

Fig. 4. Merging Changes to the Spelling Checker

The base version has only the most basic requirements: there is only one dictionary, and there are no constraints on the order of the words in the output. The first enhancement introduces the modified requirement that acronyms (which contain only capital letters) are never reported as spelling errors. The second enhancement adds a requirement for sorting the output. The result of merging the two changes includes the acronym modification, but requires sorting only in the cases where the acronym modification did not take effect. This is a consequence of the minimal change principle [8] implicit in the change merging formula. In this case, a review by an analyst concludes that the case where the sorting requirement is suspended is impossible: the dictionary (a constant in the specification) cannot be empty in any acceptable version of a spell checking system, as would be required by the second condition in the last quantifier of Figure 4. In general, application of the change merging rules can highlight cases where requirements changes interact. These cases can then be reviewed by people to check whether a subtle interaction was missed or misjudged.

The implementation of the change merging definitions for specifications is straightforward, just as is the implementation of weakest preconditions for loop-free code. The difficulty of automatic application lies in the simplification step in both cases: since most logics that are useful for specification are not decidable, it is in general impossible to do a perfect job of simplification. For these logics, there is no computable canonical form in which all tautologies reduce to the logical constant "true" and all contradictory statements reduce to the logical constant "false". In the above examples, simplification using only the propositional structure of the formulas was sufficient to get useful results, even though human judgement was needed to recognize constraints that hold in the problem domain, but are not universally true in the logical sense. However, even for decidable systems such as propositional logic, the existence of a canonical form does not solve the problem completely, because the result produced by the simplifier does not resemble the original formulas and is typically hard to read. Manual simplification was needed in the above examples to make the results readable by people. Heuristic methods that try to match the original structures as far as possible would be useful for practical decision support. This is an area for further research.

5 Conclusions

We have presented a method for merging changes to a black box software specification, particularly those expressed using logic. Since logic has a natural Boolean algebra structure, the application of standard change merging models was straightforward once the refinement ordering for the larger scale aspects of system specifications were determined. Although the definition of the Boolean difference operation for logical assertions is a direct consequence of this algebraic structure, it is an unfamiliar operation and its behavior is somewhat counter-intuitive. We found that the effects of the change merging formulas were hard to predict without performing the detailed calculations prescribed by our method.

The main issues remaining for practical application are verifying the conformance of these models to the actual intent of designers who wish to combine their changes, and providing effective automation support for assertion simplification that can put synthesized assertions into a form readily understood by people.

Our previous research has explored formal models of the chronological evolution history [21]. This model has been applied to automate configuration management and a variety of project management functions [1]. The ideas presented in this paper are a promising basis for improving these capabilities, particularly in the area of computer aid for extracting useful design rationale information from a record of the evolution of the system.

Challenges facing future research on meaning-altering changes are to span the software design space using a set of manageable changes with precise and expressive representations, to provide automatic procedures for suggesting applicable changes, and to construct automatic or computer-aided procedures for decomposing manual design changes into sequences of primitive changes. Successful research in this direction and its future applications will support software design automation with great scientific and economic impact.

References

1. S. Badr, Luqi, Automation Support for Concurrent Software Engineering, *Proc. of the 6th International Conference Software Engineering and Knowledge Engineering*, Jurmala, Latvia, June 20-23, 1994, 46–53.
2. F. Bauer et al., *The Munich Project CIP. Volume II: The Program Change System CIP-S*, Lecture Notes in Computer Science 292, Springer 1987.
3. V. Berzins, On Merging Software Enhancements *Acta Informatica*, Vol. 23 No. 6, Nov 1986, pp. 607–619.
4. V. Berzins, Luqi, An Introduction to the Specification Language Spec, *IEEE Software*, Vol. 7 No. 2, Mar 1990, pp. 74–84.
5. V. Berzins, Luqi, *Software Engineering with Abstractions: An Integrated Approach to Software Development using Ada*, Addison-Wesley Publishing Company, 1991, ISBN 0–201–08004–4.
6. V. Berzins, Software Merge: Models and Methods, *Journal of Systems Integration*, Vol. 1, No. 2, pp. 121–141 Aug 1991.
7. D. Dampier, Luqi, V. Berzins, Automated Merging of Software Prototypes, *Journal of Systems Integration*, Vol. 4, No. 1, February, 1994, pp. 33–49.
8. V. Berzins, Software Merge: Semantics of Combining Changes to Programs, *ACM TOPLAS*, Vol. 16, No. 6, Nov. 1994, 1875–1903.
9. V. Berzins, *Software Merging and Slicing*, IEEE Computer Society Press Tutorial, 1995, ISBN 0-8186-6792-3.
10. V. Berzins, D. Dampier, Software Merge: Combining Changes to Decompositions, *Journal of Systems Integration*, special issue on CAPS (Vol. 6, No. 1–2, March 1996), pp. 135-150.
11. V. Berzins, Recombining Changes to Software Specifications, *Journal of Systems and Software*, to appear, Aug, 1998.
12. M. Feather, A System for Assisting Program Change, *ACM Transactions on Programming Languages and Systems*, Vol. 4 No. 1, Jan 1982, pp. 1–20.
13. M. Feather, A Survey and Classification of some Program Change Approaches and Techniques, in *Program Specification and Change (Proceedings of the IFIP TC2/WG 2.1 Working Conference)*, L.G.L.T. Meertens, Ed., North-Holland, 1987, pp. 165–195.
14. M. Feather, Constructing Specifications by Combining Parallel Elaborations, *IEEE Transactions on Software Engineering*, Vol. 15 No. 2, Feb 1989, pp. 198–208.
15. S. Fickas, Automating the Transformational Development of Software, *IEEE Transactions on Software Engineering*, Vol. 11 No. 11, Nov 1985, pp. 1268–1277.
16. W. Johnson, M. Feather, Building an Evolution Change Library, *12th International Conference on Software Engineering*, 1990, pp. 238–248.
17. E. Kant, On the Efficient Synthesis of Efficient Programs, *Artificial Intelligence*, Vol. 20 No. 3, May 1983, pp. 253–36. Also appears in [26], pp. 157–183.

18. Luqi, M. Ketabchi, A Computer Aided Prototyping System, *IEEE Software*, Vol. 5 No. 2, Mar 1988, pp. 66–72.
19. Luqi, V. Berzins, R. Yeh, A Prototyping Language for Real-Time Software, *IEEE Transactions on Software Engineering*, Vol. 14 No. 10, Oct 1988, pp. 1409–1423.
20. Luqi, Software Evolution via Rapid Prototyping, *IEEE Computer*, Vol. 22, No. 5, May 1989, pp. 13–25.
21. Luqi, A Graph Model for Software Evolution, *IEEE Transactions on Software Engineering*, Vol. 16, No. 8, pp. 917–927, Aug. 1990.
22. Luqi, Specifications in Software Prototyping, Proc. SEKE 96, Lake Tahoe, NV, June 10-12, 1996, pp. 189-197.
23. R. Lutz, Analyzing Software Requirements: Errors in Safety-Critical Embedded Systems, TR 92-27, Iowa State University, AUG 1992.
24. D. Parnas, P. Clemens, A Rational Design Process: How and Why to Fake It, *IEEE Transactions on Software Engineering*, Vol. 12 No. 2, Feb 1986, pp. 251–257.
25. S. Horowitz, J. Prins, T. Reps, Integrating Non-Interfering Versions of Programs, *ACM Transactions on Programming Languages and Systems*, Vol. 11 No. 3, Jul 1989, pp. 345–387.
26. C. Rich, R. Waters, Eds., *Readings in Artificial Intelligence and Software Engineering*, Morgan Kaufmann, 1986.
27. D. Smith, G. Kotik, S. Westfold, Research on Knowledge-Based Software Environments at Kestrel Institute, *IEEE Transactions on Software Engineering*, Vol. 11 No. 11, Nov 1985, pp. 1278–1295.
28. W. Swartout, R. Balzer, On the Inevitable intertwining of Specification and implementation, *Communication of the ACM*, Vol. 25 No. 7, July 1982, pp. 438–440. Also appears in *Software Specification techniques*, N. Gehani, A.D. McGettrick, Eds., 1986, pp. 41–45.

Combining and Distributing Hierarchical Systems

Chris George[1] and Đỗ Tiến Dũng[2]

[1] United Nations University International Institute for Software Technology, Macau
[2] Ministry of Finance, Hanoi, Vietnam

Abstract. It is possible with RAISE to specify and do most refinement in an applicative framework, and then transform the concrete applicative specification into an imperative sequential or concurrent one. This is a change from a style more appropriate to proof of refinement to a style more appropriate to implementation.

The resulting imperative specification is typically hierarchical, with upper levels calling the functions of lower ones. This paper presents a further stage of development in which the hierarchical structure is transformed into a distributed one, and components communicate asynchronously. This also allows "horizontal" communication between components of previously separate hierarchies.

A major design aim is to reuse the hierarchical specification, as far as possible extending the existing modules by standard, generic components. The method should achieve correctness by construction, and be amenable to quality control; it is an example of an engineering approach using standard components and standard assembly techniques.

The method is illustrated by collaborative work done between UNU/IIST and the Vietnamese Ministry of Finance in developing a specification of a national financial information system.

Keywords Formal specification, development, refinement, reuse, restructuring, distributed systems, coordination, software engineering

1 Introduction

We take it that engineering, as opposed to science, creates artifacts as far as possible through combining existing components. Speed and reliability are maximised and cost minimised through having to invent from scratch as little as possible. In this process engineers exploit the known properties of the components, and the known laws of the combining activity, which allows them to compute the properties of the combinations.

In this paper we describe the development of a distributed system, a financial information system, by developing first an applicative (or functional) specification and then transforming this, first into an imperative concurrent but still hierarchical system, and then into a distributed system. The first of these transformations follows the existing ideas of the RAISE method [1]. The second transformation is new and is based on a small number of standard components. Hence it exemplifies an essentially engineering approach.

In section 2 we describe the problem we tackled, the development of a specification of a national financial information system for Vietnam. In section 3 we show how the RAISE method (outlined in appendix A) was applied to the problem to produce a hierarchical, synchronous system. In section 4 we describe how the transformation to a distributed, asynchronous system was achieved. Section 5 is a concluding discussion.

2 A Financial Information System

During 1996–7 United Nations University International Institute for Software Technology (UNU/IIST) in Macau and the Vietnam Ministry of Finance (MoF) undertook a joint project called MoFIT (Ministry of Finance Information Technology) aimed at doing the domain analysis and specification for a national financial information system for Vietnam. The aim was to specify the major components of such a system and the main activities and information flows, and also to train software engineers from Vietnam in the relevant techniques. As well as the first author from UNU/IIST, the project involved six mainly young software engineers from Vietnam: four from the MoF, one from the Institute of Information Technology in Hanoi and one from Hanoi University. During the 16 months of the project these people each spent between 6 and 12 months working at UNU/IIST. As well as the main work described here, studies were also made of other aspects like system security and the possible effects of changes in taxation policy. The results are described in two UNU/IIST technical reports [2, 3] which in turn reference a number of more detailed project reports.

Vietnam is divided into 61 provinces, provinces are divided into districts, and districts into communes. The major government ministries reflect this structure, with offices at the national, province, district and in some cases commune levels. So, much of the collection or dissemination of information follows this hierarchical structure. In collecting information about taxes, for example, districts will supply information to their provincial offices, which will merge and perhaps summarise it and send it to the national office for the final merge into national information. Changes in taxation policy, or requests for information, flow down the hierarchy in the obvious manner.

The main component concerned with generating revenue is the taxation system, which is part of the MoF. In the first phase of the project all the engineers had experience of developing software for this system, mainly packages for particular tasks for province and district taxation offices. So in this phase we concentrated on analysing and specifying the taxation system.

In the second phase we considered other components. The treasury system is concerned with the actual collection and disbursement of money, with offices at national, provincial and district levels. The budget system is concerned with collecting budgetary estimates at the commune, district, province and national levels and, after government decision on the final figures, distributing actual annual budgets at the various levels and then monitoring these budgets. We also looked at two systems which exist only at the national level: the external loans and external aid systems.

2.1 The Taxation System

Taxation in Vietnam is currently primarily on enterprises. There are various categories of tax, such as profit taxes and sales taxes that may be levied. Provincial tax departments are responsible for larger enterprises as well as for their district offices; district offices are concerned with smaller enterprises.

Province and district taxation offices therefore share the task of demanding, collecting and accounting for taxes. They need to maintain for each taxpayer

- a *roll* of comparatively static information about the taxpayer, including basic details like name and address as well as information about the kind of business the taxpayer is in, from which the applicable categories of tax can be determined
- *bases* or figures collected from taxpayers about actual turnover, profits, etc.
- *accounts* recording taxes demanded, paid and owing for each category of tax for each taxpayer in each period.

They also need the current national taxation rules, called the *regime*, for tax calculation.

National and provincial taxation offices share the tasks of collecting, merging and summarising reports from their constituent offices at the immediately lower level.

It is apparent that there are several functional or organisational components of the taxation system that one would like the design to reflect:

- accounting for each category and period for each taxpayer
- registration of taxpayers
- recording base information for taxpayers
- making, merging and summarising reports
- structurally relating districts to provinces, provinces to the national office.

Making the structure of the specification reflect the main conceptual components aids in the comprehension of the overall system. Making the components separate with the standard properties of internal coherence and minimal linkage makes them easier to develop independently and robust against changes to other components.

One would also like to specify only once shared data structures and functions over them.

2.2 The Taxation System Specification

The taxation system specification does meet these structural requirements. There are separate components for a regime, for registration, for a roll, for a base and the tax calculation from it, for a collection of bases, for an account and a collection of accounts. These combine as illustrated in figure 1 into a *group*, which provides all the functions for dealing with a collection of taxpayers. It also shares some other specifications that will be used globally: in particular an abstract description of a report format with a functions to merge and summarise reports with common formats.

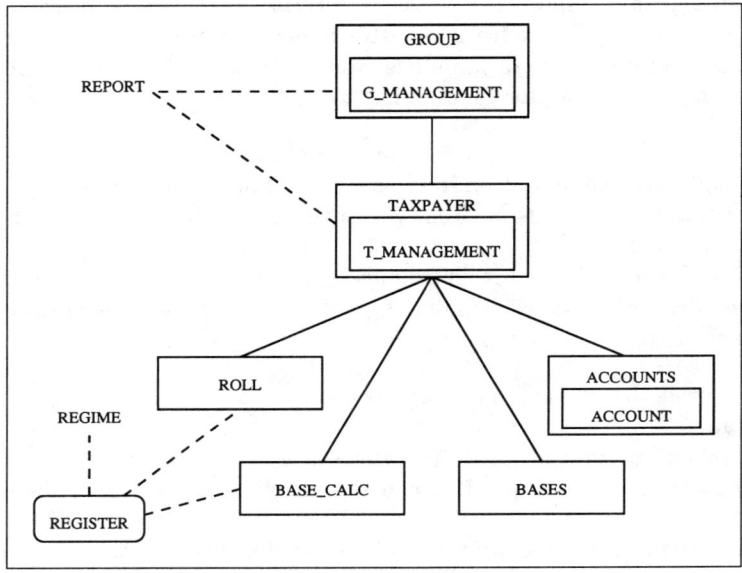

Fig. 1. Modules involved in specifying a taxation group

In figure 1 nested boxes indicate extension (inheritance), continuous lines indicate module dependency where the lower box is used to make an object in the upper one, and broken lines indicate dependency on shared modules through parameterisation.

The main structure of the specification then follows the hierarchical structure of the taxation system. Each district and province has a group; a province has a number of districts and the national or *general* taxation department (GTD) has a collection of provinces. See figure 2. For example, the type *Office* at the provincial (PTD) level is defined as a record containing its group and its district offices represented as a mapping from their identifiers to their offices:

type
    Office :: (1)
        taxpayers : GR.Group
        offices   : T.DTDid $\overrightarrow{m}$ DTD.Office

The prefixes in the type names indicate that the types are defined in other modules.

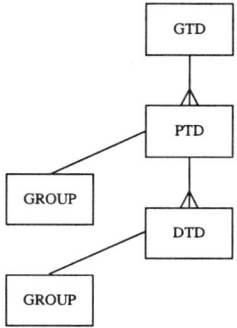

Fig. 2. Taxation system hierarchy

There is a function *mk_report* that specifies that a provincial report with a particular format is the result of collecting the district reports, merging these, creating the report from its own group, and merging this and the merged report from the districts. Thus the basic requirement that a provincial report combines these elements is clearly specified.

The specification at this point consists of about 1000 lines of RSL in 22 modules. The specification is applicative (functional). We wanted to develop it further towards a possible implementation. We had taken some account of a possible implementation strategy in that the main component of the Group module was a database (specified abstractly as a standard generic module) instantiated with a structure of information to be recorded about each taxpayer. So we separated the storage and retrieval of information about taxpayers from its processing, and provided a basis for a database implementation. Further design work would suggest possible detailed database schemas or relations that could be used for implementation. But such an implementation would be imperative, not applicative. Additionally, the actual system runs asynchronously, with different offices separated geographically and probably several concurrent users within one office. Finally, as we shall see, the taxation system communicates with other systems like the treasury and budget systems.

3 Initial Development to a Concurrent System

The general ideas in the RAISE method for specifying a system initially in an applicative, sequential style and developing this to an imperative, (synchronous) concurrent system are summarised in appendix A.

As an example to illustrate these ideas we consider the buffer that we will use later both for the message system and the in-tray of our distributed system.

We start with a parameter scheme *BUFF_PARM* which postulates a type *Elem*, a particular *null* value of this type, and a test *is_null*:

scheme BUFF_PARM =
class
   type Elem
   value
      null : Elem • is_null(null),
      is_null : Elem → **Bool**
end

The applicative specification *A_BUFFER* given here is concrete in that its type of interest *Buffer* is concrete: it is a list of *Elem* values. The function *put* is explicitly specified: it returns a new buffer with the extra value appended. The *get* function is specified implicitly. It takes a predicate as a parameter allowing it to be used either as a function to get the first element in the buffer (by making the predicate "λ x : X.Elem • **true**") or for extracting an element with some particular property. We will need this feature for the in-tray later, when we need to be able to extract a message with a particular number. Failure, because the buffer is empty or there is no element with the required property, is indicated by returning the *null* element.

scheme A_BUFFER(X : BUFF_PARM) =
class
   type Buffer = X.Elem*
   value
      put : X.Elem × Buffer → Buffer
      put(e, b) ≡ b ⁀ ⟨e⟩,

      get : (X.Elem → **Bool**) × Buffer → X.Elem × Buffer
      get(f, b) **as** (e, b′) **post**
         (∀ x : X.Elem • x ∈ **elems** b ⇒ ∼ f(x)) ∧ e = X.null ∧ b′ = b
         ∨
         (∃ b1, b2 : Buffer •
            b = b1 ⁀ ⟨e⟩ ⁀ b2 ∧
            b′ = b1 ⁀ b2 ∧ f(e) ∧
            (∀ x : X.Elem • x ∈ **elems** b1 ⇒ ∼ f(x)))
end

One way to transform the applicative *A_BUFFER* to a concurrent *C_BUFFER* is to use the former in the definition of the latter:

scheme C_BUFFER(X : BUFF_PARM) =
hide A, buff, put_ch, get_ch, get_res_ch **in**
class
   object A : A_BUFFER(X)

```
variable buff : A.Buffer := ⟨⟩
channel put_ch, get_res_ch : X.Elem, get_ch : X.Elem → Bool
value
    main : Unit → in put_ch, get_ch out get_res_ch write buff Unit
    main() ≡
        while true do
            buff := A.put(put_ch?, buff)
            ⌈⌉
            let (e, b′) = A.get(get_ch?, buff) in
                buff := b′ ; get_res_ch!e
            end
        end,

    put : X.Elem → out put_ch Unit
    put(e) ≡ put_ch!e,

    get : (X.Elem → Bool) → in get_res_ch out get_ch X.Elem
    get(f) ≡ get_ch!f ; get_res_ch?
end
```

Here we have a server process *main* that runs for ever, mostly waiting for interactions with the "interface processes" *put* and *get*. The imperative state is held in a variable *buff*, and three channels are used for communication. The variable and channels are hidden, so the only possible interactions are via the interface processes. For example, when *get* is called with actual parameter a predicate f, it will communicate with *main* by outputting f on the channel *get_ch*. *main* uses the functions defined earlier in *A_BUFFER* to compute the result from the predicate f and the current value of the variable *buff*. Then the new buffer value is assigned to *buff* and the result element sent back to *get* on the *get_res_ch* channel. *get* then terminates, returning the element value it received. It should be intuitively clear that the concurrent buffer "behaves like" the applicative one, and this can be formalised in terms of transforming applicative properties into concurrent ones. See appendix A for details.

When the types of interest of sequential modules are functions or mappings over finite types, the concurrent system has an extra level through there being RSL "object arrays". Thus the mapping in the provincial tax department of district tax department identifiers to district tax department offices results in an array of objects modelling district tax offices.

We can see the effect of this transformation for our provincial tax office. The type definition (1) of section 2.2 becomes

object
    GR : GROUP,
    DTDS[id : T.DTDid] : DTD

We have an object for the province's group of taxpayers and an array of objects representing its constituent district tax departments.

4 From Concurrent to Distributed

The construction described in the previous section was applied to the taxation specification to produce a (synchronous) concurrent description of the taxation system. The hierarchy reflects both the bureaucratic structure (districts belong to provinces, provinces to the national, "general" taxation department) and also to the data and control flow in distributing the current regime (taxation rules) and in collecting reports. The module structure is nested, as illustrated in (either half of) figure 3. In the meantime we had also worked on the treasury and budget systems. These exhibit essentially the same kind of hierarchic structure based on provinces, districts (and, for the budget system, communes). The three specifications needed to be combined into a single specification, since in practice the three systems communicate, and they do so at the local level. For example, when someone pays tax they actually pay it at the local treasury office. The treasury office sends a notification to the corresponding tax office, and also reports amounts collected to the local budget office, since this monitors budget performance. We had modelled for each system the receipt of such information but not (since we had three separate specifications) the transmission of it.

We also wanted to include the two other specifications we had done, of the external loans and external aid systems. These do not exhibit the same problems since they only have national offices.

The structure of the hierarchic specifications seemed wrong for introducing "horizontal" communication between local offices of different systems. The provincial offices are modelled by an array of objects "inside" the national one, and the district offices are similarly "inside" the provincial ones. This is really just a conceptual issue; there is no reason why a treasury office in district D of province P should not call a function named *Tax.P.D.pay* to report a tax payment, but to some members of the team it seemed wrong to apparently pass the call through the national office.

More real is the problem that communication in the hierarchic systems is synchronous, while communication in the actual systems will be asynchronous. The means of communication between offices vary, and at present very few are electronic. Asynchrony applies vertically as well as horizontally — and often the delays are longest in this direction. District treasury and taxation offices may be co-located, but some distance from their provincial offices.

So we wanted to move from the situation illustrated in figure 3 to that illustrated in figure 4.

4.1 Construction

There are two issues: how to construct the combined and distributed system, and its semantics: how to relate its properties to those of the separate hierarchical ones. The first we describe in this section 4.1, the second in section 4.2.

The aim was to achieve this restructuring of the specification while reusing as much as possible of the work done already. It was clear that the restructuring would need some additional components — the message system for a start. We

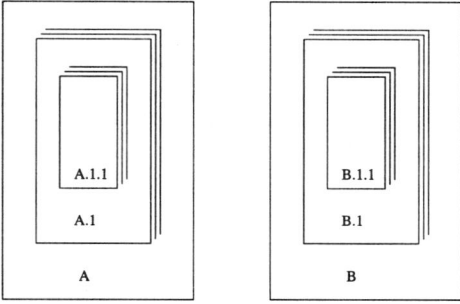

Fig. 3. Separate hierarchical systems

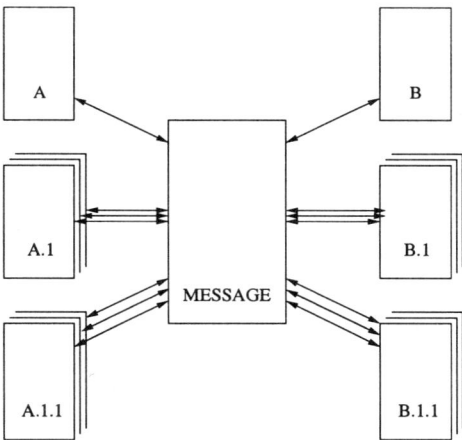

Fig. 4. Distributed and combined systems

wanted to make these components as far as possible generic and hence reusable between the systems we had and also for similar problems in the future.

Message System The message system clearly needs a universal set of addresses for offices in different systems. This is easy enough to specify. A district address, for example, has the form *System.Province.District* which makes it easy for a district treasury office, for example, to address a message to its corresponding tax office, or to its treasury provincial office.

We also apparently need a universal message type. We did not want to enforce such a type across the component systems, so instead we specified a message type for each system plus a global one, together with *encode* and *decode* functions within each system between its type and the global one. There are axioms for each system:

$$\forall\ m : \text{System\_message} \cdot \text{decode}(\text{encode}(m)) = m$$

to guarantee correct message passing within the system. This leaves open the design of suitable functions to deal with the encoding and decoding of particular kinds of messages that pass between systems without it necessarily following that the tax system, say, can read all messages intended to stay within the treasury system.

The message system is specified as an array of the concurrent buffers specified earlier in section 3, one buffer for each address. It uses *put* to add a message to a buffer and *get* to obtain the next message in a buffer.

We decided to enforce a rule that all messages are numbered (by defining a module to store and increment a number and instantiating it in each office, so that address and number together can uniquely identify an outgoing message), and include the sender's address, and a protocol that all messages are answered by at least an acknowledgement. The reply carries the same message number as the message it is answering or acknowledging. This, as we shall see, enables the automation of report collection and, if required, of other activities.

A "null" message may be the result of faulty communication, or merely the result of seeking a reply that has not yet arrived.

In-tray Each office has an in-tray for receiving incoming messages. This is an instantiation of the same buffer used to make the message system, but also uses the facility for extracting a message by number, to allow for replies to messages to be extracted.

It is interesting to note that the function to extract a reply from an in-tray is a loop — it keeps trying until a non-null message is extracted. This breaks the normal design rule that only servers must potentially loop for ever: this is an interface process intended to interact with server processes, and must be guaranteed, assuming it finishes waiting to interact with a server, to terminate. In practice such a process will need an overall time-out or repetition limit to prevent it looping for ever, and also some delay between iterations to prevent "race" conditions. We could have specified this but it did not seem worth it — it is a problem easily solved at the final implementation stage — so we indicated the problem merely by a comment.

Secretary Messages sent to the message system are placed in the appropriate destination buffer. They need to be transferred from there to the destination's in-tray. This is a traditional role for a secretary — to open the mail. The name of this module is quite intentional — in many tax, treasury, etc. offices in Vietnam this is currently a manual process and likely to be so for some time. In specifying this system we are not assuming that all of it will be implemented in software. Some instances of some components will be manual, and our specification then represents our assumptions about what will be done. In fact any specification component of a larger system has a dual role. To the other components that use it, it describes what assumptions they may make about that component; to its implementor it describes what services must be provided.

We wrote two versions of the secretary module. An "unskilled" one merely transfers messages from the message system to the in-tray. A "skilled" one is supplied with a function that decides if a particular (decoded) message can be "handled" by the secretary, in which case the appropriate function is applied and the reply encoded and dispatched to the sender of the original message. So, for example, the collection of reports within the tax system can be handled by the secretary modules since the tax "generate report" functions already exist. If desired, the recording of tax payments notified by messages from the treasury system can be done because the "pay" function in the taxation system already exists, and an acknowledgement can be sent. All that is required is to write the "handle" functions that call the appropriate existing functions according to the data in the message. This needs to be written for each office (or each class of office perhaps) but is a straightforward task.

Secretaries never handle replies to messages sent from their offices: they just place them in the in-tray. There are other components, like the stubs described in the next section, that will be waiting for them.

Stub Modules Each provincial office, for example, contains in the hierarchical version an array of objects representing its district offices. In the distributed version these objects will no longer appear inside it, but need to be replaced by simple stub modules. For each function in the hierarchical system called in a lower object from a higher, the stub module will apparently provide the same function, returning the same result. But in fact it will send an appropriate message to the office for which it is a stub, and wait for a reply (recognised by message number) to appear in its office's in-tray. It then returns the content of the reply and thus (assuming no communication faults) appears, modulo some delay, to act exactly like the function it replaced.

Changes to Existing Modules It should be apparent that the only modules that need to be changed in forming the distributed system are those for each system defining the office at the national, provincial, district and possibly commune levels. Each needs to be supplied with

- an object defining its own system message type, used to instantiate the in-tray, secretary and stub modules
- objects for the message number counter, in-tray, and secretary, which are just instantiations of generic modules
- a constant specifying its own address
- stub modules to replace the lower level modules
- can_handle and handle functions for the (skilled) secretary module to use.

Only the last two of these require more than a very few lines of specification, and are easy to write and to check because they follow a very regular pattern.

This is a very small change to the specification. For the taxation system, for example, only three modules of the 22 needed any change, and the changes only affected a very small part of these three.

4.2 Semantics

The construction of the distributed system is comparatively simple. But its semantics seem much more of a problem. In "opening up" the hierarchies and apparently allowing arbitrary asynchronous communication we are immediately faced with the notorious problem of interference which prevents us drawing reliable conclusions about concurrent systems based on the properties of their components (or, at least, considerably complicates the proof of such properties and typically necessitates the introduction of extra conditions, such as rely/guarantee [4]).

But in fact our distributed system retains some important structural properties. Although the message system is capable of allowing communication between arbitrary nodes, it is only used in very particular ways:

- The communication within, say, the tax system is still hierarchical. That is, we did not introduce any new communication paths between tax offices. The only possible communications between tax offices are those between an office and its immediate superior or inferiors in the hierarchy.
- We only introduce "horizontal" communication paths for particular purposes, such as allowing a treasury office to report a tax payment to a tax office. If we can keep the number of these paths low we can deal with them individually.
- We have adopted the protocol that all messages are replied to. This means that we can rely on either obtaining an answer to a query or deciding, after some suitable wait, that it is "null".

We stated that a major aim of the development is to reuse as much as possible of the original, synchronous, specification and also to reuse safely the validation done of that system. We have seen that reuse was achieved; now we consider validation of the asynchronous system.

We consider a number of requirements and see how we can validate the distributed system against them:

1. Taxes for taxpayers will be calculated according to the current regime on the basis of their bases and roll information.
2. Reports collected by an office will correctly reflect the current information from its group of taxpayers and/or its subsidiary offices.
3. Tax paid by a taxpayer at a treasury office will be correctly credited at the corresponding tax office.

The first requirement is mostly about the calculations that are carried out within the "Group" specification. The group is still part of a provincial or district tax office and is unaffected by the distribution. If this property was true in the original, applicative specification it will, appropriately transformed, still be true. The rules for calculating tax, in particular for calculating interest penalties on tax unpaid from previous periods, and for using payments correctly to credit against unpaid tax, are complicated. We had earlier made a rapid prototype of the taxation accounting part of the specification to check that we had specified these rules correctly. Some of the team wrote some test cases and the expected results; others did the prototype implementation (using the RAISE tool that translates a subset of RSL to C++, plus a simple command line interface). The tests revealed a few errors that were just "typos" but also revealed one conceptual error about the date from which interest should be added. It is important that such validation work should not need to be redone, and this is ensured if, as here, the specification of this part can be reused unchanged.

There are some additional questions about the "current" regime, the identification of the taxpayer's roll and base information, but it is comparatively easy to check that there is a function to transmit a regime down the tax hierarchy (and to check its receipt) and that the one transmitted is the one used until a new one is received. Similarly we can check that roll and base information is properly installed.

The second requirement is another example of a function within the tax system. In the original, applicative specification it was stated explicitly. Hence we know its concurrent counterpart holds in the hierarchical specification. The problem comes now from two sources: interference from other activities, either within the tax system (e.g. a taxpayer declares their profits and changes their base) or from another system (e.g. the treasury reports payment of some tax by a taxpayer).

Information systems like this are typically not meant to deal in very precise ways with this kind of problem. It is not in general required, say, that all district offices together "lock" their databases against all other accesses while a provincial report is compiled. It is accepted that figures may vary according to other events occurring, by chance, just before or just after the report is compiled. A report is not a single snapshot, but an amalgam of a number of component snapshots taken at roughly the same time. It is unlikely the the amalgamated picture was ever precisely true. The problem, in this case, is one of finding a specification of the "current information" that is sufficiently loose!

There may be more local serialisation issues. For example, if a taxpayer makes a payment, this amount will increase the tax paid and reduce the tax owing. If the payment transaction is decomposed in this way then the compilation of a report should not reflect the situation mid-way between the two sub-transactions: it would over-estimate tax revenue. But this is not an issue caused by the distribution: it is clear in the specification of a group and can be handled during development using standard database design techniques.

Specifying that a report correctly summarises a loose specification of what is the "current situation" in a distributed system is an example of "interface refinement" as described by Gerth et. al. [5]. But the formal machinery proposed there is rather heavy to express the freedom allowed in this system. Another possibility is to use partial orders on events as indicating causality [6], and to specify that the event of asking for a report from each district precedes the arrival of the request there, which precedes the report being sent back, which in turn precedes its receipt and merging with others. The "current information" is that existing at some point between the request arriving and the report's dispatch, and hence between the superior office's request and the merge. But we can check informally that the requirement is met if we check that each superior office sends the appropriate message to each of its subordinate ones, that such messages are properly delivered, that the subordinate offices "handle" and correctly reply with the information requested, and that the responses are correctly merged. Much of this (the production of the report in the district office, the merging of reports at the province office) is already specified in the hierarchical system and reused (unchanged) in the distributed system.

The third requirement is an example of communication between systems, so it is a requirement that the separate hierarchical systems could not have been specified to meet. But we can decompose it into

1. Payment of tax at a treasury office will be correctly reported to the appropriate tax office.
2. (Report of) payment of tax to a tax office will be correctly credited

The second of these is already a property of the "Group" and is unchanged by the distribution. So we need to check that

- each treasury office can receive tax payments
- the correct information (amount, tax category, taxpayer) is sent to the correct tax office
- the message system delivers messages to the correct recipient
- such messages can be correctly "handled" by tax offices, with the appropriate group functions called, and the appropriate acknowledgement sent.

(These need to be extended to allow for possible non-communication with checks for non-acknowledgement, resending of information, and recognition of duplicate inputs.)

We conclude that it is not feasible to have a general theory of such a distribution, but that if we have sufficient restrictions on possible communication paths, and suitable message protocols, then we can argue informally that requirements are met provided particular properties of the extra components we added for distribution are true. These are properties like

- the message system sends messages to their addressees
- messages are correctly encoded/decoded
- received messages are correctly "handled", i.e. the appropriate existing function is called with the correct parameters
- messages are replied to with the correct response, or acknowledged.

The point to notice about these properties is that they are easily stated requirements of, for example, the message system or the encode/decode functions, and hence can be part of their specification, or they are easily checked by looking at a few lines of specification. The only possible exception to this is the "there is always a reply or acknowledgement" since its generation may conceivably be some distance textually from the handling of the message it should be a response to, but in practice one can structure the specification so that it is clear. Hence these properties can be checked "by inspection" rather than by proof; they are amenable to quality control.

Or, of course, one can take a particularly critical property like "all messages are replied to or acknowledged" and perform the proof. In general we want to restrict proofs at this stage to critical properties, because of the problems of proof about concurrent systems that we remarked on earlier, and to do as much as possible by quality control.

4.3 Implementation

The specification is still a long way from implementation. But the aim of this work was not to implement the system. It was to analyse a very large system and to specify an overall architecture. The architecture reflects things that we do not expect to change very much, like the hierarchical structure of national, provincial and local offices and the broad distinctions between the separate taxation, treasury and budget systems. The specification had to avoid constraining things that are likely to change, like taxation rules and even the kinds of tax that are being collected.

Over the next few years Vietnam expects to gradually computerise many of the functions described in the specification, plus the means of communication between different offices. At any point in time the overall system will be very heterogeneous, with different degrees of computerisation and a range of technologies used both in computing and communication. Many of the "secretary" modules will be implemented by people rather than software. Detailed issues of interoperability will need to be solved as the system evolves, and these solutions will themselves need to evolve as new coordination [7] technologies become available and as the investment is made. Indeed, the ability to gradually implement such a system, and to allow heterogeneity, will be essential to its success; it cannot be implemented monolithically and switched on overnight, and to attempt to do so would be to invite disaster.

5 Conclusions

We achieved a number of aims. We were able to separate clearly the functional aspects of particular parts of the system (like tax accounting and report merging) from more organisational aspects. We were able to do this partly through adopting a "bottom-up" approach that allowed us to tackle one problem at a time. This also had a pedagogic purpose — it is particularly hard to do things top-down with people with little experience in formal specification. Much of what is done top-down is done to make things abstract and generic, and one needs to be able to foresee the effects of different kinds of module connection like parameterisation, extension and instantiation. But as long as one has the confidence that things can be put together later, the bottom-up approach has much to recommend it in keeping things simple for as long as possible, and in allowing separate parts to be worked on independently. In general, even with experienced people, it is often a good idea to look first at new, difficult problems regardless of where they will eventually appear in the specification structure.

We stated at the start of this paper that engineering involved composing entities with known properties in combinations with accompanying rules that allowed the properties of the combinations to be computed. This we have done for the applicative to imperative, sequential to concurrent transformations. We know exactly how to relate the properties of the result to the properties of the starting point. The method involves working initially with applicative specifications, perhaps refining these to more concrete versions, and perhaps even proving these refinements, or at least some important properties. Then there is a transformation step to a concurrent, synchronous specification which is simple enough to be amenable to quality control. It might be automated, though in practice there are various options that can be chosen as to how exactly to structure the variables or channels being introduced.

The further step introduced in this paper from separate hierarchical systems to a combined and distributed system uses a number of standard generic modules. The changes to the existing system are very small and, again, open to quality control.

The introduction of asynchrony, and the opening of hierarchies for independent communications between their components, makes the system semantics more complicated, and much more difficult to relate to those of the synchronous, hierarchical system. But it seems that, given sufficient architectural constraints on the possible communication paths, and reasonable protocols that enable non-reception of messages to be decided, we can still relate asynchronous properties to synchronous ones in a reasonable manner, and the required checks are again amenable to quality control. There is more work to be done to generalise and properly formalise these ideas.

The attempt to separate concerns and put things together later is not always so successful. We also looked, for example, at how the security aspects of the tax system could be specified, starting with the current policy. This uses a quite conventional system of groups of users with levels of functional access to the user-level functions and access rights for various functions and parts of the taxation database in each office.

We hoped at one point to be able to put a "shell" around the system so that user access could be controlled at the outer level without changing the specification within it. But this proved very difficult, mainly because at the abstract level it is difficult to say exactly what data is being accessed. It seemed inevitable that we would need to pass the user identities associated with top level transactions down to the level of the database accesses in order to validate them there. This is probably good practice anyway, as there is less of the system to validate against security leaks. But it involves a simple but rather tedious addition of an extra parameter to many functions.

6 Acknowledgements

The MoFIT project was carried out by all the authors of [2,3], not just by the authors of this paper. We also received helpful comments from Tomasz Janowski and an anonymous referee on earlier drafts.

References

1. The RAISE Method Group. *The RAISE Development Method*. BCS Practitioner Series. Prentice Hall, 1995.
2. Do Tien Dung, Le Linh Chi, Nguyen Le Thu, Phung Phuong Nam, Tran Mai Lien, and Chris George. Developing a Financial Information System. Technical Report 81, UNU/IIST, P.O.Box 3058, Macau, September 1996.
3. Do Tien Dung, Chris George, Hoang Xuan Huan, and Phung Phuong Nam. A Financial Information System. Technical Report 115, UNU/IIST, P.O.Box 3058, Macau, July 1997.
4. C.B. Jones. Accommodating Interference in the Formal Design of Concurrent Object-Based Programs. *Formal Methods in System Design*, 8:105–122, 1996.
5. Rob Gerth, Ruurd Kuiper, and John Segers. Interface Refinement in Reactive Systems. In Cleaveland [9].
6. Sigurd Meldal and David C. Luckham. Defining a Security Reference Architecture. Technical Report CSL-TR-97-728, Stanford University, June 1997.
7. Peter Wegner. Coordination as Constrained Interaction. In Ciancarini and Hankin [8].
8. Paolo Ciancarini and Chris Hankin, editors. *Coordination Languages and Models*, volume 1061 of *Lecture Notes in Computer Science*. Springer-Verlag, April 1996.
9. W.R. Cleaveland, editor. *Concur'92: Third International Conference on Concurrency Theory*, volume 630 of *Lecture Notes in Computer Science*. Springer-Verlag, August 1992.
10. The RAISE Language Group. *The RAISE Specification Language*. BCS Practitioner Series. Prentice Hall, 1992.
11. J.V. Guttag. Abstract data types and the development of data structures. *CACM*, 20(6), June 1977.
12. C. A. R. Hoare. *Communicating Sequential Processes*. Prentice-Hall International, 1985.
13. R. Milner. *Communication and Concurrency*. Prentice-Hall International, 1989.
14. R.E. Milne. Transforming Axioms for Data Types into Sequential Programs. In *Proceedings of 4th Refinement Workshop*. Springer-Verlag, 1991.

A The RAISE Development Method

The RAISE specification language (RSL) [10] allows specification in both applicative and imperative styles, and of both sequential and concurrent systems. The applicative/imperative and sequential/concurrent distinctions are orthogonal, giving four possible styles, but the applicative concurrent style is rarely used. So we use applicative, imperative and concurrent as abbreviations for applicative sequential, imperative sequential and imperative concurrent respectively.

RSL supports the specification of data types in the standard algebraic style, by defining abstract types (sorts) and axioms over their generators and observers.

A design goal of RSL was uniformity, and so it is also possible to specify imperative programs using axioms, and also to specify concurrent systems in the same way. This allows equational reasoning about all styles of specification.

When one speaks about an abstract data type, one is being abstract about the structure of the type. The imperative counterpart is to be abstract about the variable(s) involved (in the programming language sense of a variable as an assignable entity whose contents can later be retrieved). One can see the collection of variables (with their types) of an imperative specification as corresponding to the "type of interest" [11] of an applicative specification.

The concurrent part of RSL is based on process algebra (similar to CSP [12] and CCS [13]) with communication of values along channels. One can be abstract about the channels involved (and hence also about the possible internal communications with sub-processes).

Consider a simple example of an abstract data type with a generator *empty* and an observer *is_empty*. Here are the appropriate axioms in the three styles:

[applicative]
  is_empty(empty) ≡ **true**

[imperative]
  empty() ; is_empty() ≡ empty() ; **true**

[concurrent]
  ∀ test : **Bool** $\overset{\sim}{\to}$ **Unit** •
    (main() ∥ empty()) ∥ test(is_empty()) ≡ (main() ∥ empty()) ∥ test(**true**)

The strong equivalence "≡" between expressions compares not only results but also effects, i.e. changes to variables and communications on channels. (In the applicative case it could be replaced by "=", as there are no effects.) The applicative generator *empty* becomes in the imperative case a function of the same name that will change some variables so that the current state is "empty". The applicative observer *is_empty* becomes an imperative function that can read some or all of these variables. Thus the imperative axiom says that performing *empty* followed by performing *is_empty* is in every way equivalent to performing *empty* and returning **true**.

In the concurrent case we need a *main* or server process that mediates access to the imperative state. The functions *empty* and *is_empty* become "interface processes" that interact with the server to change or interrogate its internal state. (In object-oriented terminology these would be called "methods".) The interlock operator "‖" is like the parallel operator but allows its constituent processes to communicate only with each other until one of them terminates. The *test* process is just a technique, needed because interlock requires its arguments to be of type **Unit**. So we can read the concurrent axiom as saying that if we force the server *main* to communicate with *empty*, and the resulting process to communicate with *is_empty*, the result will be in every way equivalent to forcing the communication with *empty* and obtaining **true**.

It should be clear that all these axioms say essentially the same thing. If you make it empty, and then ask if it is, the answer will be "yes". But the effort and machinery to make this simple assertion becomes progressively more difficult as we proceed to imperative and then concurrent styles. This was certainly the experience of early users of RSL.

The difference does not apply only to specification, but also to reasoning about specifications. Whether this is done manually or with a proof tool, our experience is that proving the "same" property in the different styles for the "same" specification involves effort and difficulty on a ratio of something like 1:2:5 for the three styles. These figures are only impressions — we have made no measurements. We only want to make the point that things get much more difficult. A proof tool with better strategies could undoubtedly alleviate the problems, but we doubt the disparity can be removed.

So we conclude that (abstract) applicative specifications are easiest to construct and to reason about, but imperative or concurrent systems are what we typically need to implement. There does seem to be a notion of them being the "same" thing in some sense — or at least there being imperative and concurrent counterparts to applicative specifications. So perhaps we can transform the latter into the former. If we can supply a notion of correctness, i.e. define precisely what we mean by "same", then we have a possible development method.

This was described in the book on the RAISE method [1]. We can follow the development route illustrated in figure 5. We start with a more or less abstract applicative specification. Making this concrete essentially involves making its types concrete and defining the required functions over these concrete types. Showing refinement involves showing that these functions satisfy the axioms of the abstract specification. The concrete types typically are records or products of other types which sometimes merit being made the "types of interest" of subsidiary modules. This process naturally produces a hierarchy of modules (with some complications when we use parameterisation to make modules generic or to allow them to be "shared").

When we have a concrete applicative specification we can transform it into a concrete imperative one, using a standard set of transformation rules. This transformation operates on a module by module basis, and preserves the structure of the specification. We arrive at a similarly hierarchic specification where the

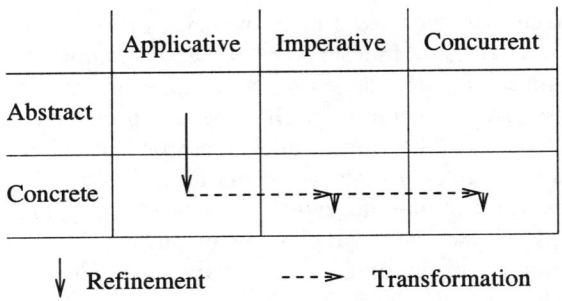

Fig. 5. Development route

"leaf" modules have variables and functions to change or report on their state. "Branch" modules normally have no variables; their functions call the functions of the leaf modules below them.

Finally there may be some small refinement steps that are best done in an imperative context, like introducing iteration to refine existentially or universally quantified expressions.

The syntax of the transformation is straightforward, but what about its semantics? What is the semantic relation between the applicative specification and the imperative one generated from it?

The imperative specification cannot be a refinement of the applicative one, because the signatures of the functions have changed: parameters corresponding to state variables have disappeared. The refinement relation in RSL is required to allow substitution in a system of a component by a refinement of it. So, such changes in signature are certainly precluded. But there is a meta-theorem (figure 6) that says if we have an abstract applicative specification **A0**, a refinement of it **A1**, and an imperative specification **I1** obtained by transforming **A1**, then:

1. There is an abstract imperative specification $I0$ (i.e. one with no explicitly defined variables) which is refined by the concrete imperative **I1**.
2. A conservative extension $I0 + D$ of this abstract imperative specification refines the original abstract applicative **A0**.

A version of this construction was originally described in [14].

The point is that there is no need to write the abstract imperative specification $I0$ or the extension D: we know they exist and we know that the concrete imperative specification constructed by transformation is "correct" with respect to the applicative one.

Another way to see this notion of correctness is to consider again the three axioms relating *empty* and *is_empty*. The transformation ensures that if the applicative specification has a property, then the imperative specification will have the corresponding imperative property, where "corresponding" is defined by the transformation.

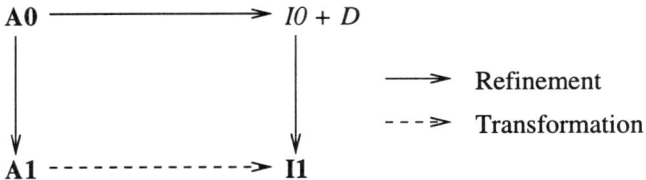

Fig. 6. Transformation theorem

Another point to note is that the method need not even start with an abstract applicative specification. It is possible to start with a concrete one, which is for most people the easiest starting point, and there is a simple abstraction method that will create an abstract applicative one from it. In the MoFIT project we did almost no refinement; most of the applicative modules have concrete types and explicit algorithms.

A further transformation, first described in [1], will produce a concrete concurrent specification from the concrete imperative one. This again applies module by module and maintains the overall structure of the specification. Leaf modules contain the imperative state components embedded in "server" processes.

The semantic relation, and hence the notion of correctness of the concurrent system, is similar to the imperative case. There will exist an abstraction from the concrete concurrent specification to an abstract concurrent one, a conservative extension of which can be shown to implement the original abstract applicative one. We can guarantee that if the applicative specification has a property, the concurrent one will have the corresponding transformed property.

The concurrent architecture has some convenient features. In particular:

- It is guaranteed to be deadlock free.
- The states of the imperative components are independent, since all communication is between leaf and branch nodes. This means in turn that it is possible for branch modules to call the interface processes of their leaf nodes in parallel instead of sequentially, with the same results; there is no interference.

Other examples we have done suggest that it is possible to further develop this calling structure, in particular to deal with "shared" nodes, so that leaves can call the interface processes of other leaves. This requires care in the proper sequencing of calls in branch modules, and also requires that the dependencies between modules are acyclic.

It is not suggested that all concurrent systems can be designed in this way, by transforming an initially applicative specification. But it does seem to apply quite conveniently to many systems and to give a very satisfactory architecture.

Software Engineering Issues for Network Computing

Carlo Ghezzi and Giovanni Vigna

Politecnico di Milano
Dipartimento di Elettronica e Informazione
Piazza Leonardo da Vinci, 32
20133 Milano, Italy
ghezzi|vigna@elet.polimi.it

Abstract. The Internet is becoming the infrastructure upon which an increasing number of new applications are being developed. These applications allow new services to be provided and even new business areas to be opened. The growth of Internet-based applications has been one of the most striking technological achievements of the past few years. Yet, there are some risks inherent in this growth. Rapid development and reduced time to market have probably been the highest priority concerns for application developers. Therefore, these developments proceed without following a disciplined approach. We argue that the resulting applications will become the legacy systems of the near future, when the quality of these systems will need improvement but, at the same time, modifications will be hard to make in an economical and reliable way. In this paper we discuss the need for a software engineering approach to the development of network applications. In particular, we discuss a possible research agenda for software engineering research by looking at two specific areas: the World Wide Web and applications based on mobile code.

Keywords and phrases: Internet, World Wide Web, mobile code, software engineering, software quality, software development process.

1 Introduction

Since the beginning of the 1990's, use of the Internet and the World Wide Web (WWW) has exploded. Today, there are more than 50 million users from about 200 countries; the yearly rate of growth has been more than 50%, and the number of forecasted users by the year 2000 is approximately 380 million [20].

In recent years, there has been a shift both in the way the Internet is used and in how its potential is perceived by technology developers, service providers, and users. The Internet is not merely seen as a communication infrastructure that allows people to communicate in a fast, cheap, and reliable way; it is increasingly seen as the infrastructure upon which new services, new applications, and even new and previously unforeseen types of social processes are becoming possible. For example, electronic commerce may revolutionize the way business is done.

As another example, interactive distance learning and tutoring may change the way knowledge is transferred and will support new kinds of learning processes.

A new field is therefore emerging: *network computing*. By this, we mean computing where the computational infrastructure is a large set of autonomous and geographically distributed computers, connected by the Internet. In this paper we discuss critically the current state of network computing, to understand the current risks that are inherent in its growth.

Rapid development and reduced time to market seem to be the major concerns that drive the developments of network computing applications. The implementation technologies used for new developments are often unstable; in some cases they are just partially developed prototypes. Applications are developed in an *ad hoc* manner, without following disciplined design approaches, and often with little concern for their qualities, such as reliability or modifiability. We argue that these systems are likely to become the legacy systems of the near future, when people will discover that these applications are difficult to maintain in an economical and reliable way. We see a similarity between the current situation and the one that existed in the sixties (see [9] and much of the work that was spurred on by that paper), when the risks due to the lack of appropriate mathematical foundations, methods, and tools were recognized, and a suitable research agenda was set for software engineering to tame those risks.

This paper is structured as follows. In Section 2, we introduce some some general concepts about network computing. In sections 3 and 4 we look into two specific important areas of the network computing domain: the World Wide Web and applications based on mobile code. For these two areas, we discuss what the main risks are and outline a possible research agenda. This is not meant to be an exhaustive account of what is needed, but rather reflects a subjective viewpoint that is based on our work and some initial results that have been achieved by our research group at Politecnico di Milano. Section 5 draws some conclusions and outlines future work.

2 Network Computing

The term network computing (or "Internet computing") is difficult to define precisely. The term is often used informally to denote the research efforts, technologies, products, and services that exploit the global network, known as the Internet (for example see [19]). One may object that network computing is just another name for the "traditional" distributed computing field. This is only partially true. Indeed, network computing is based on a distributed system, composed of a set of computational nodes connected by a network and therefore several of the methods and techniques developed so far by the distributed computing research community can be viewed as foundational background for network computing. However, there are some distinguishing characteristics of network computing that make it possible to identify a research field with new, unsolved problems. These characteristics are *large scale, autonomy, heterogene-*

ity, and *mobility*, which influences both the *communication layer* and the *computational layer* of the network.

In network computing, the communication layer is a global-scale internetwork composed of autonomous subnetworks. Each subnetwork is deployed, maintained, and evolved without a centralized control. In addition, the network is composed of heterogeneous technologies: from those used to connect computers in a LAN, to those used to interconnect LANs geographically, to those used to connect mobile computing devices. The different technologies used to provide connectivity, spanning from fiber optics to different kinds of wireless connections, provide different levels of quality of services, e.g., in terms of performance and reliability. Therefore, given two communication endpoints in the network, few assumptions can be made about the type of communication that can be established. In addition, wireless technology allows computational nodes to move while remaining still connected to the net. This supports mobile users, who may be using laptops or personal digital assistants (PDAs). Therefore, the protocols used to transfer data across the network must cope with topologies that may change dynamically.

The computational layer is the infrastructure that is responsible for supporting the execution of applications. This layer is composed of the network nodes and the operating system software associated with these nodes. Nodes are organized in clusters administered by different autonomous authorities, each with different objectives, access procedures, and use policies. In addition, the computational infrastructure includes heterogeneous platforms, ranging from PCs to workstation and mainframes. Therefore, a global-scale computational layer must be based on mechanisms that can be deployed on very diverse hardware and software platforms. The heterogeneous nature of the computational layer becomes more evident when support to mobile computations must be provided. In this case there is a need for mechanisms that allow execution of the same code on different platforms.

Network computing applications exploit the global-scale infrastructure provided by the communication and computational layer to provide services to distant users and to access resources that are dispersed across a large set of hosts. Based on a highly autonomous infrastructure, these applications tend to be autonomous themselves. This means that either a service is delivered to a user through the interaction of different autonomous components that are managed by different authorities (the World-Wide Web follows this approach), or that an application belonging to an administrative subdomain in the network can move to other domains to achieve its goals. These kinds of mobile applications are often called "mobile agents" or "software agents".

The potential of this pervasive and ubiquitous infrastructure is enormous, and it is quite difficult to anticipate the way it will evolve and how far it will go. New applications and new services are announced almost every day. Although in many cases they promise more than what they actually deliver, the speed and complexity of the evolution are such that they are difficult to dominate. It is therefore important to build a coherent framework of principles, abstractions, methods, and tools that allow network computing to be understood and practiced in a systematic fashion [11]. We claim that these are the challenges that software engineering must face in this context.

At the foundational level, we need to identify the theories that are needed to describe, reason about, and analyze network computations, where the topology and structure of the computing layer changes dynamically, while users and computations can move. From a methodology viewpoint, we need to identify process models that are suitable for describing and managing application developments for the new computing infrastructure, where applications grow in a largely independent way, no precise pre-planning is possible, and evolution/reconfiguration are the norm in an inherently chaotic, self-regulating environment.

As far as technology is concerned, we need to define a common set of mechanisms and service infrastructures that enable exploitation of the potential of a world-wide computing system in a effective, secure way. In addition, we need to understand what are the new programming language abstractions and mechanisms that are suitable for the implementation of network computing applications.

This wide spectrum of problems provides a real challenge for software engineering research. A number of efforts are already in place, but much more focused work is needed. In the next section we focus on the problem of supporting the development of World Wide Web sites. In Section 4 we describe some work on supporting developers of mobile code applications. The efforts we describe in this paper are only a small sample of what could be done in this field.

3 Software Engineering for WWW Applications

From its introduction in 1990 [3], the World Wide Web (WWW) has been evolving at a fast pace. The number of WWW sites is increasing as Internet users realize the benefits that stem from a globally interconnected hypermedia system. Each site, in fact, provides structured information as an intertwined net of hypertext resources; links can point both to local resources and to non-local resources belonging to other Web sites, thus providing a way to navigate from local to geographically distributed information sources. Companies, organizations, and academic institutions exploit the WWW infrastructure to provide customers and users with information and services.

The expectations of both providers and consumers are driving R&D efforts aimed at improving the WWW technology. Examples are represented by the introduction of active contents in static hypertext pages by means of languages like Java [16] and JavaScript [10] and by the use of the Servlet technology [22] to customize the behavior of Web servers. This technological evolution has promoted a shift in the intended use of the WWW. The Web infrastructure is going beyond the mere distribution of information and services; it is becoming a platform for generic, distributed applications in a world-wide setting.

This promising scenario is endangered by the lack of quality of many existing WWW-based applications. Although there is no well-defined and widely accepted notion of Web quality (and indeed, this would be a valuable research objective in its own), our claim is based on the following common observations that can be made as WWW users:

1. we know that a required piece of information is available in a certain WWW site, but we keep navigating through a number of pages without finding it;
2. we get lost in our navigation, i.e., we do not understand where we are in our search;
3. navigation style is not uniform (for example, the "next page in the list" link is in the bottom right corner for some pages, and in the top left corner for others);
4. we continuously encounter broken links;
5. the data we find are outdated (for example, we find the announcement of a "future" event that has already occurred);
6. duplicated information is inconsistent (for example, in a university Web site providing pages in two language versions, say English and Italian, the same instructor has different office hours).

This is only a sample list. Items 4 to 6 of the list can be defined as flaws; they affect "correctness" of the Web site. The others are related to style issues, and affect usability. Furthermore, even if we start from a Web site that does not exhibit these weaknesses, these are likely to occur as soon as the Web site undergoes modifications. Thus, maintenance of legacy Web sites becomes increasingly difficult, and Web site quality decreases. If we try to understand what the causes of these inconveniences are, we realize that they all stem from the lack of application of systematic design principles and the use of inadequate (low-level) tools during development.

Most current Web site designs are not guided by systematic design methodologies and do not follow well-defined development processes. Rather, they proceed in a unstructured, *ad hoc* manner. Developers focus too early, and predominantly, on low-level mechanisms that enable, for example, particular visual effects, without focusing on who the expected users are, what the conceptual contents of the information is, and how the information should be structured. In particular, they rarely focus on the underlying conceptual model of the information that will be made available through the Web. The lack of a conceptual model becomes evident to the users, who find it difficult to search the Web to retrieve the data they are interested in. In addition, even if a conceptual model of the information to be published has been developed, no design guidance nor adequate abstractions are available to help Web developers move down systematically towards an implementation, possibly being supported by suitable tools.

This situation reminds us of the childhood of software development when applications were developed without methodological support, without the right tools, simply based on good common sense and individual skills. WWW site development suffers from a similar problem. Most Web site developers delve directly into the implementation phase, paying little or no attention to such aspects as requirements acquisition, specification, and design. Too often, implementation is performed by using a low-level technology, such as the Hypertext

Markup Language (HTML) [24]. Using the analogy with conventional software development, this approach corresponds to implementing applications through direct mapping of very informal designs (if any) into an assembly-level language. Furthermore, the lack of suitable abstractions makes it difficult to reuse previously developed artifacts, or to develop frameworks that capture the common structure of classes of applications and allow for fast development by customization. Finally, the management of the resulting Web site is difficult and error prone, because change tracking and structural evolution must be performed directly at the implementation level. This problem is particularly critical since WWW sites, by their very nature, are subject to frequent updates and even redesigns.

Software engineering research has provided methods for requirements acquisition, languages and methods for specification, design paradigms, technologies (such as object-oriented programming languages), and tools (e.g., integrated development environments) that provide systematic support to the software development process. In principle, their availability should help software developers to deliver quality products in a timely and cost-effective manner. A similar approach has to be followed in order to bring WWW development out of its immaturity. The next two subsections discuss a possible solution to these problems by analyzing the characteristics of Web site development process and by introducing a tool that aims at providing systematic support for the development process.

3.1 A WWW Software Process

The benefits of a well-defined and supported software process are well known [14]. As for conventional software, the development of a Web site should be decomposed into a number of phases: requirements analysis and specification, design, implementation. After the site has been implemented and delivered, its structure and contents are maintained and evolved. By identifying these phases of the development process we do not imply any specific development process structure. Different process models (waterfall, spiral, prototype-based) can be accommodated in the framework. Actually, the continuous and rapid changes in business, which will be reflected in the evolution of the corresponding WWW sites, is likely to favor flexible process life cycles, based on rapid prototyping and continuous refinement. In the sequel, we briefly and informally outline the possible objectives of the different phases of WWW development, based on our own experience.

Requirements Analysis and Specification During requirements analysis, the developer collects the needs of the stakeholders, in terms of contents, structuring, access, and layout. Contents requirements define the domain-specific information that must be made available through the Web site. Structuring requirements specify how contents must be organized. This includes the definition of *relationships* and *views*. Relationships highlight semantic connections among contents. For example, relationships could model generalization (*is-a*), composition (*is-composed-of*), or domain-dependent relationships. Views are perspectives on information structures that "customize" contents and relationships according to different use situations. Different views of the same contents could be provided to different classes of users (e.g., an abstract of a document can be made accessible to "external" users, while the complete document can be made accessible to "internal" users). Access requirements define the style of information access that must be provided by the Web site. This includes priorities on information presentation, indexing of contents, query facilities, and support for guided tours over sets of related information. Layout requirements define the general appearance properties of the Web site, such as emphasis on graphic effects vs. text-based layouts. Based on our experience, we argue that existing tools supporting requirements specification and traceability of requirements through all development artifacts can be used in this context too. Further research is needed to extend the above framework and to identify the additional specific features that a tool supporting requirements for Web based applications should exhibit.

Design Based on the requirements, the design phase defines the overall structure of a WWW site describing how information is organized and how users can navigate across it. A careful design activity should highlight the fundamental constituents of a site; it should abstract away from low-level implementation details, and should allow the designer to identify recurring structures and navigation patterns to be reused [13]. As such, a good design can survive frequent changes in the implementation, fostered by —say— the appearance of new technologies.

Being largely implementation-independent, the design activity can be carried out using notations and methodologies that are not primarily Web-oriented. Any design methodology for hypermedia applications could be used; e.g., HDM [12], RMDM [2], or OOHDM [25]. Our experience is based on the adoption of the HDM (Hypertext Design Model) notation [12].

In designing a hypermedia application, HDM distinguishes between the *hyperbase layer* and the *access layer*. The hyperbase layer is the backbone of the application and models the information structures that represent the domain, while the access layer provides entry points to access the hyperbase constituents. The hyperbase consists of *entities* connected by *application links*. Entities are structured pieces of information. They are used to represent conceptual or physical objects of the application domain. An example of an entity in a literature application is "Writer". Application links are used to describe domain-specific, non-structural relationships among different entities (e.g., an application link from a "writer" to the "novels" he or she wrote). Entities are structured into *components*, i.e., clusters of information that are perceived by the user as conceptual units (for example, a writer's "biography").

Complex components can be structured recursively in terms of other components. Information contained in components is modeled by means of *nodes*.

Usually, components contain just one node, but more than one node can be used to give different or alternative views (*perspectives*, in HDM) of the component information (e.g., to describe a book's review in different languages, or to present it in a "short" vs. an "extended" version). Navigation paths inside an entity are defined by means of *structural links*, which represent structural relationships among components. Structural links may, for example, define a tree structure that allows the user to move from a root component (for example, the data-sheet for a novel) to any other component of the same entity (e.g., credits, summary, reviews, etc.)

Once entities and components are specified, as well as their internal and external relationships, the access layer defines a set of *collections* that provide users with the structures to access the hyperbase. A collection groups a number of *members*, to make them accessible. Members can be either hyperbase elements or other collections (nested collections). Each collection owns a special component called *collection center* that represents the starting point of the collection. Examples of collections are *guided tours*, which support linear navigation across members (through next/previous, first/last links), or indexes, where the navigation pattern is from the center to the members and vice versa. For example, a guided tour can be defined to navigate across all horror novels; another one can represent a survey of 14th century European writers.

Implementation The implementation phase creates an actual Web site from the site design. As a first step, the elements and relationships highlighted during design are mapped onto the constructs provided by the chosen implementation technology. As a second step, the site is populated. The actual information is inserted by instantiating the structures defined in the previous step and the cross-references representing structural and application links among the elements. Collections are then created to provide structured access to the hyperbase contents. The third step is delivery. The site implementation must be made accessible using standard WWW technologies, namely Web browsers like Netscape's Navigator or Microsoft's Internet Explorer that interact with Web servers using the Hypertext Transfer Protocol (HTTP). This can be achieved by publishing the site implementation into a set of files and directories that are served by a number of "standard" WWW servers (also called *http daemons* in the UNIX jargon).

The standard tools available today to implement Web sites are rather low-level and semantically poor. The basic abstractions available to Web developers are:

- HTML pages, i.e., text files formatted using a low-level markup language;
- directories, i.e., containers of pages; and
- references, i.e., strings of text embedded in HTML tags that denote a resource (e.g., an HTML page) using a common naming scheme.

There are neither systematic methods nor linguistic constructs to map the types that define the semantics of the application domain (entities) onto implementation-level types (pages). There are no constructs to define complex information structures, like sets of pages with particular navigational patterns, such as lists of pages or indexes. These structured sets of information must be realized manually by composing the existing constructs and primitives. In addition, there is no way to create document templates and mechanisms to extend existing structures by customization. The development of a set of documents exhibiting the same structure is carried out in an ad hoc manner by customizing sample prototypes manually. There are no constructs or mechanisms to specify different views of the same information and to present these views depending on the access context. This hampers effective reuse of information. The only form of reuse is by copy. Some authoring tools like Microsoft's FrontPage [6] and NetObject's Fusion [18] try to overcome some of these limitations by providing a site-level view on the information hyperbase. Nonetheless, these tools are strictly based on the low-level concepts of HTML pages and directories. Therefore, the developer is faced with a gap between the high-level concepts defined during design and the low-level constructs available for implementation.

Maintenance The situation described above worsens in the maintenance phase. Web sites have an inherently dynamic nature. Contents and their corresponding structural organization may be changed continuously. Therefore, maintenance is a crucial phase, even more than in the case of conventional software applications. As in conventional software, we can classify Web site maintenance into three categories: *corrective*, *adaptive*, and *perfective* maintenance [14]. Corrective maintenance is the process of correcting errors that exist in the Web site implementation. Examples are represented by internal dangling references, errors in the indexing of resources, or access to outdated information (as in the case of published data with an expiration date). Adaptive maintenance involves adjusting the Web site to changes in the outside environment. A notable example is represented by verification of the references to documents and resources located at different sites. Outbound links become dangling as a consequence of events over which the site developer has no control. Thus, adaptive maintenance is a continuous process. Perfective maintenance involves changing the Web site in order to improve the way contents are structured or presented to the end user. Changes may be fostered by the introduction of new information or by the availability of new technologies. Perfective maintenance should reflect updates to the requirements and design documents. Maintenance in general, and perfective maintenance in particular, is by far the activity that takes most of the development effort.

Presently, Web site maintenance is carried out using tools like link verifiers or syntax checkers that operate directly on the low-level Web site implementation. This approach may be suitable for some cases of corrective and adaptive maintenance, but does not provide effective support for tasks that involve knowledge of the high-level structure of the Web site. For example, since reuse is achieved by copy, modifying a reused component, like a recurring introduction paragraph for a number of documents, involves the identification of every use of the component and its consistent update. In a similar way, modification of the structure or style of a set of similar documents requires updates in all instances. For example, if we decide that the background color of the summary page of all "horror" novels must be changed to purple, this requires consistent change of all files representing these summaries. More generally, since perfective maintenance may require modification of the structure and organization of information, it should be supported by a structural view of the site and of the relationships between design elements and their implementation constructs. These relationships are of paramount importance because they allow the developer to reflect design changes onto the implementation and vice versa. Standard Web technologies do not provide the means to represent these relationships and the high-level organization of information. Another problem concerns maintenance of hypertext references. In the standard WWW technology, references are just strings embedded inside the HTML code of pages; they do not have the status of first-class objects. Therefore, their management and update is an error-prone activity.

3.2 The WOOM Approach

A number of research efforts are currently being developed to improve the methods and tools supporting WWW developments, trying to solve some of the critical issues discussed in the previous section. It will not be possible to provide a comprehensive view of such efforts here. Rather, we will bring to the readers' attention what we are currently doing in our group to support Web design, as an example of a research effort that tries to address some of the previously identified problems. In this project, we developed a WWW object-oriented modeling framework, called WOOM — *Web Object Oriented Model*. WOOM provides concepts, abstractions, and tools that help in the mapping from high-level design of a Web site (e.g., in HDM) into an implementation that uses "standard" WWW technology.

More precisely, WOOM offers three main modeling environments: a *design environment*, an *implementation environment*, and a *presentation environment*. In the design environment the developer designs the conceptual model of the information to be published through the Web site. WOOM provides a set of predefined classes that allow designs to be built following the HDM methodology. In the implementation environment the developer implements a Web site leveraging off of an object-oriented model. This model provides high-level constructs to implement the information architecture defined in the design environment. Relationships between design elements and implementation constructs are maintained explicitly to allow for change tracking and consistent updating. In the presentation environment the developer is provided with mechanisms to customize and put into context the user's view on the site contents. This is achieved by means of a dynamic publishing process.

In the following, we provide some details of the Web site model and the publishing process, which constitute the core elements of the implementation and presentation environment, respectively.

A Web Site Model According to WOOM, a Web site can be defined in terms of *components*, *links*, *sites* and *servers*.

Components are the fundamental entities of the model. They model the contents and structure of a collection of information. In WOOM there are many types of components that differ in granularity, in the type of information they represent, and in the role they play in the model. For instance, a component can be the whole contents of a site, a single hypertext page, an icon, or even a single word. In WOOM all the component types are organized by the inheritance relationship in a class hierarchy, whose root is the **Component** class. The hierarchy can be extended by developers to define new types of components. WOOM provides a predefined set of components types that can be distinguished into *resources*, *elements*, and *containers*.

Resources are the units of information. They are distinguished into *opaque resources* and *hyper pages*. Opaque resources are unstructured resources. Subclasses of this class are *images*, i.e., graphic objects, *applets*, i.e., programs that are activated on the client side, *scripts*, i.e., applications that are activated on the server side, and *external*. External resources are those types of information that are not directly supported by the current Web technology and are managed by means of external helper applications. These resources include audio and video information, PostScript files, binaries, and other similar entities. Hyper pages are hypertext pages, which may contain text, anchors, and references to pictures, sounds, and animations. HTML pages are a special kind of hyper pages.

The contents of a hyper page are modeled by a ordered list of *elements*. An element is an information fragment, like a text paragraph, an anchor, or a dotted list. Elements can be simple or complex. Simple elements are atomic data containers, while complex elements contain an ordered list of other elements. WOOM provides a predefined set of elements that model the elements of the HTML standard. For example, the image placeholder element (IMG) is a simple element, while the BODY element may be composed of some paragraphs, a table, etc.

Containers are collectors of resources. They are composed of an ordered list of components that can be resources or other containers. Containers are used by the site developer to define contexts or to organize other components in macro-objects that can be managed as a whole. WOOM provides a number of predefined container types: *lists*, *trees*, *indexes*, and *sets*. Lists organize the enclosed resources in a linear fashion. They are used to represent a sequential relationship inside a group of resources (e.g., the pages that compose a guided tour through the novels of a given writer). Trees impose a hierarchical structure to the enclosed resources. For example, the novels of a given writer can be classified into genres: horror, science fiction, etc.; science fiction novels, in turn, can be classified into, say genetics, astronomy, etc. Indexes organize the contained resources in two-level trees. For example, an author's novels can be grouped into "youth", "maturity", and "late" novels. Sets are simply used to group resources without any specific relationship among them, but characterized by some common visual or semantic property. Each container type exports an interface that allows other entities to access the enclosed resources without exposing the container's internal implementation details. Additional container types can be defined by the Web developer by extending the WOOM framework.

The containment relationship among containers, resources, and elements defines an ordered DAG in which compound components are nodes and atomic components are leaves. In a given DAG, there is a component that is not enclosed by others: it is called the DAG root. In general, a component can belong to more than one component, and there cannot be circular containment relationships. This is different from the existing Web technology in which files can be included in more than one directory only by using links in the file system. In WOOM even a single word can be shared by different hyper pages.

Every component object has an identifier. Components belonging to the same compound component cannot have the same identifier. Components are uniquely identified a pathname. The pathname for a component is the description of the path that must be followed to reach the component starting from the DAG root. The pathname is a string obtained by concatenating the identifiers of the components that constitute the path. This identification mechanism is similar to the well-known naming scheme based on pathnames adopted by file systems. A component can be identified by one or more pathnames. Each pathname is a different chain of enclosing components and identifies a different context for the component. As it will be explained later, contexts are an important concept in the WOOM model. When the information consumer requests the contents of a component, he/she specifies also one of the contexts for the component. The publishing process that produces the external representation of the component delivered to the user provides a different result on the basis of the chosen context. Thus, the same component information is "contextualized" in different ways.

Links model the navigational connections between components. Links are objects that associate a source component with a destination component within a particular context. Context information must be taken into account when creating links because a component in different contexts may assume different forms. By keeping track of the context of the destination component, WOOM links may lead to a particular version of the component. WOOM links are different from standard HTML links in two ways. First, they are first-class objects whereas in HTML links are just strings of text embedded in the HTML anchor element. Second, links can reference any component, e.g., a hyper page or a text paragraph inside a hyper page, whereas in standard HTML links may only refer to files in the file system.

Sites and servers model the mechanisms that allow the information consumer to access the components' data. A site is composed of a component DAG and one or more servers. The servers are used to define the network access points to the site contents. A server corresponds, at run-time, to an HTTP daemon process that replies to the end user's requests for components belonging to the site. Each server is characterized by a unique address and has an associated container and context that limit the scope of the components that are accessible through the server. For instance, the information contained in a Web site could be made accessible by means of two servers that are associated with two containers such that one is not the ancestor of the other in the site's DAG. Therefore, they provide access to resources that are in different contexts and the information spaces served by the two servers are cleanly separated even if there may be some components that can be accessed by both servers.

Delivering Information to the User The end-user accesses the Web site contents by requesting a component from a server. The particular component is specified by means of a path in the Web site's DAG. The server replies providing an *external representation*, or *view*, of the component's contents. The external representation is the result of a recursive publishing process that propagates in a top-down fashion from the DAG's root to the component to be published, along the path specified in the request. Before detailing the process, two WOOM mechanisms must be introduced: *transformers* and *viewers*.

Transformers are objects with an associated state and a *transform* operation that takes as parameter a component object. The transform operation modifies the component passed as parameter and eventually returns it. Transformer objects are associated with component objects in the site's DAG. A transformer associated with object O influences the publishing process of O and of all its sub-components. WOOM provides a set of predefined transformers, e.g., transformers to publish only specific parts of a component, or to add some navigational garnishment to components that are part of containers such as lists or indexes. The set of available transformers can be extended by the Web site developer.

Viewers are responsible for building the external representation of components. When a component is passed to a viewer, the viewer uses the component's data (i.e., the values of its attributes) and the external representation of its sub-components to create the component view that will be delivered to the user. WOOM provides several generic viewers that are able to produce a simple external representation for WOOM's predefined components. The Web site developer must provide viewers for any new component types introduced in the component hierarchy.

Transformers and viewers are the key mechanisms in the two phases of the publishing process, namely the *transformation process* and the *translation process*.

The transformation process is responsible for modifying the information structure according to the user's access context. Let us consider a user request for a component, say C, identified by the path $A \mapsto B \mapsto C$ in the component DAG. For the sake of simplicity, we assume that the server that received the request is associated with the DAG root (A). The publishing process starts by applying the transformation process to A. A recursively invokes the process on B, and finally B invokes the process on C. Transformers are propagated as parameters in the chain of invocations. Suppose that a transformer t_A is associated with A, and transformers t_B^1 and t_B^2 are associated with B. Therefore, A invokes the transformation process on B passing t_A as a parameter. Then, B invokes the transformation process on C passing as parameters t_A, t_B^1, and t_B^2.

The transformation process for a component follows a fixed schema. First, a shallow copy of the component is created. This copy is passed to the first transformer in the list received during the transformation invocation. The transformer modifies the copied object depending on its own state and the values of the object's attributes. The modified object is then passed to the transform method of the next transformer, until the last transformer has been applied. If the returned object is non-null then the transformation process is propagated to every contained component object. This way, the publishing process takes into account the context (i.e., the path) in which the object is accessed.

Once the transformers have modified the DAG[1] according to the context, a similar process is performed to translate the requested component object into an external representation. The translation process starts from the DAG root (A) and is recursively invoked until it reaches the requested component (C). The chain of invocations propagates the viewers from the root to the specified component. From that point on the process is invoked on any subcomponent to produce the corresponding external representation. These representations are then used to produce the external representation of the requested component. For example, suppose that C has two sub-components D and E. In addition, suppose that B is associated with viewer v_B and C is associated with viewer v_C. Then the translation process is the following: A invokes the translation on B. B invokes the translation on C passing as parameter its viewer, v_B. C invokes the translation on D and E passing as parameters v_B and v_C. Since D and E are leaves of the DAG, the recursion stops and one viewer is applied to obtain the external representation. The most specific viewer is chosen among those that have been propagated by the publishing process. If no viewers are present, the default one is used. Then, the external representations of D and E are returned. A viewer is then applied to C, passing as parameters the external representation of D and E. The result is the external representation of C. This result is passed back to the chain of recursive invocation without modifications, and it is eventually delivered to the user that requested the component.

This general publishing mechanism is used to contextualize and customize the presentation of information. For instance, consider a hyper page describing a novel (e.g., Primo Levi's *La Tregua*) that is placed in two containers. The first container is a list enclosing all the novels of a particular genre (e.g., "holocaust" novels). The second is a set collecting the novels of the same writer (e.g., Levi's books). In the first context the page must be modified to include information that highlight the relationship between the novel and the genre, and links to navigate inside the list. In the latter context, the resource must be modified to include references to the author's biography. This is achieved by associating two different transformers with the two containers. Depending on the access context (the publishing path) only one of the transformers will be applied to the hyper

---

[1] Note that since transformers are applied to copies of resources and elements, the original entities defined by the site developer are not modified.

page, resulting in the "customized" version. Since this done automatically by the publication tool, consistency is automatically preserved (only one instance of the writer's data is kept), and maintenance is greatly facilitated.

An important result of this approach is that it clearly separates the description of the data from the way the data are presented to the user. The same data can be presented differently in different contexts. This separation not only helps in designing the application, but also provides support to Web site evolution.

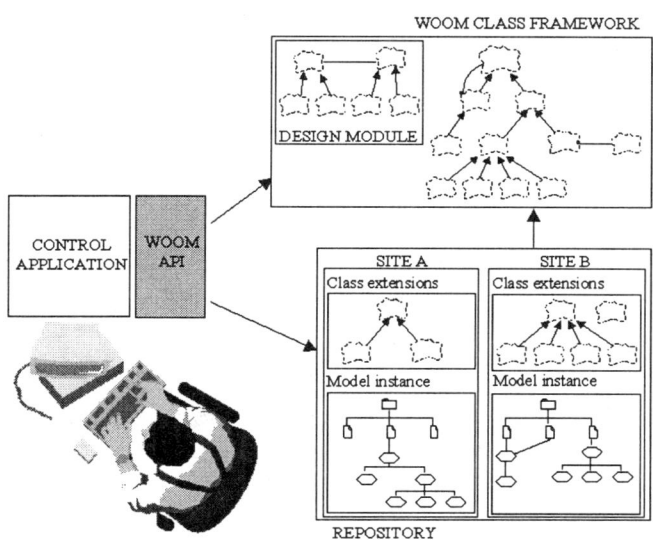

Fig. 1. The WOOM-based authoring tool.

A Tool for Web Development We developed a prototype authoring tool, written in Java, that implements the WOOM model. The tool allows the developer to use WOOM constructs to create the components in a Web site, to perform complex management operations, and to customize the publishing process that delivers a particular view of the site's information to the user. The main components of the tool are presented in Figure 1. A first component is the WOOM class framework. The framework provides the definitions of basic WOOM entities and provides some predefined constructs. The class framework provides support for representing Web site design elements into the model. This is achieved by means of an integrated, yet separate, design module. The design module is a plug-in component that provides support for a specific design notation. Currently, the HDM notation is supported. As a preliminary step in Web site implementation, the WOOM class framework is imported into the development application. Then, the developer uses the instances of the classes provided by the design module to represent the entities defined during the design phase. Once the design elements have been represented, the developer chooses which type of component will be used to implement a particular design element. To do this, the developer may use the predefined constructs offered by the WOOM class framework or may create new application-specific constructs using inheritance and composition. After suitable constructs have been identified, relationships that associate a design element with the corresponding implementation construct are created. These relationships are used in tracking changes in the implementation to the site design and vice versa. The next step consists of populating the site, by instantiating component objects of the appropriate classes, and creating application links. Structural links are automatically managed by the semantics of structured objects that implements structured design elements. Once the site has been populated, the developer specifies how contents must be presented by defining transformers, viewers, and by configuring the servers that provide access to the site's information.

Web site maintenance and management operations are performed on the WOOM model instance. The WOOM framework provides support for a set of predefined tasks like syntax checking, link updating, resource restructuring, consistency checks, shared resource management, and design change management. Web site instances, composed of site-dependent schema extensions (classes and transformers) and component objects are persistently stored in a repository module. The control application accesses the WOOM schema and instances by means of the WOOM API. The control application is a Java application that uses the primitives and services offered by the API. We are currently working on a graphical interface that allows the developer to access WOOM services in an intuitive and user-friendly way.

4 Mobile Code Applications

The global computing infrastructure realized by the Internet is still in its infancy. Even though there exist efforts to realize mechanisms to distribute the computations on a large scale (for example, CORBA [23]) there is still the need for a general-purpose, flexible, programmable infrastructure that applications can exploit to access the computing power and the resources of the hosts connected to the network. One of the most promising approaches to providing this infrastructure is represented by *Mobile Code Systems* (MCSs). MCSs allow an application to relocate part or all of its code on remote hosts, possibly together with the corresponding execution state.

MCSs are based on a common conceptual framework. In this framework, the computational infrastructure is composed of a world-wide distributed environment with several autonomous *sites* that support the computations of *agents*, that are threads of execution. Agents may change their execution site and even their code dynamically. Several MCSs, like Telescript [28], Agent Tcl [17], and Java Aglets [21] have been implemented.

The idea that software can migrate is not new. In particular, it has been exploited by several distributed systems to support load balancing. Mobile code, however, differs from distributed computing in many respects [11]. First, traditional distributed computing systems deal with a set of machines connected by a local area network, whereas in the mobile code framework mobility is exploited at a much larger scale (the Internet scale). Hosts are heterogeneous, they are managed by different authorities, and they are connected by heterogeneous links. Second, mobility is seldom supported in distributed systems. In the particular cases where it is supported, it is not provided as a feature given to the programmer to be exploited to achieve particular tasks. Rather, it is used to allow components to be automatically relocated by the system to achieve load balancing. Component relocation is not visible to the applications' programmer, since a software layer is provided on top of the network operating system to hide the concept of physical locality of software components. On the other hand, in the mobile code framework programming is location aware and mobility is under the programmer's control. Components can be moved to achieve specific goals, such as accessing resources located at remote sites.

This powerful concept originated a very interesting range of technical results recently. What is still lacking, however, is both a conceptual reference framework to describe and compare the various technical solutions and a methodological framework to support a sound development process of *Mobile Code Applications* (MCAs). In particular, we envision a process by which developers of MCAs are equipped with methods, notations, tools, techniques, and guidelines that support every phase of the development process. But much research is needed to reach this ideal stage from the current state of knowledge.

In the sequel, we illustrate some initial work done by our group in the areas of architectural design and implementation of MCAs. These phases are particularly critical because the distinction between design paradigms [5] and implementation technologies [8] is often blurred and not well understood. The goal here is to identify which are the concepts that are characteristic of architectural design, which are the issues that must be addressed during implementation, and what are the relationships between design choices and implementation choices. This way, it is possible to develop guidelines that allow the developers to select the most appropriate design paradigm for a specific application, and the most appropriate technology to implement the resulting software architecture.

4.1 Design

In the design phase the developer creates a software architecture for an application that must deliver a specified functionality. A software architecture is the decomposition of a software system in terms of software components and interactions among them [26]. Software architectures with similar patterns of interaction can be abstracted into *architectural styles* [1] or *design paradigms*, which define architectural schemas that may be instantiated into actual software architectures.

The design of MCAs is a complex task. These applications are highly dynamic from the point of view of both code and location and therefore it is necessary to take into account these concepts at the design level. We identified three prototypical design paradigms that involve code mobility: *Remote Evaluation* (REV), *Code on Demand* (COD), and *Mobile Agent* (MA). Although we cannot claim that these paradigms cover all possible design structuring styles for network-centric applications, they can be viewed as the most typical representatives.

Given two interacting components A and B of a distributed architecture, these paradigms differ in how the *know-how* of the application, i.e., the code that is necessary to accomplish a computation, the *resources*, i.e., the inputs of the computation, and the *processor*, i.e., the component responsible for the execution of the code, are distributed between the involved sites. In order to let this computation to take place, the know-how, the resources, and the component that will process the resources using the know-how have to be present at the same site. Let us assume that component A is located at site S_A and component B is located on site S_B. In addition, let A be the entity that causes the interaction and the one that is interested in its effects. Table 1 shows the distribution of the different elements before and after the interaction. The table also lists the *Client-Server* (CS) paradigm. Although CS is not a paradigm for mobile computations (no mobility of code takes place), it has been included because it is often used in designing network computing applications.

Paradigm	Before		After	
	S_A	S_B	S_A	S_B
Client-Server	**A**	know-how resources **B**	**A**	know-how resources **B**
Remote Evaluation	know-how A	resources **B**	**A**	*know-how* resources **B**
Code on Demand	resources **A**	know-how B	resources *know-how* **A**	**B**
Mobile Agent	know-how A	resources	—	*know-how* resources ***A***

Table 1. Mobile code paradigms. This table shows the location of the components before and after the service execution. For each paradigm, the component that is the processor is in bold face. Components in italics are those that have been moved.

In the CS paradigm, a server component (B in Table 1) exports a set of services. The code that implements such services is owned by the server component; thus, we say that the server holds the *know-how*. It is the server itself that executes the service; thus it is the *processor*. The client (A in Table 1) is interested in accessing some entity managed by the server, and therefore it is the server that has the *resources*.

In the REV paradigm, the executor component (B) offers its computational power (i.e., it is the *processor*) and its *resources*, but does not provide any "specific" service. It is A that sends the service code (the *know-how*) that will be executed by B in its location.

In the COD paradigm, component A initially is unable to execute its task. It is B that provides the code (i.e., the *know-how*). Once the code is received by A, the computation is carried out on A's location, thus, A is the *processor*. The computation involves only local files and local devices; thus, A holds the *resources*.

In the MA paradigm, A has the *know-how* and it is the component responsible for the execution of the task. The computation must access the *resources* that are located at B's site. Therefore, A migrates to S_B and performs the computation there.

Usually, an application (or parts thereof) may be designed following different paradigms. In principle, it would be helpful to be able to analyze the tradeoffs among the different solutions based on different paradigms at the design level, before proceeding to an implementation. For example [5] discusses a set of possible designs and evaluates their tradeoffs in the case of a distributed information retrieval application. The tradeoffs are evaluated in terms of a simple quantitative measure: network traffic. The case study shows that, in general, there is no definite winner among the different paradigms, but rather the choice depends on a number of parameters that characterize the specific problem instance.

Therefore, the developer that approaches the design of an MCA should select some parameters that describe the application behavior, together with some criteria to evaluate the parameters values. For example, one may want to minimize the number of interactions, the CPU costs, or the generated network traffic. Given different possible architectural designs, the developer should analyze the selected parameters looking for the design that optimizes the chosen criteria. This way it is possible to determine which is the most reasonable design.

4.2 Implementation

Having designed an MCA according to some paradigm, one has to choose a technology to implement it. Given a particular paradigm, which technology should be used?

We identify three classes of technologies [7]:

Message-based These technologies enable the communication between remote processes in the form of message exchange. They do not provide any native mechanism for the migration of code. A typical example is RPC [4].

Weakly mobile These technologies provide mechanisms that enable an agent to send code to be executed in a remote site together with some initialization data or to bind dynamically code downloaded from a remote site. Examples of such technologies are the *rsh* facility in UNIX, and languages like M0 [27] or Java [16].

Strongly mobile These technologies enable agents to move with their code and execution state to a different site. An example is represented by the Telescript technology.

In principle, it is possible to implement applications developed with any paradigm by using any kind of technology, given that such technologies allow for the communication between agents. However, we have found that some technologies are more suitable to implement applications designed using particular paradigms [15]. Unsuitable technologies force the developer to program, at the application level, some mobility mechanisms or force an inefficient, counter-intuitive use of the existing ones.

Technologies	Paradigms		
	CS	COD/REV	MA
Messsage-based	Well suited	Code as data Program interpretation	Code and state as data Program state restoring Program interpretation
Weakly mobile	Code is a single instruction Creates unnecessary execution threads	Well suited	State as data Program state restoring
Strongly mobile	Code is a single instruction Creates unnecessary execution units Move state back and forth	Manage migration Move state back and forth	Well suited

Table 2. Relationships among paradigms and technologies.

As shown in Table 2, message-based technologies are well suited for implementing architectures based on the CS paradigm. If they are used to implement COD-based or REV-based architectures, they force the implementation to use the basic message exchange mechanism to transfer code (viewed as data) and to program the evaluation of such code explicitly. Even worse, if message-based technologies are used to implement MA-based architectures, the programmer also has to explicitly manage state marshalling, transfer, and unmarshalling; i.e., auxiliary variables must be used to keep the state of the computation and unnatural code structures must be used to restore the state of a component after migration to a different site.

Weakly mobile technologies that allow segments of code to be executed remotely are naturally oriented towards the implementation of applications designed according to the REV and COD paradigms. These technologies provide inefficient implementations of CS architectures since they force the remote execution of segments of code composed of a single instruction. Therefore, a new thread of execution is created in order to execute this "degenerate" code. On the contrary, in order to implement applications based on the MA paradigm, the programmer has to manage, at the program level, the packing/unpacking of the variables representing the state and the restoring of the agent execution flow[2].

Strongly mobile technologies are oriented towards MA-based applications while they are not suited for implementing applications based on the CS and REV/COD paradigms. In the former case, the programmer has to "overcode" an agent in order to have it moved to the server site, execute a single operation and jump back with the results. Such implementations could be rather inefficient since the whole thread state is transmitted back and forth across the network. In the latter case, in addition to the code to be executed remotely, the implementor has to add the migration procedures. Furthermore, the state of the execution thread is to be transmitted over the network.

Summing up, technologies may reveal to be too powerful or too limited to implement a particular architecture. In the first case resources are wasted, resulting in inefficiency. In the second case, the programmer has to code all mechanisms and policies that the technology does not provide. It is therefore important to select an appropriate technology that can implement an architectural design in a natural way.

5 Conclusions

Network computing is a rapidly evolving field, which is raising much interests, both in industry and in research institutions. Indeed, it is a very promising field. Unfortunately, however, at its current stage of maturity, it is perhaps raising too many unjustified expectations. We see many interesting things being done in practice which are not backed up by adequate methods and tools. A challenge exists for software engineering research to evaluate critically how things are done today in order to identify systematic approaches to the development of network computing applications. The "just do it" approach that seems to be behind the current efforts is simply inadequate to reach the desired levels of quality standards of network applications, for example in terms of reliability and ease of change. We must, of course, keep into account what makes network applications different from most traditional applications. In particular, their intrinsic levels of flexibility, autonomy, decentralization, and continuous change that cannot be

---

[2] This is a very common situation. In fact, most existing mobile code technologies are weakly mobile, because weak mobility is easier to implement. Nonetheless, practitioners tend to think in terms of the MA paradigm. Therefore, there are many examples of mobile code applications that use awkward conditional structures to restore, at the logical level, the computational flow after migration.

pre-planned centrally. These properties must eventually be combined with the necessary discipline that allows the desired level of reliability to be reached in a measurable and economical way.

In this paper we tried to identify a possible research agenda for software engineering research in the area of network computing. We also summarized some initial work that has been done in the past few years by the Software Engineering Group at Politecnico di Milano. The work described here is the result of the joint work of several people: Antonio Carzaniga, Francesco Coda, Gianpaolo Cugola, Alfonso Fuggetta, Franca Garzotto, Gian Pietro Picco, and the authors of this paper. The results described here are only representative of some initial steps in the direction of providing systematic support for the development of network computing applications. More research is needed before we can identify a comprehensive, integrated set of useful methods and techniques, and provide tools to support them.

The authors wish to thank the participants at RTSE'97 in Bernried for very stimulating discussions and comments on the work reported here. The reviewers of the initial version of this paper provided further insightful suggestions.

References

1. G. Abowd, R. Allen, and D. Garlan. Using Style to Understand Descriptions of Software Architecture. In *Proc. of SIGSOFT'93: Foundations of Software Engineering*, December 1993.
2. V. Balasubramanian, T. Isakowitz, and E.A. Stohr. RMM: A Methodology for Structured Hypermedia Design. *Communications of the ACM*, 38(8), August 1995.
3. T. Berners-Lee, R. Cailliau, A. Luotonen, H. Frystyk Nielsen, and A. Secret. The World Wide Web. *Communications of the ACM*, 37(8), August 1994.
4. A. Birrell and B. Nelson. Implementing Remote Procedure Calls. *ACM Trans. on Computer Systems*, 2(1):29–59, February 1984.
5. A. Carzaniga, G.P. Picco, and G. Vigna. Designing Distributed Applications with Mobile Code Paradigms. In R. Taylor, editor, *Proceedings of the 19th International Conference on Software Engineering (ICSE'97)*, pages 22–32. ACM Press, 1997.
6. Microsoft Corp. FrontPage Home Page. *http://www.microsoft.com/FrontPage/*.
7. G. Cugola, C. Ghezzi, G.P. Picco, and G. Vigna. A Characterization of Mobility and State Distribution in Mobile Code Languages. In M. Mühlaüser, editor, *Special Issues in Object-Oriented Programming: Workshop Reader of the 10th European Conf. on Object-Oriented Programming ECOOP'96*. dpunkt, July 1996.
8. G. Cugola, C. Ghezzi, G.P. Picco, and G. Vigna. Analyzing Mobile Code Languages. In J. Vitek and C. Tschudin, editors, *Mobile Object Systems: Towards the Programmable Internet*, volume 1222 of *Lecture Notes on Computer Science*. Springer, April 1997.
9. E.W. Dijkstra. GOTO Statement Considered Harmful.
10. D. Flanagan. *JavaScript — The Definitive Guide*. O'Reilly & Ass., 2nd edition edition, January 1997.
11. A. Fuggetta, G.P. Picco, and G. Vigna. Understanding Code Mobility. *IEEE Transactions on Software Engineering*, 24(5), May 1998.
12. F. Garzotto, L. Mainetti, and P. Paolini. Hypermedia Design, Analysis, and Evaluation Issues. *Communications of the ACM*, 38(8), August 1995.

13. F. Garzotto, L. Mainetti, and P. Paolini. Information Reuse in Hypermedia Applications. In *Proceedings of ACM Hypertext '96*, Washington DC, March 1996. ACM Press.
14. C. Ghezzi, M. Jazayeri, and D. Mandrioli. *Fundamentals of Software Engineering.* Prentice Hall, 1991.
15. C. Ghezzi and G. Vigna. Mobile Code Paradigms and Technologies: A Case Study. In K. Rothermel and R. Popescu-Zeletin, editors, *Proceedings of the 1st International Workshop on Mobile Agents (MA '97)*, volume 1219 of *Lecture Notes on Computer Science*. Springer, April 1997.
16. J. Gosling and H. McGilton. The Java Language Environment: A White Paper. Technical report, Sun Microsystems, October 1995.
17. R.S. Gray. Agent Tcl: A transportable agent system. In *Proceedings of the CIKM Workshop on Intelligent Information Agents*, Baltimore, Md., December 1995.
18. NetObjects Inc. Fusion Home Page. *http://www.netobjects.com/*.
19. IEEE Internet Computing Magazine. IEEE Computer Society, 1997.
20. A. Kambil. Doing Business in the Wired World. *IEEE Computer*, 30(5):56–61, May 1997.
21. D.B. Lange and D.T. Chang. IBM Aglets Workbench—Programming Mobile Agents in Java. IBM Corp. White Paper, September 1996.
22. Sun Microsystems. The Java Servlet API . White Paper, 1997.
23. Object Management Group. *CORBA: Architecture and Specification*, August 1995.
24. D. Ragget, A. Le Hors, and I. Jacobs. Hypertext Markup Language 4.0 Specification. W3C Recommendation, April 1998.
25. D. Schwabe and G. Rossi. From Domain Models to Hypermedia Applications: An Object-Oriented Approach. In *Proceedings of the International Workshop on Methodologies for Designing and Developing Hypermedia Applications*, Edinburgh, September 1994.
26. M. Shaw and D. Garlan. *Software Architecture: Perspective on an Emerging Discipline.* Prentice Hall, 1996.
27. C. Tschudin. *An Introduction to the MO Messenger Language.* Univ. of Geneva, Switzerland, 1994.
28. J.E. White. Telescript Technology: Mobile Agents. In Jeffrey Bradshaw, editor, *Software Agents*. AAAI Press/MIT Press, 1996.

A Two-Layered Approach to Support Systematic Software Development

Maritta Heisel[1] and Stefan Jähnichen[2,3]

[1] Otto-von-Guericke-Universität Magdeburg, Fakultät für Informatik, Institut für Verteilte Systeme, D-39016 Magdeburg, Germany, email: heisel@cs.uni-magdeburg.de
[2] FG Softwaretechnik, Technische Universität Berlin, Sekr. FR 5-6, Franklinstr. 28/29, D-10587 Berlin, Germany, jaehn@cs.tu-berlin.de
[3] GMD FIRST, Rudower Chaussee 5, 12489 Berlin, Germany

Abstract. We present two concepts that help software engineers to perform different software development activities systematically. The concept of an *agenda* serves to represent technical process knowledge. An agenda consists of a list of steps to be performed when developing a software artifact. Each activity may have associated a schematic expression of the language in which the artifact is expressed and validation conditions that help detect errors. Agendas provide methodological support to their users, make development knowledge explicit and thus comprehensible, and they contribute to a standardization of software development activities and products.

The concept of a *strategy* is a formalization of agendas. Strategies model the development of a software artifact as a problem solving process. They form the basis for machine-supported development processes. They come with a generic system architecture that serves as a template for the implementation of support tools for strategy-based problem solving.

Keywords: Software engineering methodology, process modeling, formal methods

1 Introduction

Software engineering aims at producing software systems in a systematic and cost-effective way. Two different aspects are of importance here: first, the *process* that is followed when producing a piece of software, and second, the various intermediate *products* that are developed during that process, e.g., requirements documents, formal specifications, program code, or test cases.

To date, research on the process aspects of software engineering concentrates on the management of large software projects, whereas research on the product aspects of software engineering concentrates on developing appropriate languages to express the various software artifacts, e.g., object-oriented modeling languages, architectural description languages, specification or programming languages.

The work presented in this paper is intended to fill a gap in current software engineering technology: it introduces concepts to perform the *technical* parts of software processes in a systematic way. By ensuring that the developed products fulfill certain pre-defined quality criteria, our concepts also establish an explicit link between processes and products.

We wish to systematically exploit existing software development knowledge, i.e., the problem-related fine-grained knowledge acquired by experienced software engineers that enables them to successfully produce the different software engineering artifacts. To date, such expert knowledge is rarely made explicit. As a consequence, it cannot be re-used to support software processes and cannot be employed to educate novices. Making development knowledge explicit, on the other hand, would

- support re-use of this knowledge,
- improve and speed up the education of novice software engineers,
- lead to better structured and more comprehensible software processes,
- make the developed artifacts more comprehensible for persons who have not developed them,
- allow for more powerful machine support of development processes.

Agendas and *strategies* help achieve these goals. An agenda gives guidance on how to perform a specific software development activity. It informally describes the different steps to be performed. Agendas can be used to structure quite different activities in different contexts.

Strategies are a formalization of agendas. They aim at machine supported development processes. The basic idea is to model software development tasks as problem solving processes. Strategies can be implemented and supplied with a generic architecture for systems supporting strategy-based problem solving.

Figure 1 shows the relation between agendas and strategies. First, the development knowledge used by experienced software engineers must be made explicit. Expressed as an agenda, it can be employed to develop software artifacts independently of machine support. If specialized machine support is sought for, the agenda can be formalized as a strategy. Such a formalization can be performed systematically, following a meta-agenda. Implemented strategies provide machine support for the application of the formalized knowledge to generate software artifacts. In general, the steps of an agenda correspond to subproblems of a strategy.

Agendas and strategies are especially suitable to support the application of formal techniques in software engineering. Formal techniques have the advantage that one can positively guarantee that the product of a development step enjoys certain semantic properties. In this respect, formal techniques can lead to an improvement in software quality that cannot be achieved by traditional techniques alone.

In the following two sections, we present agendas and strategies in more detail. Related work is discussed in Section 4, and conclusions are drawn in Section 5.

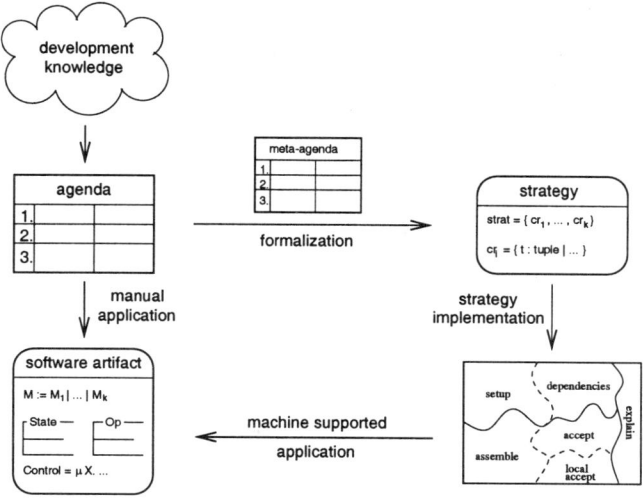

Fig. 1. Relation between agendas and strategies

2 Agendas

An agenda is a list of steps to be performed when carrying out some task in the context of software engineering. The result of the task will be a document expressed in a certain language. Agendas contain informal descriptions of the steps. With each step, schematic expressions of the language in which the result of the activity is expressed can be associated. The schematic expressions are instantiated when the step is performed. The steps listed in an agenda may depend on each other. Usually, they will have to be repeated to achieve the goal.

Agendas are not only a means to guide software development activities. They also support quality assurance because the steps of an agenda may have validation conditions associated with them. These validation conditions state necessary semantic conditions that the artifact must fulfill in order to serve its purpose properly. When formal techniques are applied, the validation conditions can be expressed and proven formally. Since the validation conditions that can be stated in an agenda are necessarily application independent, the developed artifact should be further validated with respect to application dependent needs.

2.1 An Agenda for Formally Specifying Safety-Critical Software

To illustrate the agenda concept, we present a concrete agenda that supports the formal specification of software for safety-critical applications. Because we want to give the readers a realistic impression of agendas, we present the agenda unabridged and give a brief explanation of the important aspects of software system safety and the language and methodology we use to specify safety-critical software.

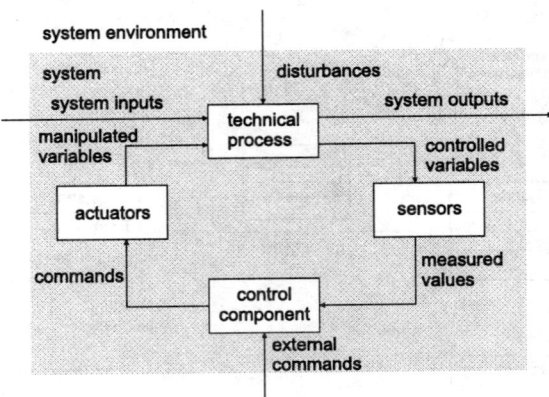

Fig. 2. System Model

The systems we consider in the following, see Figure 2, consist of a technical process that is controlled by dedicated system components being at least partially realized by software. Such a system consists of four parts: the *technical process*, the *control component*, *sensors* to communicate information about the current state of the technical process to the control component, and *actuators* that can be used by the control component to influence the behavior of the technical process.

Two aspects are important for the specification of software for safety-critical systems. First, it must be possible to specify behavior, i.e. how the system reacts to incoming events. Second, the structure of the system's data state and the operations that change this state must be specified. We use a combination of the process algebra real-time CSP [Dav93] and the model-based specification language Z [Spi92] to specify these different aspects.

In [Hei97,HS96] we have described the following principles of the combination of both languages in detail: For each system operation Op specified in the Z part of a specification, the CSP part is able to refer to the events $OpInvocation$ and $OpTermination$. For each input or output of a system operation defined in Z, there is a communication channel within the CSP part onto which an input value is written or an output value is read from. The dynamic behavior of a software component may depend on the current internal system state. To take this requirement into account, a process of the CSP part is able to refer to the current internal system state via predicates which are specified in the Z part by schemas.

There are several ways to design safety-critical systems, according to the manner in which activities of the control component take place, and the manner in which system components trigger these activities. These different approaches to the design of safety-critical systems are expressed as *reference architectures*.

We present an agenda for a reference architecture where all sensors are passive, i.e., they cannot trigger activities of the control component, and their measurements are permanently available. This architecture is often used for monitoring systems, i.e., for systems whose primary function is to guarantee safety. Examples are the control component of a steam boiler whose purpose it is to ensure that the water level in the steam boiler never leaves certain safety limits, or an inert gas release system, whose purpose is to detect and extinguish fire.

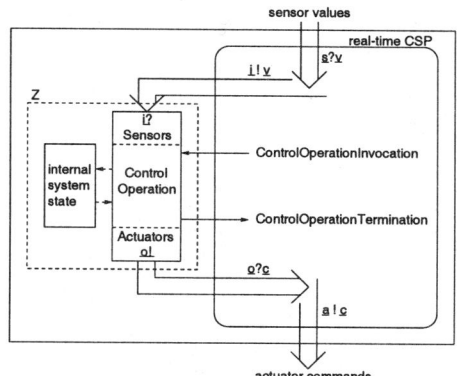

Fig. 3. Software Control Component for Passive Sensors Architecture

Figure 3 shows the structure of a software control component associated with the passive sensors architecture. Such a control component contains a single control operation, which is specified in Z, and which is executed at equidistant points of time. The sensor values $\underline{v}$ coming from the environment are read by the CSP control process and passed on to the Z control operation as inputs. The Z control operation is then invoked by the CSP process, and after it has terminated, the CSP control process reads the outputs of the Z control operation, which form the commands $\underline{c}$ to the actuators. Finally, the CSP control process passes the commands on to the actuators.

Agendas are presented as tables with the following entries for each step:
- a numbering for easy reference,
- an informal description of the purpose of the step,
- a schematic expression that proposes how to express the result of the step in the language used to express the document,
- possibly some informal or formal validation conditions that help detect errors.

The agenda for the passive sensors architecture is presented in Tables 1 and 2, where informal validation conditions are marked "∘", and formal validation conditions are marked "⊢". The dependencies between the steps are shown in Figure 4.

The agenda gives instructions on how to proceed in the specification of a software-based control component according to the chosen reference architecture. We briefly explain its steps.

No.	Step	Schematic Expressions	Validation Conditions
1	Model the sensor values and actuator commands as members of Z types.	$Type ::= \ldots$	
2	Decide on the operational modes of the system.	$MODE ::= Mode1 \mid \ldots \mid ModeK$	
3	Define the internal system states and the initial states.	$\begin{array}{\|l}\hline \textit{InternalSystemState} \\ \hline mode : MODE \\ \ldots \\ \hline \end{array}$ $\begin{array}{\|l}\hline \textit{InternalSystemStateInit} \\ \hline \textit{InternalSystemState}' \\ \ldots \\ \hline \end{array}$	○ The internal system state must be an appropriate approximation of the state of the technical process. ⊢ The internal state must contain a variable corresponding to the operational mode. ○ Each legal state must be safe. ⊢ There must exist legal initial states. ○ The initial internal states must adequately reflect the initial external system states.
4	Specify an internal Z operation for each operational mode.	$Sensors \;\widehat{=}\;$ $[InternalSystemState;$ $in1? : SType1; \ldots; inN? : STypeN \mid$ $\langle consistency\ /\ redundancy \rangle]$ $Actuators \;\widehat{=}\;$ $[InternalSystemState';$ $out1! : AType1; \ldots; outM! : ATypeM \mid$ $\langle derivation\ of\ commands \rangle]$ $OpModeJ \;\widehat{=}\; [\Delta InternalSystemState;$ $Sensors;\ Actuators \mid \ldots]$	⊢ The only precondition of the operation corresponding to a mode is that the system is in that mode. ⊢ For each operational mode and each combination of sensor values there must be exactly one successor mode. ⊢ Each operational mode must be reachable from an initial state. ⊢ There must not be any redundant modes.

Table 1. Agenda for the passive sensors architecture, part 1

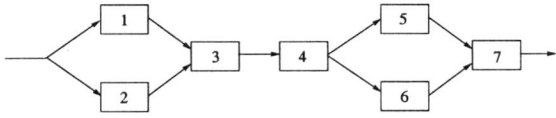

Fig. 4. Dependencies of steps of agenda for passive sensors architecture

Step 1 The defined types depend on the technical properties of the sensors and actuators. If the sensor is a thermometer, the corresponding type will be a subset of the integers. If the sensor can only distinguish a few values, the corresponding type will be an enumeration of these values. The same principles are applied to model the actuators.

Step 2 We assume that the controller is always in one of the operational modes $Mode1, \ldots, ModeK$ that are defined with respect to the needs of the technical process. The operational modes are defined as an enumeration type in Z.

Step 3 In this step, the legal internal states of the software component must be defined by means of a Z schema. The components of the internal state must be defined such that, for each time instant, they approximate the state of the technical process in a sufficiently accurate way. The state invariant defines the relations between the components. It comprises the safety-related requirements as well as the functional properties of the legal states. Initial states[1] must be specified, too.

Step 4 We must now specify how the state of the system can evolve. When new sensor values are read, the internal state must be updated accordingly. Each internal Z operation $OpModeJ$ specifies the successor mode of the current mode $ModeJ$ and the commands that have to be given to the actuators, according to the sensor values. It is normally useful to define separate schemas for the sensor values and actuator commands according to the schematic expressions $Sensors$ and $Actuators$. The internal Z operations then import these schemas.

Step 5 The central control operation defined in Z is a case distinction according to the operational modes. By importing the schemas $Sensors$ and $Actuators$ the operation has all inputs from the sensors at its disposition, and it is guaranteed that all actuator commands are defined. The inputs and the current operational mode determine the successor mode which is specified by the internal operations $OpModeI$.

Step 6 The real-time CSP control process first initializes the system, establishing an initial state. Then, the recursive process $ControlComponent_{READY}$ is executed. This process first reads all sensor values from the respective channels $(sensor1, \ldots, sensorN)$ in parallel. This is modeled using the parallel composition operator $\|$. Then it invokes the control operation. When the control operation has terminated, all output values are written to the

---

[1] The schema decoration S' of a schema S is obtained by replacing all declared variables $v_1, v_2, \ldots$ in S by their "primed" versions $v'_1, v'_2, \ldots$ of the variables. S and S' denote the state before and after execution of an operation, respectively.

respective actuator channels ($actuator1, \ldots, actuatorM$) in parallel. The process *Wait INTERVAL* does not accept any event for *INTERVAL* time units and afterwards is ready to release control. The constant *INTERVAL* must be chosen large enough, to cover the time needed to read sensor the values, to execute the control operation, and to write the actuator commands. On the other hand, it must be small enough to ensure that the internal system state always is sufficiently up-to-date.

No.	Step	Schematic Expressions
5	Define the Z control operation.	─ *Control* ──────────────── $\Delta InternalSystemState$ $Sensors$; $Actuators$ ─────────── $mode = Mode1 \Rightarrow OpMode1$ $\wedge \ldots \wedge$ $mode = ModeK \Rightarrow OpModeK$
6	Specify the control process in real-time CSP.	$ControlComponent \mathrel{\hat{=}} SystemInitExec \rightarrow ControlComp_{READY}$ $ControlComp_{READY} \mathrel{\hat{=}} \mu X \bullet$ $((sensor1?valueS1 \rightarrow in1!valueS1 \rightarrow Skip \parallel \ldots \parallel$ $sensorN?valueSN \rightarrow inN!valueSN \rightarrow Skip);$ $ControlInvocation \rightarrow ControlTermination \rightarrow$ $(out1?valueA1 \rightarrow actuator1!valueA1 \rightarrow Skip \parallel \ldots \parallel$ $outM?valueAM \rightarrow actuatorM!valueAM \rightarrow Skip)$ $\parallel Wait\ INTERVAL); X$
7	Specify further requirements if necessary.	

Table 2. Agenda for the passive sensors architecture, part 2

Usually, different phases can be identified for processes expressed as an agenda. The first phase is characterized by the fact that high-level decisions have to be taken. For these decisions, no validation conditions can be stated. In our example, these are the Steps 1 and 2. In the second phase, the language templates that can be proposed are fairly general (for example, we cannot say much more than that schemas should be used to define the internal system states and the initial states), but it is possible to state a number of formal and informal validation conditions. In our example, the second phase consists of Steps 3 and 4. In the third and last phase of an agenda, the parts of the document developed in the earlier phases are assembled. This can be done in a routine or even completely automatic way. Consequently, no validation conditions are necessary for this phase. In our example, the third phase consists of Steps 5 and 6. Step 7 allows specifiers to add specification text, if this is necessary for the particular application. The example shows that

- the agenda is fairly detailed and provides non-trivial methodological support,
- the structure of the specification need not be developed by the specifier but is determined by the agenda,
- the schematic expressions proposed are quite detailed,
- the validation conditions that help avoid common errors are tailored for the reference architecture and the structure of its corresponding specification.

2.2 Agenda-Based Development

In general, working with agendas proceeds as follows: first, the software engineer selects an appropriate agenda for the task at hand. Usually, several agendas will be available for the same development activity, which capture different approaches to perform the activity. This first step requires a deep understanding of the problem to be solved. Once the appropriate agenda is selected, the further procedure is fixed to a large extent. Each step of the agenda must be performed, in an order that respects the dependencies of steps. The informal description of the step informs the software engineer about the purpose of the step. The schematic language expressions associated with the step provide the software engineer with templates that can just be filled in or modified according to the needs of the application at hand. The result of each step is a concrete expression of the language that is used to express the artifact. If validation conditions are associated with a step, these should be checked immediately to avoid unnecessary dead ends in the development. When all steps of the agenda have been performed, a product has been developed that can be guaranteed to fulfill certain application-independent quality criteria.

Agenda-based development of software artifacts has a number of characteristics:

- **Agendas make software processes explicit, comprehensible, and assessable.**
  Giving concrete steps to perform an activity and defining the dependencies between the steps make processes explicit. The process becomes comprehensible for third parties because the purpose of the various steps is described informally in the agenda.
- **Agendas standardize processes and products of software development.**
  The development of an artifact following an agenda always proceeds in a way consistent with the steps of the agenda and their dependencies. Thus, processes supported by agendas are standardized. The same holds for the products: since applying an agenda results in instantiating the schematic expressions given in the agenda, all products developed with an agenda have the same structure.
- **Agendas support maintenance and evolution of the developed artifacts.**
  Understanding a document developed by another person is much less difficult when the document was developed following an agenda than without such

information. Each part of the document can be traced back to a step in the agenda, which reveals its purpose. To change the document, the agenda can be "replayed". The agenda helps focus attention on the parts that actually are subject to change. In this way, changing documents is greatly simplified, and it can be expected that maintenance and evolution are less error-prone when agendas are used.
- **Agendas are a promising starting point for sophisticated machine support.**
  First, agendas can be formalized and implemented as strategies, see Section 3. But even if a formal representation of development knowledge is not desired, agendas can form the basis of a process-centered software engineering environment (PSEE) [GJ96]. Such a tool would lead its users through the process described by the agenda. It would determine the set of steps to be possibly performed next and could contain a specialized editor that offers the user the schematic language expressions contained in the agenda. The user would only have to fill in the undefined parts. Furthermore, an agenda-based PSEE could automatically derive the validation obligations arising during a development, and theorem provers could be used to discharge them (if they are expressed formally).

We have defined and used agendas for a variety of software engineering activities that we supported using different formal techniques. These activities include (for more details on the various agendas, the reader is referred to [Hei97]):

- Requirements engineering
  We have defined two different agendas for this purpose. The first supports requirements elicitation by collecting possible events, classifying these events, and expressing requirements as constraints on the traces of events that may occur [HS98]. Such a requirements description can subsequently be transformed into a formal specification. The second agenda places requirements engineering in a broader context, taking also maintenance considerations into account. This agenda can be adapted to maintain and evolve legacy systems.
- Specification acquisition in general
  There exist several agendas that support the development of formal specifications without referring to a specific application area (such as safety-critical systems). The agendas are organized according to *specification styles* that are language-independent to a large extent.
- Specification of safety-critical software
  Besides the agenda presented in Section 2.1, more agendas for this purpose can be found in [HS97,GHD98,WSH98].
- Software design using architectural styles
  In [HL97], a characterization of three architectural styles using the formal description language LOTOS is presented. For each of these styles, agendas are defined that support the design of software systems conforming to the style.
- Object-oriented analysis and design
  An agenda for the object-oriented *Fusion* method [CAB[+]94] makes the de-

pendencies between the various models set up in the analysis and design phases explicit and states several consistency conditions between them.
- Program synthesis
  We have defined agendas supporting the development of provably correct programs from first-order specifications. Imperative programs can be synthesized using Gries' approach [Gri81], and functional programs can be synthesized using the KIDS approach [Smi90].

3 The Strategy Framework

In the previous section, we have introduced the agenda concept and have illustrated what kind of technical knowledge can be represented as agendas. Agendas are an informal concept whose application does not depend on machine support. They form the first layer of support for systematic software development.

We now go one step further and provide a second layer with the strategy framework. In this layer, we represent development knowledge *formally*. When development knowledge is represented formally, we can reason about this knowledge and prove properties of it. The second aim of the strategy framework is to support the application of development knowledge by machine in such a way that *semantic* properties of the developed product can be guaranteed.

In the strategy framework, a development activity is conceived as the process of constructing a solution for a given problem. A strategy specifies how to reduce a given problem to a number of subproblems, and how to assemble the solution of the original problem from the solution to the subproblems. The solution to be constructed must be *acceptable* for the problem. Acceptability captures the semantic requirements concerning the product of the development process. In this respect, strategies can achieve stronger quality criteria than is intended, e.g., by CASE. The notion of a strategy is *generic* in the definition of problems, solutions and acceptability.

How strong a notion of acceptability can be chosen depends on the degree of formality of problems and solutions. For program synthesis, both problems and solutions can be formal objects: problems can be formal specifications, solutions can be programs, and acceptability can be the total or partial correctness of the program with respect to the specification. For specification acquisition, on the other hand, we might wish to start from informal requirements. Then problems consist of a combination of informal requirements and pieces of a formal specification. Solutions are formal specifications, and a solution is acceptable with respect to a problem if the combination of the pieces of formal specification contained in the problem with the solution is a semantically valid specification. This notion of acceptability is necessarily weaker than the one for program synthesis, because the adequacy of a formal specification with respect to informal requirements cannot be captured formally. Only if the requirements are also expressed formally, a stronger notion of acceptability is possible for specification acquisition.

The strategy framework is defined in several stages, leading from simple mathematical notions to an elaborated architecture for systems supporting strategy-based problem solving. In the first stages, strategies are defined as a purely declarative knowledge representation mechanism. Experience has shown that formal knowledge representation mechanisms are (i) easier to handle and (ii) have a simpler semantics when they are declarative than when they are procedural. As for strategies, (i) agendas can be transformed into strategies in a routine way (see Section 1), and (ii) the relational semantics of strategies supports reasoning about and combination of strategies. Further stages gradually transform declaratively represented knowledge into executable constructs that are provided with control structures to guide an actual problem solving process. Figure 5 shows the different stages.

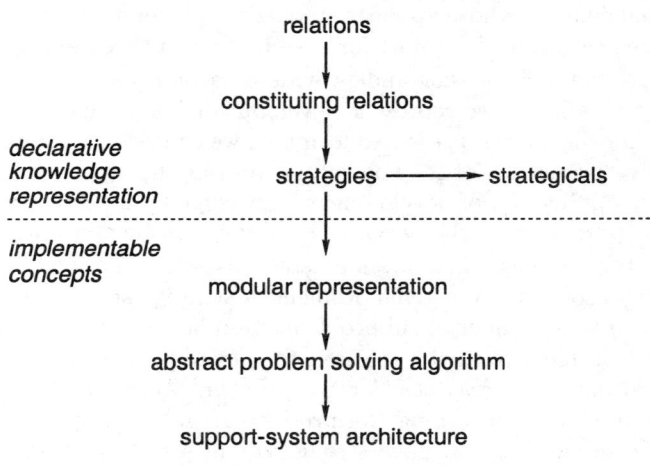

Fig. 5. Stages of definitions

The basic stage consists in defining a suitable notion of *relation*, because, formally, strategies establish a relation between a problem and the subproblems needed to solve it, and between the solutions of the subproblems and the final solution. Relations are then specialized to problem solving, which leads to the definition of *constituting relations*. *Strategies* are defined as sets of constituting relations that fulfill certain requirements. In particular, they may relate problems only to acceptable solutions. *Strategicals* are functions combining strategies; they make it possible to define more powerful strategies from existing ones.

To make strategies implementable, they are represented as *strategy modules*, which rely on constructs available in programming languages. In particular, relations are transformed into functions. The next step toward machine support consists in defining an *abstract problem solving algorithm*. This algorithm describes the manner in which strategy-based problem solving proceeds and can

A Two-Layered Approach to Support Systematic Software Development   191

be shown to lead to acceptable solutions. The *generic system architecture* provides a uniform implementation concept for practical support systems.

In the following, we sketch the definitions of the strategy framework (for details, see [Hei97]). Subsequently, we discuss its characteristics. Strategies, strategicals, and strategy modules are formally defined in the language Z [Spi92]. This does not only provide precise definitions of these notions but also makes reasoning about strategies possible.

3.1 Relations

In the context of strategies, it is convenient to refer to the subproblems and their solutions by *names*. Hence, our definition of strategies is based on the the notion of relation as used in the theory of relational databases [Kan90], instead of the usual mathematical notion of relation. In this setting, relations are sets of tuples. A tuple is a mapping from a set of *attributes* to *domains* of these attributes. In this way, each component of a tuple can be referred to by its attribute name. In order not to confuse these domains with the domain of a relation as it is frequently used in Z, we introduce the type *Value* as the domain for all attributes and define tuples as finite partial functions ($\rightarrowtail$) from attributes to values:

$$tuple : \mathbb{P}(Attribute \rightarrowtail Value)$$

where $\mathbb{P}$ is the powerset[2] operator. Relations are sets of tuples[3] that all have the same domain. This domain is called the *scheme* of the relation.

$$relation : \mathbb{P}(\mathbb{P}\, tuple)$$
$$\forall r : relation \bullet \forall t_1, t_2 : r \bullet \operatorname{dom} t_1 = \operatorname{dom} t_2$$

3.2 Constituting Relations

Constituting relations specialize relations for problem solving. The following declaration introduces the constant *const_rel* as a set of relations, whose attributes are either *ProblemAttributes* or *SolutionAttributes*. Their values must be *Problems* or *Solutions*, respectively. The types *Problem* and *Solution* are generic parameters.

$$const\_rel : \mathbb{P}\, relation$$
$$\forall cr : const\_rel \bullet \forall t : cr;\ a : scheme\ cr \bullet$$
$$scheme\ cr \subseteq (ProblemAttribute \cup SolutionAttribute) \wedge$$
$$(a \in ProblemAttribute \Rightarrow t\, a \in Problem) \wedge$$
$$(a \in SolutionAttribute \Rightarrow t\, a \in Solution)$$

---

[2] A declaration $m : \mathbb{P}\, X$ declares m to be a set of elements of X.
[3] Hence, the set *relation* of all relations is a set of sets of tuples. In such an axiomatic description, the name of the global constant is introduced above the horizontal line. Below the horizontal line, restrictions of the value of the constant may be stated. Note that in Z function applications are written without parentheses.

Acceptability, the third generic parameter, is a binary relation between problems and solutions:

$$\_acceptable\_for\_ : Solution \leftrightarrow Problem$$

By default, we use the distinguished attributes P_init and S_final to refer to the initial problem and its final solution.

The schemes of constituting relations are divided into *input attributes IA* and *output attributes OA*. Constituting relations restrict the values of the output attributes, given the values of the input attributes. Thus, they determine an order on the subproblems that must be respected in the problem solving process. Based on the partitioning of schemes, it is possible to define a dependency relation on constituting relations. A constituting relation cr_2 directly depends on another such relation cr_1 ($cr_1 \sqsubset_d cr_2$) if one of its input attributes is an output attribute of the other relation: $OA\ cr_1 \cap IA\ cr_2 \neq \emptyset$. For any given set crs of constituting relations, a *dependency relation* $\sqsubset_{crs}$ is defined to be the transitive closure of the direct dependency relation it determines.

A set of constituting relations defining a strategy must conform to our intuitions about problem solving. Among others, the following conditions must be satisfied:

- The original problem to be solved must be known, i.e. P_init must always be an input attribute.
- The solution to the original problem must be the last item to be determined, i.e. S_final must always be an output attribute.
- Each attribute value except that of P_init must be determined in the problem solving process, i.e., each attribute except P_init must occur as an output attribute of some constituting relation.
- The dependency relation on the constituting relations must not be cyclic.

Finite sets of constituting relations fulfilling these and other requirements are called *admissible*. For a complete definition of admissibility, see [Hei97].

Example. For transforming the agenda presented in Section 2.1 into a strategy, we must first define suitable notions of problems, solutions, and acceptability. A problem $pr : SafProblem$ consists of three parts: the part $pr.req$ contains an informal requirements description, the part $pr.context$ contains the specification fragments developed so far, and the part $pr.to\_develop$ contains a *schematic* Z-CSP expression that can be instantiated with a concrete one. This schematic expression specifies the syntactic class of the specification fragment to be developed, as well as how the fragment is embedded in its context. Solutions are syntactically correct Z-CSP expressions, and a solution $sol : SafSolution$ is acceptable for a problem pr if and only if it belongs to the syntactic class of $pr.to\_develop$, and the combination of $pr.context$ with the instantiated schematic expression yields a semantically valid Z-CSP specification.

3.3 Strategies

We define strategies as finite[4] admissible sets of constituting relations that fulfill certain conditions. Let $strat = \{cr_0, \ldots, cr_{max}\}$ and $scheme_s\ strat = scheme\ cr_0 \cup \ldots \cup scheme\ cr_{max}$. The set $strat$ is a strategy if it is admissible and

- the set $scheme_s\ strat$ contains the attributes P_init and S_final,
- for each problem attribute a of $scheme_s\ strat$, a corresponding solution attribute, called $sol\ a$, is a member of the scheme, and vice versa,
- if a member of the relation $\bowtie strat$[5] contains acceptable solutions for all problems except P_init, then it also contains an acceptable solution for P_init. Thus, if all subproblems are solved correctly, then the original problem must be solved correctly as well.

$strategy : \mathsf{P}(\mathsf{F}\ const\_rel)$

$\forall strat : strategy \bullet$
  $admissible\ strat\ \wedge$
  $\{P\_init, S\_final\} \subseteq scheme_s\ strat\ \wedge$
  $(\forall a : ProblemAttribute \bullet$
      $a \in scheme_s\ strat \Leftrightarrow sol\ a \in scheme_s\ strat) \wedge$
  $(\forall res : \bowtie strat \bullet$
      $(\forall a : subprs_s\ strat \bullet (res\ (sol\ a))\ acceptable\_for\ (res\ a))$
      $\Rightarrow (res\ S\_final)\ acceptable\_for\ (res\ P\_init))$

The last condition guarantees that a problem that is solved exclusively by application of strategies is solved correctly. This condition requires that strategies solving the problem directly must produce only acceptable solutions. Figure 6 illustrates the definition of strategies, where arrows denote the propagation of attribute values.

Example. When transforming an agenda into a strategy, we must decide which of the steps of the agenda will become subproblems of the strategy. If the result of a step consists in a simple decision or can be assembled from already existing partial solutions, then no subproblem corresponding to the step is necessary. Considering the agenda of Section 2.1, we decide that Steps 2, 5, and 6 need not become subproblems. Hence, we can define

$passive\_sensors = \{step\_1, steps\_2/3, step\_4, steps\_5/6/7, pass\_sol\}$

Figure 6 shows how attribute values are propagated. The constituting relation $step_1$, for example, has as P_init as its only input attribute, and P_sens/act

---

[4] A declaration $m : \mathsf{F}\ X$ declares m to be a finite set of elements of X.
[5] A *join* $\bowtie$ combines two relations. The scheme of the joined relation is the union of the scheme of the given relations. On common elements of the schemes, the values of the attributes must coincide. The operation $\bowtie$ denotes the join of a finite sets of relations.

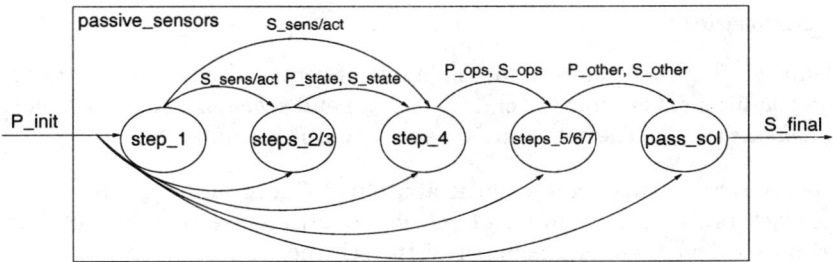

Fig. 6. Strategy for passive sensors

and S_sens/act as its output attributes. The requirements $P\_sens/act.req$ consist of the requirements $P\_init.req$ with the addition "Model the sensor values and actuator commands as members of Z types." (see Table 1). The context $P\_sens/act.context$ is the same as for P_init, and $P\_sens/act.to\_develop$ consists of the single metavariable type_defs : $Z\text{-}ax\_def$, which indicates that axiomatic Z definitions have to be developed. For the solution S_sens/act of problem P_sens/act, the only requirement is that it be acceptable. The other constituting relations are defined analogously. The complete strategy definition can be found in [Hei97].

3.4 Strategicals

Strategicals are functions that take strategies as their arguments and yield strategies as their result. They are useful to define higher-level strategies by combining lower-level ones or to restrict the set of applicable strategies, thus contributing to a larger degree of automation of the development process.

Three strategicals are defined [Hei97] that are useful in different contexts. The THEN strategical composes two strategies. Applications of this strategical can be found in program synthesis. The REPEAT strategical allows stepwise repetition of a strategy. Such a strategical is useful in the context of specification acquisition, where often several items of the same kind need to be developed. To increase applicability of the REPEAT strategical, we also define a LIFT strategical that transforms a strategy for developing one item into a strategy for developing several items of the same kind.

3.5 Modular Representation of Strategies

To make strategies implementable, we must find a suitable representation for them that is closer to the constructs provided by programming languages than relations of database theory. The implementation of a strategy should be a module with a clearly defined interface to other strategies and the rest of the system.

Because strategies are defined as relations, it is possible for a combination of values for the input attributes of a constituting relation to be related to several combinations of values for the output attributes. A type *ExtInfo* is used to select one of these combinations, thus transforming relations into functions. Such external information can be derived from user input or can be computed automatically. A strategy module consists of the following items:

– the set *subp* : P *ProblemAttribute* of subproblems it produces,
– a dependency relation *_depends_on_* : *ProblemAttribute* ↔ *ProblemAttribute* on these subproblems,
– for each subproblem, a procedure *setup* : *tuple* × *ExtInfo* ↛ *Problem* that defines[6] it, using the information in the initial problem and the subproblems and solutions it depends on, and possibly external information,
– for each solution to a subproblem, a predicate *local_accept* : *tuple* ↔ *Solution* that checks whether or not the solution conforms to the requirements stated in the constituting relation of which it is an output attribute,
– a procedure *assemble* : *tuple* × *ExtInfo* ↛ *Solution* describing how to assemble the final solution, and
– a test *accept_* : P *tuple* of acceptability for the assembled solution.

Optionally, an *explain* component may be added that explains *why* a solution is acceptable for a problem, e.g., expressed as a correctness proof.

3.6 An Abstract Problem Solving Algorithm

The abstract problem solving algorithm consists of three functions, called *solve*, *apply*, and *solve_subprs*. The function *solve* has a problem *pr* as its input. To solve this problem, a strategy *strat* must be selected from the available strategies. The function *apply* is called that tries to solve the problem *pr* with strategy *strat*. If this is successful, then the value of the attribute *S_final* obtained from the tuple yielded by *apply* is the result of the *solve* function. Otherwise, another trial is made, using a different strategy.

The function *apply* first calls another function *solve_subprs* to solve the subproblems generated by the strategy *strat*. It then sets up the final solution and checks it for acceptability. If the acceptability test fails, *apply* yields a distinguished failure element. Otherwise, it yields a tuple that lies in ⋈ *strat* (see Section 3.3).

The function *solve_subprs* has as its arguments the tuple consisting of the attribute values determined so far, and a set of subproblems still to be solved. It applies *solve* recursively to all subproblems contained in its second argument.

Problem solving with strategies usually requires user interaction. For the functions *solve*, *apply*, and *solve_subprs*, user interaction is simulated by providing them with an additional argument of type seq *UserInput*, where the type *UserInput* comprises all possible user input. User input must be converted into external information, as required by the strategy modules. To achieve this, we

---

[6] The arrow ↛ denotes a partial function, thus expressing that for some combinations of tuples and external information it may be impossible to define a corresponding problem.

use *heuristic functions*. Heuristic functions are those parts of a strategy implementation that can be implemented with varying degrees of automation. It is also possible to automate them gradually by replacing, over time, interactive parts with semi- or fully automatic ones.

It can be proven that the functions *solve*, *apply* and *solve_subprs* model strategy-based problem solving in an appropriate way: Whenever *solve* yields a solution to a problem, then this solution is acceptable.

3.7 Support-System Architecture

We now define a system architecture that describes how to implement support systems for strategy-based problem solving. Figure 7 gives a general view of the architecture which is described in more detail in [HSZ95]. This architecture is a sophisticated implementation of the functions described in Section 3.6. We introduce data structures that represent the state of the development of an artifact. This ensures that the development process is more flexible than would be possible with a naive implementation of these functions in which all intermediate results would be buried on the run-time stack. It is not necessary to first solve a given subproblem completely before starting to solve another one.

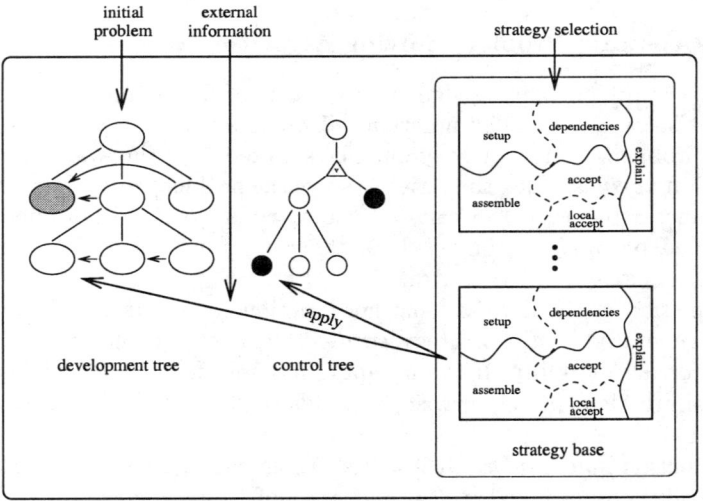

Fig. 7. General view of the system architecture

Two global data structures represent the state of development: the *development tree* and the *control tree*. The development tree represents the entire development that has taken place so far. Nodes contain problems, information about the strategies applied to them, and solutions to the problems as far as they have been determined. Links between siblings represent dependencies on other problems or solutions.

The data in the control tree are concerned only with the future development. Its nodes represent uncompleted tasks and point to nodes in the development tree that do not yet contain solutions. The degrees of freedom in choosing the next problem to work on are also represented in the control tree. The third major component of the architecture is the strategy base. It represents knowledge used in strategy-based problem solving via strategy modules.

A development roughly proceeds as follows: the initial problem is the input to the system. It becomes the root node of the development tree. The root of the control tree is set up to point to this problem. Then a loop of strategy applications is entered until a solution for the initial problem has been constructed.

To apply a strategy, first the problem to be reduced is selected from the leaves of the control tree. Second, a strategy is selected from the strategy base. Applying the strategy to the problem entails extending the development tree with nodes for the new subproblems, installing the functions of the strategy module in these nodes, and setting up dependency links between them. The control tree must also be extended.

If a strategy immediately produces a solution and does not generate any subproblems, or if solutions to all subproblems of a node in the development tree have been found and tested for local acceptability, then the functions to assemble and accept a solution are called; if the assembling and accepting functions are successful, then the solution is recorded in the respective node of the development tree. Because the control tree contains only references to unsolved problems, it shrinks whenever a solution to a problem is produced, and the problem-solving process terminates when the control tree vanishes. The result of the process is not simply the developed solution – instead, it is a development tree where all nodes contain acceptable solutions. This data structure provides valuable documentation of the development process, which produced it, and can be kept for later reference.

A research prototype was built to validate the concept of strategy and the system architecture developed for their machine-supported application. It is called IOSS (Integrated Open Synthesis System) [HSZ95] and supports the development of provably correct imperative programs from specifications expressed in first-order predicate logic.

3.8 Discussion of Strategies

The most important properties of the strategy framework are:

- **Uniformity.** The strategy framework provides a uniform way of representing development knowledge. It is independent of the development activity that is performed and the language that is used. It provides a uniform mathematical model of problem solving in the context of software engineering.
- **Machine Support.** The uniform modular representation of strategies makes them implementable. The system architecture derived from the formal strategy framework gives guidelines for the implementation of support systems for strategy-based development. Representing the state of development by

the data structure of development trees is essential for the practical applicability of the strategy approach. The practicality of the developed concepts is confirmed by the implemented system IOSS.
- **Documentation.** The development tree does not only support the development process. Is also useful when the development is finished, because it provides a documentation of how the solution was developed and can be used as a starting point for later changes.
- **Semantic Properties.** To guarantee acceptability of a solution developed with an implemented system, the functions *local_accept* and *accept* are the only components that have to be verified. Hence, also support systems that are not verified completely can be trustworthy.
- **Stepwise Automation.** Introducing the concept of heuristic function and using these functions in distinguished places in the development process, we have achieved a separation of concerns: the essence of the strategy, i.e. its semantic content, is carefully isolated from questions of replacing user interaction by semi or fully automatic procedures. Hence, gradually automating development processes amounts to local changes of heuristic functions.
- **Scalability.** Using strategicals, more and more elaborate strategies can be defined. In this way, strategies can gradually approximate the size and kind of development steps as they are performed by software engineers.

4 Related Work

Other approaches to make software engineering more systematic can be divided into product-oriented and process-oriented approaches:

Product-oriented approaches. Recently, efforts have been made to support re-use of special kinds of software development knowledge: *Design patterns* [GHJV95] have had much success in object-oriented software construction. They represent frequently used ways to combine classes or associate objects to achieve a certain purpose. Furthermore, in the field of software architecture [SG96], *architectural styles* have been defined that capture frequently used design principles for software systems. Apart from the fact that these concepts are more specialized in their application than agendas, the main difference is that design patterns and architectural styles do not describe *processes* but *products*.

A prominent example of knowledge-based software engineering, whose aims closely resemble our own, is the Programmer's Apprentice project [RW88]. There, programming knowledge is represented by *clichés*, which are prototypical examples of the artifacts in question. The programming task is performed by "inspection" – i.e., by choosing an appropriate cliché and customizing it. In comparison to clichés, agendas are more process-oriented.

In the German project KORSO [BJ95], the product of a development is described by a *development graph*. Its nodes are specification or program modules whose static composition and refinement relations are expressed by two kinds of vertices. There is no explicit distinction between "problem nodes" and "solution nodes". The KORSO development graph does not reflect single development steps, and dependencies between subproblems cannot be represented.

Process-oriented approaches. Chernack [Che96] uses a concept called *checklist* to support inspection processes. In contrast to agendas, checklists presuppose the existence of a software artifact and aim at detecting defects in this artifact.

Related to our aim to provide methodological support for applying formal techniques is the work of Souquières and Lévy [SL93]. They support specification acquisition with *development operators* that reduce *tasks* to subtasks. However, their approach is limited to specification acquisition, and the development operators do not provide means to validate the developed specification.

Astesiano and Reggio [AR97] also emphasize the importance of method when using formal techniques. They set up a *method pattern* for formal specification, consisting of context, formalism, and pragmatics. Pragmatics, in turn, contain rationale, guidelines, presentation, and documentation. Guidelines (see [Reg98] for an example) correspond to the steps of an agenda (i.e., an agenda without dependency graph, schematic expressions, and validation conditions).

The strategy framework uses ideas similar to tactical theorem proving, which has first been employed in Edinburgh LCF [Mil72]. *Tactics* are programs that implement "backward" application of logical rules. The goal-directed, top-down approach to problem solving is common to tactics and strategies. However, tactics set up all subgoals at once when they are invoked. Dependencies between subgoals can only be expressed schematically by the use of *metavariables*. Since tactics only perform goal reduction, there is no equivalent to the *assemble* and *accept* functions of strategies.

Wile's [Wil83] development language Paddle provides a means of describing procedures for transforming specifications into programs. Since carrying out a process specified in Paddle involves executing the corresponding program, one disadvantage of this procedural representation of process knowledge is that it enforces a strict depth-first left-to-right processing of the goal structure. The "second generation" process language JIL [SO97] is more flexible in this respect. Representing processes as programs has the advantage that processes are formal objects on which reasoning can be performed. On the other hand, humans find it easier to follow instructions when they are expressed on a higher level of abstraction than a programming notation can provide.

Process languages are widely used in the field of software process modeling [FKN94,FW96]. Software process modeling aims at automated support for software development processes on the level of company processes. The goal is to execute software processes like software [Ost87]. This goal implies that the language used to express processes should be similar to a programming language. Typical activities that are considered in software process modeling are filling in forms, sending emails, using a version control system to check in or check out files, or starting an editor or another tool. In contrast, agendas and strategies do not consider company processes but single documents and their semantics. They structure activities that need creativity and do not lend themselves easily to automatic enactment. Therefore, programming language notations are not necessary to express them. All in all, agendas and strategies describe activities that are considered atomic in software process modeling. Hence, process modeling techniques are a useful complement to agendas and strategies. To obtain realistic processes for larger projects, they should always be used in combination.

Humphrey [Hum95] has devised the *personal software process* to improve the performance of software engineers. Software engineers are trained to plan and analyze their activities and to perform measurements on them. Personal strengths and weaknesses are identified. Based on this knowledge, software engineers improve their personal skills. The personal software process approach is centered around individuals, not around activities, as agendas and strategies are. As with process modeling techniques, the two approaches do not exclude but complement each other. The methods captured in agendas and strategies can only be worked out by highly competent individuals.

5 Conclusions

We have shown that the concept of an agenda bears a strong potential to

- structure processes performed in software engineering,
- make development knowledge explicit and comprehensible,
- support re-use and dissemination of such knowledge,
- guarantee certain quality criteria of the developed products,
- facilitate understanding and evolution of these products,
- contribute to a standardization of products and processes in software engineering that is already taken for granted in other engineering disciplines,
- lay the basis for powerful machine support.

Agendas lead software engineers through different stages of a development and propose validations of the developed product. Following an agenda, software development tasks can be performed in a fairly routine way. When software engineers are relieved from the task to find new ways of structuring and validating the developed artifacts for each new application, they can better concentrate on the peculiarities of the application itself.

We have validated the concept of an agenda by defining and applying a number of agendas for a wide variety of software engineering activities. Currently, agendas are applied in industrial case studies of safety-critical embedded systems in the German project ESPRESS [GHD98,WSH98].

Furthermore, we have demonstrated that strategies are a suitable concept for the formal representation of development knowledge. The generic nature of strategies makes it possible to support different development activities. Strategicals contribute to the scalability of the approach. The uniform representation as strategy modules makes strategies implementable and isolates those parts that are responsible for acceptability and the ones that can be subject to automation.

The generic system architecture that complements the formal strategy framework gives guidelines for the implementation of support systems for strategy-based development. The representation of the state of development by the data structure of development trees contributes essentially to the practical applicability of the strategy approach.

In the future, we will investigate to what extent agendas are independent of the language which is used to express the developed artifact, and we will define agendas for other activities such as testing and specific contexts, e.g., object-oriented software development. Furthermore, we will investigate how different instances of the system architecture can be combined. This would provide integrated tool support for larger parts of the software lifecycle.

References

[AR97]   E. Astesiano and G. Reggio. Formalism and Method. In M. Bidoit and M. Dauchet, editors, *Proceedings TAPSOFT'97*, LNCS 1214, pages 93–114. Springer-Verlag, 1997.
[BJ95]   M. Broy and S. Jähnichen, editors. *KORSO: Methods, Languages, and Tools to Construct Correct Software*. LNCS 1009. Springer-Verlag, 1995.
[CAB+94] D. Coleman, P. Arnold, St. Bodoff, Ch. Dollin, H. Gilchrist, F. Hayes, and P. Jeremaes. *Object-Oriented Development: The Fusion Method*. Prentice Hall, 1994.
[Che96] Yuri Chernack. A statistical approach to the inspection checklist formal synthesis and improvement. *IEEE Transactions on Software Engineering*, 22(12):866–874, December 1996.
[Dav93] Jim Davies. *Specification and Proof in Real-Time CSP*. Cambridge University Press, 1993.
[FKN94] A. Finkelstein, J. Kramer, and B. Nuseibeh, editors. *Software Process Modelling and Technology*. Wiley, 1994.
[FW96]   A. Fuggetta and A. Wolf, editors. *Software Process*. Trends in Software 4. Wiley, 1996.
[GHD98] Wolfgang Grieskamp, Maritta Heisel, and Heiko Dörr. Specifying safety-critical embedded systems with Statecharts and Z: An agenda for cyclic software components. In E. Astesiano, editor, *Proc. ETAPS-FASE'98*, LNCS 1382, pages 88–106. Springer-Verlag, 1998.
[GHJV95] Erich Gamma, Richard Helm, Ralph Johnson, and John Vlissides. *Design Patterns – Elements of Reusable Object-Oriented Software*. Addison Wesley, Reading, 1995.
[GJ96]   P. Garg and M. Jazayeri. Process-centered software engineering environments: A grand tour. In A. Fuggetta and A. Wolf, editors, *Software Process*, Trends in Software 4, chapter 2, pages 25–52. Wiley, 1996.
[Gri81] David Gries. *The Science of Programming*. Springer-Verlag, 1981.
[Hei97] Maritta Heisel. *Methodology and Machine Support for the Application of Formal Techniques in Software Engineering*. Habilitation Thesis, TU Berlin, 1997.
[HL97]   Maritta Heisel and Nicole Lévy. Using LOTOS patterns to characterize architectural styles. In M. Bidoit and M. Dauchet, editors, *Proceedings TAPSOFT'97*, LNCS 1214, pages 818–832. Springer-Verlag, 1997.
[HS96]   Maritta Heisel and Carsten Sühl. Formal specification of safety-critical software with Z and real-time CSP. In E. Schoitsch, editor, *Proceedings 15th International Conference on Computer Safety, Reliability and Security (SAFECOMP)*, pages 31–45. Springer-Verlag London, 1996.

[HS97]   Maritta Heisel and Carsten Sühl. Methodological support for formally specifying safety-critical software. In P. Daniel, editor, *Proceedings 16th International Conference on Computer Safety, Reliability and Security (SAFECOMP)*, pages 295–308. Springer-Verlag London, 1997.
[HS98]   Maritta Heisel and Jeanine Souquières. Methodological support for requirements elicitation and formal specification. In *Proc. 9th International Workshop on Software Specification and Design*, pages 153–155. IEEE Computer Society Press, 1998.
[HSZ95]   Maritta Heisel, Thomas Santen, and Dominik Zimmermann. Tool support for formal software development: A generic architecture. In W. Schäfer and P. Botella, editors, *Proceedings 5-th European Software Engineering Conference*, LNCS 989, pages 272–293. Springer-Verlag, 1995.
[Hum95]   Watts S. Humphrey. *A Discipline for Software Engineering*. Addison-Wesley, 1995.
[Kan90]   Paris C. Kanellakis. Elements of relational database theory. In Jan van Leeuwen, editor, *Handbook of Theoretical Computer Science*, volume B, chapter 17, pages 1073–1156. Elsevier, 1990.
[Mil72]   Robin Milner. Logic for computable functions: description of a machine implementation. *SIGPLAN Notices*, 7:1–6, 1972.
[Ost87]   Leon Osterweil. Software processes are software too. In *9th International Conference on Software Engineering*, pages 2–13. IEEE Computer Society Press, 1987.
[Reg98]   Gianna Reggio. A method to capture formal requirements: the INVOICE case study. In M. Allemand, C. Attiogbe, and H. Habrias, editors, *Proceedings Workshop on Comparing Specification Techniques*. IRIN – Université de Nantes, 1998.
[RW88]   Charles Rich and Richard C. Waters. The programmer's apprentice: A research overview. *IEEE Computer*, pages 10–25, November 1988.
[SG96]   Mary Shaw and David Garlan. *Software Architecture*. IEEE Computer Society Press, Los Alamitos, 1996.
[SL93]   Jeanine Souquières and Nicole Lévy. Description of specification developments. In *Proc. of Requirements Engineering '93*, pages 216–223, 1993.
[Smi90]   Douglas R. Smith. KIDS: A semi-automatic program development system. *IEEE Transactions on Software Engineering*, 16(9):1024–1043, September 1990.
[SO97]   Stanley Sutton and Leon Osterweil. The design of a next-generation process language. In M. Jazayeri and H. Schauer, editors, *Proceedings of the Fifth ACM SIGSOFT Symposium on the Foundations of Software Engineering*, LNCS 1301, pages 142–158. Springer-Verlag, 1997.
[Spi92]   J. M. Spivey. *The Z Notation – A Reference Manual*. Prentice Hall, 2nd edition, 1992.
[Wil83]   David S. Wile. Program developments: Formal explanations of implementations. *Communications of the ACM*, 26(11):902–911, November 1983.
[WSH98]   Kirsten Winter, Thomas Santen, and Maritta Heisel. An agenda for event-driven software components with complex data models. In W. Ehrenberger, editor, *Proceedings of the 16th International Conference on Computer Safety, Reliablity and Security (SAFECOMP)*. Springer-Verlag, 1998. to appear.

A Framework for Evaluating System and Software Requirements Specification Approaches

Erik Kamsties and H. Dieter Rombach

Fraunhofer Institute for Experimental Software Engineering,
Sauerwiesen 6, D-67661 Kaiserslautern, Germany
{kamsties, rombach}@iese.fhg.de

Abstract. Numerous requirements specification approaches have been proposed to improve the quality of requirements documents as well as the developed software and to increase user satisfaction with the final product. However, no or only anecdotal evidence exists about which approach is appropriate in a particular context. This paper discusses the value of experimentation in requirements engineering to gain sound empirical evidence. Subsequently, a framework is suggested, which helps to structure one's research agenda for experimentation, and supports the development of experiments driven by this agenda. As an example for the application of the framework, our research agenda is outlined, focusing on requirements specification approaches for embedded systems. The experiments found in the literature regarding this topic are analyzed, issues that warrant more experimentation are identified, and finally, an additional set of experiments is proposed.

1 Introduction

Software developers who wish to improve either the productivity or the quality of the software they develop are faced with an enormous portfolio of techniques, methods, tools, and standards for requirements specification. However, no or only anecdotal evidence exist about which approach is appropriate in a particular context [1]. Open questions are often: (1) under which conditions are requirements specification approaches profitable at all, (2) which approach should be applied in which type of project, (3) how can an approach be applied most efficiently, and (4) what is the impact on related activities (e.g., testing). A typical example for an anecdotal evidence is the following statement which was taken from the brochure of a CASE tool for requirements modeling: "the maintenance costs are lowered, the quality of your applications improves, and you deliver applications to market faster".

The transfer of software engineering technology to industry is plagued with a lot of problems, which can be attributed to some degree to the lack of empirical evidence. First, new technologies are often rejected by project personnel, since these are considered not well adapted to project needs and, thus, are perceived as not beneficial. Second, new technologies are bypassed under project pressure since project personnel are not convinced enough of the benefits to take any risks and they are not supported by the project management. Project progress is often measured by the project management only in lines of code. Third, past project experiences are not reused in new projects because benefits were not demonstrated explicitly and, thus, "religious" beliefs win [2].

Empirical research provides strong methods, such as controlled experiments, to overcome the limitations of ad-hoc evaluation of software engineering technology. For instance, results from empirical research indicates that the introduction of a CASE tool actually leads to a decrease of productivity in the first year [3]. Controlled experiments have been proven to be a particularly effective means for evaluating software engineering methods and gaining the necessary understanding about their utility [4]. We will discuss their strengths and weaknesses in more detail in the next section. Moreover, an organization's software competencies are manageable assets. Software competencies are tailored technologies and methodologies that play a key role in supporting strategic capabilities of an organization[1]. Experiments are the key to building up software competencies [2].

We suggest in this paper a framework, which helps to structure one's research agenda for experimentation, and supports the development of experiments driven by this agenda. More precisely, the framework offers a template for documenting a research agenda for the comprehensive investigation of a software engineering topic. Such a research agenda is useful to analyze existing studies, to identify issues which warrant more investigation, and to derive additional experiments. The framework supports the development of individual experiments by providing high-level guidelines, and a second template for documenting experiments. However, it does not support the design or statistical analysis of experiments.

In work related to us, Basili et.al. [5], and Kitchenham, Pfleeger et.al. [6], [7] proposed frameworks to develop individual empirical studies (including design and analysis procedures). Our framework provides a "front-end" to those frameworks, namely the agenda, for describing a plan for a set of interrelated studies.

As a running example we discuss our own agenda for the investigation of *requirements specification approaches*, more precisely, of languages, of techniques, and of methods supporting the specification/documentation of requirements as well as on associated techniques to verify those requirements. It is worthwhile to investigate requirements specification approaches, since it is well-known that most of the defects found in software are caused by misconceptions in the requirements phase. Requirements specification approaches are proposed as one way of overcoming these problems. Only a few of them are applied in industrial practice. We believe that this is due to the relatively high investment compared to other improvements, for instance, the introduction of inspections, together with unproven merits. Religious beliefs in object-oriented approaches is one manifestation of this situation. Therefore, our long term goal is to provide empirical insights into this area of requirements engineering.

---

[1] Strategic capabilities are corporate goals defined by the business position of the organization and implemented by key business processes.

The remainder of this paper is organized as follows. A brief introduction into methods for empirical research is given in the next section. The third section discusses the benefits, drawbacks, and practical issues of current experimentation in requirements engineering. The fourth section outlines the suggested framework for experimentation. As an example for the application of the framework, our agenda for experimentation with requirements specification approaches is outlined. The experiments found in the requirements engineering literature are characterized according to our agenda, open issues are identified, and an additional set of experiments is proposed. A summary and an outlook on future work concludes this paper.

2 Introduction into Methods for Empirical Research

Software engineering and consequently requirements engineering is an amalgamation of influences from many fields including theoretical computer science, physical sciences, electrical engineering, behavioral and life sciences [8]. Considering requirements engineering, for instance, formal methods [9] stem from research in theoretical computer science, while ethnography [10] has its roots in the behavioral and life sciences. In general, the parent research fields were often used as sources and inspirations for technology development in software engineering, but the underlying research methods of these fields were not adopted to a large extent. Software engineering and requirements engineering research is about developing languages, techniques, methods, and tools. Their validation did not play such an integral part of research as the confirmation and validation of models and hypotheses in physical, behavioral, or life sciences. It has been claimed that in software engineering, there is a lack of experimentation to validate research results [11]. Proposing a model or building a tool is not enough. There must be some way of validating that the model or tool is an advantage over current models or tools [12]. There are some indications that this situation is beginning to change, for instance, the classification scheme used for submissions to the "International Symposium on Requirements Engineering" encourages researchers to perform either case studies (dimension D: "Case study applying a proposed solution to a substantial example") or more objective evaluations, i.e., experiments (dim. E: "Evaluation or comparison of proposed solutions") [13].

We believe that software engineering is a true engineering task. Hence, improvement of practical software development requires an "experimental" approach. Basili outlines three research paradigms which comprise experimentation, namely the scientific method, the engineering method, and the empirical method [12]. The engineering method and the empirical method are variations of the scientific method. All three methods are depicted in Fig. 1.

Basili recommends to apply the research methods as follows:

> "In the area of software engineering the scientific method might best be used when trying to understand the software process, product, people, and environment. It attempts to extract from the world some form

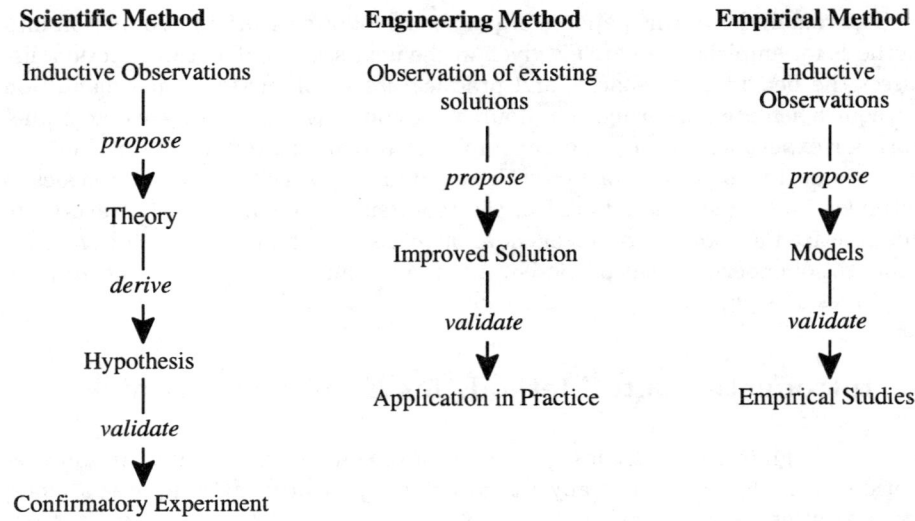

Fig. 1. Research Methods

of model which tries to explain the underlying phenomena, and evaluate whether the model is truly representative of the phenomenon being observed. It is an approach to model building. (...)

The engineering method is an evolutionary improvement oriented approach which assumes one already has models of the software process, product, people, and environment and modifies the model or aspects of the model in order to improve the thing being studied. (...)

The empirical method is a revolutionary improvement oriented approach which begins by proposing a new model, not necessarily based upon an existing model, and attempts to study the effects of the process or product suggested by the new model."

In an industrial context, the empirical method can help select and introduce a promising technique which is afterwards continually optimized by following the engineering method.

Experiments can be distinguished by several dimensions, namely, the purpose, the control over independent variables, the style of data, and the type of statistical analysis. The purpose of an experiment can be scientific learning, teaching, training, or technology/process evaluation and optimization. Examples include experiments to investigate the influence of domain knowledge on the efficiency of inspections, experiments at university to motivate software engineering principles, and industrial experiments to compare actual practices with new technologies in order to raise confidence. The degree of control over independent variables decides whether a *controlled experiment* or a *case study* is appropriate. A controlled experiment requires high level, and low difficulty of control, a case study must be performed otherwise. This decision has also an impact on the style of data gained and the type of statistical analysis. Controlled experiments are better in establishing causal relationships, while the conclusions from case studies are limited to the particular conditions of the study.

Experiments can be characterized further by the the scope of investigation as depicted by Table 1 [5]. Four different types of studies are outlined, namely blocked subject-project, replicated project, multi-project variation, and single project.

Table 1. The scope of empirical studies is related to the number of teams replicating each project and the number of different projects analyzed.

	1 Project	> 1 Project
1 Team	Single Project (Case Study)	Multi-Project Variation
> 1 Team	Replicated Project	Blocked Subject-Project

Blocked subject-project studies examine one or more objects (i.e., the examined processes, products, or models) across a set of teams and a set of projects. Replicated project studies examine object(s) across a set of teams and a single project, while multi-project variation studies examine object(s) across a single team and a set of projects. Single project studies examine object(s) on a single team and a single project. Teams are possibly single-person groups that work separately, and projects are separate programs or problems on which teams work. As the scope of examination increases, the wider-reaching a study's conclusions become and the higher the cost. Small studies can be performed in a quantitative mode while larger studies typically involve more qualitative and less quantitative analysis.

Experimentation must be guided and there must be a rational for data collection, i.e., a framework for experimentation is required. Several frameworks have been proposed to design and analyze empirical studies in software engineering including DESMET by Kitchenham, Pfleeger, et.al. [14], [7], [6]. DESMET focuses on the evaluation of methods and tools, either in a qualitative (subjective), quantitative (objective), or hybrid mode through surveys, case studies, and formal (i.e., controlled) experiments. We suggest using the following components as an experimental infrastructure:

- *Quality Improvement Paradigm* (QIP) [15], [16]
  The QIP provides an experimental framework for software development based on the scientific method (see Fig. 1). According to the QIP, projects within an organization are based on the continuous iteration of characterization, goal setting, selection of improved technology, monitoring and analysis of its effects to correct projects on-line, post-mortem analysis to understand what could be done better in future projects, and packaging the newly learned lessons so they can be reused efficiently in future projects.

- *Goal/Question/Metric Paradigm* (GQM) [15], [17], [18]
  The GQM Paradigm supports the process of stating goals, refining goals in an operational way into metrics, and interpreting the resulting data. The idea behind the GQM Paradigm is that measurement (and hence experimentation) should be based on goals. By stating goals explicitly, all data collection and interpretation activities are based on a clearly documented rationale.
- *Experience Factory* concept [19]
  The experience factory facilitates the reuse of models, gained for instance by experimentation, across project boundaries within an organization.

We will use this experimental infrastructure within our framework, which is described in section 4.

3 Empirical Research in Requirements Engineering

Experimentation in requirements engineering (RE) was discussed in a panel session at the International Symposium on Requirements Engineering in 1995 [20][2]. Experimentation was considered quite important, but nevertheless especially difficult to perform in RE research. One critique was that RE methods are not relevant objects for experimentation, since RE is in its essence about understanding and problem solving, and none of the present RE methods would support these tasks sufficiently. Thus, "requirements engineering is about insight not experimentation" [21]. We subscribe to the first part of the quotation. But as long as there are no real problem solving methods in RE, we have to apply the principles, techniques, methods, and tools that RE research has produced so far. Empirical research can contribute to RE by evaluating the truth of principles and the effectiveness of techniques, methods, and tools.

Another critique on experimental RE was that it is limited to small and unrealistic problems. This is true to some extent for replicated project and blocked subject-project treatments (see Table 1). But multi-project variation treatments can be performed in realistic environments in a quantitative mode as the field study of El Emam et.al. [22] illustrates. In this study, a model was developed which predicts the impact of user participation on the quality of RE service and on the quality of RE products in the presence of uncertainty. The model was tested using quantitative data of 39 real world software development projects from different organizations instead of using toy problems. The results indicates that as uncertainty increases, greater user participation alleviates the negative influence of uncertainty on the quality of RE service, and as uncertainty decreases, the beneficial effects on the quality of RE service of increasing user

---

[2] It is difficult to discuss experimentation in requirements engineering, since the term 'experimentation' is used differently in the literature. Some authors use it as a synonym for 'just trying out' other imply controlled experiments with it. We use the term here as comprising case studies as well as controlled experiments.

participation diminish. The interaction between user participation and uncertainty had no impact on the quality of RE products. Empirical research can contribute to RE by validating predictive models.

There are two popular approaches of gathering evidence about requirements specification approaches (the topic of our running example in section 4). The first approach is providing a sample specification of a common exemplar (e.g., library, ATM). These studies have typically a 'single project' or 'replicated project' scope of investigation (see Figure 1) and are performed by students or researchers. Examples for those studies include the library problem [23], the production cell [24], and the steam boiler [25]. The second approach is conducting studies in an industrial environment. These have typically a 'single project' or 'multi-project variation' scope of investigation and are performed by practitioners and researchers. Examples for those studies include experience reports from trial applications (e.g., of the CoRE approach [26]), and field studies of current practice (e.g., regarding scenarios by Weidenhaupt et.al. [27]). However, the advantages and disadvantages of these two approaches must be judged from two perspectives: that of the RE researcher and that of the practitioner in an organization. The major value of a common exemplar is to advance research efforts [28]. From a practitioner's perspective it is less valuable, instead, it is more likely a demonstration of existence (e.g., an ATM can be described with notation XYZ). Industrial case studies are valuable for both researchers and practitioners, since they indicate whether an approach scales up and fits into the context. Their main disadvantage is that the results are context-dependent and causal relationships often cannot be established, because of the lack of control on the independent variables. Furthermore, it can be difficult to find trial projects. Most case studies as well as exemplar studies in RE are mainly qualitative.

Controlled experiments (with a 'replicated project' or 'blocked subject-project' scope of investigation) complement common exemplar studies and industrial case studies because they allow for more quantitative analysis. They are useful for researchers since they can be replicated at different locations and varied in order to increase confidence in an requirements specification approach and to understand the influencing factors better. They are useful for practitioners since they can be used to gain confidence in new techniques before they are applied under project pressure. Experiments are increasingly performed in other areas of software engineering, e.g., inspections, or software maintenance. A problem with respect to RE is the lack of commonly accepted quantitative measures for the success of requirements engineering (requirements are not countable!). Therefore, measures must be defined first, which increases the effort for experiment preparation. An example for a validated success measure can be found in [29].

We suggest *common experiments* in analogy to common exemplars for requirements engineering. Similar to a common exemplar, a common experiment is available to everyone for replication and variation. A common experiment is either a case study or a controlled experiment, dependent on the tackled RE activities, which is developed and conducted according to our experimental infrastructure outlined in section 2. Because upstream RE activities, e.g., elicitation, negotiation, and formalization of requirements, are creative, time-consuming, and less guidance is available, they require a case study approach for investigation, since the influencing factors are not under tight control. The downstream RE activities, e.g., reviews and testing, can be investigated by controlled experiments. The basis for both types of common experiments is a common exemplar which we supplement with (1) guidelines and procedures in order to make the usage of the exemplars more controlled, and (2) goal-oriented data collection procedures in order to make comparisons possible. Common experiments differ from the before-mentioned approaches in that they are repeatable, since common exemplars are used in a controlled way. Replications are important to increase evidence for requirements specification approaches and to compare approaches. Feather et.al. [28] propose the use of 'requirements exemplars' (i.e., natural requirements) instead of 'specification exemplars' (i.e., tidied and simplified requirements) to study the upstream RE activities as well. We use both types of exemplars in our common experiments.

Furthermore, we propose *situated experiments* in addition to common experiments. A situated experiment is more convincing to practitioners because, in contrast to a common experiment, exemplars and/or processes are taken from their individual application domain. The situated experiment in combination with the common experiment allows the question of whether application domain knowledge plays a role in the efficient application of an approach to be factored out. This two step approach of empirical evaluation has been applied successfully in the area of inspections [30].

An industrial case study may be useful as a follow-up to a common experiment. The experimental results can "prove" the feasibility of requirements specification approaches in the small (replicated project, or blocked subject-project) and industrial scale case studies are performed afterwards to analyze whether the results scale up in a realistic environment (single project, or multi-project variation).

Our framework for planning and developing common and situated experiments is outlined in the next section.

4 Framework

The purpose of our framework is to facilitate experimentation. First, by means of structuring and formalizing a research agenda, and second, by an experimental infrastructure to construct experiments driven by this agenda. The framework is comprised of the following three components:

- a roadmap (i.e., research agenda) for experimentation,
- guidelines for the construction of experiments based on the QIP and GQM Paradigm (these need to be supplemented by guidelines for experimental design and statistical analysis as those discussed in section 2), and
- a set of experiment descriptions. Each description contains a characterization of the environment in which the experiment took place, the goals, the hy-

pothesis, a description of the investigated objects, the experimental design, the statistical analysis, the results, and the experiences gained.

The particular environment (e.g., university, company), in which the framework should be applied plays an important role. First, for defining a meaningful roadmap, and second, for interpreting the experimental results, since extrapolations are depending heavily on the representativeness of the sample. Fig. 2 illustrates our framework.

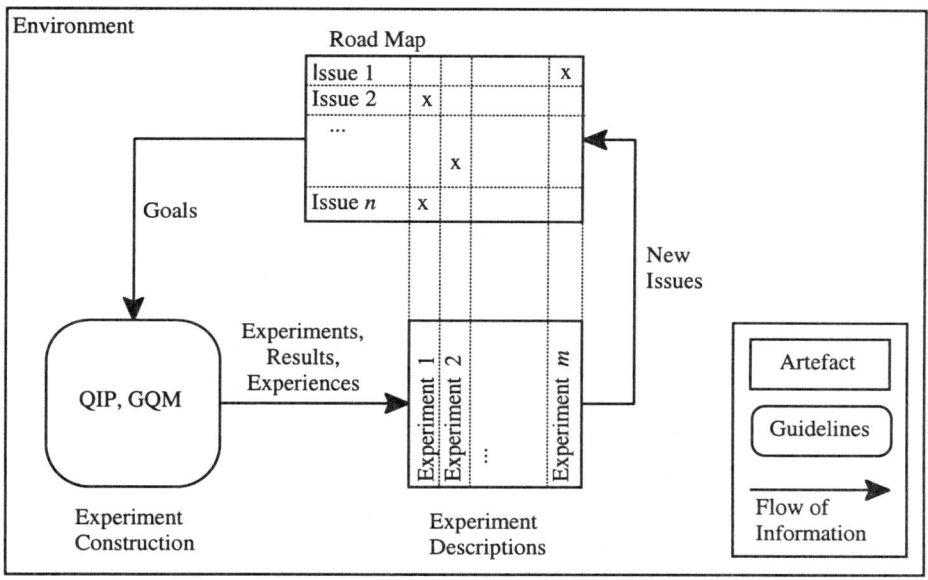

Fig. 2. Framework

The components of our framework work together in the following manner: The roadmap raises a set of issues to be addressed by experimentation and maintains pointers to descriptions of already performed experiments. The 'experiment construction' component supports the development of new experiments based on the QIP and GQM Paradigm. The roadmap can be altered in case of new issues arising from the results of experiments conducted.

The roadmap and the experiment descriptions should be stored in an experience base (not illustrated in Fig. 2) in order to facilitate reuse [19]. A prototype implementation of an experience base which contains experiment descriptions, but not a roadmap, has been created within the Special Research Project 501 at the University of Kaiserslautern [31], [32].

The framework can be applied for two purposes. First, it helps analyzing experiments found in the literature, and second, it supports the construction of new experiments. A roadmap (i.e., research agenda) has to be defined in both cases as the initial step. In the first case, the roadmap can be used then to classify and analyze experiments found in the literature. In the second case, experiments can be derived then from the roadmap. Instead of constructing new experiments, it is also possible to reuse existing ones from comparable environments. For instance, the Software Engineering Laboratory at NASA Goddard Space Flight Center performed a large number of experiments [33], which are candidates for reuse.

We discuss the framework components in the following subsections in more detail. The discussion is illustrated with a complete example of an instantiation of the framework in the context of requirements engineering for evaluating requirements specification approaches.

4.1 Road Map

The roadmap represents a research agenda for a particular environment. It consists of (1) a set of issues (i.e., questions) which arise in a particular environment concerning a specific theme, (2) a "formalization" of issues in terms of GQM goals in order to characterize experiments precisely, and (3) pointer from issues to experiments. A GQM goal is defined by the following template:

Analyze [object of study (e.g., products, processes, resources)]
for the purpose of [purpose (e.g., characterization, etc.)]
with respect to [quality focus (e.g., cost, efficiency, etc.)]
from the viewpoint of [viewpoint (e.g., researcher, practitioner, etc.)]
in the context of [description of specific context].

The facets describe what will be analyzed ("object of study"), why the object will be analyzed ("purpose"), what property/attribute of the object will be analyzed ("quality focus"), who uses the data collected ("viewpoint"), and in which environment the analysis take place ("context"). We suggest the goal template to characterize empirical studies.

The development of a relevant roadmap is a crucial task, since the issues must be relevant to the chosen viewpoint in order to create experiments which are of interest to a larger community within the particular environment. Our agenda (i.e., roadmap) for the investigation of requirements specification approaches is described in the remainder of this subsection.

Theme and Environment We currently focus on the introduction of an requirements specification approach into an purely text-based ("prosaic") RE process. Those approaches promise a lot of advantages, for example early detection of requirements problems (since the requirements engineer is forced to analyze the requirements more thoroughly), or the possibility for automating some tasks (e.g., verification). Furthermore, these approaches gain more and more interest from industry, as we observed at the RE seminars that we are offering to practitioners. The overall rationale behind our roadmap is to substantiate the recommendations we make to practitioners during our consulting and training

A Framework for Evaluating Requirements Specification Approaches

activities with experimental data. The following subsection introduces the issues of our current agenda.

Issues A set of issues (i.e., questions) arise with respect to the theme described before:

- *Informal vs. formal.* What are the differences of applying semi-formal or formal requirements specification languages compared to relying entirely on textual requirements? The benefits of semi-formal and formal languages are often claimed: they help to avoid misunderstandings due to ambiguity, inconsistency, or incompleteness. Nevertheless a significant number of software development projects are conducted with completely informal requirements documents. There are several reasons for this situation, one of them is that there are doubts that the promised improvements can be reached in practice.
- *Languages.* Which language for requirements specification is best suited for a particular environment? A lot of requirements specification languages/approaches have been proposed in the past years. For instance, state-based approaches seem to be easy to apply since their theoretical foundation is taught in most lectures on computer science. Nevertheless, the expressiveness is somewhat limited (which is indicated for instance by the high number of extensions to statecharts). Therefore, more powerful languages have been proposed, for example, to describe timing properties in real-time systems more concisely.
- *Verification.* Which verification technique is most effective for requirements specifications written in a particular language? A requirements specification must be verified, first, to ensure correctness and completeness with respect to the customer's needs, and second, to ensure specification-internal consistency and completeness. Several techniques have been proposed ranging from general purpose reading techniques (e.g., perspective-based reading [34]) to specialized techniques for requirements (e.g., forward and backward search [35]).

Each "informal" issue is "formalized" by a GQM goal as described in the following subsection.

Goal Definition A goal is defined by a 5-tuple (object, purpose, quality focus, viewpoint, context). We discuss in the following the facets of the goals with respect to the investigation of requirements specification approaches.

> **Object** The objects of study are either requirements specifications written in different languages, or verification techniques. There is a danger to compare "apples and oranges" since there are some requirements specification approaches such as Structured Analysis, in which the language is inherently coupled to a method. Others, such as Z are merely languages.

Purpose The purposes of our empirical studies with requirements specification approaches are understanding, characterization, and evaluation.

Quality Focus The quality focus is a quantitative description of subjective terms like "better" used in the description of an issue. Possible foci are the quality of the requirements specification (e.g., understandability), the effectiveness and efficiency of requirements specification related activities (e.g., verification), or the effort for further development activities (e.g., implementation, testing).

Viewpoint The viewpoint in our first investigations is that of the researcher. Other possible viewpoints include practitioner, manager, etc..

Context The experiments have to be performed with students at the university. This limits the choice of objects because of the required training effort.

Pointer to experiments This part of the roadmap contains a pointer (e.g., a literature reference) to a particular study, if available. A brief discussion of the degree to which a study covers an issue and the open questions shall be provided for each study, too.

Example The issues raised before are used to characterize experiments found in the RE literature and to identify areas which up to now have been neglected or which warrant more investigation. Table 2 represents our roadmap. It lists the experiments we found in the RE literature as well as our proposal for an additional set of experiments. The focus is on experiments with 'repeated project' or 'blocked subject-project' scope and quantitative analysis. The degree to which a study covers an issues is omitted from Table 2.

There are several more quantitative experiments in the RE literature targeting on issues, which are not concerned by our roadmap. Vessey&Conger [41] investigated methodologies (object-, process-, and data-oriented), Jankowski [42] investigated CASE tools, and Gowen&Collofello investigated the verification of safety-critical software [43].

Most obvious in Table 2 is that all issues raised before are already tackled by experiments. A more detailed analysis reveals:

- None of the experiments consider new technology (e.g., object-oriented approaches, or formal methods). Prevalent are Structured Analysis and its derivates.
- The impact of the application domain was not studied.
- The verification of requirements using general-purpose reading techniques was studied, but specialized techniques were not used in experiments so far.
- The quality focus of the experiment by Yadav et.al. is questionable to some extent. Can we really attribute differences among specifications with respect to completeness, consistency, and correctness to the used language? These

Table 2. Roadmap for the Investigation of Requirements Specification Approaches

Issue	Goal Definition	Pointer
Informal vs. formal	*Analyze* documents written in natural language and Structured Analysis *for the purpose of* evaluation *with respect to* understandability, reviewability, modifiability, efficiency and reliability of constructing specifications *from the viewpoint of* the researcher *in the context of* computer science students.	Takahashi et.al. [36]
	Analyze documents written in natural language and Real-Time Structured Analysis *for the purpose of* evaluation *with respect to* the effectiveness of functional testing *from the viewpoint of* the researcher *in the context of* the National Institute of Standards and Technology.	Mills [37]
Languages	*Analyze* documents written in IDEFo (SADT), DFD *for the purpose of* evaluation *with respect to* completeness, consistency, correctness, ease of learning, ease of use, overall utility *from the viewpoint of* the researcher *in the context of* a lab lecture at the Texas Tech University	Yadav et.al. [38]
	Analyze documents written in SCR, OMT *for the purpose of* evaluation *with respect to* understandability, verifiability, testability, and modifiability *from the viewpoint of* the researcher *in the context of* a lecture at the University of Kaiserslautern.	*Our proposal (see section 4.3)*
Verification	*Analyze* adhoc, checklist, scenario-based reading *for the purpose of* evaluation *with respect to* the effectiveness and efficiency of different reading techniques on SCR specifications *from the viewpoint of* the researcher *in the context of* a lecture at the University of Maryland.	Porter et.al. [39]
	Analyze adhoc, perspective-based reading *for the purpose of* evaluation *with respect to* the their effectiveness and efficiency on textual requirements *from the viewpoint of* the researcher *in the context of* NASA/GSFC and the University of Kaiserslautern.	Basili et.al. [40] Laitenberger [34]

differences depending to our experience on humans and their domain knowledge, cognitive skills, etc..

Therefore, we gave the 'language' issue the highest priority and propose experiments using an object-oriented and a "classical" requirements specification approach. Our proposal for this additional set of experiments is discussed in detail in section 4.3. The following subsection describes how to develop experiments from the roadmap.

4.2 Experiment Construction

The Quality Improvement Paradigm (QIP) are used here as an overall process for constructing experiments (i.e., planning, designing, executing, analyzing, etc. them) [44]. The basic steps, adapted to experiments, are:

1. Characterize the experiment and the environment in which it take place
2. Define the goals of the experiment with the GQM and derive hypotheses
3. Develop the experimental design
4. Execute the experiment
5. Analyze the collected data, create follow-up hypotheses
6. Package the experiences and the results

Step 1 ('Characterize') and step 2 ('Define goals') are part of the roadmap. We give no detailed guidelines for the steps 3 ('Develop the experimental design')–5 ('Analyze the collected data'), because there can be found good advice in the software engineering literature (e.g., by Pfleeger et.al. [7]) as well as in the general literature on experimentation (e.g., [45]). Furthermore, guidelines can be derived from analyzing existing experiments, as it was done by Lott et.al. [4] for controlled experiments in the area of defect detection techniques. Step 6 ('Package') is supported by the experiment description component of our framework, which is described in the following subsection.

4.3 Experiment Descriptions

Experiments are described according to Basili et.al. [5] by four categories which reflect the phases of an empirical study:

1. Definition (i.e, study goals, scope, and hypotheses)
2. Planning (i.e, objects of study, subjects, experimental tasks to be performed, experimental design, metrics, etc.)
3. Operation (i.e, data collection, validation, and analysis procedures)
4. Interpretation

In the remainder of this subsection our proposal for experiments with requirements specification approaches is presented according to the above scheme.

We have started to define and perform a first set of controlled experiments regarding the evaluation of different languages provided by requirements specification approaches. This issue has been addressed so far merely by qualitative studies (scope: single, or replicated project). We used initially the Unified Modeling Language (UML) [46] together with the OMT method [47] and the SCR style tabular requirements technique (SCR = Software Cost Reduction) [48]. The motivation for these experiments is two-fold. First, object-oriented requirements analysis (OORA) approaches are becoming more and more popular. They claim to facilitate understanding, since objects map directly to real-world entities. OMT is the most applied OORA approach, which is especially used in technical domains. However, since the behavioral specification in OMT is distributed over a set of collaborating objects, it is not easy to tell whether an analysis model satisfies the required end-to-end behavior. The UML is the de-facto standard for documenting object-oriented models. Second, SCR is a widely-known *black-box* specification technique for technical domains (embedded real-time systems) where its tabular notation is claimed to be readily understandable. It is easy to verify, since system-internals are not described.

Our initial experiments are aimed at understanding the effects of the methodological choice between the black box and white box specification style. Four experiments numbered '(a)' – '(d)' are proposed in the following.

Definition

Goal: *Analyze* techniques $T_1, T_2, \ldots, T_n$ to express requirements
- T_1: UML language with OMT method
- T_2: SCR style tabular requirements technique
- T_n: further requirements specification approaches

for the purpose of evaluation
with respect to understandability (a), verifiability (b), testability (c), and modifiability (d)
from the viewpoint of the researcher
in the context of a lecture at the University of Kaiserslautern.
Scope: Replicated project or blocked subject-project
Hypothesis: There is a difference with respect to (a) understandability, (b) verifiability, (c) testability, (d) maintainability.

Plan

Objects: Documents in T_1 and T_2
Subjects: Students
Tasks: several tasks are to be performed:
- Answer questions regarding behavioral and functional aspects of the specification (a)
- Check completeness and consistency with respect to informal requirements (b)
- Perform changes on the specification (c)
- Design test cases based on the specification (d)

Table 3. Overview on independent and dependent Variables

Independent Variables	Dependent Variables
Run (run 1 and run 2)	Understandability measured via questionnaire (i.e., time needed to complete the questionnaire, correctness of answered questions, completeness of answered questions)
Requirements Specification Approach (T_1, T_2)	Verifiability measured via defect form (i.e., number of inconsistencies found, time needed)
Type of Document	Testability measured via test cases (i.e., time required to write test cases)
Experience of Subjects	Modifiability measured via success of changes (i.e., time needed to perform changes, completeness of changes, correctness of changes, modification rate)

Table 4. 2 x 2 Within-subjects factorial design (random assignment to groups A, B)

Run	Technique (Document)	
	$T_1(D_1)$	$T_2(D_2)$
1	A	B
2	B	A

The independent and dependent variables are summarized in Table 3. The experimental design is depicted in Table 4.

The 'operation' and 'interpretation' categories are omitted in this experiment description since this is only a proposal. These experiments are open for variation. It should be relatively easy to exchange the used specifications, or both the employed requirements specification approaches and the used specifications.

5 Summary and Future Work

In this paper we have discussed the role of experimentation in requirements engineering in overcoming the lack of empirical evidence in the field. A framework for experimentation in software engineering, not only requirements engineering, was suggested which facilitates experimentation by means of structuring and formalizing a research agenda (i.e., roadmap), and by an experimental infrastructure for developing experiments according to this agenda. The experimental infrastructure provides an overall process for experimentation and supports the definition of the goals of a study, however, it does not comprise guidelines for experimental design or statistical analysis.

We have presented our agenda for experimentation with requirements specification approaches to illustrate the application of the framework. The agenda was also used to characterize already existing experiments in the literature, to identify open issues. We found only a few experiments performed in requirements engineering with a 'replicated project' or 'blocked subject-project' scope of investigation and quantitative analysis. Only the experiments with reading techniques by Porter&Basili et.al. are *controlled* experiments. Based on our literature review, we made a proposal for an additional set of experiments regarding languages for expressing requirements.

The application of the framework gave us a clear indication for the framework's utility. We do not plan a larger validation of the framework, because it extends already proven concepts. Instead, we plan to perform the proposed experiments.

We hope that the framework will also serve as a means for communicating research agendas (with respect to experimentation) within a research community.

This paper describes work in progress. We performed one of the proposed experiments at the University of Kaiserslautern in December 1997 [49]. Currently, we are capturing experiences made in other environments—e.g., the NASA Software Engineering Laboratory—, developing further experiments, and extending our agenda. The proposed framework, the agenda, and the experiments are parts of a PhD thesis that is currently being performed at the Fraunhofer Institute (IESE).

Performing experiments in requirements engineering is beneficial for students, practitioners, and the research community. Students can experience the relative strengths and weaknesses of the requirements engineering approaches that are introduced in their lectures. Professionals can gain confidence in new approaches before they are applied under project pressure. The research community can accumulate a body of knowledge regarding the utility of various approaches under varying project characteristics. We therefore recommend that replicable experiments be adopted as a standard part of both education and technology transfer programs.

The empirical evaluation of requirements engineering approaches cannot be the effort of a single person or a single research group. Many experiments are too large for any single organization, they must be repeated in different environments. The International Software Engineering Research Network (ISERN) is a community that believes software engineering research needs to be performed in an experimental context. ISERN has facilitated the development of experiments and their replication in different environments. Organizations interested in joining ISERN may access the World-Wide Web information available from the following URL http://wwwagse.informatik.uni-kl.de/ISERN/isern.html or send an email to isern@informatik.uni-kl.de.

6 Acknowledgments

We thank our colleagues in the Software Engineering Research Group at the University of Kaiserslautern and in the Fraunhofer Institute for their suggestions, especially Colin Atkinson, and Khaled El Emam. Furthermore, we wish to thank the participants of the RTSE '97 workshop in Bernried who refereed this paper for their comments on previous versions.

References

1. Norman Fenton. How effective are software engineering methods? *Journal of Systems and Software*, 22(2):141–146, August 1993.
2. H. Dieter Rombach. Experimentation as a vehicle for software technology transfer: A family of software reading techniques. In *Proceedings of the 1st International Conference on Empirical Assessment & Evaluation in Software Engineering*, Keele (UK), March 1997. Keynote talk.
3. Robert L. Glass. Do measuring advocates measure up? In *Proceedings of the 3rd International Conference on Applications of Software Measurement*, pages 1.02–1.12, 1992.
4. Christopher M. Lott and H. Dieter Rombach. Repeatable software engineering experiments for comparing defect-detection techniques. *Journal of Empirical Software Engineering*, 1996.
5. Victor R. Basili, Richard W. Selby, and David H. Hutchens. Experimentation in software engineering. *IEEE Transactions on Software Engineering*, SE-12(7):733–743, July 1986.
6. Barbara Ann Kitchenham. Evaluating software engineering methods and tools. Parts 1 to 8. *ACM SIGSoft Software Engineering Notes*, 1996 and 1997.
7. Shari Lawrence Pfleeger. Experimental design and analysis in software engineering. Parts 1 to 5. *ACM SIGSoft Software Engineering Notes*, 1994 and 1995.
8. Bill Curtis. A methodological and empirical basis for research in software engineering. Technical report, Microelectronics and Computer Technology Corporation, 1988.
9. Jonathan P. Bowen, Ricky W. Butler, David L. Dill, Robert L. Glass, David Gries, Anthony Hall, Michael G. Hinchey, C. Michael Holloway, Daniel Jackson, Cliff B. Jones, Michael J. Lutz, David Lorge Parnas, John Rushby, Hossein Saiedian, Jeannette Wing, and Pamela Zave. An invitation to formal methods. *IEEE Computer*, 29(4):16–30, April 1996.
10. Ian Sommerville, Tom Rodden, Pete Sawyer, Richard Bentley, and Michael Twidale. Integrating ethnography into the requirements engineering process. In *Proceedings of the IEEE International Symposium on Requirements Engineering (RE93)*, pages 165–173, San Diego, California, USA, January 1993.
11. Walter F. Tichy, Paul Lukowicz, Lutz Prechelt, and Ernst A. Heinz. Experimental evaluation in computer science: A quantitative study. *Journal of Systems and Software*, 28(1):9–18, January 1995.
12. Victor R. Basili. The experimental paradigm in software engineering. In H. D. Rombach, V. R. Basili, and R. W. Selby, editors, *Experimental Software Engineering Issues: A critical assessment and future directions*, pages 3–12. Lecture Notes in Computer Science Nr. 706, Springer–Verlag, September 1992.
13. Pamela Zave. Classification of research efforts in requirements engineering. *ACM Computing Surveys*, 29(4):315–321, 1997.
14. W-E.A. Mohamed, C. J. Sadler, and D. Law. Experimentation in software engineering: A new framework. In *Proceedings of Software Quality Management '93*, pages 417–430. Elsevier Science, Essex U.K., 1993.
15. Victor R. Basili and H. Dieter Rombach. The TAME Project: Towards improvement–oriented software environments. *IEEE Transactions on Software Engineering*, SE-14(6):758–773, June 1988.
16. Victor R. Basili. Software development: A paradigm for the future. In *Proceedings of the 13th Annual International Computer Software and Application Conference (COMPSAC)*, pages 471–485, Orlando, Florida, September 1989.

17. Victor R. Basili, Gianluigi Caldiera, and H. Dieter Rombach. Goal Question Metric Paradigm. In John J. Marciniak, editor, *Encyclopedia of Software Engineering*, volume 1, pages 528–532. John Wiley & Sons, 1994.
18. L. Briand, C. Differding, and D. Rombach. Practical guidelines for measurement-based process improvement. In *Proceedings of the International Software Consulting Network Conference (ISCN'96)*, 1996.
19. Victor R. Basili, Gianluigi Caldiera, and H. Dieter Rombach. Experience Factory. In John J. Marciniak, editor, *Encyclopedia of Software Engineering*, volume 1, pages 469–476. John Wiley & Sons, 1994.
20. Kevin Ryan. Let's have more experimentation in requirements engineering. In *Proceedings of the 2nd IEEE International Symposium on Requirements Engineering*, page 66, York, U.K., March 1995. Panel session.
21. Michael Jackson, 1995. Concluding statement at the panel session on "Let's have more Experimentation in Requirements Engineering" at the International Symposium on Requirements Engineering (RE'95).
22. Khaled El Elmam, Soizic Quintin, and Nazim H. Madhavji. User participation in the requirements engineering process: An empirical study. *Requirements Engineering Journal*, 1(1):4–26, 1996.
23. Jeannette M. Wing. A study of 12 specifications of the library problem. *IEEE Software*, pages 66–76, July 1988.
24. Claus Lewerenz and Thomas Lindner (Eds.). Case study "production cell". FZI-Publication 1/94, Forschungszentrum Informatik (FZI), Universität Karlsruhe, Germany, 1994.
25. J.-R. Abrial, E. Börger, and H. Langmaack (Eds.). *Formal Methods for Industrial Applications: Specifying and Programming the Steam Boiler Control*. Lecture Notes in Computer Science. Springer, 1996.
26. S. R. Faulk, L. Finneran, J. Kirby, and J. Sutton. Experience applying the CoRE method to the Lookheed C-130J. In *Proceedings of the 9th Annual Conf. on Computer Assurance*, pages 3–8, Gaithersburg, MD, USA, June 1994.
27. Klaus Weidenhaupt, Klaus Pohl, Matthias Jarke, and Peter Haumer. Scenarios in system development: Current practice. *IEEE Software*, pages 34–45, March 1998.
28. Martin S. Feather, Steven Fickas, Anthony Finkelstein, and Axel van Lamsweerde. Requirements and specification exemplars. *Automated Software Engineering*, 4(4):419–438, October 1997.
29. Khaled El Elmam and Nazim H. Madhavji. Measuring the success of requirements engineering processes. In *Proceedings of the 2nd IEEE International Symposium on Requirements Engineering*, pages 204–211, York, UK, March 1995.
30. Oliver Laitenberger and Jean-Marc DeBaud. Perspective-based reading of code documents at Robert Bosch GmbH. *Information and Software Technology*, 39:781–791, 1997.
31. Raimund L. Feldmann, Jürgen Münch, and Stefan Vorwieger. Experiences with systematic reuse: Applying the EF/QIP approach. In *Proceedings of the European Reuse Workshop*, Brussels, Belgium, November 1997.
32. Raimund L. Feldmann and Stefan Vorwieger. The web-based Interface to the SFB 501 Experience Base. SFB-501-TR- 01/1998, Sonderforschungsbereich 501, Dept. of Computer Science, University of Kaiserslautern, 67653 Kaiserslautern, Germany, 1998.
33. Victor Basili, Gianluigi Caldiera, Frank McGarry, Rose Pajersky, Gerald Page, and Sharon Waligora. The Software Engineering Laboratory – an operational Software Experience Factory. In *Proceedings of the 14th International Conference on Software Engineering*, pages 370–381, May 1992.

34. Oliver Laitenberger. Perspective-based reading: Technique, validation, and research in future. ISERN- 95-01, University of Kaiserslautern, Kaiserslautern, Germany, 1995.
35. R. R. Lutz and R. M. Woodhouse. Requirements analysis using forward and backward search. In Nancy R. Mead, editor, *Software Requirements Engineering*, volume 3 of *Annals of Software Engineering*, pages 459–475. Baltzer Science Publishers, September 1997.
36. Kenji Takahashi, Atsuko Oka, Shuichiro Yamamoto, and Sadahiro Isoda. A comparative study of structured and text-oriented analysis and design methodologies. *Journal of Systems and Software*, 28(1):69–75, January 1995.
37. Kevin L. Mills. An experimental evaluation of specification techniques for improving functional testing. *Journal of Systems and Software*, 32(1):83–95, January 1996.
38. Surya B. Yadav, Ralph R. Bravoco, Akemi T. Chatfield, and T. M. Rajkumar. Comparison of analysis techniques for information requirements determination. *Communications of the ACM*, 31(9):1090–1097, September 1988.
39. Adam A. Porter, Lawrence G. Votta, and Victor R. Basili. Comparing detection methods for software requirements inspections: A replicated experiment. *IEEE Transactions on Software Engineering*, 21(6):563–575, June 1995.
40. Victor R. Basili, Scott Green, Oliver Laitenberger, Filippo Lanubile, Forrest Shull, Sivert Sorumgard, and Marvin V. Zelkowitz. The empirical investigation of perspective-based reading. *Journal of Empirical Software Engineering*, 1(2):133–164, 1996.
41. Iris Vessey and Sue A. Conger. Requirements specification: Learning object, process, and data methodologies. *Communications of the ACM*, 37(5):102–113, May 1994.
42. David Jankowski. Computer-aided systems engineering methodology support and its effects on the output of structured analysis. *Journal of Empirical Software Engineering*, 2:11–38, 1997.
43. Lon D. Gowen and James S. Collofello. Assessing traditional verification's effectiveness on safety-critical software systems. *Journal of Systems and Software*, 26(2):103–115, August 1994.
44. Oliver Laitenberger and Jürgen Münch. Ein Prozeßmodell zur experimentellen Erprobung von Software-Entwicklungsprozessen. SFB-501-TR- 04/1996, University of Kaiserslautern, Special Research Project 501, 1996. In german.
45. R. Moen, T. Nolan, and L. Provost. *Improving Quality Through Planned Experimentation*. McGraw-Hill, Inc., 1st edition, 1991.
46. Rational Software Corporation. *Unified Modeling Language*, 1997. Version 1.
47. James Rumbaugh, Michael Blaha, William Premerlani, Frederick Eddy, and William Lorensen. *Object-Oriented Modeling and Design*. Prentice Hall, 1991.
48. A. John van Schouwen. The A-7 requirements model: Re-examination for real-time systems and an application to monitoring systems. CRL Report No. 242, McMaster University, CRL, Telecommunications Research Institute of Ontario (TRIO), Hamilton, Ontario, Canada, February 1992.
49. Erik Kamsties, Antje von Knethen, and Ralf Reussner. An empirical evaluation of two requirements specification techniques. Technical report, University of Kaiserslautern, Kaiserslautern, Germany, 1998. In preparation.

Formal Methods and Industrial-Strength Computer Networks *

Joy Reed

Oxford Brookes University, Oxford, UK
jnreed@brookes.ac.uk

Abstract. Two case studies involving the application of formal methods to industrial-strength computer networks are described. In both case studies, the formal method (CSP/FDR) was thought sufficiently mature for these applications. However in both cases, for the formal method to be effective it was necessary to develop techniques requiring expert knowledge in the theory underpinning the formal method. These examples illustrate that there remain significant technical challenges to effective use of formal methods, which come to light only through large-scale applications. **Keywords**: Formal Methods, Network Protocols, CSP, FDR.

1 Introduction

There are many varieties of formal methods, a term referring to the application of mathematics and mathematically derived techniques to the specification and development of program code and hardware. They all have the same purpose: improving the quality and reliability of computer software and hardware.

There are also numerous applications of formal methods. The overwhelming majority of these applications have been conducted by specialists in the formal techniques rather than by specialists in the application domain. I will describe two industrial-strength case studies, which help illustrate why application specialists do not yet effectively use formal methods. In both cases the formal method had previously been thought sufficiently mature for technology transfer; but disappointingly the method was found to have an inadequate match of existing techniques to the particular application domain. Happily in both cases the theory underlying the formal method was further investigated and focussed on the problem at hand, in order to provide suitable techniques; and the case-studies were successfully completed. However, developing suitable techniques which rendered the application problems tractable required considerable knowledge of the finer points of theory underpinning the formal method - of the sort it is not realistic to expect practitioners to possess.

The first case study briefly described below involves a specification and verification of a signalling protocol for a realistic pots, "plain old telephone system" [KR93]. The work was done in the late 1980's as a part of the REX project, which was an ESPRIT collaboration among academia and industry. We

---

* This work was supported in part by the US Office of Naval Research.

constructed a high-level specification of the system using Timed CSP (TCSP) [RR86] and a refinement also using TCSP, and proved that the refinement met the specification. The problem was one of an excess of formal expressions at even the top-most abstract level so as to render the specifications (related by refinement) collectively so large that proof was intractable by hand, or otherwise. We solved this problem by developing proof conditions whereby constraints which were relied on by one component were guaranteed by another component. This "rely and guarantee" technique significantly reduced the size of the specifications which had to be constructed and manipulated. However it was important that we establish that the these proof rules were theoretically sound, in particular, that they did not produce circular reasoning.

The second case study described below is part of ongoing research involving application of an automated property checker, FDR [FDR], to modern high-speed, multiservice networks. FDR is a finite-state model checker for the process-algebraic language of CSP. Modern multiservice networks such as the Internet typically use protocols designed to operate with arbitrary numbers of interacting components. A problem in employing finite-state model checkers for these protocols is that the model checkers can not directly handle end-to-end properties of arbitrary but unbounded numbers of subcomponents. In order to use FDR for the Internet reservation protocol, we first had to develop an inductive approach for establishing properties of interest, including deadlock and livelock freedom, for such end-to-end protocols.

2 CSP and FDR

CSP [Hoa85] models a system as a *process* which interacts with its environment by means of atomic *events*. Communication is synchronous; that is, an event takes place precisely when both the process and environment agree on its occurrence. CSP comprises a process-algebraic programming language together with a related series of semantic models capturing different aspects of behaviour. A powerful notion of refinement intuitively captures the idea that one system implements another. Mechanical support for refinement checking is provided by Formal Systems' FDR refinement checker, which also checks for system properties such as deadlock or livelock. There are a variety of model checkers for checking properties of finite-state systems. CSP/FDR is distinctive in that it uses a form of CSP (CSP_M [Ros97,S98,FDR]) for expressing both properties and models, it is compositional, and it uses effective compression techniques for state-space reduction.

The simplest semantic model identifies a process as the sequences of events, or *traces* it can perform. We refer to such sequences as *behaviours*. More sophisticated models introduce additional information to behaviours which can be used to determine liveness properties of processes.

We say that a process P is a refinement of process S, written $S \sqsubseteq P$, if any possible behaviour of P is also a possible behaviour of S. Intuitively, suppose S (for "specification") is a process for which all behaviours are in some sense acceptable. If P refines S, then the same acceptability must apply to all behaviours of P. S can represent an idealised model of a system's behaviour, or an abstract property corresponding to a correctness constraint, such as deadlock freedom.

The theory of refinement in CSP allows a wide range of correctness conditions to be encoded as refinement checks between processes. FDR performs a check by invoking a normalisation procedure for the specification process, which represents the specification in a form where the implementation can be validated against it by simple model-checking techniques. When a refinement check fails, FDR provides the means to explore the way the error arose. The system provides the user with a description of the state of the implementation (and its subprocesses) at the point where the error was detected, as well as the sequence of events that lead to the error. The definitive sourcebook for CSP/FDR can now be found in [Ros97].

Unlike most packages of this type, FDR was specifically developed by Formal Systems for industrial applications, in the first instance at Inmos where it is used to develop and verify communications hardware (in the T9000 Transputer and the C104 routing chip). Existing applications include VLSI design, protocol development and implementation, control, signalling, fault-tolerant systems and security. Although the underlying semantic models for FDR do not specifically address time (in contrast to Timed CSP formalism [RR86,TCSP92,KR93]), work has been carried out modelling discrete time with FDR [Sid93,Ros97,R98]. A class of embedded real-time scheduler implementations [Jac96] is analysed with FDR by extracting numerical information from refinement checks to show not only that a timing requirement is satisfied, but also to determine the margin by which it is met.

3 A POTS Signalling Protocol

In [KR93] we described a Timed CSP specification of a telephone exchange, together with a decomposition into a design also described using TCSP. We provided selected proofs establishing that the design satisfies the specification. The work was based on a large specification given in SDL by a telecommunications software company which formed a major part of the REX Esprit Project. The specification was not concerned with billing and data-transfer, rather with safety and liveness properties of the signalling phase of a "Plain Old Telephone Service". It treated awkward race conditions such as a caller replacing just as the callee telephone is about to ring.

We found that for this relatively large, complex application there was a tension between writing strong specifications (in order to achieve desired behaviour, and reduce the sheer weight of formal expressions and state explosion for both the specification and further refinements) and keeping the specification weak enough that it could be implemented. This tension does not reveal itself in the small sized examples underlying the intuition and test beds for much of the theoretical work on formal methods.

Strong specifications for individual subcomponents allow us to prove many properties about the composite system made up of these components. However, it may be impossible or impractical to implement a component which satisfies a desired specification in every possible environment. For these cases it is desirable to relax (or weaken) component specifications but not so much that it becomes impossible to prove the composite system correct. We developed a *Rely and Guarantee* method for CSP which controls this relaxation by explicitly describing a component's intended environment. An added benefit is that the method can greatly reduce the sheer volume of formal expressions needed for a specification.

An example of a proof rule (stated intuitively for two components) for safety properties is the following: if (1) S_p and S_q are initially true, that is, true for the empty trace and (2) the events which cause S_p and S_q to be untrue are mutually exclusive, then

$$\frac{P \text{ sat } S_p \Rightarrow S_q \qquad Q \text{ sat } S_q \Rightarrow S_p}{P||Q \text{ sat } S_p \wedge S_q}$$

We use the above proof rule when we want to design a system to meet safety properties S_p and S_q, but we do not want to implement S_p and S_q unconditionally for P and Q respectively. Rather the implementor of P can assume S_q while implementing S_p, and the implementor of Q can assume S_p while implementing S_q, that is the pair of weaker constraints $S_p \Rightarrow S_q$ and $S_q \Rightarrow S_p$. There is an apparent circularity here in that if Q fails (i.e., fails to satisfy S_q), then P is no longer constrained and so may fail too, thus justifying Q's failure. The side conditions (1) and (2), which are formalised in [KR93], achieve a resolution by ensuring that P and Q are initially correct, and cannot go wrong simultaneously. The idea is that the set of events which can cause S_p and S_q to become false must be disjoint, thereby preventing a single (shared) event to cause both predicates to become false. Analogous but more complex rules are formulated for liveness properties.

These side conditions are automatically true (hence requiring no additional burden of proof) if there are no safety assumptions (constraints) placed on inputs. In general, this condition is automatically satisfied if there are no safety constraints placed on inputs. For example, using this technique we must never specify something of the form "*a* onlyif *b*" in the case that *a* is an input event for P. This makes intuitive sense because otherwise we would require the implementor to filter inputs according to value - something not always appropriate or efficient to do. For systems such as signalling protocols, components must sensibly deal with whatever inputs they are given, so these side conditions are automatically met.

We developed an architectural structure for organising and manipulating the specifications which substantially reduces the sheer volume of formal objects to be handled using this technique. The rely and guarantee parts of the specification could be collected together to form interface specifications, making for a high-level of organisation with a minimum of effort. This reduction in the volume of formal expressions, aligned with an associated reduction in effort of manipulating specification components, proved crucial to effectively formalising and verifying the protocol.

The details of this rely and guarantee technique can be found in [KR93]. The observation of interest here is that for the TCSP formal method to be effective for this industrial-strength application, a new technique (the rely and guarantee) first had to be developed. There were two aspects of this new technique:

- The proof rules which had to be shown sound using the underlying theory of TCSP, and
- The architectural organisational/structuring conventions which substantially reduced the volume of detail.

The structuring conventions were somewhat application related and it might be hoped that application specialists could have developed such enabling techniques "in house", where necessary. However, establishing that the proof rules were sound required special expertise which we should not realistically expect application specialist to possess.

4 An Internet Reservation Protocol

Our second case study of interest involves certain aspects of the Internet RSVP protocol. We (J Reed, D Jackson, B Deianov and G Reed) used CSP/FDR to model and automatically check properties satisfied by the end-to-end protocol [R98].

RSVP is a protocol for multicast resource reservation intended for IP based networks. The protocol addresses those requirements associated with a new generation of applications, such as remote video, multimedia conferencing, and virtual reality, which are sensitive to the quality of service provided by the network. These applications depend on certain levels of resource (bandwidth, buffer space, etc.) allocation in order to operate acceptably. The RSVP approach is to create and maintain resource reservations along each link of a previously determined multicast route, with receivers initiating the resource requests. Thus it is analogous to a signalling phase prior to packet/cell transmission (such as found in ATM networks) during which virtual channels with associated resource assignments are put in place. The multicast may consist of several senders and several receivers.

The full technical specification for RSVP as given by its developers appears as a working document of the Internet Engineering Task Force [BZB96]. The protocol assumes a multicast route, which may consist of multiple senders and receivers. RSVP messages carrying reservation requests originate at receivers and are passed upstream towards the senders. Along the way if any node rejects the reservation, a RSVP reject message is sent back to the receiver and the reservation message discarded; otherwise the reservation message is propagated as far as the closest point along the way to the sender where a reservation level greater than or equal to it has been made. Thus reservations become "merged" as they travel upstream; a node forwards upstream only the "maximum" reservation request.

Receivers can request confirmation messages to indicate that the request was (probably) successful. A successful reservation propagates upstream until it reaches a node where there is a (pending) smaller or equal request; the arriving request is then merged with the reservation in place and a confirmation message sent back to the receiver. Thus the receipt of this confirmation is taken to be a (high-probability) indication rather than a guarantee of a successful reservation. There is no easy way for a receiver to determine if the reservation is ultimately successful. Enhancements involve control packets travelling downstream following data paths, which contain pertinent information to predict the result.

Several interesting aspects emerge from the intuitive description of the RSVP protocol. The protocol is defined for *arbitrary* routing graphs consisting of several senders and receivers. Confirmations sent by intermediate nodes to receivers are ultimately valid only for the receiver making the largest request; i.e., a requester may receive a confirmation although subsequently the end-to-end reservations fails because of further upstream denial. Clearly we are dealing with end-to-end properties inherently involving arbitrary configurations of intermediate nodes. Global views involving intermediate nodes, (e.g., a successful reservation propagates upstream until it reaches a node where there is a (pending) smaller or equal request) present serious problems indeed for building models consisting of predetermined sets of components.

Previous CSP/FDR network applications primarily centre on protocols, but these applications do not specifically address arbitrary network topologies. There are numerous examples of formalisations of layered protocols using a variety of techniques and approaches, including Ethernet - CSMA/CD (in non-automated TCSP [Dav91]) (in non-automated algebraic-temporal logic [Jma95]), TCP (in non-automated CSP [GJ94]), DSS1 / ISDN SS7 gateway (in LOTOS [LY93]), ISDN Layer 3 (in LOTOS [NM90]), ISDN Link Access Protocol (in Estelle [GPB91]), ATM signalling (in TLT, a temporal logic/UNITY formalism [BC95]).

There are a variety of different techniques based on induction for reducing a system of unbounded processes to a finite-state problem. Not surprisingly all of these, as well as ours described below, rely on proof obligations corresponding to a base case and an inductive case. The methods differ in the particular mechanisms, derived from their underlying process theory, for abstracting away the unbounded parts of the system. Techniques appearing in the literature include formulations in process algebra illustrated with bounded buffer and token ring [wl89], network grammars and abstraction illustrated on token ring algorithm and binary tree parity checker [cgj95], general induction theorem illustrated with a distributed replication algorithm and dining philosophers [km89], and PVS model checking illustrated with a mutual exclusion protocol [Shan].

4.1 End properties of network protocols

We approached this problem by developing an induction scheme which lets us infer properties about arbitrary (but finite) collections of nodes from a small number of proofs about fixed numbers of nodes. For example, we might wish to establish deadlock or livelock freedom for an end-to-end protocol which operates with an arbitrary number of intermediate network nodes. We would therefore want to express models and properties in a topology independent manner. To achieve this, we base our specification on a fixed number of single network nodes together with their immediate neighbours, and inductively establish the property for arbitrary chains of such nodes.

Suppose we can characterise the interface which a sender or routing node presents to the next node downstream by a property P. Considering a single node (or partial node where splitting has been used to avoid cycles), if we can demonstrate that under the assumption that all incoming interfaces satisfy P then so do all outgoing interfaces, we have established an inductive step which allows arbitrary acyclic graphs to be built up, always presenting an interface satisfying P to the nodes downstream. The essential base condition, of course, is that an individual data source meets P. The symmetric case starting with a property of a receiving node and building back towards a source is equally sound. A rigorous presentation of this inductive technique is given in [CR,Cre]. Our technique differs from the ones mentioned above in that it relies on the compositionality of CSP to abstract the unbounded parts of the network into a fixed-size component, which serves an invariant (inductive) property of the entire network.

The essence of the method applied to the reservation protocol is to check an assertion effectively stating that if "upstream" channels of a module satisfy property P, then the "downstream" ones do likewise. Figure 1 illustrates the FDR mechanism to do this: assert that the parallel composition of a given module with a property satisfying P, with all upstream channels and all but one downstream channels appropriately hidden (made internal), refines P itself.

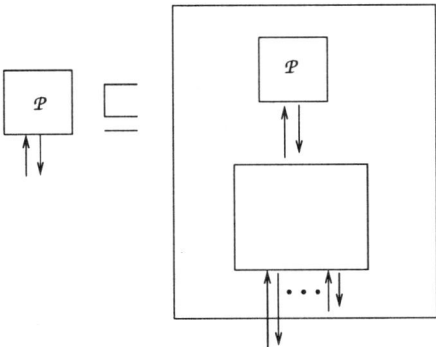

Fig. 1. Simple Induction Scheme

The power of this modelling strategy depends on the ability to reduce a collection of arbitrary n processes to a fixed number of processes, which can then be mechanically model-checked. The reduction is possible if an arbitrary process is defined recursively. In our examples, the state space is kept finite by limiting the resource set to a fixed number, and bounded by reducing an arbitrary chain of processes to one or two. The technique can be especially valuable for establishing deadlock or livelock freedom for end-to-end protocols. However, we note that some properties modelled with CSP/FDR are not inductive in the sense indicated in Figure 1. For example, properties having the following nature;

> If a node exhibits desirable behaviour along a link within t for some time t, then an arbitrary composition of nodes exhibits desirable behaviour along the link within t' for some t'.

must be established using another form of abstraction. The most we can show by model checking is that such properties are link-to-link. It is interesting to note that although certain behaviours are inductive in the above sense, it could be significant that they fail to be inductive in our model-checking sense. For some protocols, link reaction delays could accumulate to an unacceptable end-delay.

Again as in the first case-study described, in order for the formal technique to be effective (in this case, usable at all for the problem at hand), we had to first develop some techniques requiring specialist knowledge in the underlying theory. In this case, we had to make especially clever use of the CSP hiding operator for properly building an inductive structure, and we had to use "lazy abstraction" (previously used only for establishing security properties [Ros97]) to ensure that our checks were sufficiently strong. We also needed to recognise which end properties required a conventional approach, rather than an inductive approach which would have failed.

5 Conclusions

I have described two case studies from my experience with computer networks which illustrate that all too often, existing techniques in our formal methods tool bags do not match industrial-strength problems. Encouragingly for formal methods advocates, with some extra work effective techniques were developed which solved the problem at hand. These techniques required specialist knowledge in the theory underpinning the formal method. Significantly, however, the theoretical basis for the formal semantics did not have to be extended or redefined in any way. Rather we had to appeal to the theory in order to establish soundness of the new techniques.

It is generally recognised that although there has been considerable work in formal methods involving theoretical foundations, standards, and even case-studies, industrial uptake of formal methods is low. Historically for computer networks such as the Internet, correctness potentially offered by formal methods has not been considered a problem; the Internet is characterised by best-effort rather than guaranteed service, and bug fixes have typically been cheap and easy (simply download an update from the Internet). However the success of such multiservice networks is bringing demands for such concerns as security and financial integrity, where establishing correctness is deemed essential.

If formal methods are to be effective for this new generation of network applications, it is essential that the methods are mature enough to be usable by people who are specialists in their application areas rather than in the formal theory. It is unrealistic to expect application specialists, even intelligent and knowledgeable ones, to have the expertise, time or inclination to develop techniques requiring particular knowledge of the finer points of theory underpinning the formal method. The case studies described here illustrate that there remain significant technical challenges for practical use of formal methods which come to light only through application to realistic, large-scale problems. It continues to be important for formal methods specialists to apply the methods to a variety of industrial-strength problems, and make available any resultant techniques which contribute to the maturity and applicability of the methods.

References

[BC95] D Barnard and Simon Crosby, The Specification and Verification of an Experimental ATM Signalling Protocol, *Proc. IFIP WG6.1 International Symposium on Protocol Specification, Testing and Verification XV*, Dembrinski and Sredniawa, eds,Warsaw, Poland, June 1995, Chapman Hall.

[But92] R Butler. A CSP Approach to Action Sysems, DPhil Thesis, University of Oxford, 1992.

[BZB96] R Braden, L Zhang, S. Berson, S. Herzog and S. Jamin. Resource reSerVation Protocol (RSVP) – Version 1, Functional Specification. Internet Draft, Internet Engineering Task Force. 1996.

[cgj95] E.M. Clarke and O. Grumberg and S. Jha, Verifying parameterized networks using abstraction and regular languages, *Proceedings of CONCUR'95"*, 1995, LNCS 962, Springer.

[Cre] S Creese, An inductive technique for modelling arbitrarily configured networks, MSc Thesis, University of Oxford, 1997.

[CR] S Creese and J Reed, Inductive Properties and Automatic Proof for Computer Networks, (to appear).

[Dav91] J Davies, Specification and Proof in Real-time Systems, D.Phil Thesis, Univ. of Oxford, 1991.

[FDR] Formal Systems (Europe) Ltd. Failures Divergence Refinement. *User Manual and Tutorial*, version 1.4 1994.

[ftpe] Estelle Specifications, ftp://louie.udel.edu/pub/grope/estelle-specs

[GJ94] JD Guttman and DM Johnson, Three Applications of Formal Methods at MITRE, *Formal Methods Europe*, LNCS 873, M Naftolin, T Denfir, eds, Barcelona 1994.

[GPB91] R Groz, M Phalippou, M Brossard, Specification of the ISDN Linc Access Protocol for D-channel (LAPD), CCITT Recommendation Q.921, ftp://louie.udel.edu/pub/grope/estelle-specs/lapd.e

[Hoa85] CAR Hoare. *Communicating Sequential Processes*. Prentice-Hall 1985.

[ISOE] ISO Recommendation 9074, The Extended State Transition Language (Estelle), 1989.

[ISOL] ISO: Information Processing System - Open System Interconnection - LOTOS - A Formal Description Technique based on Temporal Ordering of Observational Behavior, IS8807, 1988.
[Jac96] DM Jackson. Experiences in Embedded Scheduling. *Formal Methods Europe*, Oxford, 1996.
[Jma95] M Jmail, An Algebraic-temporal Specification of a CSMA/CD Protocol, *Proc. IFIP WG6.1 International Symposium on Protocol Specification, Testing and Verification XV*, Dembrinski and Sredniawa, eds,Warsaw, Poland, June 1995, Chapman Hall.
[KR93] A Kay and JN Reed. A Rely and Guarantee Method for TCSP, A Specification and Design of a Telephone Exchange. *IEEE Trans. Soft. Eng.*. 19,6 June 1993, pp 625-629.
[km89] R.P. Kurshan and M. McMillan, A structural induction theorem for processes, *Proceedings of the Eighth ACM Symposium on Principles of Distributed Computing*, 1989.
[LY93] G Leon, JC Yelmo, C Sanchez, FJ Carrasco and JJ Gil, An Industrial Experience on LOTOS-based Prototyping for Switching Systems Design, *Formal Methods Europe*, LNCS 670, JCP Woodcock and DG Larsen, eds., Odense Denmark, 1993.
[NM90] J Navarro and P s Martin, Experience in the Development of an ISDN Layer 3 Service in LOTOS, *Proc. Formal Description Techniques III*, J Quemada, JA Manas, E Vazquez, eds, North-Holland, 1990.
[PS91] K Paliwoda and JW Sanders. An Incremental Specification of the Sliding-window Protocol. *Distributed Computing*. May 1991, pp 83-94.
[R98] JN Reed, DM Jackson, B Deianov and GM Reed, Automated Formal Analysi of Networks: FDR Models of Arbitrary Topologies and Flow-Control Mechanisms, ETAPS-FASE98 European Joint Conference on Theory and Practice of Software; Fundamental Approaches to Software Engineering, Lisbon Portugal, March 1998.
[RGG95] AW Roscoe, PHB Gardiner, MH Goldsmith, JR Hulance, DM Jackson, JB Scattergood, H ierarchical compression for model-checking CSP or How to check 10^{20} dining philosphers for deadlock, Springer LNCS 1019.
[Ros97] AW Roscoe. *The CSP Handbook*, Prentice-Hall International, 1997.
[RR86] GM Reed and AW Roscoe, A timed model for communicating sequential processes, Proceedings of ICALP'86, Springer LNCS 226 (1986), 314-323; *Theoretical Computer Science* 58, 249-261.
[S98] B. Scattergood, Tools for CSP and Timed CSP, University of Oxford, DPhil Thesis, (forthcoming 1998).
[Shan] N Shankar, Machine-Assisted Verification Using Automated Theorm Proving and Model Checking, *Math. Prog. Meothodology*, ed. M Broy.
[Sid93] K Sidle, Pi Bus, *Formal Methods Europe*, Barcelona, 1993.
[Sin97] J Sinclair, Action Systems, Determinism, and the Development of Secure Systems, PHd Thesis, Open University, 1997.
[Tan96] AS Tanenbaum. *Computer Networks*. 3rd edition. Prentice-Hall 1996.
[TCSP92] J Davies, DM Jackson, GM Reed, JN Reed, AW Roscoe, and SA Schneider, Timed CSP: Theory and practice. *Proceedings of REX Workshop, Nijmegen*, LNCS 600, Springer-Verlag, 1992.
[Tur86] JS Turner. New Directions in Communications (or Which Way to the Information Age). *IEEE Commun. Magazine*. vol 24, pp 8 -15, Oct 1986.

[wl89]   P. Wolper and V. Lovinfosse, Verifying Properties of Large Sets of Processes with Network Invariants, *Proceedings of the International Workshop on Automatic Verification Methods for Finite-State Machines* 1989, LNCS 407, Springer-Verlag.
[wwwl]   LOTOS Bibliography, http://www.cs.stir.ac.uk/ kjt/research/well/bib.html
[ZDE93] L Zhang, S Deering, D Estrin, S Shenker and D. Zappala. RSVP: A New Resource ReSerVation Protocol. *IEEE Network*, September 1993.

Integration Tools Supporting Development Processes

Stefan Gruner

Graduiertenkolleg für Informatik und Technik, RWTH Aachen, 52056 Aachen (Germany)
gruner@kolleg.informatik.rwth-aachen.de

Manfred Nagl

Lehrstuhl für Informatik III, RWTH Aachen, 52056 Aachen (Germany)
nagl@i3.informatik.rwth-aachen.de

Andy Schürr

Inst. für Softwaretechnologie, Univ. der Bundeswehr München, 85577 Neubiberg (Germany)
schuerr@informatik.unibw-muenchen.de

Abstract. Development processes of various engineering disciplines are usually rather complex. They consist of many interacting subprocesses, which are carried out by different developers. Each subprocess delivers its own documents, which are part of the overall result. All involved documents and their mutual, fine-grained dependencies are subject to permanent changes during the life-time of their development process. Keeping these documents in a consistent state is a most important prerequisite for the success of any engineering project.

As completely automatic change control between documents is often impossible, interactive consistency monitoring and (re-)establishing tools are necessary, which we call integration tools. This paper reports about experiences in building integration tools for software engineering environments and about ongoing efforts to build similar integration tools for chemical process engineering. Furthermore, the paper describes an object-oriented and graph-grammar-based formal method for specifying integration tools and sketches how their implementations are derived from their high-level specifications.

Keywords. development processes, document integration, tool specification, fine-grained interdocument relations, coupled graph grammars.

1 Development processes and their results

Development Processes (DP) in areas such as software development, computer integrated manufacturing, or chemical process control usually involve different developers. Each developer produces a certain set of *documents*, which is part of the overall DP result. His documents have to be kept in a *consistent state* with documents produced by other developers.

Between documents, *directed* and *mutual consistency dependencies* have to be taken into account. A software design specification, which depends on a requirement specification, is an example of a directed dependency. The different perspectives of a requirement specification —such as a data-oriented view and a function-oriented view— are an example for mutual document dependencies.

Simultaneous engineering [BW96] aims at accelerating DPs by starting dependent subprocesses as early as possible with preliminary results (prereleases) of preceding subprocesses. *Concurrent* engineering [Re+93], on the other hand, allows to develop different perspectives of the same product part in parallel.

1.1 Development subprocesses and their results

A key problem in the development of any engineering product is *change control,* especially in the case of simultaneous or concurrent engineering. Changes are carried out due to detected errors, due to changed design decisions but also, in the extreme case, due to changed requirements in an ongoing project. In the course of a usual development process many errors are made and the construction of required results is often not straightforward. Thus we can state that both development and maintenance of engineering products have to deal with permanent changes of intermediate or final DP results.

In any application area mentioned above complex document configurations are built up and maintained. They do not only consist of the final configuration (e.g. the source code of a software system) but also of many further subconfigurations responsible for describing the requirements, the architectural plan, documenting the developed ideas and met decisions, assuring quality, or managing the whole development process. Such an *overall configuration* consists of many documents which, in turn, may have a complex inner structure.

Produced *documents* often have many fine-grained *dependencies between* their *constituents* (increments). For the quality of the whole product and the efficiency of the total process these dependencies are of minor importance. A single developer is usually responsible for the internal consistency of a document. He should be able to keep all local consistency requirements in mind and, in many cases, he is supported by suitable document processing tools such as a syntax-directed diagram editor or a CASE analysis tool.

The *fine-grained dependencies between documents* correspond to the interfaces between the work of different developers. As we show in section 2, no suitable support is available for keeping these interdocument dependencies in a consistent state. Therefore, we concentrate on this problem in the following. We use the relations between a requirement specification and the design of a software system as a running example.

For *coordinating* a *team* of *developers,* management information (administration configuration) about a project has to be built up and maintained. We distinguish between process, product (configuration and version), resources, and department or company information, and we regard their mutual relations in order to coordinate a team of developers working. Management in this sense has to be supported by suitable tools. There, interesting problems arise as the administration configuration is changed in its structural form, when a development process is carried out [Kra98]. In this paper, however, we concentrate on the support of technical developers and the interfaces of their results.

Many DP *documents*, which are the results of technical development subprocesses, have a *semiformal form*. Some documents are completely informal, as the nonfunctional requirements specification, where we find plain text possibly presented in a standardized (sub-)chapter form. Rather seldom we find formal documents, as e.g. a specification in a logic-based language such as Z. A standard case is that we find documents in diagrammatic, tabular, pictorial, or textual form which altogether possess an underlying structure and a more or less well-defined syntax. Examples of this kind are OO-analysis diagrams, module descriptions in a software design description language, and so on. So, "semiformal" either means that formalization of a certain DP result is not carried out completely or, even more, that the underlying document description language is only formalized to a certain extent.

Having most documents in a semiformal form, the fine-grained *relations* between documents are *semiformal, too*. Often, we can state that a certain increment (subpart) of one document may be related to an increment of another document if both increments are instances of corresponding types, have compatible properties, and appear in a certain context within their documents. A technical documentation may, for instance, contain a section for each module of a related software design document, and a section may contain a subsection for each exported resource of the related module.

1.2 Preserving consistency of dependent documents

Language correspondences have to be elaborated, which define legal interdocument relations, before supporting tools can be built [Jan92]. This is usually called *method integration* [Krö93].

In some cases method integration rules require that instances of some type T_A in a document A are always related to instances of type some T_B in a document B, as it was the case with modules in software design and sections in technical documentation documents, respectively. This is called a bijective *(1:1) correspondence* between increment types of documents. In many cases, however, we have *(m:n) correspondences* on the type level such that further information is needed in order to decide whether an increment of type T_A of document A may be related to an increment of type T_B in document B. Such a decision may depend on

- local properties of inspected increments,
- their contexts in the regarded pair of documents,
- and manual design decisions of an involved developer.

Usually, consistency establishing subprocesses of a development process *cannot be automated*. The development of some document B_j, which is the result of one subprocess, often depends on the result of another subprocess, delivering some master document A, in a rather imprecisely defined way. Exceptions are generating an NC program from a CAD document, or generating module frames from a software design document etc. In these rare cases, the increments of involved documents are closely related to each other and a complete formal definition of the corresponding interdocument dependencies is feasible.

The standard case is that subprocesses are *creative* in the sense that a developer is not able to come up with a precise and complete formal definition of a procedure (method, plan) how changes of a master document A have to be translated into corresponding changes of dependent documents B_j (Fig.1). As an example, regard the development of a coarse-grained software design for a given requirements specification. The design may be one of the "structured world", an object-based or an object-oriented one [Nag90], and it is *influenced by many factors* such as the underlying middleware or the decision to (re-)use certain libraries or frameworks. As a consequence, there is no chance to automate the transition from requirements engineering to software design completely. However, the transition can be simplified by tools, which perform trivial subtasks on their own and keep track of once established relations between the requirements for and the design of a software system (see below).

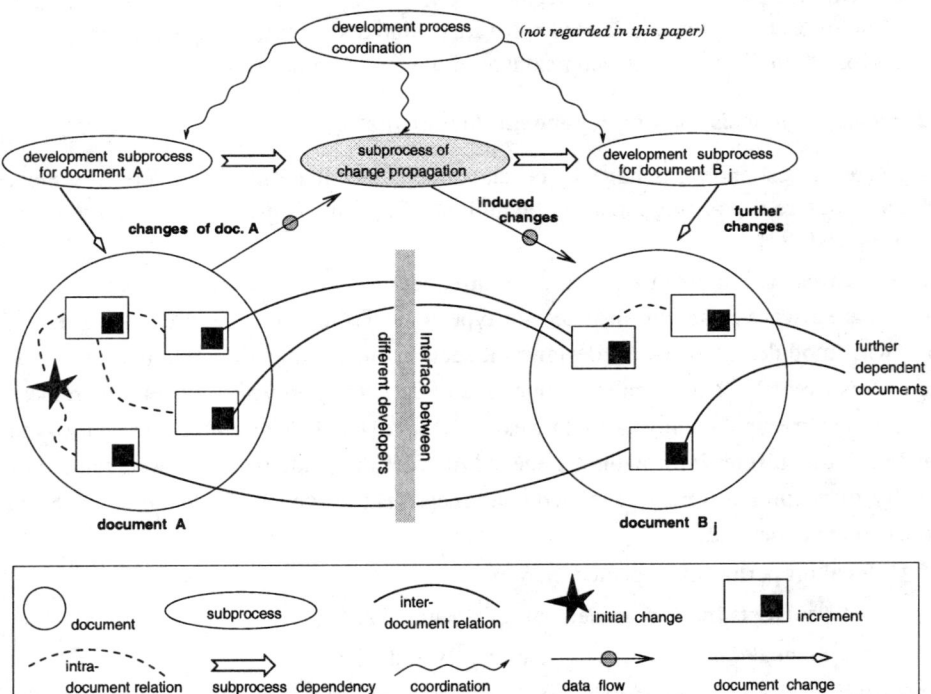

Fig.1 Dependent documents and their development subprocesses

Changes within a master document A require changes in a dependent document B_j, which then require further changes in dependent documents of B_j. There are many *different possibilities* how *to translate* an update of a master document into updates of its dependent documents. Furthermore, rather *different strategies* may be used *to propagate* necessary changes along chains of dependent documents. One possibility is called batch-oriented. It reestablishes first complete consistency between a document A and all its directly dependent documents B_j w.r.t. a sequence of updates on A, before proceeding with the dependent documents of B_j. Another possibility is called trace-oriented. It propagates one performed update on a document A to all directly or indirectly affected dependent documents after the other. Both strategies have their specific advantages and disadvantages and should be supported by integration tools.

The following sections discuss the *specification* and *realization* of *various types* of *integration tools*, which are responsible for monitoring and (re-)establishing consistency of dependent documents. These tools have to regard the semiformal structure of corresponding documents. They have to give substantial support for fine-grained integration by regarding the current form of documents and offering different possibilities how to propagate changes, which are selected based on creative design decisions. Furthermore, they must not enforce certain orders of process steps as quite different consistency reestablishing strategies are possible. Finally, it should be possible to work with already existing and a-posteriori integrated tools, when manipulating the corresponding documents.

2 Available support for interdocument consistency control

The available and industrial support for monitoring and maintaining fine-grained consistencies of related documents is on a considerably lower level than the tight integration tools sketched in the previous section. The standard procedure is that developers exchange documents is some low-level *standard format* (Postscript, SGML, HTML etc.). In any case, the developer of a dependent document has to find out which changes have taken place on a master document A and then has to perform the adequate changes on the dependent documents B_j.

Another wide-spread approach, especially in the software engineering community [SB93], is to implement *batch-oriented* and *automatic converters* after the corresponding method integration has taken place. So, neither incremental changes of some master document A can be handled, nor do these tools regard that dependent documents B_j are already elaborated to a certain state. Also, no creative design decisions of developers can be taken into account. Furthermore, such converters are usually hand-coded. As many documents in different languages as well as different method integration approaches exist, hand-coding of integration tools has to be replaced by generating tools from high-level specifications.

A similar problem occurs with industrial *document exchange standards* such as STEP with its data modeling language EXPRESS [ISO] or CDIF [EIA94]. They define big class diagrams (data models) for certain types of engineering documents, but mostly disregard consistency relations between different types of documents. The data modeling language EXPRESS allows, for instance, to define the data model of each type of documents as a separate module and to import the data model of one module into another one. Furthermore, EXPRESS offers rules for defining static integrity constraints across document boundaries. It is very difficult, however, to derive consistency establishing operations from these static integrity constraints. As a consequence, EXPRESS data models are not a suitable source of input for generating integration tools.

Also *hypertext systems*, as introduced in [NK91], do not offer an appropriate solution for preserving the consistency of a set of related documents. They have no knowledge about the semantics of links and just offer basic mechanisms to insert unspecific links and to browse along them. Consistency control is on a low level, namely detection of dangling links. Finally, all links have to be established by the user. He has no profit if he is forced to insert all links manually and then only receives warnings that a part of them is dangling.

More refined concepts can be found in (meta) software development environments, where documents are internally represented as *attributed syntax trees*. Support is given for propagating changed attribute values up and down the syntax tree. This allows to specify and generate analysis tools, which check interdocument consistency constraints [KKM87] if all regarded documents are modeled as subtrees of a common syntax tree. Other systems offer better support for the required nesting of documents. Gate nodes and door attributes of a distributed syntax tree model the transition from one document's language to another one [Bo+88].

All syntax tree based systems mentioned above have problems with the specification of *active transformation tools* (in contrast to passive consistency checking tools). Attribute coupled grammars and variants thereof [GG84] [RT88], tree pattern matchers [AGT89], and context-sensitive tree transformation tools [CC93] are promising attempts to overcome these problems. They are useful for purposes like concrete syntax generation (unparsing) or compiler back-end generation. The still remaining problem with these approaches is that generated transformation tools are unidirectional, batch-oriented, and not interactive.

Yet a further integration approach can be found in the software project KORSO [BJ95]. The key idea of this project is to provide means for the development of *correct software* by *specification* and *program transformation* within a framework of formally sound meta tools. However, it is not easy to transfer formal integration methods for software engineering to other document development domains (e.g. engineering or project management). In industrial application domains we find that the "universe of discourse" is not completely formalizable, or that indeterminism is a dominant factor.

There is at least another RTSE'97 workshop contribution dealing with consistency management, especially in requirements engineering [JN98]. In that paper, a so-called *meta meta model* is employed together with consistency rules that can incrementally be called on demand. This fully user-oriented approach is based on logic formulas for *consistency description* and goals for *inconsistency monitoring* in data bases. Methods for an incremental and semi-automatic resolution of discovered inconsistencies are not reported. This paper is related to the *View Point* approach of consistency management in [FNK94] [FS96]. The View Point approach offers *actions* for semi-automatic (userdriven) inconsistency resolution. The main difference between the View Point approach and our approach is the way of specifying integration tools. In our opinion, it is more difficult and less intuitive to transfer the required expert knowledge into logic formulas than to operate with "visible" graph structures and graph transformations that can be easily understood by non-computer-science project partners and customers, too.

Federated data base systems [SL90] represent another form of data integration. They offer a common global schema for different local data base systems, which usually is used for retrieval of data but not for updates (update problem). Active data base systems [DHW95] offer event-trigger mechanisms to keep data bases consistent. Event-trigger mechanisms play about the same role for the data-oriented integration paradigm as messages do for the control-oriented integration paradigm of broadcast message servers [Rei90] [Fro90] [Fra91]. Event-trigger mechanisms and broadcasted messages are still rather *low level means* to simplify the implementation of integration tools and to propagate updates between related documents or processing tools.

For the sake of completeness we should mention tools, which coordinate development subprocesses and their results on a *coarse-grained level*, i.e. without taking the internal structure of documents and the fine-grained interdocument relations between them into account. There, we find CAD frameworks [HN+90] or EDM systems [McI95] for managing project data bases. Workflow systems [GHS95] coordinate development subprocesses. Furthermore, we find configuration and version control tools on coarse- as well as fine-grained level [Da+97] [SS95]. However, the latter are usually unspecific w.r.t. the structure of their documents [Wes98].

3 Some experiences in building integration tools

Our experiences in building integration tools date back to 1988, when the implementation of our first integrated CASE tool prototype was finished [Lew88]. Its most important integration tool has the task to keep a program's design in a consistent state with its technical documentation. This tool can be used in two different modes. Its *free format mode* allows to create arbitrary links between increments of the design document and sections or paragraphs of the accompanying technical documentation. In this case, the tool supports browsing along hyperlinks and issues warnings that once created hyperlinks are now dangling or that sources or targets of hypertext links are modified. The integration tool's more sophisticated *fixed format mode* enforces a structure of the technical documentation, which is closely related to the structure of its software design document. Any module of the design document corresponds to a section of the technical documentation, any exported module resource to a paragraph of the enclosing section. Section headlines are automatically derived from module names.

This integration tool for software design and technical documentation thus realizes a combination of a hyperlink *browser,* a consistency *checker,* and a consistency reestablishing *transformator* (as any other integration tool presented here). Updates of the design document are immediately propagated as *change messages* to the dependent technical documentation. These messages are then asynchronously processed and —partly automatically, partly manually— translated into appropriate updates of the technical documentation. The integration tool was manually implemented without any kind of reuse of basic components and without a formal specification of its expected behavior. Needed hyperlinks were stored as pairs of unidirectional pointers in related documents.

Some years later an incrementally and automatically working integration tool for software design and Modula-2 was built using a more elaborate specification and implementation approach [Wes91]. First of all, the EBNF syntax definitions of both involved types of documents were related to each other and then manually translated into a *programmed graph rewriting specification* of the integration tool's functional behaviour. Based on the graph rewriting specification, an integration tool was (manually) implemented, that keeps a software system's design and the corresponding configuration of Modula-2 interface documents in a consistent state. The main progress of this integration tool —compared with the previous integrator— is that hyperlinks are now stored in a separate *integration document*. This allows the integration of already implemented types of documents more easily, simplifies multi-user access to related documents, and offers the appropriate data base for storing information about an ongoing integration process.

The needs to build an integration tool, which keeps requirements engineering documents and software design documents in a consistent state, forced us to generalize the integration tool specification and implementation approach [Jan92]. The most challenging feature of this integration tool for requirements engineering (RE) and software design was the required interaction between the computation of applicable transformations rules and the manual selection of actually applied rules. This is due to the fact that consistency relations between Structured Analysis (SA) diagrams and Entity Relationship (ER) diagrams on one hand and design documents on the other hand are rather vague and context-dependent. An SA data flow diagram (DFD) may be translated into a module or a procedure of a design document depending on the number of applied occurrences of the DFD in its SA document, the way how related SA increments were already translated into software design increments, and creative design decisions of the involved integration tool user.

Fig.2 shows one example of an SA document and a graphical as well as a textual view of its related design document. The top left DFD **SellProduct** contains the three processes **AcceptChoice, CheckPayment,** and **CalculatePrice** as well as the two data stores **CoinCharacteristics** and **PriceTable**. The latter two provide needed input data for **CheckPayment** and **CalculatePrice**, respectively. The DFD in the left bottom corner of figure 2 represents the refinement of the process **CheckPayment**. All involved

DFDs —except **CheckPayment**— are translated into so-called F(unction) modules, all data stores into so-called O(bject) modules. The occurrence of a certain process or data store Y in a DFD X corresponds to an import between the related modules X and Y. The data flows between processes as well as the input and output ports of DFD **SellProduct** (the small rectangles labeled **Input** and **Message** on its left-hand side) are disregarded on this level of granularity. They may be useful later on for determining formal parameter lists of generated procedures. The missing module **CheckPayment** together with all its dependent components is just under construction. The black background color of DFD **CheckPayment** in the SA document informs the integration tool's user that this SA increment has not yet any counterpart in the corresponding program design. It is up to the user to decide whether it is worthwhile to build a separate module for **CheckPayment**, too, or whether the functionality of **CheckPayment** may be implemented as a single local function of module **SellProduct**.

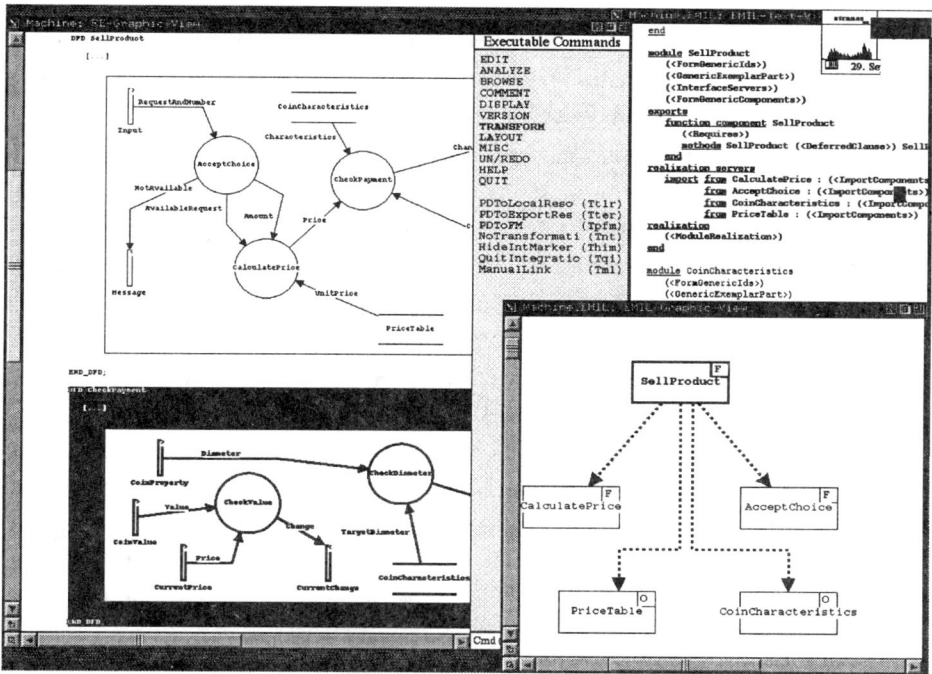

Fig.2 Requirements engineering and program design integration tool

The syntax of the regarded requirements engineering and software design documents with their diagrammatic notations was no longer defined in the form of EBNFs, but in the form of (extended) ER diagrams. As a consequence, a new meta modeling approach was employed to identify corresponding entity types of ER diagrams instead of corresponding nonterminal classes of previously used EBNFs. Similar approaches to relate entity types of different (data base) schemas by deriving them from the same meta class can be found in the data base community for solving data base migration problems, see for example [JJ95].

Unfortunately, it is often not possible to derive consistency checking or document transformation code directly from constructed meta models. The problem is that entity type correspondences, such as DFD is either related to module or to procedure, are not precise enough to define the wanted behavior of integration tools. Therefore, we returned to the idea presented in [Wes91] to describe the syntax of documents by means of grammars and to specify dependencies between documents by coupling these grammars. The main difference between the old proceeding in [Wes91] and the new proceeding in [Lef95] is that the former one uses context-free string grammars (EBNFs) for this purpose, whereas the latter one is based on *context-sensitive graph grammars,* as already suggested in [Pra71].

Following this approach, the specification and realization of document integration tool proceeds now as follows:

1. The internal structures of dependent documents are modeled as *directed graphs,* which contain different classes (types) of attributed nodes and edges for different kinds of increments and intradocument relations.
2. UML[1] *class diagrams* are then constructed to define the relevant components of regarded document graphs from a static point of view.
3. Next, *correspondences* between UML class diagrams are established in accordance with the meta modeling approach of [Jan92]. They identify possibly related increment classes (node types) of dependent documents.
4. Afterwards, *object diagrams* are used to define corresponding substructures (subgraphs) of related document graphs more precisely on the instance level.
5. These object diagrams are translated into *graph grammars* that generate those subsets of schema consistent document graphs, which consist of previously defined object diagrams only (thereby excluding intermediate inconsistent or incomplete document editing results as valid integration tool inputs).
6. Finally, the constructed *graph grammars are coupled* such that each production of a master document graph is related to a set of productions of a dependent document graph.

All needed kinds of integration tools may be derived from a single coupled graph grammar specification of the corresponding interdocument consistency relation. This includes a *forward transformation* tool, which propagates updates from a master document to the dependent document, a *reverse transformation* tool, which propagates updates

---

[1]. UML, the Unified Modeling Language [FS97], is the new standard notation for object-oriented analysis and design. It is now an accepted standard of the Object Management Group OMG.

from a dependent document back to its master document, or a pure *analysis* tool, which checks consistency of dependent documents without changing their contents.

Up to now, all integration tools are manually derived from a given coupled graph grammar specification, based on a *reusable framework* for the construction of integration tools [Nag96]. The reusable framework offers, for instance, various forms of document traversing and comparing strategies as well as a standard implementation of integration documents. These integration documents, which were first introduced in [Wes91], are now used for storing all hyperlinks between two dependent documents together with all design decisions of users how to translate updates of master documents into updates of dependent documents.

Some of the tools described above have found their way to *industrial products*. Within *cap debis* company, that was our partner in the ESF and COMPLEMENT projects [FO90] [Krö93], integration tools from requirements engineering to design have been realized as part of their CASE tool set [Hru91]. Furthermore, in [EJS88] an industrial development environment is described sharing common concepts and tool behaviour with [Lew88].

It is the subject of ongoing research activities to translate coupled graph grammar specifications, which define interdocument consistency relations in a purely declarative manner, automatically into *programmed graph rewriting specifications*, which define the functional behavior of specific integration tools in the form of complex document graph transformations [JSZ96], and to extend the methodological framework of our approach. Those graph rewriting specifications may be translated into equivalent C or Modula-2 code, using the compiler of the PROGRES graph grammar development environment [SWZ95].

The presented integration tool development process is explained in more detail in the following section 4. It was already successfully used for realizing another version of the integration tool for requirements engineering and software design as well as for realizing new integration tools between software designs and Eiffel programs or between SA and ER diagrams [Lef95]. Furthermore, related graph grammar based approaches were used for translating relational DBMS schemas into object-oriented DBMS schemas [JSZ96] and for integrating commercial SA editors with a research prototype for high-level timed Petri nets [BOP97]. Last but not least a refined version of the presented integration approach is currently used for integrating software tools for chemical process engineering [NM97] [NW98].

4 Specifying interdocument integration tools

The previous section presented a number of graph grammar based integration tools and sketched their development. It is the purpose of this section to explain the graph grammar based development of integration tools in more detail, using the running example of the integration tool for RE and software design. As already mentioned, the development of such a tool starts with modeling all involved types of documents as directed graphs. Different types of increments —such as **DFD** or **Process**— correspond to different types (classes) of nodes, different types of intradocument relations —such as **DFD contains Process** or **DFD defines Process**— are introduced as different types of directed edges (associations). Furthermore, node attributes are needed to represent local properties of increments, such as the **Name** of a **DFD** or a **Process**.

4.1 UML class and object diagrams as interdocument relation descriptions

The needed components of document graphs and their relations are introduced as so-called *graph schemas*. It is a matter of taste whether an ER-diagram-like notation or an UML-class-diagram notation is used for this purpose. Within this paper, we prefer the upcoming standard OO notation UML, which allows to draw class diagrams as well as object diagrams [FS97]. Furthermore, UML offers the concept of packages, which allows to encapsulate document graph schemas and to distinguish between local and externally visible document graph components.

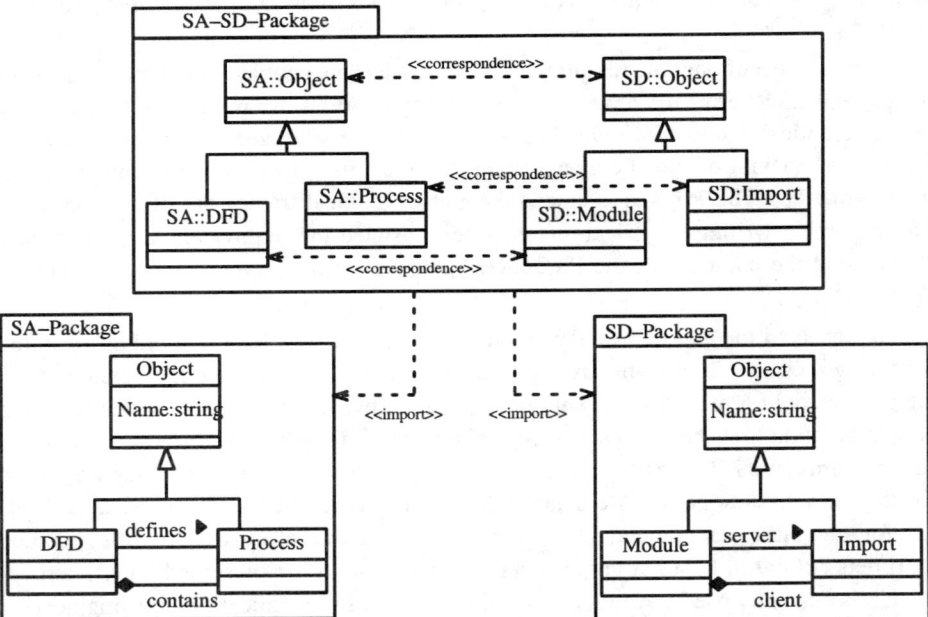

Fig.3 Corresponding SA and SD document graph schema definitions

Fig.3 shows a cut-out of the graph schema definitions for Structured Analysis (SA) and software design (SD) documents. Its packages **SA** and **SD** display only those definitions of classes and associations which are needed for the translation of a **DFD** and a **Process** into a **Module** and an **Import**, respectively. Both packages introduce a superclass **Object** to declare a **Name** attribute for **DFD** and **Process** on one side and for **Module** and **Import** on the other side. Please note that the **Import** relation is modeled as part of its **client Module** (source) and possesses the **Name** of its **server Module** (target) as its own

Name. This reflects the way how import relations (clauses) are defined in the textual software design document representation of Fig.2.

The additional **SA–SD** package imports all externally visible classes of its dependent packages **SA** and **SD** and introduces the required class correspondences between the two (abstract) **Object** superclasses and between their subclasses **DFD** and **Module** as well as between their subclasses **Process** and **Import**. Many classes and class correspondences have been omitted in Fig.3 due to lack of space, as e.g. the SD class **Procedure** and its correspondence to the SA class **DFD**.

Some constraints have to be postulated concerning legal and illegal combinations of generalization relationships with graph schema crossing correspondence relationships. These constraints prohibit e.g. the definition of a correspondence relationship between the classes **SA::DFD** and **SD::Object** in the presence of a correspondence relationship between the classes **SA::Object** and **SD::Module**. This is considered as a contradiction between the requirement that any **SA::Object** is mapped onto a **SD::Module** and the fact that a **SA::DFD**, a special kind of **SA::Object**, may be mapped to any **SD::Object**.

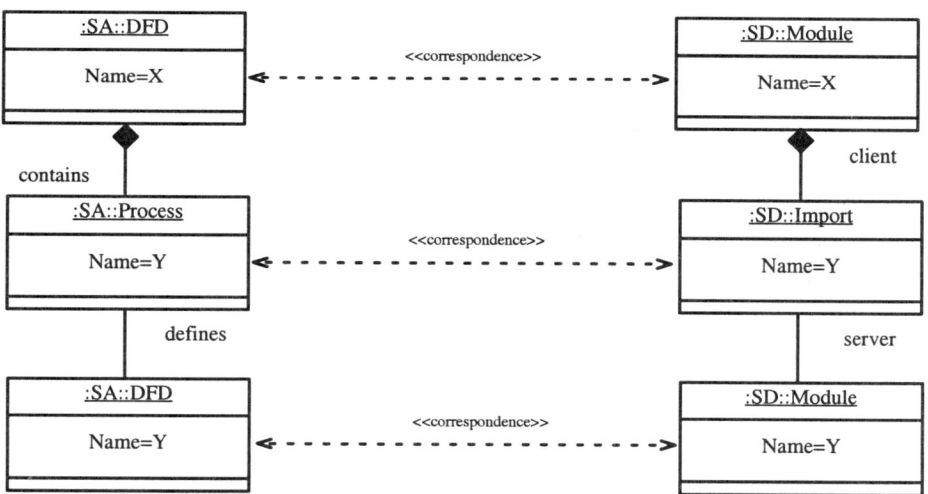

Fig.4 Object diagram definition of corresponding SA and SD subgraphs

Based on graph schema correspondences, which define a superset of all possible relations between SA increments and SD increments, it is now necessary to identify existing interdocument consistency relations more precisely. Experiences showed that object diagrams are the most appropriate notation for this purpose. They allow one to define pairs of subgraphs (subpatterns, substructures) on the instance level, which relate certain configurations of SA increments to corresponding configurations of SD increments and viceversa. Fig.4 presents one example of this kind. It states that a **DFD** X, which contains a **Process** Y with its own **DFD** definition, may be related to a **Module** X, which contains an **Import** clause for **Module** Y. Furthermore, it requires that the **DFD** instances X and

Y correspond to **Module** instances X and Y, and that the **Process** instance of Y in DFD X corresponds to the **Import** clause for **Module** Y in **Module** X.

Many object diagrams of this kind are necessary to define the set of all relevant interdocument relations between SA and SD document graphs. Unfortunately, it is not possible to establish useful consistency or completeness criteria for the resulting set of object diagrams in the general case. This is due to the fact that subgraphs of different object diagrams may overlap and that certain document subgraphs on one side may not have corresponding document subgraphs on the other side. Our running example requires e.g. the construction of another object diagram, which relates the same SA subgraph as in Fig.4 to a **Module** X, which contains a **Procedure** Y. As a consequence, it is not possible to interpret the constructed set of object diagrams as the consistent definition of a deterministic function, which translates SA documents into SD documents. The completeness criteria is violated by the fact that there may be some SA documents without corresponding SD documents. There is perhaps no rule how to translate a **DFD** X, which contains a **Process** X as a forbidden self-reference, into a corresponding SD document substructure.

4.2 From class and object diagrams to coupled graph grammars

The UML class diagrams and object diagrams of the previous subsection are the appropriate means to discuss the functionality of an integration tool with its future users. These users have the needed knowledge about the regarded application domain for building the appropriate set of class and object diagrams as well as for checking consistency and completeness of these diagrams. The following step of the integration tool building process is on a more technical level and may be performed without any assistance of application domain experts. It concerns the translation of a set of object diagrams into a *coupled graph grammar specification*. Each object diagram is translated into one or more coupled graph grammar productions. Each coupled graph grammar production is a pair of two regular graph grammar productions plus the definition of a correspondence relationship between the nodes on the left- and right-hand sides of the combined productions.

Fig.5 shows two examples of coupled graph grammar productions, which were produced by taking the object diagram of Fig.4 as input. The main problem of the transition from object diagrams to coupled graph grammars is that we have to distinguish between *context nodes*, which are part of a production's left- and right-hand side, and *new nodes*, which are only part of a production's right-hand side. It is, for instance, not useful to define a graph grammar production, which creates a **Process** Y as part of a **DFD** X together with its **DFD** definition Y. As a consequence, we would not be able to deal with a **DFD** without any applied **Process** occurrences or with more than one occurrence. It is, therefore, better to translate the object diagram of Fig.4 into two coupled graph grammar productions, as presented in Fig.5. The first one, **Create–DFD&Module**, consists of two regular graph grammar subproductions, which have connected grey rectangles as background. Both subproductions have an empty left-hand side and a single node on the right-hand side. The SA subproduction creates an isolated **DFD** node with **Name** = Y in the

SA document graph, the SD subproduction a corresponding **Module** node with the same **Name** in the related SD document graph.

The following coupled graph grammar production **Create–Process&Import** of Fig.5 matches two pairs of corresponding **DFD** and **Module** nodes with the left-hand sides of its two subproductions. These nodes together with their correspondence relationship are preserved by the given subproductions due to the fact that the defined right-hand sides contain their left-hand sides as subgraphs. Furthermore, the coupled subproductions create a new **Process** occurrence of **DFD Y** in **DFD X** as well as a corresponding **Import** clause with **Module X** as **client** and **Module Y** as **server**.

coupled production Create–DFD&Module =

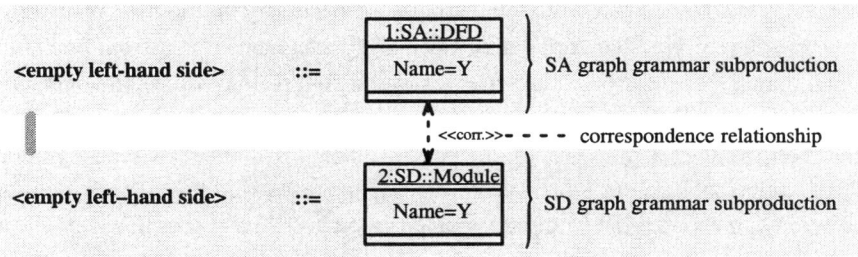

coupled production Create–Process&Import =

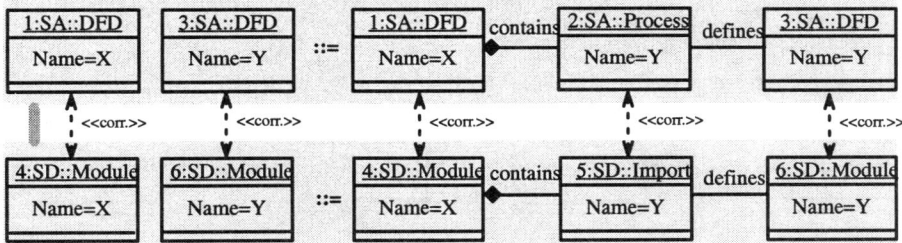

Fig.5 Two coupled graph grammar productions derived from figure 4

4.3 From coupled graph grammars to integration tool specifications

As already mentioned, one coupled graph grammar serves as the specification for a number of related but nevertheless quite differently behaving integration tools. The same coupled SA–SD graph grammar may for instance be used to develop an incrementally working forward engineering tool, which translates SA document updates into SD document updates, and a batch-oriented reverse engineering tool, which takes a complete SD document as input and produces a corresponding SA document as output. This is a consequence of the fact that coupled graph grammar productions do not distinguish between master documents and dependent documents and that they do not prescribe how and when consistency between dependent documents is (re-)established.

Coupled graph grammars, which are constructed using a set of object diagrams as input, never contain node or edge deleting productions, i.e. the left-hand sides of their productions are always subgraphs of their right-hand sides. The restriction to non-deleting productions is not as severe as it seems to be at a first glance. This is due to the fact that the productions of a coupled graph grammar are *not* the editing operations for the involved types of documents. Document graph editing operations are defined without having certain interdocument consistency relations in mind. Furthermore, they do not only create, but modify and delete document components. Last but not least the editing operations for a certain type of document graphs may be used to manipulate subgraphs, which are irrelevant and therefore hidden for the regarded document integration task; (see [Nag96] for further details concerning the definition of document views for integration tools).

The restriction to non-deleting productions is the necessary prerequisite for being able to derive different kinds of (efficiently operating) integration tools from one coupled graph grammar specification. Otherwise, we would be forced to parse pairs of document graphs w.r.t. to unrestricted types of graph grammars in order to be able to check interdocument consistency relations (i.e. to solve the membership problem for type 0 grammars, which is undecidable in the general case). Having the restriction to non-deleting productions in mind, it is possible to translate coupled graph grammar productions into different sets of ordinary graph transformation rules. One set of transformation rules defines the functional behavior of a forward transformation integration tool, another one the behavior of the corresponding reverse transformation integration tool, a third one the behavior of a consistency checking tool, and so on.

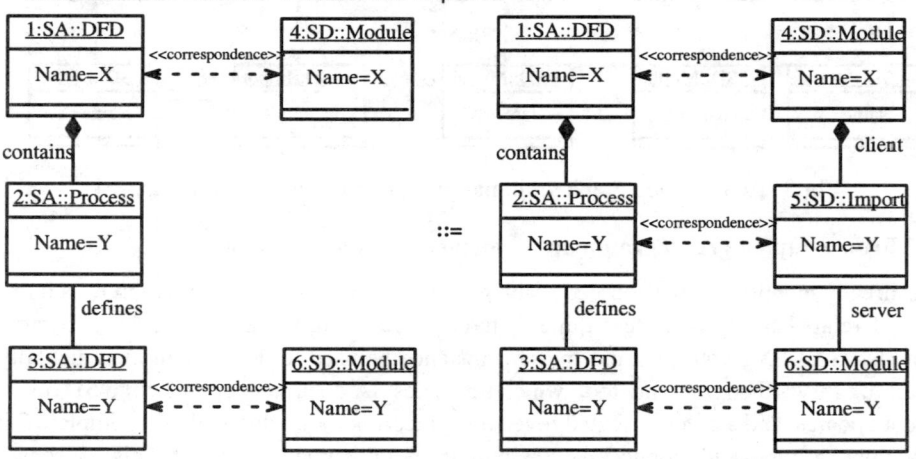

Fig.6 A forward graph transformation rule from SA to SD

Fig.6 shows one example of a derived SA–SD forward transformation rule. It translates a **Process** occurrence of **DFD** Y in **DFD** X of the SA document into an **Import** between the related **Modules** X and Y of the SD document. This rule was constructed as follows: its left-hand side is the combination of the right-hand side of the corresponding SA production with the left- and side of the corresponding SD production in Fig.5, its right-hand side is the combination of the right-hand sides of the two coupled SA and SD productions.

An SD–SA reverse transformation rule may be constructed by simply exchanging the roles of SA and SD productions in the previous paragraph. A consistency checking and correspondence relationships establishing transformation rule may be built by merging the constructed forward and reverse transformation rules.

4.4 From tool specifications to tool implementations

All generated transformation rules have to be combined with a reusable framework, which determines the order of rule applications and which processes needed user interactions. Furthermore, the framework provides a certain bookkeeping strategy for not yet transformed document parts or already transformed but afterwards changed document parts. Please note that "real" graph transformation rules are more complex than the one presented in Fig.6. They use a more sophisticated representation of correspondence relationships (as nodes and edges of separate integration document graphs) and manipulate therefore three related subgraphs of a hierarchical graph instead of one flat graph only [Nag96].

The finally needed translation from forward or backward graph transformation rules to efficiently executable C or Modula-2 code is supported by the PROGRES graph grammar environment [SWZ95]. This environment represents an integrated set of tools for syntax-directed editing, analyzing, and executing single graph transformation rules or complex graph transformation programs. Two execution modes are supported: (1) direct interpretation of created specifications and (2) compilation into lower level programming languages such as C and Modula-2. Generated program fragments may be combined with hand-crafted code as the integration tool framework mentioned above.

For further details concerning the construction of graph transformation rules from coupled graph grammars and the implementation of the needed framework the reader is referred to [Nag96] [JSZ96]. In [CGN98] we describe how the graph transformation approach can be transferred from a software engineering to a chemical process engineering domain. In that contribution we also discuss some details of tool specification with graph grammars, which are omitted in this paper due to lack of space.

5 Formal background of coupled graph grammars

The preceding sections introduced a graph grammar based method for the specification and implementation of document integration tools on a rather informal level. A complete formal definition of graph grammars, their underlying graph data models, and the definition of appropriate graph grammar coupling mechanisms is outside the scope of this paper. The interested reader is referred to [RS96] for a formal treatment of restricted types of graph grammars as a visual language syntax definition and parsing formalism and to the chapter 7 of the Handbook of Graph Grammars [Sch97] for the formal definition of a very general class of programmed graph transformation systems.

For further details concerning the usage of programmed graph transformation systems as a tool specification and implementation mechanism the reader is referred to [Nag96]. Further information concerning the design and implementation of the very high-level programming language PROGRES and its programming environment may be found in [SWZ95].

Last but not least the reader is referred to [Sch94] for a formal definition of coupled graph grammars, which is based on a very simply graph data model (without different types of nodes or edges and without attributes) and a simple form of graph grammar productions. A formal definition of coupled graph grammars for a more complex UML-compatible graph data model and more complex forms of productions is under development. It provides the formal background for the definition of correspondences between graph schemas (UML class diagrams) and the definition of coupled graph grammar productions, which respect the previously defined schema correspondences.

6 Summary and future work

Development processes of various engineering disciplines are usually rather complex. They consist of many interacting subprocesses, which are carried out by different developers. Various *approaches* are propagated nowadays how to support developers in executing their *subprocesses* and how to guarantee the overall *consistency* of their results, rather complex configurations of dependent technical documents. One may use the experience of developers

- by recording traces of successfully executed subprocesses and transforming them into repeatable process chunks [PDJ94],
- by offering means for direct multi-media communication, which are tightly integrated with technical document manipulating tools [Her96],
- and by realizing interactive integration tools, which help their users to monitor and (re-)establish interdocument consistency relations.

These three different approaches complement each other and may be combined with appropriate management tools to support engineering processes on a very high level (tasks and task dependencies) [NW98].

As argued in the introductory section, integration tools for fine-grained interdocument consistency relations have a special importance for development processes if they support change subprocesses, leave space for creativity and allow different forms of change propagation strategies. They are valuable, especially, if we have *well-structured* documents on both sides of change subprocesses. Due to the vast amount of configuration and document structures as well as methods to be applied, there is no chance of realizing such tools in an hand-crafting manner.

For dealing with the necessity of mechanical tool derivation this paper presented a graph grammar based method for deriving efficiently working integration tool implementations from very high-level interdocument consistency specifications. It is worthwhile to notice that the presented method requires not a complete formal specification of the (semantics of the) considered types of documents and the involved modeling languages and methods. It is sufficient if all regarded documents have a well-defined internal structure (syntax definition) and if we have some knowledge about possibly corresponding patterns of increments in related documents.

The functionality of presented integration tools varies from a low-level hypertext editor, where all interdocument relations have to be created and maintained manually (if almost no knowledge about interdocument consistency relations is available) to an automatically working document transformation tool (if interdocument consistency relations may be defined as a total and deterministic function). In many cases the available knowledge about regarded document dependencies lies between these two extremes, such that the resulting integration tools are able to perform trivial consistency (re-)establishing tasks on their own and to compute sets of possible consistency (re-)establishing actions in the general case.

It is the subject of ongoing research activities to generalize the presented coupled graph grammar formalism w.r.t. the form of permitted coupled subproductions. Furthermore, we are planning to realize a new generation of graph grammar coupling tools, based on the experiences reported in [JSZ96] (with a rather ad hoc approach to use the PROGRES environment for this purpose). Our tools shall offer appropriate support for entering graph schema correspondences and coupled graph grammar productions, for checking the consistency between graph schema correspondences and coupled productions, and for translating coupled graph grammar specifications into ordinary PROGRES specifications of needed integration tools [Gru98].

Finally, we are making our first experiences with *changing* our *focus* from tightly integrated software engineering environments to tightly integrated *chemical process engineering environments* [NM97] [NW98]. The new application domain forced us to complement coupled graph grammars with UML class and object diagrams as more appropriate means of communication between domain experts and future users of integration tools and their developers. In [CGN98] we discuss a trade-off between the complexity of integration tool specification and tool realization. The main challenge of the new application domain, however, is that we have to generalize the presented integration approach from the a-priori integration of self-made software engineering tools to the a-posteriori integration of already existing chemical process engineering tools.

Acknowledgements

The German Research Community DFG (Deutsche Forschungsgemeinschaft) is granting one of the authors of this paper with a scholarship, and is also financially supporting our ongoing project in the Collaborative Research Centre SFB 476 [NM97].

References

[AGT89]   A. V. Aho / M. Ganapathi / S.W.K. Tijang: *Code Generation Using Tree Matching and Dynamic Programming,* TOPLAS 11/4, pp.491–516 (1989).

[BJ95] M. Broy / S. Jähnichen (Eds.): *KORSO – Methods, Languages and Tools for the Construction of Correct Software*, LNCS 1009, Berlin: Springer–Verlag (1995).

[BOP97] L. Baresi / A. Orso / M. Pezzè: *Introducing Formal Specification Methods in Industrial Practice*, in: Proc. 19th Int. Conf. on Software Engineering (ICSE'19), IEEE Computer, pp.56–66 (1997).

[Bo+88] P. Borras et al.: *Centaur: The System*, in P. Henderson, Proc. 3rd ACM Softw. Eng. Symp. on Practical Software Development Environments, ACM Software Engineering Notes 13/5, pp.14–24 (1988).

[BW96] H.J. Bullinger / J. Warschatt (Eds.): *Concurrent Simultaneous Engineering Systems*, Berlin: Springer–Verlag (1996).

[CC93] J.R. Cordy / J.H. Carmichael: *The TXL Programming Language Syntax and Informal Semantics Version 7*, Technical Report 93–355, Computing and Information Science at Queen's University, Kingston (1993).

[CGN98] K. Cremer / S. Gruner / M. Nagl: *Graph Transformation based Tools for chemical Process Engineering*, in H. Ehrig / G. Engels / G. Rozenberg (Eds.), Handbook of Graph Grammars and Computing by Graph Transformation (Vol.II), Singapore: World Scientific (1998), to appear.

[Da+97] P. Dadam et al.: *Interaction Expressions – a Powerful Formalism for Describing Inter–Workflow Dependencies*, Technical Report: Informatik–bericht 97–04, Universität Ulm (1997).

[DHW95] U. Dayal / E. Hanson / J. Widom: *Active Database Systems*, in Kim (Ed.): Modern Database Systems, pp.434–456, New York: ACM (1995).

[EIA94] EIA / CDIF: *CDIF Family of Standards* (1994).

[EJS88] G. Engels / T. Janning / W. Schäfer: *A Highly Integrated Tool Set for Program Development Support*, Proc. ACM SIGSMALL Conf.'88, pp.1–10 (1988)

[FNK94] A. Finkelstein / B. Nusibeh / J. Kramer: *A Framework Expressing the Relationships between Multiple Views in Requirements Specifications*, IEEE Transactions on Software Engineering 20/10, pp.760–773 (1994).

[FO90] C. Fernström / L. Ohlsson: *The ESF Vision of a Software Factory*, in N.H. Madhavji et al., SD & F1, pp.91–100, London: Pitman (1990).

[Fra91] B. Frankel: *The ToolTalk Service*, Sun Microsystems (1991).

[Fro90] D. Fromme: *HP Encapsulator: Bridging the Generation Gap*, HP–Journal, pp.59–68 (1990).

[FS96] A. Finkelstein / I. Sommerville: *The View Points FAQ*, Software Engineering Journal 11/1, pp.2–4 (1996).

[FS97] M. Fowler / K. Scott: *UML Distilled*, New York: Addison Wesley (1997).

[GG84] H. Ganzinger / R. Giegerich: *Attribute Coupled Grammars*, in Proc. ACM Symp. on Compiler Constr., SIGPLAN Notices 17/6, pp.172–184 (1984).

[GHS95] D. Georgakopoulos / M. Hornick / A. Sheth: *An Overview of Workflow Management: From Process Modelling to Workflow Automation Infrastructure*, Distributed and Parallel Databases 3, pp.119–153 (1995).

[Gru98] S. Gruner: *Why should Chemo–Engineers be interested in Graph Grammars?* Accepted for presentation at the TAGT'98 6th Workshop on Theory and Application of Graph Transformation (Ed.: Engels), Paderborn (1998).

[Her96]   O. Hermanns: *Multicast Communication in Cooperative Multimedia Systems* (in German), Doct. Dissertation, RWTH Aachen (1996).

[HN+90]   D. Harrison / A. Newton / R. Spickelmeir / T. Barnes: *Electronic CAD Frameworks*, Proc. IEEE 78/2, pp.393–419 (1990).

[Hru91]   P. Hruschka (Ed.): *CASE in Application – Experiences with the Introduction of CASE* (in German), München: Hanser–Verlag (1991).

[ISO]   ISO CD 10303: *Product Data Representation and Exchange*, NIST Gaithersburg, USA.

[Jan92]   T. Janning: *Requirements Engineering and Programming in the Large* (in German), Doct. Dissertation RWTH Aachen, Wiesbaden: Deutscher Universitätsverlag (1992).

[JJ95]   M. Jeusfeld / U. Johnen: *An Executable Metamodel For Re-Engineering of Database Schemas*, Int. Journal of Cooperative Information Systems, 4 (2/3), pp.237–258 (1995).

[JN98]   M. Jarke / H. Nissen: *Requirements Engineering Repositories – Formal Support for Informal Teamwork Methods*, in M. Broy / B. Rumpe (Eds.): RTSE'97 Workshop; LNCS: this volume, Berlin: Springer–Verlag (1998).

[JSZ96]   J. Jahnke / W. Schäfer / A. Zündorf: *A Design Environment for Migrating Relational to Object-Oriented Data Base Systems*, in: Proc. Int. Conference on Software Maintenance 1996, IEEE Computer Society Press, pp.163–170 (1996).

[KKM87]   G. E. Kaiser / S. M. Kaplan / J. Micallef: *Multi-user, Distributed, Language-based Environment*, IEEE Software 4/6, pp.58–67 (1987).

[Kra98]   C. A. Krapp: *An Adaptable Environment for the Management of Development Processes*, Doct. Diss. RWTH Aachen, Aachen: Verlag der Buchhandlung Augustinus, Series ABI, Vol. 22, (1998).

[Krö93]   K. Kronlöf: *Method Integration*, Chicester: Wiley (1993).

[Lef95]   M. Lefering: *Integrating Tools in a Software Development Environment* (in German), Doct. Diss. RWTH Aachen, Aachen: Shaker–Verlag (1995).

[Lew88]   C. Lewerentz: *Interactive Design of Large Program Systems* (in German), Doct. Diss. RWTH Aachen, Series IFB, Vol. 194, Berlin: Springer–Verlag (1988).

[McI95]   K.G. McIntosh: *Engineering Data Management – A Guide to Successful Implementation*, Maidenhead: McGraw-Hill (1995).

[Nag90]   M. Nagl: *Software Engineering: Methodical Programming in the Large* (in German), Berlin: Springer–Verlag (1990).

[Nag96]   M. Nagl (Ed.): *Building Tightly Integrated Software Development Environments: The IPSEN Approach*, LNCS 1170, Berlin: Springer–Verlag (1996).

[NK91]   J.M. Nyce / P. Kahn: *From Memex to Hypertext: Vanevar Bush and the Mind's Machine*, London: Academic Press (1991).

[NM97]   M. Nagl / W. Marquardt: *SFB 476 IMPROVE: Support for Overlapping Developing Processes in Chemical Process Engineering* (in German), in Jarke/Pasedach/Pohl (Eds.): Informatik '97, Series Informatik aktuell, pp.143–154, Berlin: Springer–Verlag (1997).

[NW98] M. Nagl / B. Westfechtel: *Integration of Development Systems in Engineering Applications* (in German), Berlin: Springer–Verlag (1998).

[PDJ94] K. Pohl / R. Dömges / M. Jarke: *Decision-oriented Process Modelling*, Proc. 9th Intern. Software Process Workshop, ISPW 9, Airlie (1994).

[Pra71] T.W. Pratt: *Pair Grammars, Graph Languages and String-to-Graph Translations*, Journ. of Comp. and System Sciences 5, pp.560–595 (1971).

[Re+93] R. Reddy et al.: *Computer Support for Concurrent Engineering*, IEEE Computer 26/1, pp.12–16 (1993).

[Rei90] S. Reiss: *Interacting with the Field Environment*, Software–Practice and Experience 20/S1, pp.89–115 (1990).

[RS96] J. Rekers / A. Schürr: *Defining and Parsing Visual Languages with Layered Graph Grammars*, Journ. of Visual Languages and Computing 8/1, pp.27–55 (1997).

[RT88] T. Reps / T. Teitelbaum: *The Synthesizer Generator Reference Manual*, New York: Springer–Verlag (1988).

[SB93] D. Schefström / G. v. d. Broek (Eds.): *Tool Integration*, New York: Wiley (1993).

[Sch94] A. Schürr: *Specification of Graph Translators with Triple Graph Grammars*, in Tinhofer (Ed.): Proc. WG '94 Int. Workshop on Graph-Theoretic Concepts in Computer Sc., LNCS 903, pp.151–163, Berlin: Springer–Verlag (1994).

[Sch97] A. Schürr: *Programmed Graph Replacement Systems*, in Rozenberg (Ed.): Handbook of Graph Grammars and Computing by Graph Transformation (Vol.I), pp.479–546, Singapore: World Scientific (1997).

[SL90] A. P. Sheth / J. A. Larson: *Federated Database Systems for Managing Distributed, Heterogeneous and Autonomous Databases*, Comp. Surveys 22/3, pp.183–236 (1990).

[SS95] S. Sachweh / W. Schäfer: *Version Management for Tightly Integrated Software Engineering Environments*, Proc. 7th Int. Conference on Software Engineering Environments, IEEE Computer Society Press (1995).

[SWZ95] A. Schürr / A.J. Winter / A. Zündorf: *Graph Grammar Engineering with PROGRES*, in Schäfer/Botella (Eds.): Proc. 5th ESEC, LNCS 989, pp.219–234, Berlin: Springer–Verlag (1995).
The PROGRES environment is available as free software by
http://www–i3.informatik.rwth–aachen.de/research/progres/index.html

[Wes91] B. Westfechtel: *Revision and Consistency Control in an Integrated Software Development Environment* (in German), Doct. Diss., RWTH Aachen, Series IFB, Vol. 280, Berlin: Springer–Verlag (1991).

[Wes98] B. Westfechtel: *Graph–based Models and Tools for Managing Development Processes*, Habilitation Thesis, RWTH Aachen (1998).

Formal Models and Prototyping*

Luqi

Computer Science Department, Naval Postgraduate School
Monterey, CA 93943, USA

Abstract. Rapid prototyping is a promising approach for formulating accurate software requirements, particularly for complex systems with hard real-time constraints. Computer aid is needed for realizing the potential benefits of this approach in practice, because the problems associated with software evolution are greatly amplified in the context of iterative prototyping and exploratory design. This paper presents our newest models of software evolution products and processes, and explains the models and engineering automation capabilities they support via examples.

1 Introduction

The software industry remains far short of the mature engineering discipline needed to meet the demands of our information age society. Symptoms of the problem are large sums spent on cancelled software projects [38], costly delays [19], and software reliability problems [13].

Lack of sound domain models for rapidly emerging application areas makes software engineering more difficult than other engineering disciplines. Requirements for complex systems are nearly always inaccurate initially and evolve throughout the life of the systems. Requirements and specification problems have been found to be the dominant cause of faults in the Voyager/Galileo software [34], and we believe this applies to most large and complex systems.

Evolutionary prototyping can alleviate this problem by providing an efficient approach to formulating accurate software requirements [27]. Simple models reflecting the main issues associated with the proposed system are constructed and demonstrated, and then incrementally reformulated to better match customer concerns, based on specific critiques and the issues they elicit. The models are refined only as needed to resolve open issues, and the issues arising at one level of detail are resolved as much as possible before considering the next level of detail, or the next aspect of the system. This process systematically explores plausible alternatives and gradually increases confidence in the aspects of requirements models that withstand stakeholder scrutiny under a variety of scenarios.

---

* This research was supported in part by the National Science Foundation under grant number CCR-9058453 and by the Army Research Office under grant number 30989-MA.

Engineering automation is needed to realize the rapid, economical and effective changes demanded by evolutionary prototyping. The capabilities of designers can be amplified by simplifying design models to remove some considerations from their attention. However, this introduces stringent requirements for design automation, because design attributes that are hidden in this way must be derived automatically, accurately, and in a way that produces good designs.

Formal models of various aspects of software development and evolution are needed to achieve reliable and quantifiable automation of design subtasks. We have found that this approach works for complex real-time systems, and suggest that engineering automation should be a focus of future work on formal models and methods to increase practical impact of software research.

It has been necessary to interleave our formalization efforts and theoretical work with experimental validation and adjustment of the models to better fit practical reality. Software development and evolution are extremely complex problem domains, and engineering automation systems have correspondingly complex requirements that manifest all of the difficulties identified above. We have applied the evolutionary prototyping approach to the development of techniques and software for supporting the evolutionary prototyping approach itself. This strategy has been successful for developing accurate models, effective automation capabilities and decision support methods for evolution of software and system requirements.

For example, we modeled the behavior of real-time systems using the simplest formulation we could find, a refinement of data flow models that incorporates declarative control and timing constraints. The prototype system description language PSDL [25] was based on this model and was evaluated experimentally by using it to prototype representative real-time control systems. In response to feedback from these experiences, the model was refined to cover distributed computation [30], a formal semantics of PSDL was developed [22], and the part of the model addressing real-time requirements was used to develop our initial scheduling methods [26]. We developed a series of simple hardware models [30], and found that these together with the original real-time requirements models could support scheduling methods for multi-processor and distributed target hardware configurations [7, 32]. The models and language have been found to be adequate for representing a variety of complex systems, including a generic C3I station [29] and a wireless acoustic monitor for preventing sudden infant death syndrome [36].

Software evolution is a critical aspect of prototyping [27]. In the early stages of requirements formulation the purposes of the proposed system are highly uncertain and major changes to a prototype are frequent. We therefore need the capability to repeatedly and rapidly change a design while maintaining it in a form that can be quickly understood and reliably modified. Planning, version control, and team coordination are key project management issues and design rationale is a key technical issue in this context. Formal models of software evolution are needed to enable engineering automation related to these issues.

Our initial step towards formalizing software evolution in the large was a graph model of the evolution history [28]. This work led to the insights that the essence of project history lies in dependencies among versions of project documents and the activities that produce them, that the formal structures of project history and project plans are essentially the same, and that integrated modeling and support for software configuration management and project management enables higher automation levels for both [1]. More recent work suggested that hypergraphs may be useful [33], and that integration with personnel models and rationale models enables decision support for the problematic early stages of critique analysis and change planning [8].

Section 2 of this paper presents our most recent model and explores some automated processes that it can support. Section 3 illustrates our ideas with an example and section 4 sketches how they can support the evolution of reusable component libraries.

Models of software architectures and methods for realizing and evolving them can also contribute to rapid modifiability of prototypes and maintaining the understandability of evolving designs. Section 5 presents some of our recent ideas about how this can best be accomplished. Section 6 contains conclusions and suggestions about what to do next.

2 Software Evolution

This section presents the current version of our model of software evolution. Conceptually, the plans and complete history of a project are permanently recorded in an evolution record. This reflects the hypothesis that real development projects cannot afford to lose information about their development history. In implementations of the model, practical considerations dictate that older parts of the history may have to be compressed and/or migrated to off-line storage media when disk space gets low, but it should always be possible to retrieve that information when needed.

The purpose of the model is to characterize the structure of the products and processes involved in software development and evolution in sufficient detail to enable automation support for subtasks such as summarizing relevant aspects of the evolution history, determining the rationale for past design decisions, project scheduling, configuration management, team coordination, and evaluating the effectiveness of evolution processes and tools. These functions are important for prototyping because in this context changes are typically severe, quick modifications are desired, and different alternatives are often explored in parallel. In such a context the history, plans, and design document configurations have a more complex structure than in other development efforts, and decision support is needed to enable flexible exploration of the design space without getting lost in the maze of information related to these aspects of the project state.

The model presented in this section has a better representation of hierarchical structures of components and processes than previous formulations and has been extended to provide explicit representations of plan changes. In particular, decompositions of steps and the associated consistency constraints are modeled in detail for the first time in this paper.

The model can also serve as the conceptual basis for an object-oriented schema of a project database that contains all the technical and management data, and for the decision support tools that operate on project history and project plans. The refinement concept associated with the hierarchies is useful for helping developers and planners cope with the complexity of large projects.

To achieve simplicity, we focus on a minimal set of general object types, and introduce specialized subclasses only when necessary for accurate modeling. The model has only three main types of objects: component, step, and person.

The component type represents any kind of versioned object, including critiques, issues, requirements, designs, programs, manuals, test cases, plans, etc. These include the information products produced by software evolution processes. The main characteristics of components are that they represent frozen versions of evolving objects, they are partially ordered by derivation dependencies, and they may be decomposed into sets of subcomponents. Components that have subcomponents are *composite*, and those that do not are *atomic*.

The step type represents instances of any kind of scheduled software evolution activity, such as analysis, design, implementation, testing, inspection, demonstration, etc. Steps are processes that create components. These processes are usually carried out by people, although they may be partially or completely automated. When viewed in the context of evolution history, steps represent derivation dependencies among the components produced by the scheduled activities. Steps that are not yet completed represent parts of project plans. Steps are a subclass of component because they can have versions, to provide a record of how project plans evolved. Steps typically have substeps if their products are composite components.

The person type represents the people involved in the software evolution activity, including the stakeholders of the evolving system, software analysts, designers, project managers, testers, software librarians, system administrators, etc. We need to represent the people involved to be able to trace requirements back to the original raw data, and to link it to the roles the authors of critiques play in the organizational structure. This is a part of the rationale of the system that helps to identify viewpoints and analyze tradeoffs between conflicting requirements. The people in the development team must be modeled because of concerns related to project scheduling and authorization to access project information. Person is also a subclass of component, and therefore versioned, to provide a record of how the roles and qualifications of the people involved in the project change with time. People with subcomponents represent organizations.

Our formal model follows.

An **evolution record** $[N, E, I, O, C, S]$ is a labeled acyclic directed hypergraph where

1. N is a set of **nodes**, representing version identifiers for components,
2. E is a set of **edges**, representing identifiers for steps,
3. $I : E \to 2^N$ is a function giving the set of **inputs** of each edge,

4. $O : E \to 2^N$ is a function giving the set of **outputs** of each edge, such that $O(e) \cap O(e') \neq \emptyset$ implies $e = e'$,
5. $C : N \to component$ is a partial function giving the **component** associated with each node, and
6. $S : E \to step$ is a 1:1 function giving the **step** associated with each edge.

Intuitively an evolution record represents an archival project database that records the entire history of a software development project. An evolution record is intended to evolve monotonically: information can be added to an evolution record, but not removed. Specifically, new edges and new nodes can be added to the hypergraph, and the partial function C can be extended. These are the only kinds of changes allowed in the model. A consequence of the monotonicity restriction is that all past states of an evolution record are subsets of its current state.

The edges of the hypergraph represent steps. Steps have extensible sets of attributes that include scheduling policies, a finite state model of their authorization/completion status, and the people responsible for carrying out the step [8]. ¿From the user's point of view steps have states that can change, subject to consistency constraints and management approval. It is therefore convenient to model steps as objects in the object-oriented programming sense, and to associate these objects with the edges of the hypergraph via a 1:1 mapping. ¿From the perspective of the formal model, however, steps are versioned objects that change only via creation of new versions. The evolution record contains a complete history of all the versions that ever existed for each step, as discussed in greater detail below.

The edges connect the components on which a step depends to the new components the step produces. Hence edges can also be viewed as dependencies between components. Processes such as change impact analysis and requirement tracing involve following paths in the hypergraph, either forwards or backwards.

Since a step cannot be completed until all of its input components are available, a step with circular dependency could never be carried out. The hypergraph must therefore be acyclic.

In usual practice a step is not allowed to start until all its input components become available. If we accept this policy then the precedence constraints for the project schedule can be determined from the edges via the following rule: $O(e) \cap I(e') \neq \emptyset$ implies $S(e)$ precedes $S(e')$.

Nodes represent components, i.e. particular versions of objects that can have multiple versions. The mapping from nodes to components is partial because the evolution record can contain steps that are still in the planning stage or in progress. The output nodes of such steps are part of the evolution record, which implies that the version identifiers for the output components of a step are assigned when the step is created. However, the contents of these components are not yet available. The domain of the mapping C consists of precisely all the nodes that are outputs of completed steps, and is extended whenever a step completes.

C is not required to be 1:1 because it is possible for a subsequent step to undo the effects of a previous step. For example, suppose step $S(e_1)$ produces component $C(n_1)$, step $S(e_2)$ enhances it to produce $C(n_2)$, and step $S(e_3)$ undoes the enhancement to produce $C(n_3)$. In this case we have two different versions n_1 and n_3 that have different version identifiers and different roles in the evolution history, but the same contents, namely $C(n_1) = C(n_3)$. Maintaining the distinction between version identifiers and version contents helps to avoid circular dependencies in models of situations like this, which do arise in real projects.

The restriction on the output function O says that each component is produced by a unique step. This establishes clear lines of responsibility and produces a record of component authorship when each step completes.

The set of nodes and the set of steps are not disjoint. This reflects the fact that steps are a kind of component, and hence can be created and updated by other steps. We can avoid an infinite regress by distinguishing between ground steps and meta steps: the outputs of meta steps are ground steps, while the outputs of ground steps are components that are not steps. Every ground step is created by a meta step and is scheduled by an automated process upon management approval.

The meta steps provide a record of planning and management decisions that can be queried for assessment and improvement of development processes. Meta steps are not part of the plan or schedule and cannot be updated. The processes that create meta steps are not part of an evolution record and are not represented in our formal models.

In an implementation, meta steps would be created and immediately carried out by evolution support tool actions. These actions occur when a stakeholder interactively proposes a ground step or a project manager creates or edits a ground step in the plan. Completion of a meta step causes the schedule to be recomputed and the people responsible for any ground steps updated by the meta step to be notified that the plan has changed.

Hierarchical structures are modeled using a second level graph with mappings that indicate how the evolution record is refined in each level of increasingly detailed views of the structure. Such summary views are necessary in practice because evolution records get very complex even for small projects. The formalization of this aspect follows. Let $\mathcal{H}$ denote the set of evolution records.

A **hierarchical evolution record** $[V, R, H, T, N^*, E^*]$ is a labeled acyclic directed graph where

1. V is a set of **nodes** representing views of the hierarchical evolution record,
2. R is a set of **edges** representing view refinements,
3. $H : V \to \mathcal{H}$ is a function giving the **evolution record** representing each view in the refinement hierarchy,
4. $T : R \to step$ is a function giving the **target step** refined by an edge,
5. $N_v^* : H(v).N \to 2^{H(v).N}$ where $v \in V$ is an indexed family of functions that give the **node decompositions** in the view v of the hypergraph,
6. $E_v^* : H(v).E \to 2^{H(v).E}$ where $v \in V$ is an indexed family of functions that give the **edge decompositions** in the view v of the hypergraph,

7. $[v_1, v_2] \in R$ implies $H(v_1)$ is a subhypergraph of $H(v_2)$. This means that $H(v_1).N \subseteq H(v_2).N$, $H(v_1).E \subseteq H(v_2).E$, $H(v_1).I \subseteq H(v_2).I$, $H(v_1).O \subseteq H(v_2).O$, $H(v_1).C \subseteq H(v_2).C$, and $H(v_1).S \subseteq H(v_2).S$.
8. $r = [v_1, v_2] \in R$ implies there is an $e \in H(v_1).E$ such that
   - $T(r) = H(v_1).S(e)$,
   - $E^*_{v_1}(e) = \emptyset \neq E^*_{v_2}(e)$
   - $E^*_{v_1}(e') = E^*_{v_2}(e')$ if $e' \in H(v_1).E$ and $e' \neq e$, and
   - if $N^*_{v_1}(n) \neq N^*_{v_2}(n)$ then $N^*_{v_1}(n) = \emptyset$ and $n \in (I(e) \cup O(e))$.
9. The graph has a single root (a node with no incoming edges) representing the most abstract view and a single leaf (a node with no outgoing edges) representing the most detailed view.
10. The graph has a refinement edge $r = [v_1, v_2]$ with target $T(r) = S(e)$ for any hyperedge e such that $E^*_{leaf}(e) \neq \emptyset$ and any view v such that $E^*_v(e) = \emptyset$ and $e \in H(v).E$.
11. Any two paths p_1 and p_2 from the root that have the same target step set $\{T(r) | r \in p_1\} = \{T(r) | r \in p_2\}$ end in the same node.
12. The decompositions of the nodes and edges are well founded. This means that the transitive closures of the subcomponent and substep relations are acyclic in every view, where n_1 is a subcomponent of n_2 in a view v if and only if $n_1 \in N^*_v(n_2)$, and e_1 is a substep of e_2 relative to a view v if and only if $e_1 \in E^*_v(e_2)$.

Each node of a hierarchical evolution record represents a view of the evolution history. The root node is the most abstract view, containing only the top level steps and the top level components those steps produce, where a top level component is not part of the decomposition of any other component. The leaf node is the most detailed view, which contains the top level steps and components together with all direct and indirect substeps and subcomponents. Intermediate nodes in the graph represent views of the evolution process at intermediate levels of detail.

Each edge of a hierarchical evolution record represents a refinement of a single composite step, which is the *target step* of that edge. The target step is refined by adding all of its substeps to the evolution record, along with the input and output components of the substeps that are not present in the summary view. These are the only items that can be added in a single refinement. Note that a refinement does not remove or replace anything.

The refinement graph of a hierarchical evolution record is complete in the sense that any step that is composite in the leaf view can be refined from any view in which that step is atomic. A step $S(e)$ is atomic in a view v if and only if none of its substeps are visible in that view, i.e. $E^*_v(e) = \emptyset$.

The decompositions in an evolution record must be well founded, because otherwise the graph of views would contain infinite paths, and hence could not have a reachable leaf node due to the completeness property. This restriction implies a recursive program component cannot be modeled as a subcomponent of itself, and mutually recursive program components cannot be modeled as subcomponents of each other. Given that the number of subcomponents of each component is always finite in practice, this restriction implies the evolution record associated with the leaf node is finite as well. Automated processes can therefore safely construct or search the expanded form of the evolution record, which is useful in scheduling, navigation, and other decision support functions.

An evolution record captures derivation dependencies that can be used to reconstruct design rationale and to estimate costs of proposed changes. Since the model includes early artifacts such as critiques, issues, and requirements as kinds of components, the model supports generalized requirement tracing analyses by following the edges in the hypergraphs backwards. Requirements are linked to issues, issues are linked to critiques of prototype behavior, and critiques are linked to the specific people who voiced their opinions. The model therefore provides the information needed to reconsider design tradeoffs in the light of new information and new situations. The same people can be asked to reconsider their opinions given new goals or new issues. The dependency links can also be followed forward from impacted issues to find the alternatives for resolving those issues that had been considered in the past. For the alternatives that had been explored to the point of a prototype demo, queries against the forward links could find relevant critiques regarding alternative resolutions of active issues, helping to shed light on why particular decisions were made.

The evolution record model can be used to automatically schedule steps, automatically locate and deliver the proper versions of the input components to the developer assigned to carry out the step, and to automatically check in the new components produced when the step is completed. It can also be used to generate default plans, to maintain the consistency of plans, and to help managers and developers navigate through the plan and document structures of an evolutionary prototyping or development effort.

The model is intended as a framework for navigation through the possible views of the evolution record at different levels of abstraction. It is not intended to be an implementation structure. A hierarchical evolution record has a large number of nodes that do not all need to be stored explicitly. Practical implementations will materialize only those nodes that are actually visited.

3 Example

This section illustrates how evolution records and processes based on them can provide decision support for design decisions that arise in system evolution efforts. Figure 1 shows an example of a top level evolution record. In this example, the first version of a requirement ($R1$) is used to derive the first version of a prototype ($P1$), which is demonstrated to system stakeholders and elicits a critique ($C1$). When a step ($S3$) to derive the second version of the requirement ($R2$) from the critique is proposed, the system automatically proposes a step ($S4$) to create the second version of the prototype ($P2$), because the prototype depends on the requirement and the requirement will be updated. The proposed steps are scheduled automatically when they are approved by the project management.

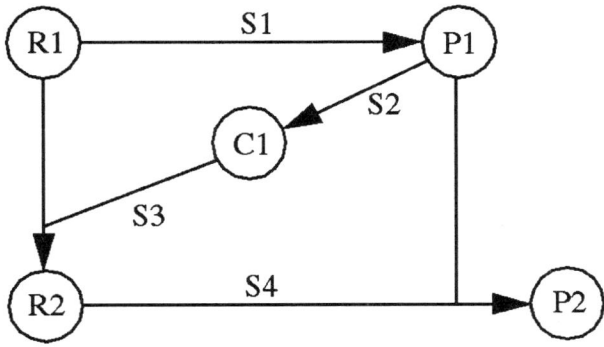

Fig. 1. Top Level Evolution Record

The concrete context of this example is iterative requirements formulation for an airline reservation system. The interpretations of the components shown in Figure 1 are given below.

- R1: version 1 of the requirement that the airline reservation system must help travel agents sell airline tickets.
- R2: version 2 of the requirement that the airline reservation system must help travel agents sell airline tickets.
- P1: version 1 of a prototype of an airline reservation system.
- P2: version 2 of a prototype of an airline reservation system.
- C1: a critique from a travel agent elicited by a demonstration of P1. The travel agent objects to the facility for finding flights a customer might want because it does not account for cities that have more than one airport.

The distinction between R1 and R2 is not apparent at the top level of abstraction.

Figure 2 shows the refinement of step $S1$ of the top level evolution record shown in Figure 1. Both $S1$ and its substeps $S1.1$ and $S1.2$ are present in the refined evolution record. The top level steps are shown with thicker lines. The component $R1$ was decomposed into the subcomponents $Ra1$ and $Rb1$ because these components are inputs to the substeps, and $P1$ is decomposed into $Pc1$ and $Pd1$ because these are the outputs of the substeps.

The interpretations of the subcomponents visible in this refined view follow.

- Ra1: version 1 of the requirement that the airline reservation system must find all flights from one airport to another.
- Rb1: version 1 of the requirement that the airline reservation system must help travel agents manage reservations on flights.
- Pc1: version 1 prototype of the flight finder subsystem.
- Pd1: version 1 prototype of the reservation management subsystem.

The decomposition mappings for the subcomponents are denoted by geometrical containment in the figures. The decomposition relations for the steps are

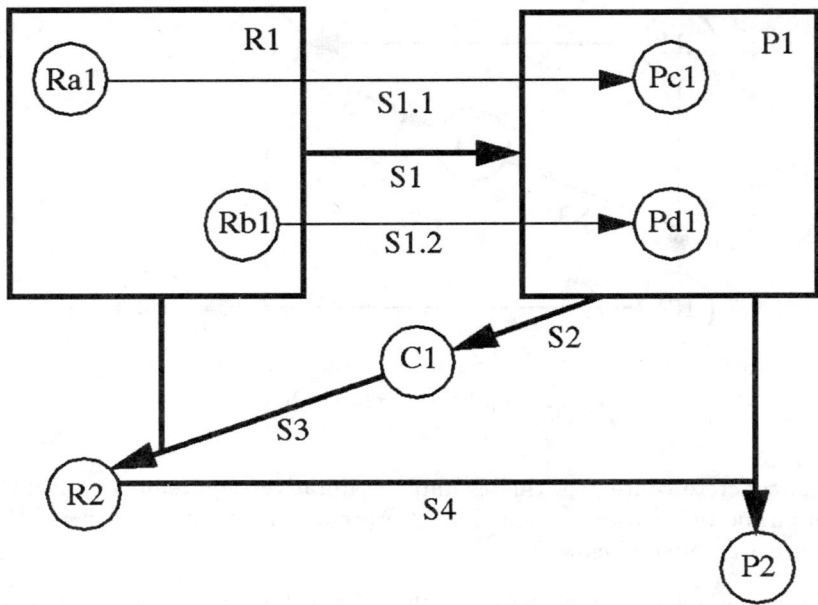

Fig. 2. Refinement of Step S1

indicated only via the structure of the step names. Note that the graphical display would get crowded if the decomposition relations were explicitly displayed as hyper-edges.

Figure 3 shows a further refinement of the evolution record shown in Figure 2 that expands all of the top-level steps. Note that the subrequirement $Rb1$ is shared by both versions of the requirement R, because it is not affected by the elicited critique. The subsystem $Pd1$ of the prototype that depends only on this subrequirement is also shared by both versions of the prototype P. We can see that the diagram is getting crowded even for this very small example.

The interpretations of the new subcomponents visible in this refined view follow.

- Ra2: version 2 of the requirement that the airline reservation system must find all flights from one city to another.
- Pc2: version 2 prototype of the flight finder subsystem.

Our goal is to provide tools based on this model that will make it easier to discover and manage large scale structures of this variety. In realistic situations, there can be many more nodes in the evolution records. We are currently exploring automatic mechanisms for determining and displaying small neighborhoods of these structures that are relevant to particular planning and analysis tasks and are small enough to be understood. Some initial results along these lines can be found in [23].

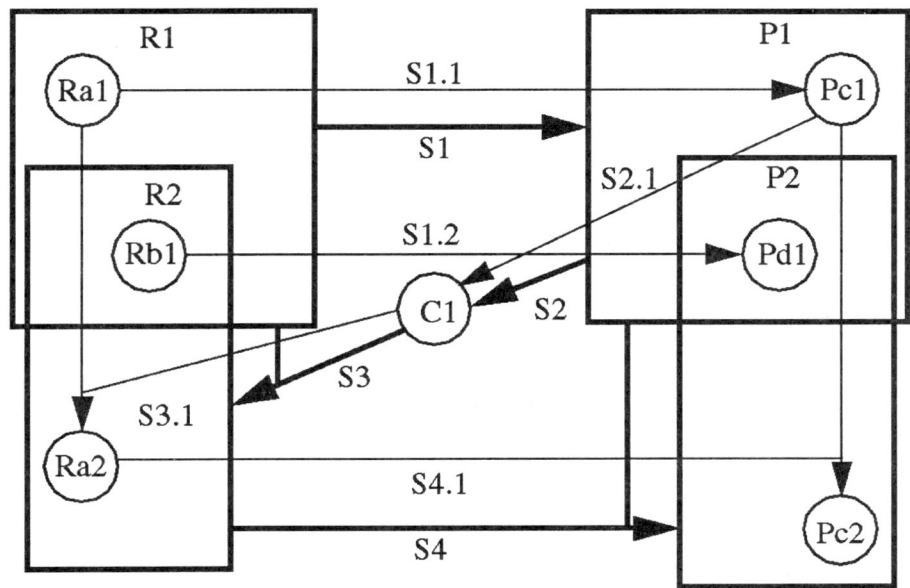

Fig. 3. Refinement of Steps S1-S4

A different approach to this problem is to apply the concept of slicing to evolution records. A slice extracts the subset of a dependency network on which a given aspect of the system depends. Program slicing has been used in a variety of ways to provide decision support for various aspects of program design, including debugging, testing, change merging [9], and software reengineering. We can apply slicing to the problem of extracting useful design rationale information from large scale evolution records. The following example illustrates the idea.

Figure 4 shows an example of a history slice. The purpose of the slice is to reconstruct the design rationale for the subsystem Pc2. The slice is constructed by following the edges backwards, to include only the components that affect the subsystem in question. In this case we find two versions of the requirement on which the design was based, along with the critique that motivated the reformulation of the initial version of the requirement. Note that airports have been replaced by cities in the requirement Ra in response to the critique C1. This information is part of the rationale for the design of the second version of the flight finder subsystem. It can be recovered from the constructed slice by judicious application of a text difference tool.

4 Evolution of Reuse Libraries

Software reuse is a critical part of prototyping for real-time systems because efficiency is of the essence in the time-critical parts of these systems. The highest

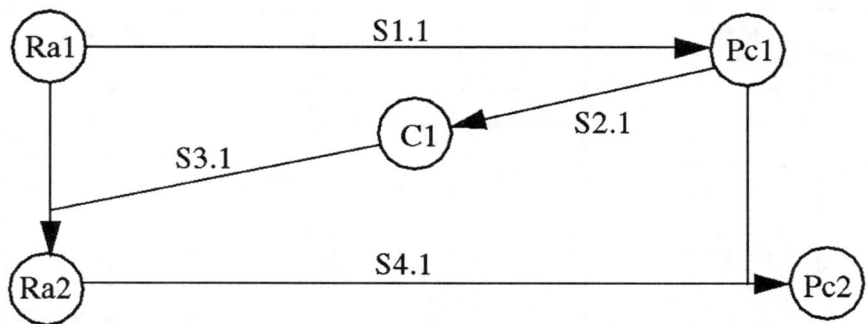

Fig. 4. History Slice at Pc2

levels of efficiency can only be achieved by intensive engineering and refinement of sophisticated algorithms and data structures, which usually takes large amounts of time and effort, and produces designs that depend on intricate chains of reasoning. The easiest way to take advantage of such components in a process that must be cheap and rapid is to use a previously constructed library of standard and well-optimized components.

The most immediate concern in following this strategy is how to find the needed reusable parts from a large library. Search methods must trade off precision (retrieving only relevant components) against recall (finding components if they are relevant). We have developed a software component search method that can simultaneously achieve high levels of precision and recall, based on algebraic queries representing symbolic test cases. Initial experimental assessments indicate that the approach is practically effective for finding reusable components.

Another concern is managing the contents of the reuse library and the systems that depend on it. The evolution record model introduced in section 2 can help to address this question.

If the evolution history of the components in the library is maintained as an evolution record, we can use the dependency information the model provides to manage the library, to propagate benefits of library improvements to applications, and to quantify the benefits of reuse and to compare the reuse value of different components in the library.

The evolution record can help maintain the rationale for the components in the library, and if the requirements and issues addressed by the reusable components are suitably recorded in the evolution record, these links can help identify when new or improved components subsume the services of older versions of the components. If the applications and the library components are part of the same evolution record, then the dependency links (which would include component reuse steps) could be used to automatically identify which applications should be updated when components in the library are improved. The same generic project scheduling rules and mechanisms discussed earlier would automatically propose steps to update the affected systems and automatically add them to project plans, awaiting management assessment of priorities and approval for implementation of the proposed steps.

Forward slicing with respect to the dependency links of the evolution record starting from all the components in the reuse library would locate all versions of applications that made use of the library components. This information coupled with records of the actual time and effort spent on developing the reused components can be used as the basis of an estimate of the economic benefit due to reuse. The steps involved in evolving the reuse library would contain information about the cost of the effort needed to build and maintain the library, which could be used to monitor the net gain or loss due to the reuse effort.

The same types of links from individual components could be used to identify the most heavily used components, find critiques related to library components, and guide decisions on how to allocate effort for improving library components to get the greatest future benefit.

5 Evolution of Software Architectures

We are currently working on models and notations that support explicit definitions of software architectures for solving given classes of problems independently from the rules that determine a particular instance of the architecture that solves a given instance of the problem. This should make it easier for software architectures and associated program generation capabilities to evolve.

Architecture evolution provides a practical path for quickly obtaining automation capabilities for new problem domains, and to gradually improve those capabilities by adding solution techniques that expand the problem domain and incorporating optimizations for specialized subproblems that improve performance. This has practical importance because it provides a path to overcome the investment barrier to technology transfer. The most attractive applications of new technology can begin to deliver tangible benefits at reasonable cost and within a reasonable time frame. It is acceptable for those benefits to be modest at first if there exists a systematic method for gradually but steadily improving the rate of return on investment. Evolvable architectures that provide program generation capabilities provide a reasonable approach to create such a method.

Formalizing these aspects of software architectures and developing the corresponding engineering automation methods will eventually enable us to certify that all programs possibly generated from a mature architecture are free from given classes of faults or that they work correctly for all possible inputs. These steps will bring us closer to the point where product-quality software can be economically produced using the same engineering automation technology that enables evolutionary prototyping and helps analysts home in on good requirements models. Our vision is to eliminate the current conflict between rapid development and high software quality.

We believe that an evolutionary approach to architecture-based program generation provides a practical path to this vision because whenever a fault in an architecture or the associated program generation rules is discovered and repaired, it not only fixes the system in which a failure was observed, but also prevents that particular fault from recurring in the systems that are generated in the future. This provides a way to steadily improve the reliability of software generation for a particular domain. Because improvements in the process can be amortized over many applications, it may become practical to do formal analysis and certification of architectures and architecture-based program generation methods. We believe the best path is a blend of prototyping to achieve good requirements and a working initial version of the tools with concurrent theoretical work and formal analysis to bring the final product into sharp focus and to achieve very high reliability. This approach will eventually reach a level where we can realistically expect that typical software products in mature application domains will always work reliably, if it can be consistently followed by the engineering research community over an extended period of time.

A necessary initial step to reach this goal is to develop a uniform representation and a tractable theory of program generation schemata that can support engineering automation for the development of architecture-based program generation capabilities for a variety of application domains.

6 Conclusions

Our previous research has explored formal models of the chronological evolution history [28]. This model has been applied to automate configuration management and a variety of project management functions [1]. The ideas presented in this paper provide a basis for improving these capabilities, particularly in the area of computer aid for understanding the record of the evolution of the system to extract useful information from it. Some recent work on improving the project scheduling algorithms based on these models has enabled scheduling 100,000 tasks in less than a minute [14]. These results suggest that the project scheduling support will scale up to projects of formidable size. We believe that further development of the model presented in this paper and associated methods and algorithms can result in unpredented levels of effective automation support for coordination of engineering efforts performs by distributed teams.

Our ultimate research goal is to create conceptual models and software tools that enable automatic generation of variations on a software system with human consideration of only the highest-level decisions that must change between one version and the next. Realization of this goal will lead to more flexible software systems and should make prototyping and exploratory design more effective. A continuing challenge is to construct effective models of the relevant decision spaces that can serve as a practical bridge between human skills and software tools for design automation.

References

1. S. Badr, Luqi, Automation Support for Concurrent Software Engineering, *Proc. of the 6th International Conference Software Engineering and Knowledge Engineering*, Jurmala, Latvia, June 20-23, 1994, 46–53.

2. F. Bauer et al., *The Munich Project CIP. Volume II: The Program Change System CIP-S*, Lecture Notes in Computer Science 292, Springer 1987.
3. V. Berzins, On Merging Software Enhancements *Acta Informatica*, Vol. 23 No. 6, Nov 1986, pp. 607–619.
4. V. Berzins, Luqi, An Introduction to the Specification Language Spec, *IEEE Software*, Vol. 7 No. 2, Mar 1990, pp. 74–84.
5. V. Berzins, Luqi, *Software Engineering with Abstractions: An Integrated Approach to Software Development using Ada*, Addison-Wesley Publishing Company, 1991, ISBN 0-201-08004-4.
6. V. Berzins, Software Merge: Models and Methods, *Journal of Systems Integration*, Vol. 1, No. 2, pp. 121–141 Aug 1991.
7. V. Berzins, Luqi, M. Shing, Real-Time Scheduling for a Prototyping Language, *Journal of Systems Integration*, Vol. 6, No. 1-2, pp. 41–72, 1996.
8. V. Berzins, O. Ibrahim, Luqi, A Requirements Evolution Model for Computer Aided Prototyping *Proceedings of the 9th International Conference on Software Engineering and Knowledge Engineering*, Madrid, Spain, June 17-20, 1997, pp. 38–47.
9. D. Dampier, Luqi, V. Berzins, Automated Merging of Software Prototypes, *Journal of Systems Integration*, Vol. 4, No. 1, February, 1994, pp. 33–49.
10. V. Berzins, Software Merge: Semantics of Combining Changes to Programs, *ACM TOPLAS*, Vol. 16, No. 6, Nov. 1994, 1875–1903.
11. V. Berzins, *Software Merging and Slicing*, IEEE Computer Society Press Tutorial, 1995, ISBN 0-8186-6792-3.
12. V. Berzins, D. Dampier, Software Merge: Combining Changes to Decompositions, *Journal of Systems Integration*, special issue on CAPS (Vol. 6, No. 1–2, March 1996), pp. 135-150.
13. M. Dowson, The ARIANE 5 Software Failure, *ACM Software Engineering Notes*, Vol. 22 No. 2, March 1997, p. 84.
14. J. Evans, Software Project Scheduling Tool, MS Thesis, Computer Science, Naval Postgraduate School, Sep. 1997.
15. M. Feather, A System for Assisting Program Change, *ACM Transactions on Programming Languages and Systems*, Vol. 4 No. 1, Jan 1982, pp. 1–20.
16. M. Feather, A Survey and Classification of some Program Change Approaches and Techniques, in *Program Specification and Change (Proceedings of the IFIP TC2/WG 2.1 Working Conference)*, L.G.L.T. Meertens, Ed., North-Holland, 1987, pp. 165–195.
17. M. Feather, Constructing Specifications by Combining Parallel Elaborations, *IEEE Transactions on Software Engineering*, Vol. 15 No. 2, Feb 1989, pp. 198–208.
18. S. Fickas, Automating the Transformational Development of Software, *IEEE Transactions on Software Engineering*, Vol. 11 No. 11, Nov 1985, pp. 1268–1277.
19. W. Gibbs, Software's Chronic Crisis, *Scientific American*, SEP 1994, pp. 86–94.
20. W. Johnson, M. Feather, Building an Evolution Change Library, *12th International Conference on Software Engineering*, 1990, pp. 238–248.
21. E. Kant, On the Efficient Synthesis of Efficient Programs, *Artificial Intelligence*, Vol. 20 No. 3, May 1983, pp. 253-36. Also appears in [35], pp. 157–183.
22. B. Kraemer, Luqi, V. Berzins, Compositional Semantics of a Real-Time Prototyping Language *IEEE Transactions on Software Engineering*, Vol. 19, No. 5, pp. 453–477, May 1993.

23. D. Lange, Hypermedia Analysis and Navigation of Domains, MS Thesis, Computer Science, Naval Postgraduate School, Sep. 1997.
24. Luqi, M. Ketabchi, A Computer Aided Prototyping System, *IEEE Software*, Vol. 5 No. 2, Mar 1988, pp. 66–72.
25. Luqi, V. Berzins, R. Yeh, A Prototyping Language for Real-Time Software, *IEEE Transactions on Software Engineering*, Vol. 14 No. 10, Oct 1988, pp. 1409–1423.
26. Luqi, Handling Timing Constraints in Rapid Prototyping *Proceedings of the 22nd Annual Hawaii International Conference on System Sciences*, IEEE Computer Society, Jan. 1989, pp. 417–424.
27. Luqi, Software Evolution via Rapid Prototyping, *IEEE Computer*, Vol. 22, No. 5, May 1989, pp. 13–25.
28. Luqi, A Graph Model for Software Evolution, *IEEE Transactions on Software Engineering*, Vol. 16, No. 8, pp. 917–927, Aug. 1990.
29. Luqi, Computer-Aided Prototyping for a Command-and-Control System Using CAPS, *IEEE Software*, Vol. 9, No. 1, pp. 56–67, Jan. 1992.
30. Luqi, Real-Time Constraints in a Rapid Prototyping Language, *Journal of Computer Languages*, Vol. 18, No. 2, pp. 77–103, Spring 1993.
31. Luqi, Specifications in Software Prototyping, *Proc. SEKE 96*, Lake Tahoe, NV, June 10-12, 1996, pp. 189-197.
32. Luqi, Scheduling Real-Time Software Prototypes, *Proceedings of the 2nd International Symposium on Operations Research and its Applications*, Guilin, China, December 11-13, 1996, pp. 614–623.
33. Luqi, J. Goguen, Formal Methods: Promises and Problems, *IEEE Software*, Vol. 14, No. 1, Jan. 1997, pp. 73–85.
34. R. Lutz, Analyzing Software Requirements: Errors in Safety-Critical Embedded Systems, TR 92-27, Iowa State University, AUG 1992.
35. C. Rich, R. Waters, Eds., *Readings in Artificial Intelligence and Software Engineering*, Morgan Kaufmann, 1986.
36. D. Rusin, Luqi, M. Scanlon, SIDS Wireless Acoustic Monitor (SWAM), *Proc. 21st Int. Conf. on Lung Sounds*, Chester, England, International Lung Sounds Association, Sep. 4-6, 1996.
37. D. Smith, G. Kotik, S. Westfold, Research on Knowledge-Based Software Environments at Kestrel Institute, *IEEE Transactions on Software Engineering*, Vol. 11 No. 11, Nov 1985, pp. 1278–1295.
38. Chaos, Technical Report, The Standish Group, Dennis, MA, 1995, http://www.standishgroup.com/chaos.html.
39. W. Swartout, R. Balzer, On the Inevitable intertwining of Specification and implementation, *Communication of the ACM*, Vol. 25 No. 7, July 1982, pp. 438–440. Also appears in *Software Specification techniques*, N. Gehani, A.D. McGettrick, Eds., 1986, pp. 41–45.

Abstraction and Modular Verification of Infinite-State Reactive Systems *

Zohar Manna,
Michael A. Colón, Bernd Finkbeiner,
Henny B. Sipma and Tomás E. Uribe

Computer Science Department
Stanford University
Stanford, CA. 94305-9045
manna@cs.stanford.edu

Abstract. We review a number of temporal verification techniques for reactive systems using modularity and abstraction. Their use allows the verification of larger systems, and the incremental verification of systems as they are developed and refined. In particular, we show how deductive verification tools, and the combination of finite-state model checking and abstraction, allow the verification of infinite-state systems featuring data types commonly used in software specifications, including real-time and hybrid systems.

1 Introduction

Reactive systems have an ongoing interaction with their environment. Many systems can be seen as reactive systems, including computer hardware, concurrent programs, network protocols, and concurrent software. *Temporal logic* is a convenient language for expressing properties of reactive systems [Pnu77]. A *temporal verification methodology* provides methods for proving that a given reactive system satisfies its temporal specification [MP95].

Computations of reactive systems are modeled as infinite sequences of states. For *finite-state* systems, the possible system states are determined by a fixed number of variables with finite domain, so there are finitely many such states. Algorithmic verification (model checking) can automatically decide the validity of temporal properties over such finite-state systems [CE81,QS82], and has been particularly successful for hardware [McM93].

Software systems, on the other hand, are usually *infinite-state*, since they contain system variables over unbounded domains, such as integers, lists, trees, and other data types. Most finite-state verification methods cannot be applied directly to such systems. The application of temporal verification techniques to

---

* This research was supported in part by the National Science Foundation under grant CCR-95-27927, the Defense Advanced Research Projects Agency under NASA grant NAG2-892, ARO under grant DAAH04-95-1-0317, ARO under MURI grant DAAH04-96-1-0341, and by Army contract DABT63-96-C-0096 (DARPA).

software systems is further limited by the size and complexity of the systems analyzed. Such limitations already appear in the verification of large finite-state systems, e.g., complex hardware, where the state-explosion problem, and the limitations of symbolic methods, restrict the number of finite-state variables that can be considered by automatic methods.

Deductive verification, which relies on general theorem-proving and user interaction, provides complete proof systems that can, in principle, prove the correctness of any property over an infinite-state system, provided the property is indeed valid for that system. However, these methods are also limited by the size and complexity of the system being analyzed, becoming much more laborious as the system complexity grows.

To overcome these limitations, verification methods analogous to those used to manage complexity in software design are being investigated. *Modular verification* follows the classic divide-and-conquer paradigm, where portions of a complex system are analyzed independently of each other. It holds the promise of proof reuse and the creation of libraries of verified components. *Abstraction* is based on ignoring details as much as possible, often simplifying the domain of computation of the original system. This may allow, for instance, abstracting infinite-state systems to finite-state ones that can be more easily model checked.

This paper presents an overview of a number of abstraction and modular verification methods that we have recently investigated, geared to the verification of general infinite-state reactive systems. These methods are being implemented as part of the STeP (Stanford Temporal Prover) verification system (see Section 2.3). We show how they help design and debug complex systems, modularly described.

Outline: Section 2 presents the basic preliminary notions, and the STeP verification system. In Section 3 we briefly present abstraction, describing a number of simple (infinite-state) examples and their abstractions, generated and verified using STeP. Section 4 presents modular verification, including a larger example of a hybrid system that is modularly specified and verified, again using STeP. Section 5 presents our conclusions and briefly discusses related work.

2 Preliminaries

2.1 System and Property Specification

Transition Systems: We use *transition systems* [MP95] to model finite- and infinite-state reactive systems. An *assertion language*, usually based on first-order logic, is used to represent sets of system states, described in terms of a set of *system variables* $\mathcal{V}$. A reactive system is given by $\mathcal{V}$, a set of *initial states* θ, and a set of *transitions* $\mathcal{T}$. The *initial condition* Θ is described by an assertion over $\mathcal{V}$, and transitions are described by *transition relations*, assertions over the set of system variables $\mathcal{V}$ and a set of primed system variables $\mathcal{V}'$, giving the value of the system variables at the next state. A *run* of the system is an infinite sequence of states $s_0, s_1, \ldots$ where s_0 satisfies θ, and for each $i \geq 0$, there is some transition $\tau \in \mathcal{T}$ such that (s_i, s_{i+1}) satisfies ρ_τ, the transition relation of τ.

Transitions can be *just* (weakly fair) or *compassionate* (strongly fair), indicating that they cannot be enabled infinitely often (continuously, in the case of justice) but never taken. A *computation* is a run that satisfies these fairness requirements. See [MP95] for details.

Temporal Logic: To express properties of reactive systems, we use *linear-time temporal logic* (LTL) [MP95], where we allow first-order quantification at the state-level.

Real-Time and Hybrid Systems: Real-time and hybrid systems can be modeled using *clocked* and *phase transition systems* [MP96], which use the basic transition system representation. Real-valued *clock variables* are updated by a *tick* transition that advances time, constrained by a global progress condition. In the case of hybrid systems, other continuous variables evolve over time, as given by a set of differential equations. This allows the reuse of the standard deductive verification techniques [MS98,KMP96].

Timed automata and hybrid automata can be easily translated into these formalisms. Furthermore, by adopting the general transition system representation, clocked and phase transition systems can model systems with an infinite-state control component. This includes, for instance, software with real-time constraints and software-controlled hybrid systems. No extension of temporal logic is required, since clock variables (including the global clock) can be directly referred to in specifications. For real-time and hybrid systems, fairness constraints are usually replaced by upper bounds on how long transitions can be enabled without being taken. Only runs that are *non-zeno*, where time grows beyond any bound, are considered to be computations.

2.2 Deductive and Algorithmic Verification

As mentioned in Section 1, the two main approaches to the verification of temporal properties of reactive systems are deductive verification (*theorem-proving*) and algorithmic verification (*model checking*). In deductive verification, the validity of a temporal property over a given system is reduced to the general validity of first-order verification conditions. In algorithmic verification, a temporal property is established by an exhaustive search of the system's state space, usually searching for a counterexample computation.

Model checking procedures are automatic, while deductive verification often relies on user interaction to identify suitable lemmas and auxiliary assertions. However, model checking is usually applicable only to systems with a finite, fixed number of states, while the deductive approach can verify infinite-state systems and *parameterized* systems, where an unbounded number of components with similar structure are composed.

2.3 The STeP System

The Stanford Temporal Prover (STeP) supports the computer-aided formal verification of reactive, real time and hybrid systems based on their temporal specifications, expressed in linear-time temporal logic. STeP integrates algorithmic and deductive methods to allow the verification of a broad class of systems, including parameterized (N-component) circuit designs, parameterized (N-process) programs, and programs with infinite data domains.

STeP is described in [BBC+95,BBC+96]. The latest release of STeP, version 2.0, is described in [MBB+98].

3 Abstraction

Abstraction reduces the complexity of a system being verified by considering a simpler *abstract system*, where some of the details of the original *concrete system* are hidden. There is much work on the theoretical foundations of reactive system abstraction [CGL94,DGG94,LGS+95,Dam96], usually based on the ideas of *abstract interpretation* [CC77].

Most abstractions *weakly preserve* temporal properties: if a property holds for the abstract system, then a corresponding property will hold for the concrete one. However, the converse will not be true: not all properties satisfied by the concrete system will hold at the abstract level. Thus, only positive results transfer from the abstract to the concrete level. This means, in particular, that abstract counterexamples will not always correspond to concrete ones.

Abstractions that remove too much information from the concrete system and are thus too *coarse* will fail to prove the property of interest. They then can be *refined*, by adding more detail, until the property can be proved or a concrete counterexample is found.

3.1 From Infinite- to Finite-State

The intuition that motivates the use of abstraction in the verification of software systems is the often limited interaction between control and data. The particular values taken on by data variables are often unimportant. Rather, it is the relationship between these variables which is relevant to verifying the system. For example, to decide which branch of a conditional statement will be taken, it is sufficient to know whether its guard is true or false, and this information can often be gleaned by an analysis of how each system transition affects the truth value of that guard.

Example: Bakery: Consider the version of Lamport's Bakery algorithm for mutual exclusion shown in Figure 1, as specified in the Simple Programming Language (SPL) of [MP95]. (STeP automatically translates such a program into the corresponding fair transition system.) This system contains two infinite-domain variables, y_1 and y_2, ranging over the non-negative integers. There is no

$$\text{local } y_1, y_2 : \text{integer where } y_1 = 0 \land y_2 = 0$$

$$\left[\begin{array}{l}\text{loop forever do} \\ \left[\begin{array}{ll}\ell_0: & \textbf{noncritical} \\ \ell_1: & y_1 := y_2 + 1 \\ \ell_2: & \textbf{await } (y_2 = 0 \lor y_1 \leq y_2) \\ \ell_3: & \textbf{critical} \\ \ell_4: & y_1 := 0\end{array}\right]\end{array}\right] \;\|\; \left[\begin{array}{l}\text{loop forever do} \\ \left[\begin{array}{ll}m_0: & \textbf{noncritical} \\ m_1: & y_2 := y_1 + 1 \\ m_2: & \textbf{await } (y_1 = 0 \lor y_2 < y_1) \\ m_3: & \textbf{critical} \\ m_4: & y_2 := 0\end{array}\right]\end{array}\right]$$

$$\text{--P1--} \hspace{10em} \text{--P2--}$$

Fig. 1. Program BAKERY

upper bound on the values that these variables can take in a computation of the system. Thus, the system is infinite-state, and cannot be directly model checked.

However, knowing only the truth value of the assertions

$$b_1 : y_1 = 0,$$
$$b_2 : y_2 = 0$$
$$b_3 : y_1 \leq y_2$$

is sufficient to determine which branches of the conditional statements are feasible. Using these assertions to replace the original integer variables, and maintaining the finite-domain control variables, we can construct a finite-state abstraction of the Bakery algorithm, shown in Figure 2. This abstract program can be given to a model checker to verify the basic safety properties of the original system, including *mutual exclusion*,

$$\Box \neg (at\_\ell_3 \land at\_m_3) \;,$$

stating that the two processes can never be both in their critical section at the same time, and *one-bounded overtaking*:

$$\Box (at\_\ell_2 \rightarrow \neg at\_m_3 \, \mathcal{W} \, (at\_m_3 \, \mathcal{W} \, (\neg at\_m_3 \, \mathcal{W} \, at\_\ell_3))) \;,$$

which states that if process P1 is waiting to enter its critical section, then process P2 can only enter its critical section at most once before P1 does.

All transitions in the concrete BAKERY program are just, except for the **noncritical** statements at ℓ_0 and m_0. Under certain conditions, the abstract transitions can inherit the fairness properties of the original ones [KMP94,CU98]. This is the case here, so we can also prove *accessibility*,

$$\Box (at\_\ell_1 \rightarrow \Diamond at\_\ell_3) \;,$$

by model checking the abstract system with the inherited fairness requirements.

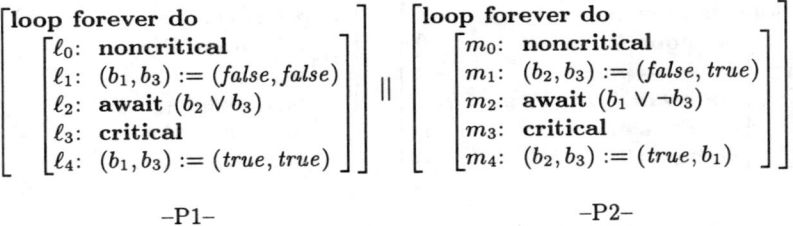

Fig. 2. Abstraction of Program BAKERY

3.2 Generating Abstractions

Constructing abstract systems manually can be time-consuming, and requires that the correctness of the abstraction be checked during a separate phase. If this is not done formally, a new potential source of error is introduced.

The Bakery example in the preceding section is an instance of *assertion-based abstraction*, where a finite number of assertions $\{b_1, \ldots, b_n\}$ are used as boolean variables in the abstract system, replacing the concrete variables they refer to. An algorithm that generates an abstract system automatically, given such a set of assertions (called the *basis* of the abstraction), is presented in [CU98]. The algorithm uses a validity checker to establish relationships between the basis elements, compositionally abstracting the transition relations of the system to directly produce abstract transition relations. This algorithm has been implemented as part of STeP, using the STeP validity checker, and automatically generated the abstractions in this section.

Example: Fischer: As a second example, consider Fischer's mutual exclusion algorithm, as shown in Figure 3. This is a real-time system, with lower and upper bounds L and U on the amount of time that each process can wait at any control location. Provided that $2L > U$, the program satisfies mutual exclusion [MP96].

The program can be modeled as a clocked transition system, with clock variables c_1 and c_2 measuring the time each process has been waiting at each control location. Because of these clock variables, the system is infinite-state and cannot be model checked directly.[1]

Examining the system suggests that the truth value of the assertions

$$b_1 : c_1 \geq L$$
$$b_2 : c_2 \geq L$$

together with the value of the finite-domain variables, is sufficient to determine when transitions can be taken. However, these two assertions are not inductive,

---

[1] Specialized model checkers for real-time and hybrid systems, such as HyTech [HH95] and Kronos [DOTY96], can automatically prove properties of such systems, but are restricted to linear hybrid systems with finite control.

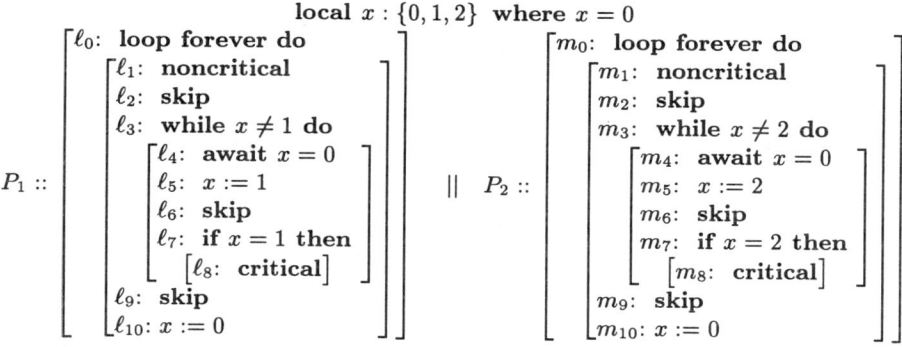

Fig. 3. Fischer's mutual exclusion algorithm.

i.e., the system contains transitions for which knowing the truth values of these assertions is not sufficient to determine them after the transitions are taken. To remedy this situation, we also consider the assertions:

$$b_3 : c_1 \geq c_2$$
$$b_4 : c_2 \geq c_1$$
$$b_5 : c_1 \geq c_2 + L$$
$$b_6 : c_2 \geq c_1 + L$$

These additional assertions yield sufficient information about the relationships between the clock variables to generate a finite-state abstraction fine enough to establish mutual exclusion: $\Box \neg (at\_\ell_4 \wedge at\_m_4)$.

Example: BRP: Finally, we turn to the bounded retransmission protocol (see, e.g. [HS96,GS97,DKRT97]). The protocol consists of two processes, a sender and a receiver, communicating over two lossy channels. The sender sends a list of items (of some unspecified type) one by one, by repeatedly transmitting a frame containing the current item until the frame is acknowledged. The receiver repeatedly waits for a frame to arrive, acknowledges it, and appends the corresponding item to the end of its own list.

To detect the arrival of duplicate frames and acknowledgements, each process maintains a bit that is compared against a bit included in the frames and acknowledgements. Which each outgoing frame, the sender attaches its bit, which the receiver later copies into the acknowledgement it sends for that frame (if the frame is not lost in transit). The sender ignores any acknowledgements that arrive with the wrong bit, and flips its bit upon the arrival of a correct acknowledgement. The receiver acknowledges every frame it receives, but only appends the carried item to its list if the frame's bit agrees with its own, and flips its own bit in this case. If the number of retransmissions of any frame exceeds a fixed, predetermined bound, the sender aborts transmission. The sender and receiver each report the status of the transmission when they terminate. Both sender and receiver report OK (resp. NOT_OK) when they detect that the transmission has succeeded (resp. failed). In addition, the sender may report DONT_KNOW should it happen to abort while transmitting the last item of the list.

One property we would like to establish is that the status reports are consistent: either both processes report OK, both report NOT_OK, or the sender reports DONT_KNOW and the receiver OK or NOT_OK. This is specified as the invariance of:

$$\begin{array}{l} \text{sendDone} \land \text{recvDone} \rightarrow \\ \left[\begin{array}{c} (\text{sendStatus} = \text{OK} \land \text{recvStatus} = \text{OK}) \lor \\ (\text{sendStatus} = \text{NOT\_OK} \land \text{recvStatus} = \text{NOT\_OK}) \lor \\ \text{sendStatus} = \text{DONT\_KNOW} \land (\text{recvStatus} = \text{OK} \lor \text{recvStatus} = \text{NOT\_OK}) \end{array} \right] \end{array}$$

The system cannot be directly model checked: not only are the sender and receiver lists unbounded, but the retransmission count sendCount is unbounded as well, since the retransmission bound is unspecified. However, a finite-state abstraction of the system can be generated. The assertion

$$b_1 : \text{sendList} = \text{nil}$$

determines if the sender has successfully transmitted and received acknowledgements for all the items to be sent. In this case, the sender cannot abort transmission. The assertions

$$b_2 : \text{sendList} = \text{cons}(\text{head}(\text{sendList}), \text{nil})$$
$$b_3 : \text{sendCount} = 0$$

ensure that the generated abstraction accurately models the sender's behavior when it chooses to abort with one item remaining to be sent. In that case, the sender can report NOT_OK only if it has yet to transmit the last item. Otherwise, the sender must report DONT_KNOW, since it is unclear whether the frame or its acknowledgement was lost in transmission.

Using this basis ($\{b_1, b_2, b_3\}$) to abstract the unbounded variables, and preserving the finite-domain variables (which includes all the variables in the invariant to be proved), STeP automatically generates a finite-state abstraction for which the above invariance is then model checked, automatically as well.

Another property we would like to establish is that the list is correctly transmitted if the sender does not abort. That is, we would like to prove

$$\varphi : \Box(\text{sendDone} \land \text{sendList} = \text{nil} \rightarrow \text{recvList} = \text{LIST})$$

where LIST is the complete list being transmitted. Again, we use abstraction. The assertions

$$b_1 : \text{sendList} = \text{nil}$$
$$b_2 : \text{recvList} = \text{LIST}$$

let us track the formula φ to be proven over the abstract system. The assertion

$$b_3 : \text{frameItem} = \text{head}(\text{sendList})$$

tracks the current item as it moves from sender to receiver. Finally,

$$b_4 : \texttt{recvList++sendList} = \texttt{LIST}$$
$$b_5 : \texttt{recvList++tail(sendList)} = \texttt{LIST}$$

where ++ is the list concatenation operator, capture an inductive relationship between the sender's and the receiver's lists at any point in time, and the list being transmitted; $b_4 \vee b_5$ is an invariant of the system. Given this basis, $\{b_1, \ldots, b_5\}$, STeP automatically generates and model checks a finite-state abstraction.

4 Modular Specification and Verification

The advantages of modular description and development of complex systems are well-known. From the formal verification point of view, decomposing systems into modules allows verification that more closely follows the design structure of the system. For instance, general properties of a parameterized module can be proved once and then reused when the module is instantiated.

[FMS98] presents *modular transition systems*, a system specification formalism that allows systems to be built from transition modules. Modules consist of an *interface*, which describes the interaction with the environment, including a list of shared variables and the name of exported transitions, and a *body*, which describes the module's actions, as transitions that can be synchronized or interleaved with those of other modules.

Complex modules are constructed from simpler ones by module expressions. The description language includes recursive module definitions, module composition and instantiation, variable hiding and renaming, and augmenting and restricting module interfaces. Composition can be synchronous or asynchronous; transitions with the same label are composed synchronously, while the rest are interleaved. This modular system specification language is being added to STeP, together with the corresponding modular proof rules.

When designing a system modularly, one would like to prove simple properties of individual modules, and combinations of modules, before the entire system is specified. *Assumption-guarantee reasoning* is often used to prove properties of a module that depend on its environment, before that environment is fully specified. Abstraction can facilitate this process: Modular properties can be model checked for abstractions, relative to assumptions on the environment. Furthermore, for real-time and hybrid systems, part or all of the complex real-time behavior can be abstracted away when debugging individual modules. More expensive verification methods should only be used after the design components and some of their combinations pass these simple (and fast) checks.

4.1 Example: Steam Boiler Case Study

The *steam boiler* case study [ABL96] is a benchmark for specification and verification methods for hybrid controlled systems. At the time of its appearance we

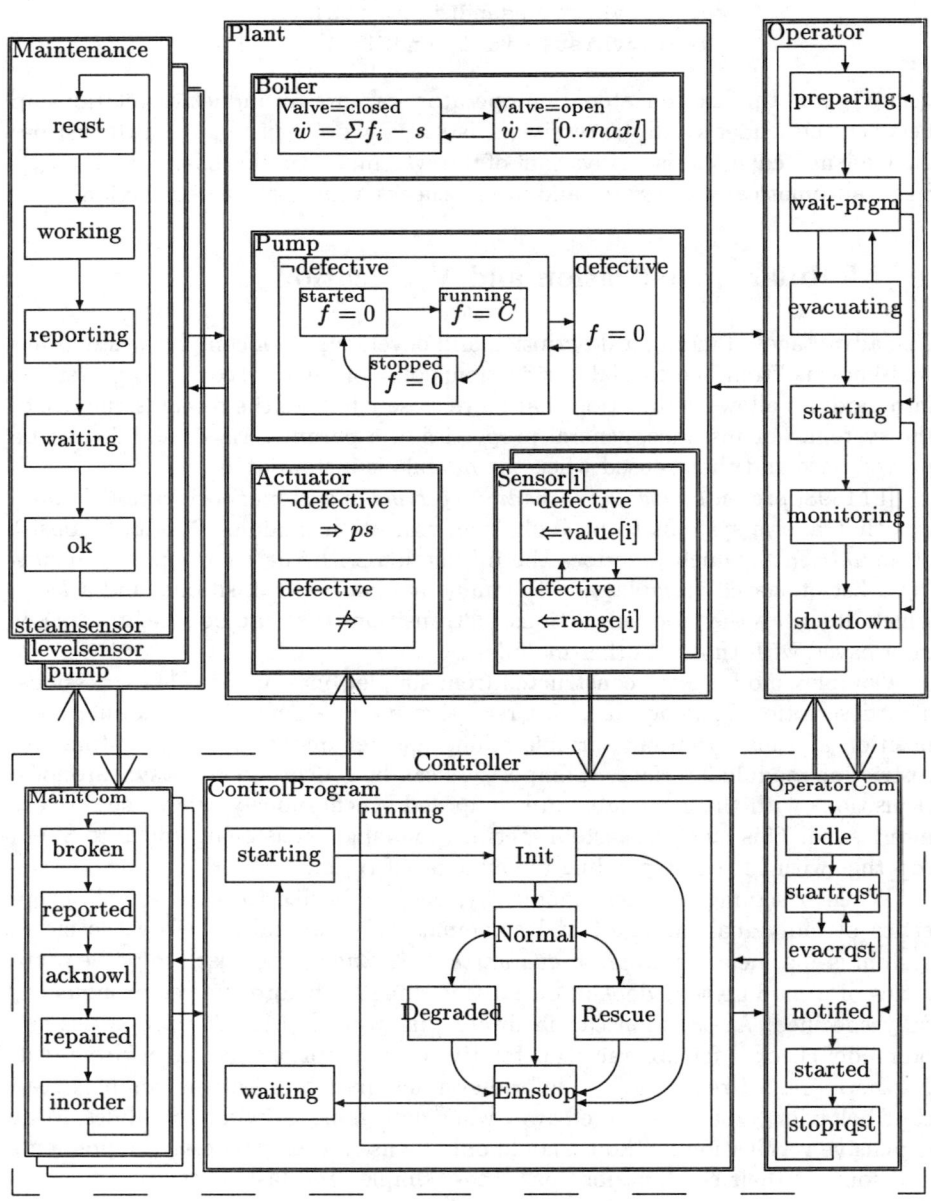

Fig. 4. Schematic overview of the Steam Boiler system

developed a STeP implementation of the system, including both the plant and the controller, consisting of some 1000 lines of STeP SPL code.

However, at that time STeP did not provide any modularity or abstraction techniques. Although we managed to prove some simple properties over that program and discovered numerous bugs in our model of the system, we quickly decided that full verification was not feasible with the tool at hand.

With modularity and abstraction techniques in place in STeP, the case study was revived. The system was rewritten as a modular transition system consisting of ten modules with a total of 80 transitions, 18 real-valued variables, and 28 finite-domain variables. In the following we briefly describe the system, and then present some of the techniques we have used to analyze it.

System Description: Our specification of the system is shown schematically in Figure 4. The system consists of a *physical plant*, a *controller*, a *maintenance department* and an *operator desk*.

The plant, at the top of Figure 4, contains the *boiler* itself, a *pump* that supplies water to the boiler, *sensors* that measure the water level in the boiler and the steam flow out of the boiler, and an *actuator* that can start and stop the pump.

The controller, at the bottom of Figure 4, consists of three sub-modules: the *control program* processes the sensor values and determines the output to the actuator, and generally monitors the plant. It is responsible to detect unsafe conditions and faulty equipment and, if necessary, generate an emergency stop. The *maintenance communication* sub-module, MaintCom, keeps track of equipment status, based on input from the maintenance department and the central control program. The *operator communication* sub-module, OperatorCom, processes the input from the operator desk during the start-up phase.

Space considerations prohibit showing the entire system, but to illustrate our modular description language, Figure 5 shows the top-level composition of the various modules. There are eight basic modules: Maintenance, MaintCom, Operator, OperatorCom, ControlProgram, Boiler, Pump and Environment. The sensor and actuator are incorporated into the boiler and the pump, respectively.

The MaintFun module is the parallel composition of instances of the MaintCom and Maintenance modules. Multiple instances of the same module may be used in a composition. For example, the full system, module BoilerSystem, contains three instances of the MaintFun module, one for the steam flow sensor, one for the level sensor, and one for the pump. In each case the generic variables equipmentDefective and equipmentState are instantiated as the variable specific to the corresponding piece of equipment. The Environment module specifies how variables may be modified by the physical environment of the plant. Finally, we *close* the system by hiding all shared variables, indicating that their behavior is determined completely by the modules included in the system.

Modules can communicate with each other through shared variables or by synchronization of transitions. For example, the Maintenance, Boiler, Pump and Operator modules communicate via shared variables, as do the three parts of the ControlProgram, whereas the communication between the Controller and

```
Module MaintFun: (M: Maintenance) || (MC: MaintCom)

Module OperatorFun: (O: Operator) || (MO: OperatorCom)

Module BoilerSystem:
        Hide(  levelEqState, steamEqState, pumpEqState,
               levelDefective, steamDefective, pumpDefective in
             ( (C:ControlProgram) || (B:Boiler) || (P:Pump)
                || Rename((SteamMaint:MaintFun)
                        equipmentDefective = steamDefective;
                        equipmentState     = steamEqState)
                || Rename((LevelMaint:MaintFun)
                        equipmentDefective = levelDefective;
                        equipmentState     = levelEqState)
                || Rename((PumpMaint:MaintFun)
                        equipmentDefective = pumpDefective;
                        equipmentState     = pumpEqState)
                || (Ops: OperatorFun) || (E: environment)))
```

Fig. 5. Top-level modular specification of the Steam Boiler system

the other modules is solely via synchronized transitions. This reflects the fact that the controller only has access to the current plant data at the time that sensors are sampled.

4.2 System Analysis: Modularity and Inheritance

The modular structure of the system allows us to prove properties of the system at various levels. For example, we may want to prove the consistency between the internal states of the Maintenance and the MaintCom modules for all the pieces of equipment. It is attractive to prove this property over the MaintFun module and then let all of its instances in the full system inherit it, rather than proving it directly over the entire system; furthermore, since the MaintFun module is finite-state, we can use a model checker for the modular proof, whereas the full system contains real-valued variables, ruling out the use of a model checker within STeP.

The MaintFun module contains two shared variables, equipmentDefective and equipmentState. To be able to inherit properties, we must assume that these variables can be arbitrarily modified by the module's environment. However, to prove the consistency property we need a stronger assumption on the environment.

We provide two ways to state such assumptions: the most general way is to specify the property as an *assume-guarantee* property, of the form $\mathcal{A} \rightarrow \mathcal{G}$, where the assumption $\mathcal{A}$ is discharged upon parallel composition of the module with its environment. However, in some cases this leads to rather large, unintuitive temporal formulas. A second, weaker way to specify an assumption is to include an explicit *environment restriction* in the module. This restriction becomes part of the environment transition when the modular property is proven. When a module with an environment restriction is composed, the transition relations of the composing modules are required to satisfy the restriction. We now show an example of each approach:

Environment Restriction: Specifying the consistency property as an assume-guarantee property is possible, but rather awkward, mainly because within a temporal formula it is hard to separate the actions of the module from those of its environment. On the other hand, we can include the assertion

$$(\text{equipmentState}' = \text{equipmentState}) \lor (\text{equipmentState}' = \text{broken})$$

as an environment restriction for the MaintFun module, stating that the environment can set equipmentState to broken, but cannot modify it in any other way. We can then prove the property directly over the MaintFun module. Subsequently, we ensure that the modules composed with MaintFun satisfy this property when building the full system.

Assume-Guarantee Reasoning: An example of a temporal property for which an assume-guarantee proof is well-suited is

$$\mathcal{G} : \Box(\text{equipmentDefective} \rightarrow \Diamond \text{equipmentState} = \text{inOrder}) ,$$

stating that if a piece of equipment is defective then it will eventually be in working order again.

The sequence of events in an equipment failure are as follows: At an arbitrary time, the environment can set any equipment to be defective, resulting in either a faulty sensor reading, or the pump failing to start when requested. The Controller detects that the equipment is broken, and sets the corresponding equipment status to broken. The maintenance function of the Controller then informs the maintenance department, which acknowledges the report and repairs the equipment, eventually setting the equipment to inOrder. All of the steps involved in achieving the inOrder condition are controlled by the MaintFun module, except for the detection of the failure, which is done by the ControlProgram module. Thus we can specify the property $\mathcal{G}$ under assumption $\mathcal{A}$, as $\mathcal{A} \rightarrow \mathcal{G}$:

$$\Box(\text{equipmentDefective} \rightarrow \Diamond \text{equipmentState} = \text{broken})$$
$$\rightarrow$$
$$\Box(\text{equipmentDefective} \rightarrow \Diamond \text{equipmentState} = \text{inOrder})$$

This implication can be model checked over the MaintFun module.

When the MaintFun module is instantiated, the full system inherits three assume-guarantee properties of the form $\mathcal{A}' \rightarrow \mathcal{G}'$:

$$\Box(\text{steamDefective} \rightarrow \Diamond \text{steamEqState} = \text{broken})$$
$$\rightarrow$$
$$\Box(\text{steamDefective} \rightarrow \Diamond \text{steamEqState} = \text{inOrder})$$

for the steam sensor,

$$\Box(\text{levelDefective} \to \Diamond \text{levelEqState} = \text{broken})$$
$$\to$$
$$\Box(\text{levelDefective} \to \Diamond \text{levelEqState} = \text{inOrder})$$

for the level sensor, and

$$\Box(\text{pumpDefective} \to \Diamond \text{pumpEqState} = \text{broken})$$
$$\to$$
$$\Box(\text{pumpDefective} \to \Diamond \text{pumpEqState} = \text{inOrder})$$

for the pump. We then need separate proofs for each of the three assumptions, specific to the particular failure detection method of that piece of equipment.

4.3 System Analysis: Abstraction

As we saw in Section 3, abstraction can reduce an infinite-state system to a finite-state one by capturing relationships between infinite-domain variables, in the form of assertions. As an example of the use of abstraction, consider the property

$$\varphi : \Box \left(\begin{array}{c} \text{steamEqState} = \text{inOrder} \land \neg\text{steamDefective} \\ \to (\text{steamEqState} = \text{inOrder} \; \mathcal{W} \; \text{steamDefective}) \end{array} \right),$$

stating that as long as the steam flow sensor is not defective its status will be inOrder. That is, the controller will not detect a failure in nondefective equipment. This property is certainly desirable, since the failure status of a piece of equipment may cause a plant shutdown. We will prove it over the full system.

To check whether the steam flow sensor is operating correctly, at each cycle the controller predicts the range of possible sensor readings for the next reading, based on a minimum and maximum assumed gradient in the flow. If the reading is outside this range, it is considered defective, and the controller will set its status to broken.

Although the property involves only finite-domain variables, its validity is obviously dependent on real-valued variables such as the actual and predicted steam flow. However, the property does not depend on the particular values of these variables, but only on certain relationships between them. The following assertion basis is sufficient to prove the property:

$$b_1 : \text{steamflow} = \text{C.s}$$
$$b_2 : \text{C.s} = \text{B.sf}$$
$$b_3 : \text{C.s} \geq \text{C.sPredLow}$$
$$b_4 : \text{C.s} \leq \text{C.sPredHigh}$$
$$b_5 : \text{C.s} \leq \text{B.sf} - \text{mingrad} * \text{delta}$$
$$b_6 : \text{C.s} \geq \text{B.sf} - \text{maxgrad} * \text{delta}$$
$$b_7 : \text{C.s} = \text{C.sLow}$$
$$b_8 : \text{C.s} = \text{C.sHigh}$$
$$b_9 : \text{C.sPredLow} = \text{C.s} + \text{mingrad} * \text{delta}$$
$$b_{10} : \text{C.sPredHigh} = \text{C.s} + \text{maxgrad} * \text{delta}$$

Here, `steamflow` is the sensor reading, `C.s` is the local value of the steam flow within the controller, and `B.sf` is the actual steam flow going out of the boiler. Parameters `mingrad` and `maxgrad` are the minimum and maximum gradients of the steam flow, and `delta` is the sampling interval. We assume that `mingrad` < 0, `maxgrad` > 0, and `delta` > 0.

The addition of these variables to the system allows us to remove all real-valued variables and construct a finite-state abstraction that contains sufficient information to prove the property.

Abstraction Test Points: When constructing abstract transition relations, the algorithm of [CU98] uses a set of *test points*, built from the abstraction basis $\{b_1, \ldots, b_n\}$, to determine the effect of a transition on the truth value of the basis elements under different circumstances. By default, the test points used are of the form $\{p_1 \to p_2'\}$, where p_1 and p_2 are basis elements or their negation. When generating the abstraction, a validity checker is used, in essence, to check the implication

$$p_1 \wedge \rho_\tau \to p_2'$$

for every transition (compositionally over the structure of the formula that describes the transition relation); if valid, the implication is added to the abstracted transition relation.

These default test points are enough to generate the abstractions described in Section 3. However, in some cases a more precise abstraction is required to prove the desired property, which could have been obtained if more complex relationships between basis elements had been explored.

Thus, our implementation allows additional test points to be specified explicitly for particular transitions, letting p_1 and p_2' above be general boolean combinations of basis elements. This has the effect of refining the abstracted system, producing an abstraction for which more properties can be proved.

To illustrate the abstraction process, some examples of concrete and corresponding abstract transition relations are given below. The evolution of the physical system, modeled by the concrete relation

$$\rho_{Ev}^C : \text{B.sf}' \geq \text{B.sf} + \text{mingrad} * \text{delta} \wedge \text{B.sf}' \leq \text{B.sf} + \text{maxgrad} * \text{delta}$$

is abstracted to

$$\rho_{Ev}^A : (b_2 \to b_5' \wedge b_6') \wedge preserve(\{b_1, b_3, b_4, b_7, b_8, b_9, b_{10}\}) \ ,$$

where $preserve(S)$ stands for $\wedge_{x \in S}(x' = x)$.[2]

The two transitions involved in the prediction of the acceptable steam flow range are

$$\rho_{P1}^C : \begin{array}{l} \text{C.steamReliable} \wedge \text{C.sLow}' = \text{C.s} \wedge \text{C.sHigh}' = \text{C.s} \\ \vee \ (\neg \text{C.steamReliable} \wedge \ \ldots) \end{array}$$

---

[2] We only include the transition relation fragments relevant to the abstraction; in particular, finite-state control variables that are retained are not included. We plan to make the entire concrete and abstract systems available elsewhere.

and
$$\rho_{P2}^C : \begin{array}{l} \text{C.sPredLow}' = \text{C.sLow} + \text{mingrad} * \text{delta} \\ \land\ \text{C.sPredHigh}' = \text{C.sHigh} + \text{maxgrad} * \text{delta} \end{array}.$$

They are abstracted to
$$\rho_{P1}^A : \begin{array}{l} \text{C.steamReliable} \to b_7' \land b_8' \land preserve(\{b_1, \ldots, b_6, b_9, b_{10}\}) \\ \land\ \neg\text{C.steamReliable} \to \ldots \end{array}$$

and
$$\rho_{P2}^A : (b_7 \to b_3' \land b_9') \land (b_8 \to b_4' \land b_{10}') \land preserve(\{b_1, b_2, b_5, b_6, b_7, b_8\}) .$$

For these transition relations, the default test points suffice. The transition that models the sensor sampling, BoilerSensorsC, is a synchronized transition between the Boiler and the ControlProgram modules, with transition relation
$$\rho_S^C : \begin{array}{l} \text{C.s}' = \text{steamflow}' \land \\ \text{steamflow}' = \text{if steamDefective then outofrange else B.sf} \end{array}.$$

This transition requires an extra test point in order to establish a sufficiently strong postcondition, namely:

$\{\neg\text{steamDefective} \land b_5 \land b_6 \land b_9 \land b_{10}\}\ \text{BoilerSensorsC}\ \{b_3 \land b_4\}$.

This results in the abstract transition relation
$$\rho_S^A : \begin{array}{l} b_1' \land (\neg\text{steamDefective} \to b_2' \land b_5' \land b_6') \land \\ (\neg\text{steamDefective} \land b_5 \land b_6 \land b_9 \land b_{10} \to b_1' \land b_2' \land b_3' \land b_4') \end{array} .$$

This abstraction allows us to prove the desired property φ above.

5 Conclusions and Related Work

We have shown how abstraction and modularity allow for more automatic and incremental verification of reactive systems. Deductive methods allow the verification and abstraction of infinite-state systems, including the unbounded data types used in software systems.

Clearly, much has to be done before these techniques are practical for large-scale software system design. In practice, a combination of formal and informal methods is required. However, we believe that abstraction, refinement and modularity will be useful in all of these settings.

Proving simple properties can help debug systems while they are being designed. The abstraction and verification of individual modules can be regarded as a "lightweight" formal method, in the sense of [JW96], which can be used before moving on to more "heavyweight" ones. Initial negative results can help debug the system; positive results will establish simple properties that will be useful in more complex, global proofs.

In the important special case of hybrid and real-time systems, untimed components can be isolated and debugged using model checking, and timed components can be abstracted to model checkable ones.

Related Work

Abstraction and Deductive Verification: The methods for *automatic invariant generation* presented in [BBM97] are a special case of abstraction, where abstract interpretation is carried out using pre-defined abstract domains for which fixpoints (or their approximations) can be efficiently computed. These methods are implemented in STeP, automatically generating local, linear, and polyhedral invariants, depending on the abstract domain used.

Verification diagrams [MP94,BMS95] provide a visual representation of the proof of the system validity of particular temporal properties. *Deductive model checking* [SUM98] interactively explores and refines an abstraction of the system state-space in search for a counterexample. Both of these verification methods can be seen as providing an appropriate assertion-based abstraction, when they succeed. Furthermore, they incorporate well-founded domains, for those cases where a finite-state abstraction does not exist.

Abstraction, Modularity and Model Checking: A procedure that explicitly generates an abstract state-space for an assertion-based abstraction, similar to our abstraction algorithm, is presented in [GS97]; another automatic abstraction procedure that uses validity checking is presented in [BLO98].

In [HLP98], a system specified in LISP code is abstracted, manually, to a model-checkable finite-state system, uncovering significant flaws in the original design. [DGH95] investigates the separation of control and data in infinite-state systems, combining model checking with the generation of verification conditions that are established deductively. [Lon93,CGL94] show how abstraction and modularity can be combined for finite-state systems that are synchronously composed and symbolically model checked.

Refinement: In general, refinement can be seen as the dual of abstraction, and used as a formal system design methodology [dBdRR90,KMP94]: first, a high-level version of the algorithm can be verified to meet the desired specifications. Then, implementation details can be added to the system, while ensuring that the desired properties still hold.

STeP: [BMSU97] presents the modular specification and verification of the well-known *generalized railroad crossing* real-time case study. Invariants are proved, or automatically generated, separately for each module. They are then used to prove properties for combinations of modules which, in turn, are used to prove the desired properties for the entire system.

Other STeP test cases are reported in [BLM97,MS98]. For more information, including abstraction and verification examples, see the STeP web pages at:

http://www-step.stanford.edu/

Acknowledgements: We thank Nikolaj Bjørner and Anca Browne for their comments.

References

[ABL96] J.R. Abrial, E. Boerger, and H. Langmaack, editors. *Formal Methods for Industrial Applications: Specifying and Programming the Steam Boiler Control*, vol. 1165 of *LNCS*. Springer-Verlag, 1996.

[AHS96] R. Alur, T.A. Henzinger, and E.D. Sontag, editors. *Hybrid Systems III: Verification and Control*, vol. 1066 of *LNCS*. Springer-Verlag, 1996.

[BBC+95] N.S. Bjørner, A. Browne, E.S. Chang, M. Colón, A. Kapur, Z. Manna, H.B. Sipma, and T.E. Uribe. STeP: The Stanford Temporal Prover, User's Manual. Technical Report STAN-CS-TR-95-1562, Computer Science Department, Stanford University, November 1995.

[BBC+96] N.S. Bjørner, A. Browne, E.S. Chang, M. Colón, A. Kapur, Z. Manna, H.B. Sipma, and T.E. Uribe. STeP: Deductive-algorithmic verification of reactive and real-time systems. In R. Alur and T.A. Henzinger, editors, *Proc. 8th Intl. Conference on Computer Aided Verification*, vol. 1102 of *LNCS*, pages 415–418. Springer-Verlag, July 1996.

[BBM97] N.S. Bjørner, A. Browne, and Z. Manna. Automatic generation of invariants and intermediate assertions. *Theoretical Computer Science*, 173(1):49–87, February 1997. Preliminary version appeared in 1st *Intl. Conf. on Principles and Practice of Constraint Programming*, vol. 976 of LNCS, pp. 589–623, Springer-Verlag, 1995.

[BLM97] N.S. Bjørner, U. Lerner, and Z. Manna. Deductive verification of parameterized fault-tolerant systems: A case study. In *Intl. Conf. on Temporal Logic*. Kluwer, 1997. To appear.

[BLO98] S. Bensalem, Y. Lakhnech, and S. Owre. Computing abstractions of infinite state systems compositionally and automatically. In *Proc. 10th Intl. Conference on Computer Aided Verification*, vol. 1427 of *LNCS*, pages 319–331. Springer-Verlag, July 1998.

[BMS95] A. Browne, Z. Manna, and H.B. Sipma. Generalized temporal verification diagrams. In *15th Conference on the Foundations of Software Technology and Theoretical Computer Science*, vol. 1026 of *LNCS*, pages 484–498. Springer-Verlag, 1995.

[BMSU97] N.S. Bjørner, Z. Manna, H.B. Sipma, and T.E. Uribe. Deductive verification of real-time systems using STeP. In *4th Intl. AMAST Workshop on Real-Time Systems*, vol. 1231 of *LNCS*, pages 22–43. Springer-Verlag, May 1997.

[CC77] P. Cousot and R. Cousot. Abstract interpretation: A unified lattice model for static analysis of programs by construction or approximation of fixpoints. In 4th *ACM Symp. Princ. of Prog. Lang.*, pages 238–252. ACM Press, 1977.

[CE81] E.M. Clarke and E.A. Emerson. Design and synthesis of synchronization skeletons using branching time temporal logic. In *Proc. IBM Workshop on Logics of Programs*, vol. 131 of *LNCS*, pages 52–71. Springer-Verlag, 1981.

[CGL94] E.M. Clarke, O. Grumberg, and D.E. Long. Model checking and abstraction. *ACM Trans. on Programming Languages and Systems*, 16(5):1512–1542, September 1994.

[CU98] M.A. Colón and T.E. Uribe. Generating finite-state abstractions of reactive systems using decision procedures. In *Proc. 10th Intl. Conference on Computer Aided Verification*, vol. 1427 of *LNCS*, pages 293–304. Springer-Verlag, July 1998.

[Dam96]   D.R. Dams. *Abstract Interpretation and Partition Refinement for Model Checking*. PhD thesis, Eindhoven University of Technology, July 1996.
[dBdRR90] J.W. de Bakker, W.P. de Roever, and G. Rosenberg, editors. *Stepwise Refinement of Distributed Systems: Models, Formalisms, Correctness*, vol. 430 of *LNCS*. Springer-Verlag, 1990.
[DGG94]   D.R. Dams, O. Grümberg, and R. Gerth. Abstract interpretation of reactive systems: Abstractions preserving ∀CTL*, ∃ECTL*, CTL*. In *IFIP Working Conference on Programming Concepts, Methods and Calculi (PROCOMET 94)*, pages 573–592, June 1994.
[DGH95]   W. Damm, O. Grümberg, and H. Hungar. What if model checking must be truly symbolic. In *First Intl. Workshop on Tools and Algorithms for the Construction and Analysis of Systems (TACAS 95)*, vol. 1019 of *LNCS*, pages 230–244. Springer-Verlag, May 1995.
[DKRT97] P.R. D'Argenio, J.P. Katoen, T. Ruys, and G.T. Tretmans. The bounded retransmission protocol must be on time! In *3rd Workshop on Tools and Algorithms for the Construction and Analysis of Systems (TACAS)*, vol. 1217 of *LNCS*, pages 416–432. Springer-Verlag, 1997.
[DOTY96] C. Daws, A. Olivero, S. Tripakis, and S. Yovine. The tool KRONOS. In Alur et al. [AHS96], pages 208–219.
[FMS98]   B. Finkbeiner, Z. Manna, and H.B. Sipma. Deductive verification of modular systems. In *International Symposium on Compositionality, COMPOS'97*, LNCS. Springer-Verlag, 1998. To appear.
[GS97]   S. Graf and H. Saidi. Construction of abstract state graphs with PVS. In O. Grumberg, editor, *Proc. 9th Intl. Conference on Computer Aided Verification*, vol. 1254 of *LNCS*, pages 72–83. Springer-Verlag, June 1997.
[HH95]   T.A. Henzinger and P. Ho. HYTECH: The Cornell hybrid technology tool. In *Hybrid Systems II*, vol. 999 of *LNCS*, pages 265–293. Springer-Verlag, 1995.
[HLP98]   K. Havelund, M. Lowry, and J. Penix. Formal verification of a space craft controller. Technical report, NASA Ames Research Center, 1998.
[HS96]   K. Havelund and N. Shankar. Experiments in theorem proving and model checking for protocol verification. In *Formal Methods Europe*, pages 662–681, March 1996.
[JW96]   D. Jackson and J. Wing. Lightweight formal methods. *IEEE Computer*, April 1996.
[KMP94]   Y. Kesten, Z. Manna, and A. Pnueli. Temporal verification of simulation and refinement. In J.W. de Bakker, W.P. de Roever, and G. Rosenberg, editors, *A Decade of Concurrency*, vol. 803 of *LNCS*, pages 273–346. Springer-Verlag, 1994.
[KMP96]   Y. Kesten, Z. Manna, and A. Pnueli. Verifying clocked transition systems. In Alur et al. [AHS96], pages 13–40.
[LGS+95] C. Loiseaux, S. Graf, J. Sifakis, A. Bouajjani, and S. Bensalem. Property preserving abstractions for the verification of concurrent systems. *Formal Methods in System Design*, 6:1–35, 1995.
[Lon93]   D.E. Long. *Model Checking, Abstraction, and Compositional Verification*. PhD thesis, School of Computer Science, Carnegie-Mellon University, Pittsburgh, PA, July 1993.
[MBB+98] Z. Manna, N.S. Bjørner, A. Browne, M. Colón, B. Finkbeiner, M. Pichora, H.B. Sipma, and T.E. Uribe. An update on STeP: Deductive-algorithmic verification of reactive systems. In *Tool Support for Sys-*

[McM93]   tem *Specification, Development and Verification*, pages 87–91. Christian-Albrechts-Universitat, Kiel, June 1998. Bericht Nr. 9803.

[McM93]   K.L. McMillan. *Symbolic Model Checking*. Kluwer Academic Pub., 1993.

[MP94]   Z. Manna and A. Pnueli. Temporal verification diagrams. In M. Hagiya and J.C. Mitchell, editors, *Proc. International Symposium on Theoretical Aspects of Computer Software*, vol. 789 of *LNCS*, pages 726–765. Springer-Verlag, 1994.

[MP95]   Z. Manna and A. Pnueli. *Temporal Verification of Reactive Systems: Safety*. Springer-Verlag, New York, 1995.

[MP96]   Z. Manna and A. Pnueli. Clocked transition systems. Technical Report STAN-CS-TR-96-1566, Computer Science Department, Stanford University, April 1996.

[MS98]   Z. Manna and H.B. Sipma. Deductive verification of hybrid systems using STeP. In T. Henzinger and S. Sastry, editors, *Hybrid Systems: Computation and Control*, vol. 1386 of *LNCS*, pages 305–318. Springer-Verlag, 1998.

[Pnu77]   A. Pnueli. The temporal logic of programs. In *Proc. 18th IEEE Symp. Found. of Comp. Sci.*, pages 46–57. IEEE Computer Society Press, 1977.

[QS82]   J. Queille and J. Sifakis. Specification and verification of concurrent systems in CESAR. In M. Dezani-Ciancaglini and U. Montanari, editors, *Intl. Symposium on Programming*, vol. 137 of *LNCS*, pages 337–351. Springer-Verlag, 1982.

[SUM98]   H.B. Sipma, T.E. Uribe, and Z. Manna. Deductive model checking. To appear in *Formal Methods in System Design*, 1998. Preliminary version appeared in *Proc. 8th Intl. Conference on Computer Aided Verification*, vol. 1102 of *LNCS*, Springer-Verlag, pp. 208–219, 1996.

NSA's *MISSI* Reference Architecture – Moving from Prose to Precise Specifications[†]

Sigurd Meldal

Computer Science Department
CalPoly
smeldal@calpoly.edu

David C. Luckham

Computer Systems Laboratory
Stanford University
dcl@pavg.stanford.edu

Abstract. We discuss the definition and modeling of reference architectures, and the notion of *conformance*. NSA's MISSI (Multilevel Information System Security Initiative) security reference architecture is used as an illustrative example.
We demonstrate that an ADL should have not only the capability to specify interfaces, connections and operational constraints, but also to specify how it is related (or conforms) with other architectures or to implementations. A reference architecture such as MISSI is defined in Rapide [14] as a set of hierarchical interface connection architectures [17]. Each Rapide interface connection architecture serves as a reference architecture – an abstract architecture that allows a number of different implementations, but which enforces a common structure and communication rules. The hierarchical reference architecture defines the MISSI policies at different levels and identifies standard components, communication patterns and policies common to MISSI compliant networks of computer systems.
Key Words and Phrases: Software architectures, security, conformance, reference architecture, software engineering, specification, testing.

1 Introduction

Everybody knows what an *architecture* is – it is a set of *components* and *connections* between them. However, that is as far as agreement goes. What the proper methods of defining these entities are, what *conformance* means, what the distinctions are be-

---

[†] This project was funded by TRW under contract 23679HYL6M, DARPA under F30602–95–C–0277 (subcontract C-Q0097), and by NFR under contract 100426/410.

tween an *architecture*, and *architecture style* and a *reference architecture*, these are issues that are unresolved (and presumably unresolvable, as they are questions closely related to world-views, methods and consequently often come down to pseudo-religious beliefs).

Architectures are used in different situations, and for distinct reasons. The most concrete use is in designing software systems, to make an initial sketch of it in terms of its module decomposition architecture in the top-down tradition of design, focusing on the high-level components and their means of interaction [35]. Architectures are also used to define *references* against which implementations can be checked for compliance. Such reference architectures define the functional components of the architecture and how the components may interact, but need not require that distinct components in the architecture necessarily be distinct also in the implementation. The use of reference architectures allows a separation of concerns in the system specification – distinct reference architectures address distinct aspects of the system (*e.g.*, there might be one reference architecture stating fault-tolerance requirements, another (such as the MISSI reference) stating security requirements, another (such as the ISO OSI reference stack) addressing communication protocols, etc.).

The presence of a component or connection between components in a reference architecture may signify different requirements, depending on which aspect of the system the reference addresses. *E.g.*, does the lack of a connection between two modules indicate a prohibition against their direct interaction (*i.e.*, is the interaction graph as given by the architecture supposed to be complete)? Does a connection between two components indicate that they *will* communicate (*i.e.* a connection represents not only a potential for interaction, is it also a requirement that such an interaction shall occur)? Moreover, what is the concept of interaction anyway? Does an architecture imply what protocol an interaction shall adhere to? *E.g.* RPC vs. buffered pipes vs. passive, reactive systems vs. event broadcasting, etc.

In the end, what distinguishes one kind of architecture from another is the *conformance requirements* imposed by the architecture.

This article discusses how one can capture a security reference architecture in a manner amenable to analysis and automatic conformance checking. We shall start by pointing out in section 2 that the notion of *abstraction* changes when we move from *prescriptive* to *descriptive* specifications. This works well with the notion of conformance w.r.t. *multiple perspectives* (or *reference architectures)*, which we touch upon in section 3. After giving a brief overview of the Rapide ADL and some important notions regarding secure architectures in sections 4 and 5, we present in section 6 the process of architecting using the Rapide ADL, giving examples from the MISSI reference architecture. In section 7 we go through all the top level requirements of the MISSI reference architecture one by one, showing how they are captured in the Rapide ADL. In section 8 we shall look briefly at how the reference architecture can be put to use for (semi-) automatic checking, visualization and analysis of implementation system conformance.

2 Abstract activity

Modern programming languages contain constructs for defining abstract *objects*. One of the consequences of "information hiding" is that an abstract object may accept many different implementations, as long as they are consistent with its abstract definition.

Similarly, the *activity* of a program, or system, may also be defined abstractly. On the one hand there is the operational abstraction embodied in the procedure and function concepts of most languages. There is also an abstraction mechanism inherent in the definition of *events* and *actors of interest* in a concurrent system. By identifying the classes of actors and activity we want to consider in describing the behavior of a system we establish a granularity of observation, ignoring details of implementation and the potentially composite nature of a single "event" or "actor."

In moving from procedural (imperative and state oriented) abstraction to behavioral (observational and event oriented) abstraction, a problem arises. A refinement of a procedural abstraction is accomplished by defining the abstraction in terms of other, more detailed procedural elements. This works well, since a procedural abstraction is *invoked* – low level activities are initiated by a higher level, the program invocation itself being the most abstract (figure 1).

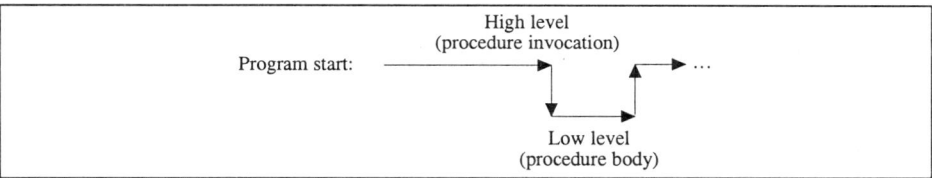

Fig. 1. Mapping from abstract to concrete activity

Furthermore, the identity of the invoker does not change as the program is refined, *e.g.* a high level procedure of a module and its invocation are retained in the final, fully detailed program.

The analogous observation does not necessarily hold true for an event based model. A process or event at some level of abstraction may not exist at a lower level. In specifying a lift system for instance, the concept of "lift" is natural, and a specification is readily given in terms of activities of such lifts. However, when implementing a lift system, there may be no distinct syntactical (or physical) entity corresponding to a particular lift of the abstract architecture (a lift being much more than simply the box itself – multiple lifts may share motors, sensor systems, etc.). The implementation of a lift may be in terms of motors, door sensors, arrays of buttons, etc., possibly shared among the abstract lifts. Events abstractly generated by a lift may be particular *patterns* of events at a level of increased detail. The abstract event of a lift moving from one floor to the next may correspond to the sequence of events "sense doors closed, signal controller, controller starts motor, sense reached next floor, signal controller, controller stops motor" in the implementation.

The result is a Copernican revolution: The causal relationship is one of concrete events and actors giving rise to more abstract ones (figure 2).

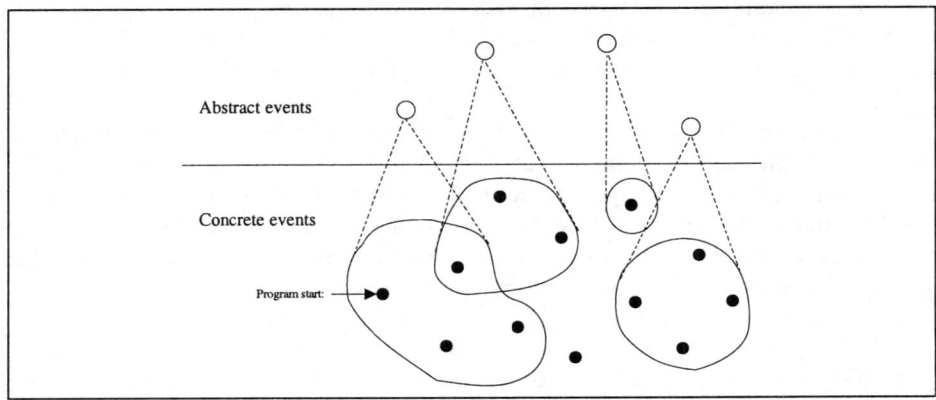

Fig. 2. Mapping from sets of concrete to abstract events

3 Multiple Perspectives on a System

Consider a description of a hotel. In *describing* such an entity one might want to partition it in a number of different ways. One way could be according to domains – there is a domain of publicly accessible facilities, another of behind-the-scenes service facilities, etc. (figure 3).

These domains may then be further subdivided, *e.g.* the public facilities one into restaurants, internal transportation (public lifts), etc., and the service facilities into kitchens, internal transportation (service lifts), etc., into the final, solid structure which is the implemented hotel.

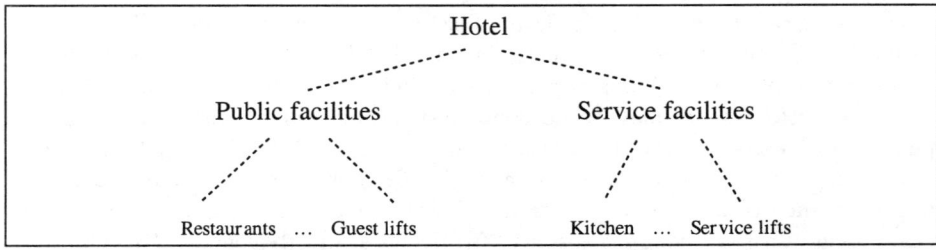

Fig. 3. Conceptual decomposition

In describing the functionality of the hotel, another decomposition may be more appropriate, for instance a partitioning of the hotel into domains of technical responsibility, *e.g.* electrical components, plumbing, etc. (figure 4). This decomposition may also be refined through layers of less and less abstraction to the details of the finally implemented hotel.

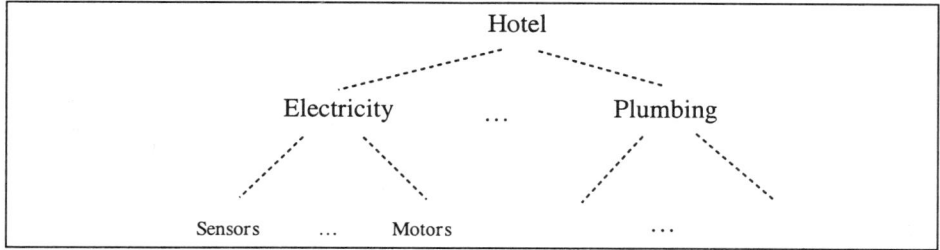

Fig. 4. Functional decomposition

There is no a priori reason to pick one decomposition over the other – both offer reasonable composition structures *for specification purposes*. They are *conceptual architectures* (in Soni et al.'s [38] terminology).

Moving from concrete architectures (such as the hotel above) to *software* architectures the discontinuity between architecture levels and between architectures and their implementation as a running system may become more problematic, in terms of what conformance entails. Soni et al. [38] distinguishes between four architectural perspectives on a given system: The *conceptual* architecture, the *module interconnection* architecture, the *execution* architecture and the *code* architecture, and the transition from one to another may result in different identification of modules, connections etc., requiring a non-trivial definition of when (say) a module interconnection architecture conforms to a given conceptual architecture.

We realize that there is an established tradition of insisting on a distinguished architecture defining the structure of the soft- and hardware components intended to implement a particular system. Such a *module interconnection architecture* [17, 38] usually defines the components and connections of a system in terms of aggregation hierarchies, laying out an implicit implementation strategy.

The module interconnection architecture may be identified as one of the (possibly many) conceptual architectures, particularly if such a conceptual architecture is *prescriptive* and *complete*.

We seem to be caught on the horns of a dilemma. On the one hand, we need to be able to *describe* system behavior under different, often competing, perspectives. On the other hand, an architecture may also be used to *prescribe* behavior, indicating in some detail how the system shall generate the behavior the descriptions require.

4 An Architecture Definition Language

In reading an architecture description, the question of what the description actually *means* needs to be resolved unambiguously in the readers' and designers' mind in order to evaluate and then implement a given architecture. Without a clear understanding of the semantics of a notation (be it graphical – boxes and arrows – or textual) one cannot be sure that whatever is extracted from it (be it implementation strategies, modeling results, etc.) is implied by the description given, and understood by other readers of the architectural description.

An *interface connection architecture* [17] is defined by identifying

- *Components*: the primary elements of the architecture, and their means of interaction with other components. Components are considered black boxes constrained only by the definitions of their *interfaces*.
- *Connections*: the lines of interaction between components.
- *Conformance*: identifying minimum requirements of how an implementation may satisfy the architecture.

The *Rapide* model of architectures is *event based* – a basic notion being that architecture components are defined by the kinds of events they may generate or react to. An interface also identifies the semantics of a conforming component by giving event based *constraints*, specifying whether particular protocols are to be adhered to, identifying causal relationships between events, etc. Such constraints form the basis for analysis and testing tools, such as run-time checking for conformance violations [11, 31].

A successful ADL requires a high degree of flexibility in how an architecture can be refined. Naturally, one wants to be able to refine interface definitions, making use of subtype substitutivity when extending an interface with new capabilities or by adding further constraints. In addition to this basic capability, an ADL should enable the definition of *hierarchies* of architectures, where one architecture can be interpreted quite flexibly as an implementation (or refinement) of another. The *Rapide map* construct gives the designer the tool to explicitly define how complex patterns of events in one architecture correspond to more abstract events of another, thereby enabling a powerful and checkable notion of *conformance*.

The literature presents a number of distinct ways of distinguishing *kinds* of architectures (*e.g.*, Soni et al. [38] makes a distinction between *object* and *function* decomposition architectures, among others, Shaw and Garlan [35] identifies *patterns* of object decomposition architectures). We prefer the notion that

> "an architecture description conveys a set of views, each of which depicts the system by describing domain concerns."
>
> Ellis et al. [5]

The distinction between different architecture descriptions then becomes one of a *difference of conformance requirements*. In moving from (say) a *module decomposition architecture* to an implementation, conformance would require that distinct components of the architecture be realized by disjoint sets of implementation modules. In contrast, in checking whether a *reference architecture* is satisfied by a particular implementation one would only make the weaker conformance requirement that there be a *mapping* of components and events at the implementation level to components and events of the reference architecture.

This perspective on what an architecture is allows a clean separation of concerns. One can specify multiple architectures for any given implementation, each focusing on a particular aspect of the system, each with an appropriate set of conformance requirements. For instance, when specifying a distributed object system it is reasonable to separate *security* concerns from *fault tolerance* concerns. Part of the security architecture for the system would state the conformance requirement that information should flow *only* along connections defined in the architecture; the architecture identifies the *maximal* connectivity of an information flow graph. In contrast, part of the fault tolerance architecture for the system would be to state the conformance requirement that information should be able to flow *independently* along all connections defined in the architecture, making no restrictions on the presence of extra connections; the architecture identifies the *minimal* connectivity of an information flow graph. In claiming that a particular implementation satisfies both perspectives the implementor would explicitly give the two maps, from the implementation to each of the reference architectures, showing the conformance argument.

The vocabulary of the *Rapide* ADL [14] incorporates and extends the basic vocabulary of interface connection architectures.

- *Events:* Representing that something happened. What that something *is* may vary from architecture to architecture, and with varying degrees of abstraction.
  Syntactically events are labeled by *name*, possibly with a set of *parameters*.
- *Causality*: In *Rapide,* one can specify whether particular (patterns of) events should be independent or causally related. This allows a very precise description of information flow.
  Causal relationships are represented syntactically as binary operators. e1 → e2 is valid if the event (or event set, see below) e1 causally *precedes* the event(s) e2, *e.g.* that e1 represents writing of data and e2 represents reading of that data, or e1 represents the sending of a message and e2 its receipt.
  e1 | | e2 is valid if the event (or event set, see below) e1 is causally completely *independent* of the event(s) e2 .
- *Patterns:* Descriptions of how events may be related by causality, time or other relations. Patterns are described using an extension of regular expressions with placeholders (free variables) to describe partial orders of events. Besides the causal operators, there are logical operators (conjunction, disjunction, etc.).
- *Constraints:* Predicates, usually in the form of prescribed or proscribed patterns of behavior, indicating the intended functionality of a component.
- *Maps:* Relating architectures to one another (and specifically, implementations to one or more architectures), indicating how conformance is obtained.

We shall give examples of these constructs later, explaining the syntax and semantics as we go along. For a full exposition of the *Rapide* pattern and constraint languages, see [16, 26, 27, 28].

Rapide's object-oriented type- and module definition sublanguage provides features for code refinement and reuse (through inheritance and polymorphism) and specification refinement and reuse (through subtyping and polymorphism).

The semantic model of *Rapide* emphasizes causal and temporal relationships among events of a system, one can be quite specific about how components of an architecture may (or may *not*) interact. *E.g.*, the focus on causal relationships allows the *Rapide* user to state in very general terms assumptions about the presence of covert channels. Furthermore, it allows tools to investigate the causal relations between events, distinguishing between temporal relationships that are causally significant and those that are not.

The *Rapide* pattern and constraint languages supports the definition of operational policies and specific protocols, which can take into account *causal-* as well as *time-* relationships between events.

The *Rapide* map construct supports explicit statements of conformance. The implementor of an architecture can state *exactly* how the implementation conforms: it defines which (sets of) components of the implementation play the role of particular components of the architecture, how patterns of events in the implementation correspond to more abstract events used in the architecture, etc. Since maps are given explicitly, they allow tools to check for conformance automatically, adding an extra degree of confidence that any conformance violations will be caught, offering a valuable supplement (or alternative) to formal reasoning.

The map construct is also a valuable tool whenever an architecture is given a *hierarchical structure*. *E.g.*, if one level of structure is defined in terms of federations of *enclaves* connected via *wide area networks*, and another level as network-connected *workstations*, *certificate servers*, etc., then maps are the means whereby the distinct levels can be related in the architecture definition. For instance, through the definition of appropriate maps the designer can identify how the set of networks, workstations and servers aggregate into enclaves and WANs.

5 Secure Architectures

There are a number of perspectives one may apply when discussing the security aspects of a software architecture. In particular, in this document we shall address two aspects of the MISSI reference architecture:

1. *Structures*: That the secure architecture has a certain structure [35], requiring the existence of certain components (such as "certificate authorities," or "enclaves" [13]). The structures may be defined at different levels of abstraction, with different conformance requirements. We shall deal with
2. a *global* level, focusing on the main components and the overall constraints on their interaction. At this level general policies about information flow and the like may be stated, without regard to how these policy constraints are ensured by particular protocols, functional units, etc.
3. *a concept of operations* ("*conops*") level, focusing on the functional decomposition of the architecture, identifying the events of interest, the main functional components and their potential for interaction.

4. an *execution* level, describing the dynamic, modular decomposition structure of the system.

The architectures at each of these levels are related to one another and impose different conformance requirements on the implementation. Both the relationships and the conformance requirements must be defined.

5. *Information flow integrity*: That certain policies and procedures regarding the authorization and acceptability of information are adhered to as it is being generated and propagated. Such policies may be in terms of any of the three levels listed above and could also involve references to cryptographic and encoding requirements, as well.

6 The Architecting Process

The MISSI reference architecture is defined in a series of prose documents, some with first order predicate logic definitions of MISSI policies. In this exposition we shall stay with the overview document, given in full in [13]. The overview is an executive summary of the reference architecture, but contains enough detail to evaluate the utility of *Rapide* to specify the architecture.

We find the *process* of *constraints capture* in itself very useful. This process can be quite enlightening – interpreting the prose and giving it an unambiguous meaning often identifies potential contradictions or holes in the original definitions of the reference architecture. Even in the case where the final reference document is given in prose, we find that the exercise of formalizing the prose as it is being developed may help the development team, by enhancing their understanding of the interplay of their own statements.

Reference documents are also subject to mishaps, resulting from typographical mistakes through incomplete version control to out-right conceptual misunderstandings. The sheer size of most such documents make them hard to check for consistency and correctness unless such checks are assisted by (semi-)automatic tools. Consequently, the presence of supporting tools should be almost mandatory in the definitions of standards. Tools require the existence of (parts of) the standard in a machine-manipulatable form, *i.e.*, in the form of a formalized set of definitions.

6.1 Prose and Constraints Capture

The process leading up to a formal capture of an architecture has three main steps: (1) identifying the components, (2) identifying how they are connected, and (3) identifying how the connections are used. The three steps are accompanied by a fourth, stating the conformance requirements, when relating the architecture to an implementation (or model, or a more detailed version). We'll go through the process of capturing the MISSI reference overview, giving examples of each of these steps.

Capturing the interface connection architectures defined in the MISSI specification, we first identify the *levels* of the reference architecture. In this article we shall deal with two levels, the *global* and the *concept of operations* levels (see section 5 above).

For each level we proceed to identify and define the *components* of the level by defining their interfaces (section 6.2), and then going on to define the *connections* among them (section 6.3) and how they are used (section 6.4).

As appropriate, we then go on to define how the components and activities of one level conform to those of another.

6.2 What Are the Components?

For each kind of component (such as an *enclave* at the global level) we define a *Rapide type*, whose interface is developed as the architecture is being refined. Part of this definition may identify how one type is a refinement or *subtype* of another [22]. Of course the interface definitions themselves rely on other types (such as *security classifications* and *security tokens*) already having been defined.

Rapide architecture components – modules – are strongly typed (within a very flexible type system). Types are declared as **interfaces**, declaring the interface between objects of the type and their environment. The declaration establishes syntactic as well as semantic structure, and may include constraints on the operational behavior of modules implementing the declared type.

A very first approximation of an *enclave* type is given in figure 5.

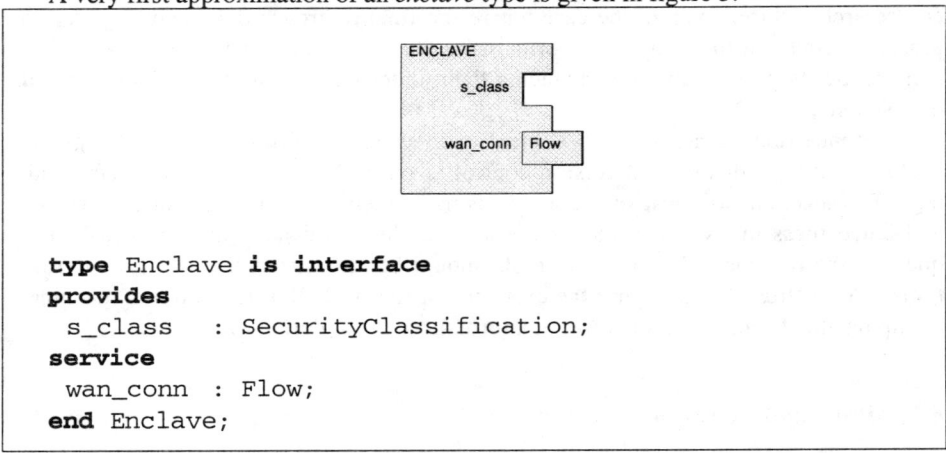

```
type Enclave is interface
provides
  s_class    : SecurityClassification;
service
  wan_conn   : Flow;
end Enclave;
```

Fig. 5. The definition of an enclave type

It identifies two important characteristics of an enclave:

1. The *provides* declaration of s_class makes it possible to refer to the security attributes (here exemplified by it having a security classification) of every en-

clave. The *Rapide* keyword **provides** introduces public elements of the interface.
2. The *service* declaration of wan_conn states that every enclave interface contains a Flow entity, which (as we shall see) defines the minimum communication capabilities of enclaves. A **service** declaration is shorthand for a (possibly complex) set of **provides** declarations.

Architecture component interfaces can be highly structured. It may be helpful to think in terms of *plugs* and *sockets* [17]: a component's interface offers a set of distinguishable means of connecting it to its environment, similarly to what one expects in the hardware world. Such a means of connecting come in dual forms (as in *plugs* and *sockets* being duals in hardware), and may have further substructures (as in a single plug carrying pins/sockets for a number of wires).

It is natural to depict the Flow service type graphically (figure 6), similarly to how we depict the Enclave interface definition in figure 5. We can see that the wan_conn attribute has a structure; the declaration of its type, Flow, shows that wan_conn consists of two **action** declarations.

```
                    accept      accept
                    release     release
              Flow            Dual of Flow

type Flow is interface
action
   out      release    (data : Data; destination : Address);
   in       accept     (data : Data; destination : Address);
end Flow;

type DualFlow is interface
action
   in       release    (data : Data; destination : Address);
   out      accept     (data : Data; destination : Address);
end Flow;
```

Fig. 6. Plugs and sockets

An *out* action declaration indicates that the component may generate events which its environment may observe, an *in* action declaration indicates that the component may react to events generated by the environment. The wan_conn declaration is therefore in fact a bi-directional communication interface offering both a means of sending messages to the environment (intended to be a WAN) as well as of accepting such messages from the environment.

In *Rapide*, such structured communication interfaces are called *services*. The dual of the wan_conn service will be part of the interface of the wide area network component of the architecture, and is naturally depicted as the inverse of the Flow type (*i.e.*, it forms a plug to the Flows socket). Where the type Flow has an *out action* there will be a corresponding *in action* of the dual, and vice versa. One need not declare dual types explicitly, but can instead use the keyword dual. We have given the dual of Flow explicitly in figure 6.

Though plausible as a first approximation in the global view of a distributed system, we may want to add some instrumentation points to the definition of an enclave. Consequently, in figure 7 we create a subtype of the Enclave type. The keyword **include** declares that the MISSI_Enclave type is an extension (and thus a subtype) of the interface type Enclave – all the declarations of the Enclave interface are declarations of the MISSI_Enclave interface. In addition we introduce a new out action called internal to be able to speak about things going on within the enclave (leaving the notion of "Activity" uninterpreted for now). As we shall see later, this turns out to allow an interesting architectural constraint about the existence of covert channels. (Some of the other actions and functions will be used later. For each, the comment succeeding the declaration identifies where it is used.)

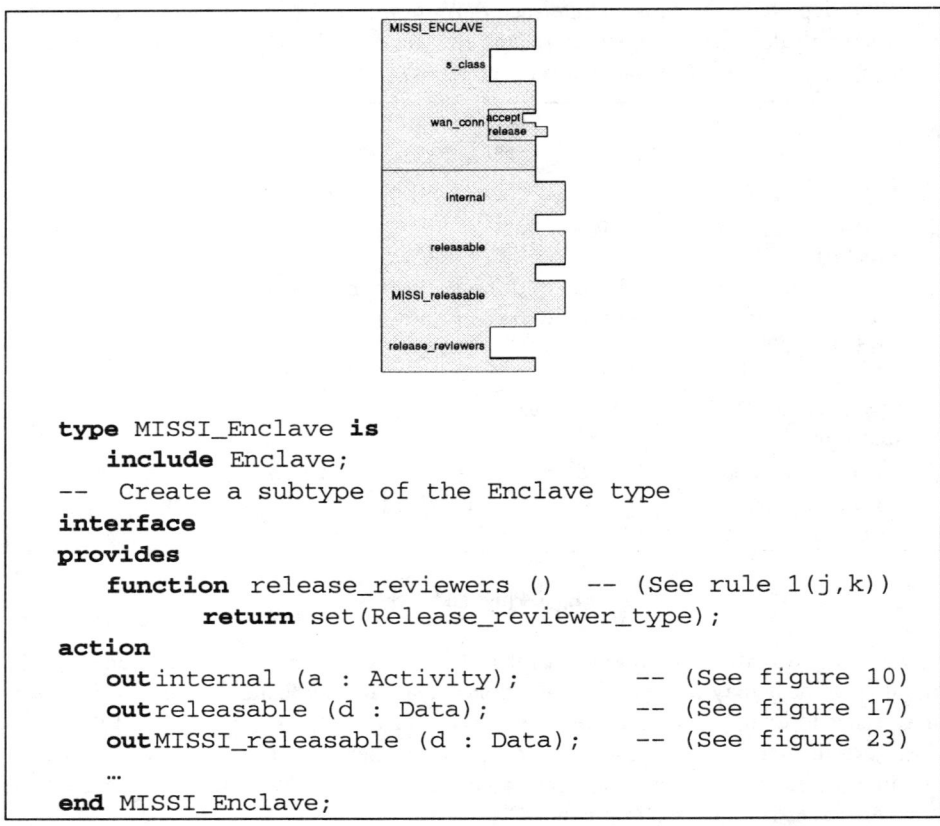

```
type MISSI_Enclave is
    include Enclave;
--  Create a subtype of the Enclave type
interface
provides
    function release_reviewers ()    -- (See rule 1(j,k))
        return set(Release_reviewer_type);
action
    out internal (a : Activity);          -- (See figure 10)
    out releasable (d : Data);            -- (See figure 17)
    out MISSI_releasable (d : Data);      -- (See figure 23)
    ...
end MISSI_Enclave;
```

Fig. 7. Extending the definition of an enclave

Having identified the *types* of components that make up the architecture, we define their number (if known), their structure (if any) and whether new components can be created while the system evolves, and whether existing components can terminate and remove themselves before the architecture terminates.

In the case of the MISSI reference architecture there is not much structure at the global level, and the architecture does not address the issue of dynamic component creation or removal. In its purest form, we may simply state that the components of the architecture are a *set* of enclaves, a single WAN (a simple routing model) and directory service agent and a set of unclassified (*i.e.*, non-DoD) sites, as in figure 8.

This is deceptively simple, but then the architecture *is* rather simple, *at this level*. The complexity arises primarily at the lower level architecture, where we see a wide variety of architecture components and policies.

```
architecture MISSI( ) is
    internet  : WAN;
    DNS       : DirectoryServiceAgent;
    enclaves  : set(MISSI_Enclave);
    sites     : set(Site);
    ...
end MISSI;
```

Fig. 8. The components of the MISSI reference architecture

6.3 How Are Components Connected? Adding Structural Constraints

Having identified the types and numbers of the components of the architecture, we proceed to define how they may interact. At this level of abstraction, the interaction is quite simple: The enclaves and sites are all connected to the WAN through their respective wan_conn services (figure 9).

```
connect
    for e: Enclave in enclaves.enum() generate
        internet.socket to e.wan_conn;
end;
```

Fig. 9. Connecting architecture components

A *Rapide* **connect** statement declares the topology of architecture connections (be it dynamic or static). A **connect** statement connects out actions of one component with in actions of others, or in more general terms, connects a service of one component with the dual service of another. The result is that when a component generates an event by invoking an out action in its interface, then that event is also labeled as being of the in action of another component as identified by a **connect** statement. **connect** statements can efficiently set up more complex connections than simple one-to-one, *e.g.*, in figure 9 we connect the internet.socket service of the WAN to the wan_conn service of *all* enclaves.

The role of the connection definitions is domain specific. In secure systems architectures, the interpretation of the set of connections would be that they identify *all* possible means of interaction among the architecture components. There is an implied frame axiom for the architecture specification that information shall flow only along those lines and in those forms explicitly defined by the connection definitions for the architecture (see figure 10, discussed below).

We notice that since all the enclaves are given a bi-directional connection to the internet, we have that the enclaves are all indirectly connected to each other. This is a common pattern – that components of an architecture communicate via intermediaries that allow for communication transformation, filtering, routing, etc. Such intermediaries are called *connectors*.

6.4 How Are Connections Used? Adding Operational Constraints

After we have specified the structural properties of the global architecture, we go on to specify some *operational* requirements that implementations have to obey. Operational requirements define protocols and possibly other restrictions on the behavior of components of the architecture. Where a connection between two components indicates a *potential* for interaction, the operational specifications will indicate precisely under what circumstances such interaction actually can (or *must*) take place, as well as indicating when interaction shall *not* occur.

In the constraint sublanguage of the Rapide ADL one can specify simple protocols for interaction (such as handshaking, etc.), as well as more sophisticated requirements regarding information flow, causal relationships, etc. At the global level the most powerful security constraint would be that

> *No information should flow from one enclave to another without going through official network connections.*

There are a number of different ways to make such a statement precise, and the Rapide formalization of the architecture specification allows us to clearly identify and thus discuss the alternatives. The strictest interpretation is probably that

> *There shall be no internal activity in two distinct enclaves such that they are causally related without intervening* wan_conn *events.*

Stated in Rapide (see figure 10), the semantics may be more immediately apparent: whenever we see a causal chain of events from an internal activity of one enclave to an internal activity of another enclave, then there must be two wan_conn events within that chain, one sending (from the originating enclave), and one receiving (at the other end). The variables ?e1, ?e2 are free, indicating that the constraint holds for *all* enclaves.

In detail: The **observe** <pattern1> **match** <pattern2> **end**; construct requires that whenever we find a match for <pattern1> then that match *also* has to be a match for <pattern2>.

In this particular constraint we are looking for *any* two MISSI_Enclaves e1, e2 – akin to existentially quantified variables here – such that e1 and e2 are distinct enclaves ("?e1 ≠ ?e2"), each generates an internal event ("?e1.internal", "?e2.internal"), these events are ordered ("... → ... → ...") with any number of events along the causal chains from one to the other ("... → any() → ..."), these events being represented by the upper cloud in figure 10.

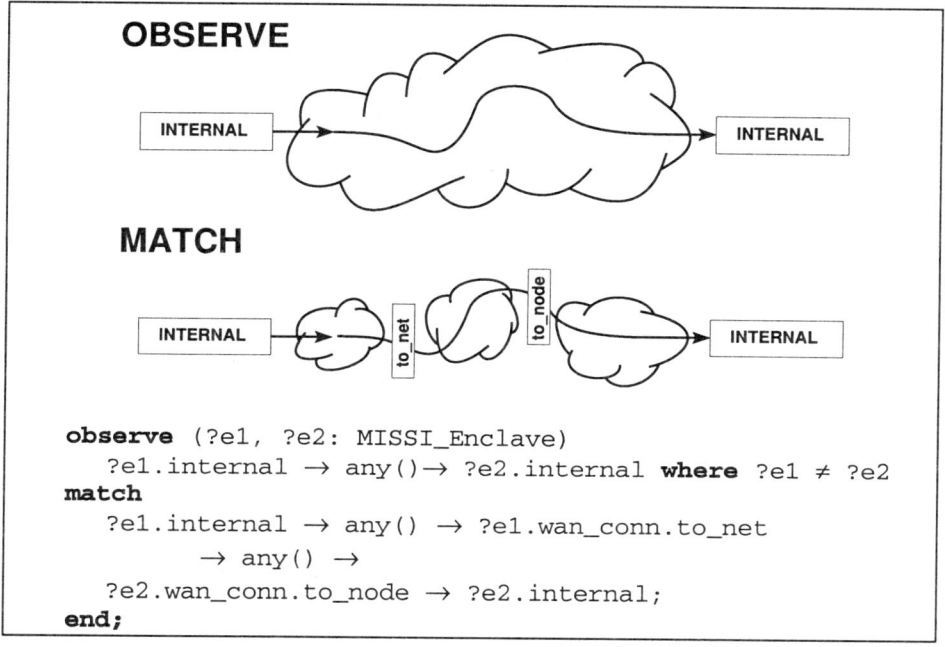

```
observe (?e1, ?e2: MISSI_Enclave)
    ?e1.internal → any()→ ?e2.internal where ?e1 ≠ ?e2
match
    ?e1.internal → any() → ?e1.wan_conn.to_net
        → any() →
    ?e2.wan_conn.to_node → ?e2.internal;
end;
```

Fig. 10. A security constraint

The constraint then goes on (in the **match** <pattern2> part), requiring that any such matching set of events must *also* match the pattern that the "cloud" (*i.e.*, the set of events matching the "any()" part of the observed pattern) be partitioned into three "clouds" such that there is a single, causally intervening wan_conn.to_net between the first and second "cloud," and similarly a single, causally intervening wan_conn.to_node event between the second and third "cloud."

Or stated in prose: any causal chain between two enclaves must be mediated by an explicit (authorized) release of information to the net and by a subsequent explicit (authorized) receipt of that information.

This formalization in terms of causal chains is a significantly stronger (and to-the-point) constraint than what we would obtain by stating the requirement in terms of *time*. If we interpreted "a → b" as "a happened before b in time," then the above constraint would be satisfied if two enclaves were (legitimately) interacting with high frequency while information were to flow covertly from the one to the other at a lower frequency. The fact that there would be legitimate wan_conn events interspersed between the sending and the receipt of covert information would legitimize the communication of the covert information. On the other hand, the interpretation of

"→" as representing *causal* dependency correctly precludes such a scenario from being acceptable.

6.5 Repeat as Needed ... The *Concept of Operations* Level

The next level of architecture is a *concept of operations* ("*conops*") architecture. The conops architecture specifies the structure of *enclaves*, and how the operations within an enclave are carried out by its various components (including human beings).

As with the global architecture, the definition of the conops architecture identifies (1) the components of an enclave, (2) their connections and (3) how these connections may (or may *not*) be used.

What are the components?
The components are such entities as *users* and *workstations, confidentiality* and *authentication servers* as well as other servers such as *firewalls*. We shall not enumerate all the component types of the conops architecture. However, the MISSI document [13] does give us an example of a nontrivial decision we face when formalizing the definitions of the component types. It says:

2(a) "*An authorized releaser for a particular enclave must be a MISSI certificate holder and reside within the enclave.*"

This paragraph introduces the component type "*authorized releaser.*" It can be interpreted in two different ways, depending on our interpretation of the word "must." If an authorized releaser *by definition* is a MISSI certificate holder, then one makes the type `releaser` a subtype of the type `certificate_holder`. A consequence of such a choice would be that one cannot entertain (or formally specify) situations where a releaser is *not* a certificate holder, just as one cannot entertain the notion that an even number not be an integer.

Another tack would be to identify the relationship between an enclave and its set of releasers, each of which is of the generic `MISSI_user_type`. In which case we are obliged to define a function from such user components to their set of certificates (in order to state that all releasers hold certificates) as well as a residency relation between enclaves and its residents (in order to state that the residency requirements should hold). Such functions and relations can be defined as being *part* of a component (*i.e.,* an attribute of it), or as a function or predicate external to the component. We chose the latter approach.

We are faced with a similar decision in paragraph 1(b):

1(b) "*All legitimate MISSI users must have a valid certificate for some classification level they are cleared to read.*"

Is this a definition of what a "legitimate MISSI user" *is* (in which case we define the type `legitimate_MISSI_user` and add the requirement that the attribute `certificate_set` be non-empty)? Or is it a definition of when a MISSI-user is "*legitimate*" (in which case we define the type `MISSI_user` with the attribute legitimate, which is true if and only if the attribute certificate_set is non-empty)? We settled for the latter interpretation.

How are components connected?
At the enclave level we also see a number of requirements regarding access and connectivity, such as:

1(a) "Authorized certificate authorities (and no others) must be provided with access to certificate generation functions."

As with many of the MISSI requirements this one has both a prescriptive as well as a restrictive aspect: There shall be access for one class of components, and such access by any other component is prohibited. The former is reasonably interpreted as a structural requirement, the latter may either be structural (that there simply be no physical accessibility), or one of protocol (that there shall be no attempts at exercising the certificate generation functions without proper authorization.)

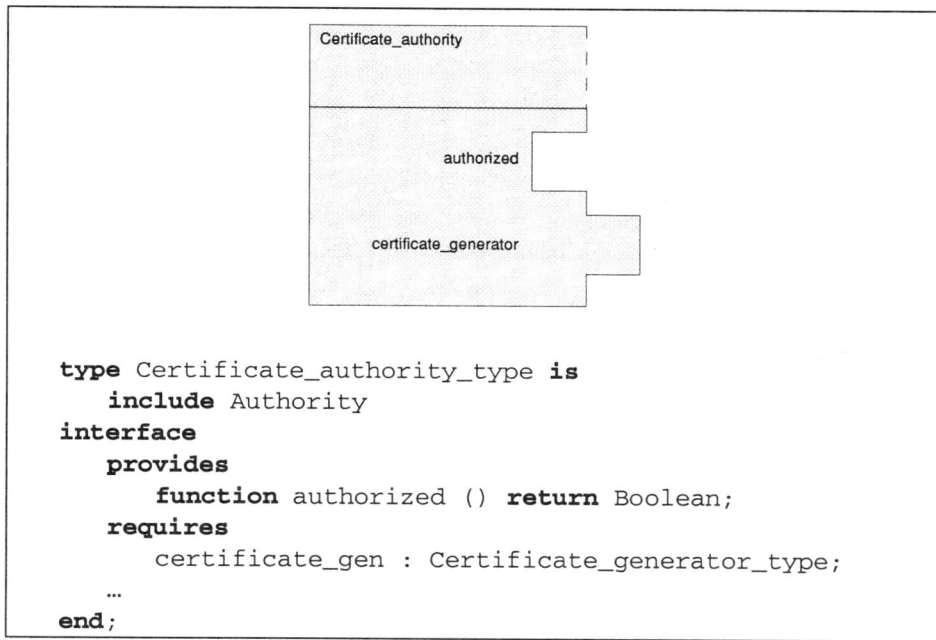

Fig. 11. An enclave component identifying its requirements

The prescriptive part of the requirement is easily modeled with in *Rapide* using interface type definitions (see figure 11). The presence of a **requires** clause in the definition lists all the entities a Certificate_authority_type module expects to be able to use without further ado – it is up to the architecture implementation to supply it with a suitable module to satisfy this requirement. The **requires** section of a type specification indicates what the environment – the *architecture* – has to make available to objects of type `Certificate_generator_type`. This mechanism differs from the usual object-oriented approach of employing parameterization of the type or the object constructors of the type.

Rapide distinguishes syntactically between interface definitions (types) and module definitions. Instead of including constructor functions as part of an interface declaration (as one defines constructors as part of class declarations in many other object-oriented languages), *Rapide* separates the constructors as separate entities called *module constructors*. The declaration of a module constructor is syntactically similar to the declaration of a function, with the implicit inclusion of all the interface component declarations. The result of an invocation of a module constructor is an object of the declared return type, with the structure as defined in the module body.

If one were to employ the alternative of supplying the server references as parameters to module constructors as in figure 12, then we would bury a key implicit element of the prose requirements; that the assignment of a server to a user is an *architectural* one, which may change over time as the system evolves and the user acquires or relinquishes certificates.

```
module certificate_authority
       (certificate_gen : Certificate_generator_type;... )
       return Certificate_authority_type is
          ...
   end;
```

Fig. 12. An implicit architecture dependency

Rapide allows us to make the style distinction between parameterized *definitional dependencies* (which are identified by the parameter lists of type definitions), parameterized *implementation dependencies* (which are identified by the parameter lists of module constructors) and *(dynamic) architectural dependencies* (which are identified by **requires** sections in interface definitions).

The restrictive part of the requirement (*"...and no others..."*) can be addressed explicitly or implicitly. By using the frame axiom for security architecture conformance (*i.e.,* in the absence of any connections, no information flow shall take place) we can deduce this restriction from the absence of any explicit connections between modules that are *not* authorized certificate authorities and certificate generators. Such a *structure-oriented* representation of the requirement would be using conditional connections in the architecture itself to set up the connections for all the authorized certificate authorities (see figure 13). Here the *architecture specification* makes clear that access to the `new_token` function will be given only to those `certificate_authority_type` components that have the `authorized` attribute set to true.

However, a requirements document that relies on the *absence* of certain statements might be asking for too much of the reader.

If one instead wishes to make this requirement explicit in the formal version of the reference architecture then it is naturally rephrased as a *protocol requirement*; that all modules attempting to make use of the certificate generators are duly authorized. Since this is a usage restriction relevant to certificate generators, it is reasonable to locate it within the definition of the `Certificate_generator_type` interface (see figure 14).

```
connect
    (?c : Certificate_authority_type)
       ?c.new_token where ?c.authorized
to
       certificate_gen.new_token;
```

Fig. 13. A conditional connection

When it states *"Authorized certificate authorities (and no others)..."* the constraint interprets the *"(and no others)"* as meaning not only all non-authorized certificate authorities, but also all other entities of other categories. The mechanism is through observing *all* calls to the `new_token` function (*i.e.*, all matches for the pattern of events representing a single call to the function `new_token` – a singleton set). And then requiring that each of these calls be made by components of the `Certificate_authority_type`, where that component also has the `authorized` attribute set to true (*i.e.*, the performer has to be of the `Certificate_authority_type` and a check of the `authorized` function will return true).

```
type Certificate is interface ... end;

type Certificate_generator_type is interface
provides
    function new_token(...) return Certificate;
    ...
constraint
    observe new_token'call
    match (?c : Certificate_authority_type)
       new_token'call(performer is ?c)
                                where ?c.authorized;
    end;
    ...
end Certificate_generator_type;
```

Fig. 14. A restrictive protocol definition

A number of the requirements – 1(c, d, e, g, h, i, k), are on the same form:

"*All MISSI certificate holders must be provided with access to appropriate <keyword> functions for each classification level they are cleared to read.*"

(Where the <keyword> identifies the distinct functions, such as *confidentiality*, *integrity*, and *certificate validation*.)

There are two elements to each of these requirements as well:

1. There is a reference to what a confidentiality (and similarly integrity-, certificate validation-, etc.) function *is*. That aspect deals with definitions of functions and abstract data types, and is best dealt with using an ADT- or object specification formalism. *Rapide* incorporates the data type specification capabilities of ANNA [15], but since the specification of datatypes impinges minimally on our discussion of architectures, we shall not pursue this aspect.
2. That for a particular functionality the actual function supplied may differ depending upon which access level is being exercised by the certificate holder. Consequently, access to server functions may change over time, as certificates are acquired or relinquished. Furthermore, there is no requirement that the appropriate function for a given access level be fixed for the duration of the system – consequently, the formalization should allow for a conforming system to supply different functions at different times for a given access level and user.

To state or allow for the latter is a challenge to ADLs and specification formalisms based on (first order) logics, which do not address the issue of *time*. In *Rapide* time is implicitly present throughout a specification, and can be made explicit as necessary through references to clocks or events.

We shall assume (see 1 above) that we can define precisely what is expected of a set of *confidentiality functions* (and similarly for the other functionalities).

Given such definitions of the server functions, we specify the access requirements explicitly (figure 15). Each `MISSI_user_type` object will assume the (external) existence of a function returning a reference to a confidentiality server (assuming that the types `Key_type`, `Wrap_info_type`, and `Wrapped_type` are defined elsewhere), an integrity server and a validation server.

This requirement is formalized using the **requires** clause of *Rapide*. In so doing we signal that a `MISSI_user_type` object may call the function `confidentiality_server` with the expectation that the architecture (*i.e.*, the environment) will supply a binding for it. The architecture may change this binding during the execution of the system. By adding the "**constraint** (classification.element(c))" to the function declaration we identify that the function is only required and accessible for a particular classification level if the `MISSI_user` actually is cleared at that level (*i.e.*, that c is an element of the module's set of classifications).

The "*(and no others)*" part of requirements 1(j, k) are dynamic prohibitions and are formalized in the same way we made precise the similar injunction in 1(a), *i.e.*, as a check that whenever there is a call for a `confidentiality_server` it is from a component with the proper clearance.

```
type Confidentiality_ref is Confidentiality_server
        (Key_type, Wrap_info_type, Wrapped_type);
- - and similarly for the other servers

type MISSI_user_type is interface
   provides
       classification : set(Classification_type);
   ...
   requires
      function confidentiality_server
         (c: Classification_type)
            return Confidentialy_ref
            constraint (classification.element(c));
      function integrity_server
         (c: Classification_type)
            return Integrity_ref
            constraint (classification.element(c));
      function validation_server
         (c: Classification_type)
            return Validation_ref
            constraint (classification.element(c));
      ...
end MISSI_user_type;
```

Fig. 15. Capturing access requirements

How are connections used?

Finally, there are the policy requirements, stating preconditions for information flow within the enclave or from the enclave to the outside. An example is

2(c) *"All data transferred outside of a secret-high enclave and addressed to a MISSI certificate holder must be protected by a confidentiality service, a proof of origin non-repudiation service and a recipient authentication service."*

This can be modeled either as the data having certain properties (essentially having stamps of approval from the respective servers), or as a precondition on the *history* leading up to a release of data outside a secret-high enclave. We recommend the latter approach, in which case we make use of the *Rapide* pattern language to identify the protocol that defines a data release: it fits the pattern of figure 16, *i.e.*, that for any piece of data, if it is released to the outside then that release has to be preceded by the three services checking it off. (The *Rapide* operator "~" represents partitioning: to match a pattern p1 ~ p2 a set has to be partitionable into two sets s1 and s2, with s1 being a match for p1, and s2 a match for p2. A set matching the pattern declared in figure 16 thus consists of four events (a conf_service, origin_service, recip_service and data_release event), all of them with the same data attribute, and the three former are all causal precursors to the data_release. There are no requirements regarding the causal relationships among the three.)

```
pattern outside_release_ok(?d : Data) is
      (conf_service(?d) ~
       origin_service(?d) ~
       recip_service(?d))
    → data_release(?d)
end;
```

Fig. 16. Abstracting patterns

6.6 Defining Relationships Between Architectures

At this point in our process we have a definition of the global level of the reference architecture, whose principal components are MISSI_enclaves and WANs, and the conops level, whose principal components are workstations, firewalls, LANs, and servers.

Part of the definition of a reference architecture with multiple levels of abstraction identifies precisely how the levels are related. There are clear relationships between these two levels – *e.g.*, the enclave architectures of the lower level are modeling the MISSI_enclaves at the top level, the activities of the firewalls at one level represent release and accept events at the higher level, the simple wan_conn of the abstract enclave definition corresponds to the firewall_type objects of the conops architecture. But in the conops level definition there is no action "internal" which may play such a crucial role in the constraints of the global level architecture – the reference architecture must define what conops-level events correspond to the internal events of the global level.

It would not be a good idea to merge the definitions from the two levels into one unstructured definition of the notion of "enclave." Instead, we use *Rapide maps* to relate components and activities of the conops architecture to their corresponding components and activities in the global architecture.

Figure 17 gives an example of such an abstraction map. It consists of three *rules*, each of which defines how occurrences of patterns of events at the conops level correspond to more abstract events at the global level.

The first rule indicates that *any* event in the conops enclave ("(?e : event) ?e@") will be mapped up to ("||>") the abstract internal event, indicating that something happened (but where we abstract away from the particulars of what happened). The second rule maps each transmission of data from the firewall to the WAN ("@firewall.wan_conn.to_net") to the abstract event release, representing the flow of information out of the enclave, abstracting away the particulars of how the information became public. The last rule is an example of how a more complex pattern of events may represent a single abstract event: Whenever a piece of information (represented by the placeholder ?content) has been approved by the validation, integrity, and encryption servers then the information becomes releasable, abstracting away from the actual protocol required for attaining this status.

```
map abstract_enclaves
    from e: Enclave_architecture to MISSI_enclave is
rule
    rule_1:
        (?e : Event) ?e@
        ||> internal(?e);

    rule_2:
        (?d : Data, ?a : Address)
            @firewall.wan_conn.to_net(?d,?a)
        ||> wan_conn.release(?d,?a);

    rule_3:
        ((?ws : COTSWorkstation; ?content : Data)
            ?ws.net_conn.to_node
                (certificate_Validation, ?content)
            ~
            ?ws.net_conn.to_node
                (integrity, ?content)
            ~
            ?ws.net_conn.to_node
                (encryption, ?content))
        ||>
            releasable(?content);;
    ...
end;
```

Fig. 17. Three abstraction maps

Figure 18 shows an excerpt from a computation, indicating the two levels of abstraction and the relationship between a set of events at the lower level with a single abstract event at the higher.

As we see, there is no prohibition against a single concrete event participating in more than one abstract event (as each of the server events are both represented as abstract internal events as well as being part of the releasable event).

If one of the steps in the protocol is missing (for instance, if the Validation never took place), we would not get the required Releasable global event. The result would be as in figure 19, and would result in a violation of a global level constraint.

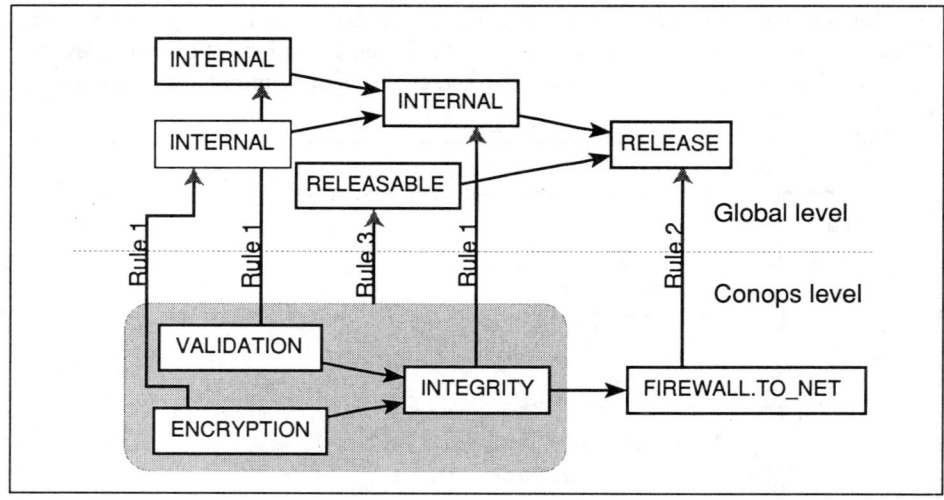

Fig. 18. Events at two levels of architectural abstraction

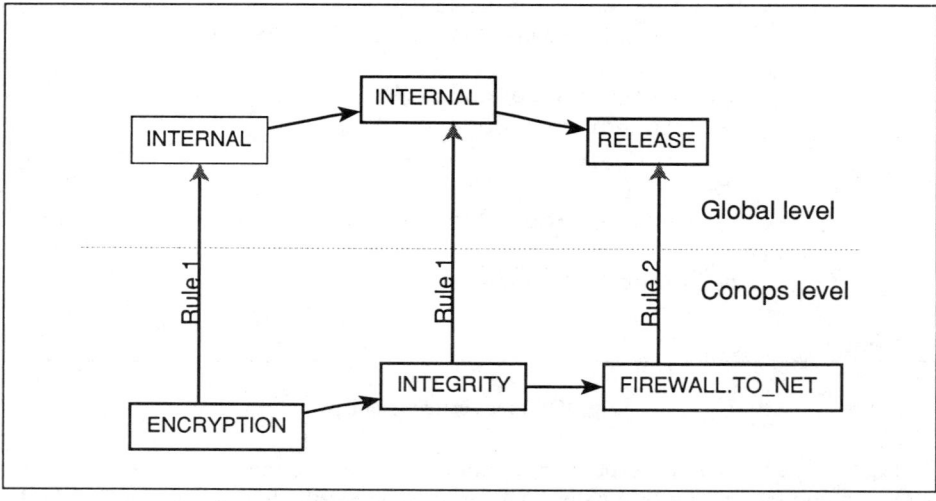

Fig. 19. A lack of a conops event results in a missing global event

7 Formalizing the MISSI requirements summary

In this section we go through all the requirements of the MISSI overview, showing how we would capture them in *Rapide*.

We have already dealt with the very first requirement (section 6.5):

1(a) *"Authorized certificate authorities (and no others) must be provided with access to certificate generation functions."*

We have also touched upon the next requirement earlier (section 6.2):

1(b) *"All legitimate MISSI users must have a valid certificate for some classification level they are cleared to read. Entities with valid certificates must be legitimate MISSI users."*

If this is a definition of when a MISSI-user is *"legitimate"* we define the type MISSI_user with the attribute legitimate, which is true if and only if the attribute "certificate_set" is non-empty.

The last constraint implies the first, of course, but in the interest of clarity of intention we state both explicitly, since redundancy adds rather than detracts from the confidence we have in the specification.

An alternative representation would define two types; MISSI_user_type and legit_MISSI_user_type <: MISSI_user_type. The latter would be constrained always to have in hand appropriate certificates, the former would allow its transformation into a legit_MISSI_user_type object after performing the appropriate checks.

The next three requirements – 1(c,d,e) – as well as the later 1(g, h, i, k), all contain a requirement on the same form:

"All MISSI certificate holders must be provided with access to appropriate <keyword> functions for each classification level they are cleared to read."

(Where the *<keyword>* identifies the distinct functions, such as *confidentiality*, *integrity*, and *certificate validation*.) They have been discussed extensively earlier, in section 6.5).

Requirements 1(j, k) strengthens the access requirements by adding that accessed functionality be

"...for the enclave in which they reside. (All <entities> are MISSI certificate holders and reside in the enclaves in which they perform their task.)"

These are simply invariants over the relationships between components and enclaves, and could be stated in those terms, *e.g.*, in the subtype release_reviewer_type of the MISSI_user_type there is the invariant that:

...
not certificates().empty;
residency().release_reviewers().element(**self**);
...

Sections 2 and 3 of the requirement set identify the circumstances under which information may be released from or accepted into an enclave.

2(a) *"An authorized releaser for a particular enclave must be a MISSI certificate holder and reside within the enclave."*

2(a) is similar to the requirements of 1, and is dealt with in the same way.

```
type MISSI_user_type is interface
provides
    function classification ()
        return set(Classification_type);
    function certificates ()
        return set(Certificate_type);
    function legitimate ()
        return Boolean;
    ...
    function residency ()
        return Enclave;
    ...
constraint
    legitimate() = not certificates().empty;
    legitimate() implies
    not map( Certificate_type,
             Classification_type,
             certificates(),
             security_level)
                    .intersect(classification())
                    .empty();
end MISSI_user_type;
```

Fig. 20. An invariant constraint. The polymorphic function map takes two types S and T (the source and target type), an object M of type set(S) and a function F with signature S→T, and returns an object of type set(T), each of whose elements is the result of applying F to some element of M. The function security_level is assumed to map certificates to security levels.

2(b) *"All data transferred outside of a secret-high enclave must have been sent by an authorized releaser in the originating enclave, must be protected by an integrity server, and must pass a releasability check in the originating enclave."*

2(b) establishes protocol precursors for the event representing the release of data from an enclave. Assuming that data is being released by means of the firewall communicating to the network, the notion of data being *releasable* was captured earlier. Given that, 2(b) becomes a constraint of the abstract enclave definition. Observing releasable and release events (figure 21), every communication to the net of a piece of data has to be preceded by a releasability event (but not the other way around – releasable data is not required to actually be released).

In *Rapide* terms: whenever we observe the set of releasable and release events (the **from** clause), with a secret-high classification then that set of events can be partitioned into a set of (possibly overlapping) causally ordered pairs of releasable-release events, (the **union** relation, the * indicating that there may be any number of them), and a set of dangling releasable events without a subsequent release.

The use of the **union** relation over the set of pairs of releasable and release events allows a single releasable event to justify multiple actual releases (as in figure 21).

Note that there must be a *causal* chain from establishing releasability to the actual release.

If the requirement specified that all releasable data actually be released then we would omit the second component of the union collecting all the dangling releasable events.

2(c) "All data transferred outside of a secret-high enclave and addressed to a MISSI certificate holder must be protected by a confidentiality service, a proof of origin non-repudiation service, and a recipient authentication service."

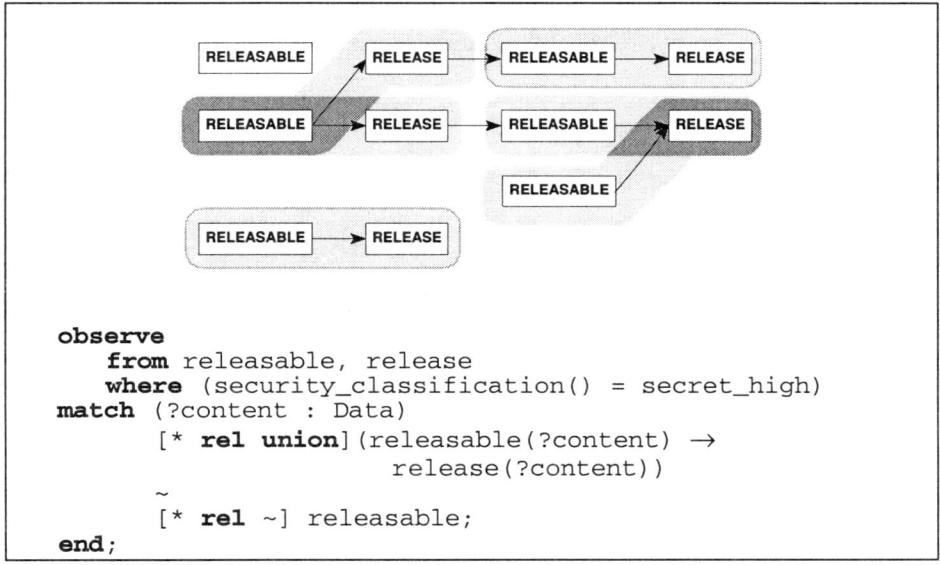

```
observe
   from releasable, release
   where (security_classification() = secret_high)
match (?content : Data)
      [* rel union](releasable(?content) →
                              release(?content))
      ~
      [* rel ~] releasable;
end;
```

Fig. 21. Satisfying the releasability requirement. Each shaded area represents a releasable event justifying the corresponding release event. There is an example of a single releasable justifying multiple releases, as well as a single release being justified by multiple releasable events.

2(c) is similarly structured to 2(b), the main difference being that we limit our interest to data addressed to MISSI certificate holders. By implication, this requires a global (specification) function mapping addresses to attributes of the addressee[1]. Figure 22 gives a variant on the 2(b) requirement. The global event MISSI_releasable is defined in figure 23, and is similar to the definition of releasable (see figure 17),

---

[1] This mapping seems methodologically dubious, but it does not offer any problems for the transformation of the prose into precisely formalized requirements.

as a mapping from a protocol pattern at the conops level to a single event at the global level. We assume that the function `Recipient : Data → Root` gives us the identity of the intended recipient of the data, and then use subtyping to limit the applicability of the mapping to those messages that have `MISSI_users` as recipients.

```
observe
    from MISSI_releasable, wan_conn.release
        where (security_classification() = secret_high)
match  (?content : Data)
        [* rel union] (MISSI_releasable(?content)
                        → wan_conn.release(?content))
        ~
        [* rel ~] MISSI_releasable;
end;
```

Fig. 22. MISSI releasability restriction

```
rule
  (?ws : COTSWorkstation; ?content : Data)
    (?ws.net_conn.to_node(confidentiality,?content)
     ~
     ?ws.net_conn.to_node(non_repudiation,?content)
     ~
     ?ws.net_conn.to_node(recipient_validation,?content))
||>
    MISSI_releasable(?content);;
```

Fig. 23. A variant on the releasability definition

2(d) *"If a recipient is capable of providing authentic receipts and the originator of the data requests a receipt, all data transferred outside of a secret-high enclave must be protected by a proof of receipt non-repudiation service."*

This requirement mixes references to capabilities of enclaves (offering an authentication service) and events (the data being transferred with a return receipt request). To be "receipt confirmation capable" is modeled by adding a node `Receipt_authentication_enclave` to the type structure, introducing a subtype of the `Enclave` type. Stated in protocol terms, a receipt acknowledgment must be generated whenever data leaves a secret-high enclave addressed to a receipt confirmation capable component. There are a number of ways one can phrase this. As a negative, one can write that for each `release` event and all its (causally) subsequent acknowledgments for the receipt of the release, the set of acknowledgments cannot be empty (figure 24).

In *Rapide* terms: observe the set consisting of a `release` event with secret_high classification (make note of the intended recipient enclave from the address), and all its subsequent `receipt_acknowledge` events. This set should not match the pattern consisting of the `release` event by itself (*i.e.*, there must be at least one acknowledgment).

```
observe
    (?content   : Data;
     ?recipient : Receipt_authentication_enclave;
     ?address   : Address)
    wan_conn.release(?content, ?address)
        where (security_classification() = secret_high
               and ?recipient = ?address.enclave),
        → ([* rel ~] receipt_acknowledge(?content.ack))
not match
    wan_conn.release;
end;
```

Fig. 24. A negative form of constraint *2(d)*

Alternatively, one can write it in positive terms – for each release event and all its (causally) subsequent acknowledgments for the receipt of the release, the set of acknowledgments has to contain at least one acknowledgment (figure 25).

```
observe
    (?content   : Data;
     ?recipient : Receipt_authentication_enclave;
     ?address   : Address)
    wan_conn.release(?content, ?address)
        where (security_classification() = secret_high
            and ?recipient = ?address.enclave),
        → ([* rel ~] receipt_acknowledge(?content.ack))
match
    wan_conn.release
        → ([+ rel ~] receipt_acknowledge);
end;
```

Fig. 25. A positive form of constraint *2(d)*

In both cases, the *Rapide* form is one of (1) filtering the set of events to extract those subsets (possibly overlapping) that are of interest (in this case to each single `release` and its (possibly empty) set of responding acknowledgments), and then (2) specifying the pattern these events have to comply with (in this case that the set of acknowledgments be non-empty).

3(a) *"An authorized receiver for an enclave must be a MISSI certificate holders and reside within the enclave in question."*

3(a) is similar to 2(a), and is dealt with in the same way.

3(b) *"Any data admitted to a secret-high enclave from the outside must be protected by an integrity service, must pass an admissibility check for the enclave, and must have a designated recipient within the enclave who is authorized to receive external data."*

3(b) is similar to 2(b), and is dealt with in the same way.

4(a) *"All sensitive administrative data must be protected by an integrity service while in transit or in storage."*

As with 2(b) and (c) there are two, quite distinct, perspective on this kind of constraint.

One can either view the requirements as related to *state*, *i.e.*, every piece of (administrative) data has some state attribute indicating whether it is in storage, in transit or in (possibly) other modes. In which case the natural mode of expression is one of first order logic (as in [13]), but at the cost of reduced checkability and increased complexity of expression – data and other basic types would acquire an ever-growing set of more or less obvious attributes, an attribute collection which may become intractable as the abstract notion of data becomes refined.

Or one can view it more dynamically, and focus on the *action* of storing or putting into transit a piece of data, in which case the assertion of being protected by an integrity service is tied to the transitional event itself. This is the path taken in the formalization of 2(b) and (c), and would be repeated for 4(a), here.

8 Putting a *Rapide* reference architecture to use

Given a *Rapide* formalization of the reference model we can put it to a number of different uses. The most obvious is as a precise definition of the model itself – being expressed in a formal language it allows us to draw unambiguous conclusions from the formalization based on testable arguments within a formal framework (in the case of *Rapide* constraints the framework is a simple one of sets and partial orders).

Since *Rapide* is supported by a growing toolkit of visualization and testing modules [29, 30], the reference architecture can be the target for *conformance testing* by implementations purporting to satisfy the architecture's requirements. Such automatic conformance testing requires two things:

- An instrumentation of the implemented system that supplies the tools with the information required to compare the implementation to the reference architecture. In many cases such instrumentation can be generated automatically by a modified

set of compilers,[2] generating the code necessary to create events and maintain the dependency graph.
- An abstraction *map* essentially defining how the patterns of events generated by the instrumentation correspond to the types of events and components referred to in the architecture.[3]
- Such a map makes the conformance argument precise, and adds documentation as to how the implementor thought her system relates to the reference architecture.

Given such instrumentation and the argument how conformance is obtained, the system conformance test becomes automatic, and can become a standard part of any regression test one might wish to subject the system to as its implementation evolves.

Furthermore, the instrumentation together with its conformance map can become an embedded, permanent part of the production system. The result is another layer of security checking, where the different perspective on the system offered by the conformance argument may detect architecture violations that might otherwise go unnoticed.

A variant of the conformance testing is the use of the tools for *scenario* testing and presentations. The Rapide toolkit has been applied to such diverse models as the SPARC V9 reference hardware architecture and a stock market model, as well as a simple scenario for security protocols based on elements of the MISSI reference architecture.

In the security model scenario we constructed a model vertically partitioned into three layers.

At the bottom layer, we defined an executable conops model of *users, workstations, protocol servers, firewalls*, and *networks*.

The topology was one of a set of LANs, each with its workstations, firewalls and servers, and each workstation with its users. The LANs were connected by means of a WAN, through their respective firewall modules.

All the networks were broadcast networks.

This bottom layer corresponds to an actual system, a flat, relatively unorganized set of components communication hither and thither – possibly in conformance with the requirements of the reference architecture. On the other hand, possibly not – that is what the toolkit checks.

The second level is an intermediate one. Each architecture is an *enclave*, each of which is accompanied by a set of the enclave-related requirements (such as 2(b), about releasability). Each enclave in the intermediate architecture is the target for a *Rapide* map, which transforms patterns of conops model behaviors into activities defined for enclaves (*e.g.,* as in the definition of the releasability map, see figure 17). Some components of an enclave is shown in figure 26 (from an animation of the conformance check), an enclave with two users, two workstations, a LAN and a firewall (besides the local servers, not shown in this figure).

---

[2] Such an instrumented compiler-set exists for Java, Verilog and CORBA IDL besides for Rapide itself.

[3] We have already made use of such maps in defining how the abstract `releasable` event occurs as an abstraction from a pattern of lower-level events.

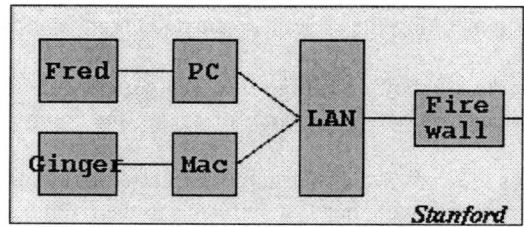

Fig. 26. Some components of an intermediate level model architecture

The third level is that of the *global* architecture, consisting of *enclaves, WANs,* etc. Figure 27 gives an abbreviated view, from an animation of the reference architecture conformance test of a model with four enclaves.) At this level we check the constraints relating to multi-enclave concerns, such as the global requirement prohibiting covert channels. The architecture level can be obtained by maps directly from the conops model, or in two stages: by the maps from the conops model to the intermediate level, and then maps from the intermediate level on to the global level. Which of these one chooses is a question of whether the intermediate models contain all the information required for the global architecture model (*e.g.,* the notion of general internal activity) or not.

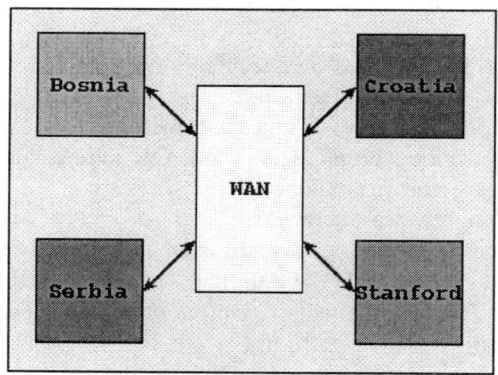

Fig. 27. A global level architecture

A model (or a system in testing or production) typically generates a large number of events. When investigating data for possible non-conformance it is critical that the number of data elements – events of possible interest – be reduced as early as possible. The *Rapide* toolkit offers two means to achieve this end. The first is the use of architecture maps in structuring the instrumentation. Each map construct results in the automatic construction of a *transformational filter* (or *sieve*). The filter passes on only those events that are considered significant in the abstraction, possibly transformed so as to aggregate event patterns into single events or simpler event patterns.

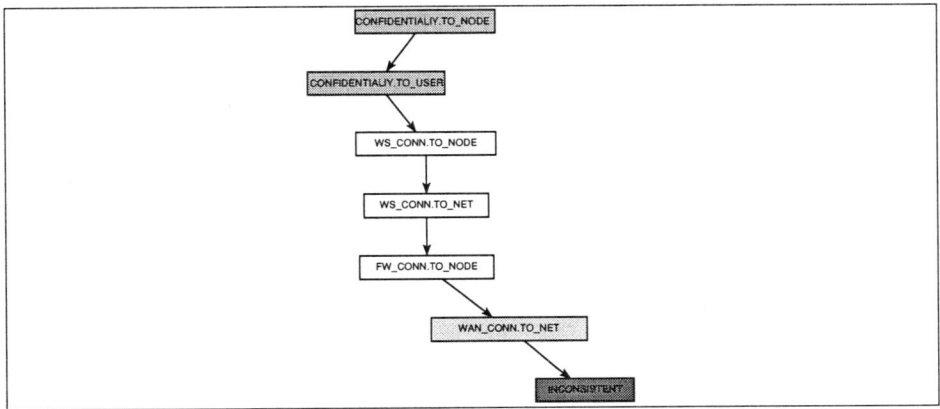

Fig. 28. Detecting a protocol violation

The second is the visualization toolset of *Rapide*. This part of the toolset allows the user to apply various patterns of events to a given execution, displaying only those events fitting patterns of interest. Combined with the *Raptor* [30] animator this makes it possible to watch an animation of a running system at a chosen level of abstraction. Then, if interesting events (such as protocol violations) are detected, the user can move to the POV (*poset visualizer*) [29] and use it to investigate the causal patterns leading up to the events that piqued her interest. In particular, the POV allows the efficient removal of extraneous information, to ease the identification of interesting events among the clutter of all the events of the system.

As an example, consider the events of figure 28. These were culled from the execution of a network model, after the occurrence of an *inconsistent* event was observed at the global level. (An *inconsistent* event signals the system's detection of a constraint violation, in this case the global releasability constraint of figure 22). By moving from the global architecture to the conops architecture, using the POV, and then following the causal links past-wards from the *inconsistent* event, we identify its cause: the absence of the Integrity and Encryption steps of the protocol making a piece of information releasable. As the user only engaged the Confidentiality server, once the information was transmitted from the firewall to the WAN, she was in violation of the reference architecture constraints.

9 *Rapide's* Relationship to Other ADLs

Architecture description languages and tools have not yet attained the maturity of programming languages. The conceptual relationships among them are still fluid, and one cannot partition the set of ADLs into families with conceptually similar basis with quite the same ease as one does programming languages (*i.e.*, imperative vs. constraint-oriented vs. function-oriented, etc.). ADLs range from meta-programming generators [3, 37] to domain-specific algorithm development tools [6].

Rapide is very much in the object-oriented tradition, with rich polymorphism, and with the full complement of inheritance and subtyping mechanisms. Being an ADL rather than a programming language, *Rapide* emphasizes the distinction between interface and implementation more than is common among object-oriented programming languages. As do UniCon [36] and Wright [2], *Rapide* distinguishes between *components* and *connections*. However, *Rapide* tends to leave connections simple as far as their protocols go – protocols being perceived as interface components rather than connector elements (protocols can be abstracted, of course).

With its emphasis on *conformance* and *reference architectures*, *Rapide* gives the specifier the opportunity to define architectures and components in a descriptive rather than a prescriptive manner. The operational description of a *Rapide* component tends to be in terms of observations matching certain patterns rather than in terms of specifying how the patterns are generated. Though a *Rapide* interface can be given a prescriptive definition in a manner similar to that of CSP, the specifier does not have to be that complete. This sets *Rapide* apart from most formalisms based on process algebras such as CCS [21] and CSP [12].

The de-emphasis of completeness of description arises naturally from the observation that a single system may be viewed through multiple perspectives – *i.e.*, there may be more than one architecture describing a particular system [32]. Since each architecture need only focus on particular aspects, a completeness requirement would violate the basic idea of separation of concerns. *Rapide* encourages such separation.

The use of abstraction maps from one architecture to another is a particularly distinguishing aspect of *Rapide*. It gives the specifiers and developers an opportunity to explicitly state conformance arguments, and to have these arguments checked by tools. Since the maps are *from* the purported implementation *to* the more abstract architecture *Rapide* sidesteps the issue of non-linear development inherent in imperative and function-oriented top-down design.

At a more detailed conceptual level, *Rapide* differs from most other event-oriented formalisms in that it adopts a partial order model rather than the more common trace-based view. Though posets introduce conceptual complexities – most human beings tend to experience the world sequentially, and our perspectives on the world reflect this – we find that posets are appropriate when one describes real-world, concurrent systems [33, 39].

The *Rapide* toolkit emphasizes observation, modeling and experimentation. Since there is a wide range of tools for ADLs, often with rather disparate ideas about what an architecture *is*, there is a challenging need for general tool frameworks that allows specifiers and developer to use toolkits associated with different ADLs when developing a particular architecture. Steps in that direction have been taken by Garlan et al., in their development of Acme [10]. In [8] Garlan and Wang report the successful combined application of Wright, *Rapide* and Aesop to a single architecture, using Acme.

Rapide makes no claim to universality. It adopts a particular world-view: that of components and connections, with events as the basic concept of its operational semantics. For architectures that do not fit these terms, one should look elsewhere.

10 Conclusion

We have indicated how one may use the event-based language of *Rapide* to capture elements of a reference architecture. Both the structural and the operational requirements of the architecture can be stated precisely in *Rapide*, and the resulting specification may become the basis for (1) analysis, (2) model checking, (3) implementation conformance testing and (4) production code conformance surveillance.

A key element in the successful application of an architecture description language to the design of reference or other software architectures is the degree to which it allows one to state *all* aspects of the architecture, and the flexibility of the *abstraction* mechanisms that may be applied when the conformance requirements are stated (as part of the architectural design). Distinct architectural perspectives require distinct abstraction mappings, and it is important that the designer be able to separate such perspectives from each other – giving separate reference architectures for each perspective, as appropriate.

Furthermore, an ADL is only as good as the tools that support it – in the absence of tool support, design capture and conformance reasoning easily devolves into vague hand-waving. The tool support should help automate conformance testing and other aspects of architecture design analysis, as well as allowing the designer to construct test scenarios and visualize the behavior of architecture conforming systems.

We have found that the *Rapide* ADL with its supporting toolset offers an interesting approach to the design of distributed architectures. In particular, the event orientation of the system, coupled with its sophisticated ability to identify causal chains and patterns of behaviors where causal relationships may play an integral role are quite enticing.

References

1. Allen, R., Garlan, D.: Formalizing architectural connection. In Proceedings of the Sixteenth International Conference on Software Engineering. IEEE Computer Society Press, May 1994.
2. Allen, R.J.: *A Formal Approach to Software Architecture*, Ph.D. Thesis, Carnegie Mellon University, Technical Report Number CMU-CS-97-144, May, 1997.
3. Batory, D., Geraci, B.J.: Composition Validation and Subjectivity in GenVoca Generators, *IEEE Transactions on Software Engineering* (special issue on Software Reuse), February 1997, pp. 67-82.
4. Boehm, B.W.: Software Process Architectures. In *Proceedings of the First International Workshop on Architectures for Software Systems*. Seattle, WA, 1995. Published as CMU–CS–TR–95–151.

5. Ellis, W.J. et al.: Toward a Recommended Practice for Architectural Description. In *Proceedings 2nd IEEE International Conference on Engineering of Complex Computer Systems,* Montreal, Canada, 1996
6. Englehart, M., Jackson, M.: *ControlH: A Specification Language and Code Generator for Real-Time N&C Applications,* Honeywell Technology Center, 1993.
7. Garlan, D., Shaw, M.: *An Introduction to Software Architecture.* Volume I. World Scientific Publishing Company, 1993.
8. Garlan, D., Wang, Z.: *A Case Study in Software Architecture Interchange,* Submitted for publication, March 1998.
9. Garlan, D.: Research directions in software architectures. *ACM Computing Surveys,* 27(2): 257–261. 1995.
10. Garlan, D., Monroe, R.T., Wile, D.: Acme: An Architecture Description Interchange Language, In *Proceedings of CASCON '97,* November 1997.
11. Gennart, B.A., Luckham, D.C.: Validating Discrete Event Simulations Using Pattern Mappings. In *Proceedings of the 29th Design Automation Conference (DAC),* IEEE Computer Society Press, June 1992, pp. 414–419.
12. Hinchey, M G., Jarvis, S.A.: *Concurrent Systems: Formal Development in CSP* McGraw-Hill International Series in Software Engineering, 1995.
13. Johnson, D.R., Saydjari, F.F., Van Tassel, J.P.: MISSI security Policy: A Formal Approach. R2SPO Technical Report R2SPO–TR001–95, NSA/Central Security Service, July 1995.
14. Luckham, D.C., Vera, J.: An event-based architecture definition language. *IEEE Transactions on Software Engineering,* 21(3):253–265, June 1993.
15. Luckham, D.C.: *Programming with Specifications: An Introduction to ANNA, A Language for Specifying Ada Programs,* Springer-Verlag, Texts and Monographs in Computer Science, October, 1990.
16. Luckham, D.C.: Rapide: A Language and Toolset for Simulation of Distributed Systems by Partial Orderings of Events, DIMACS Partial Order Methods Workshop IV, Princeton University, July 1996.
17. Luckham, D.C., Vera, J., Meldal, S.: *Key Concepts in Architecture Definition Languages.* Submitted to the CACM. Also published as technical report CSL-TR-95-674, Stanford University, 1996.
18. Meldal, S.: Supporting architecture mappings in concurrent systems design. In *Proceedings of the Australian Software Engineering Conference.* IREE Australia, May 1990.
19. Meszaros, G.: Software Architecture in BNR. In *Proceedings of the First International Workshop on Architectures for Software Systems.* Seattle, WA. 1995. Published as CMU–CS–TR–95–151.
20. Milner, R.: Operational and Algebraic Semantics of Concurrent Processes, In: *Handbook of Theoretical Computer Science,* Vol. B, Elsevier Science Publishers and MIT Press, 1990.
21. Milner, R.: *Communication and Concurrency,* Prentice Hall, December 1995.
22. Mitchell, J.C., Meldal, S., Madhav, N.: An Extension of Standard ML Modules with Subtyping and Inheritance. In *Proceedings of the 18th ACM Symp. on the Principles of Programming Languages,* ACM, ACM Press. 1991, pp. 270-278. Also published as Technical Report CSL-TR-91-472, Computer Systems Laboratory, Stanford University.
23. Monroe, R.T., Garlan, D.: Style Based Reuse for Software Architectures, *Proceedings of the 1996 International Conference on Software Reuse,* April 1996.

24. Moriconi, M., Qian, X.: Correctness and composition of software architectures. In *Proceedings of ACM SIGSOFT'94: Symposium on Foundations of Software Engineering.* New Orleans, LA. December 1994.
25. PAVG: The *Rapide* Architecture Description Language Reference Manual. http://pavg.stanford.edu/rapide/lrms/architectures.ps
26. PAVG: The *Rapide* Constraint Language Reference Manual. In preparation.
27. PAVG: *Rapide* Examples. In preparation.
28. PAVG: The *Rapide* Pattern Language Reference Manual. http://pavg.stanford.edu/rapide/lrms/patterns.ps
29. PAVG: *POV–a partial order browser* http://pavg.stanford.edu/rapide/tools-release.html
30. PAVG: *Raptor–animating architecture models.* http://pavg.stanford.edu/rapide/tools-release.html
31. PAVG: *Rapide* toolset information. http://pavg.stanford.edu/rapide/tools.html
32. Perry, D., Wolf., A.L.: Foundations for the Study of Software Architecture, *ACM Software Engineering Notes,* 17(4), October 1992.
33. Pratt, V.R.: Modeling concurrency with partial orders, *International Journal of Parallel Programming,* 15(1), pp. 33-71, February 1986.
34. Santoro, A., Park, W.: *SPARC-V9 architecture specification with Rapide.* Technical report CSL, Stanford University (to appear).
35. Shaw, M., Garlan, D.: *Software Architecture: Perspectives on an Emerging Discipline.* Prentice-Hall, 1996.
36. Shaw, M., DeLine, R., Zelesnik, G.: Abstractions and Implementations for Architectural Connections. In *Proceedings of the 3rd International Conference on Configurable Distributed Systems,* May 1996.
37. Solderitsch, J., Wickman, G., Kweder, D., Horton, H.: An Architecture and Generator for an Army IEW Domain. *Software Technology Conference 1995.*
38. Soni, D., Nord, R.L., Hofmeister, C.: Software Architecture in Industrial Applications. In *Proceedings of the 17th International Conference in Software Engineering.* ACM, April 1995.
39. van Glabbeek, R.: *Comparative Concurrency Semantics and Refinement of Actions,* PhD Thesis, Vrije Universiteit te Amsterdam, Centrum voor Wiskunde en Informatica, May 1990.

Requirements Engineering Repositories: Formal Support for Informal Teamwork Methods

Hans W. Nissen and Matthias Jarke

RWTH Aachen, Informatik V (Information Systems)
Ahornstr. 55, 52072 Aachen, Germany
{nissen|jarke}@informatik.rwth-aachen.de

Abstract. Relationships among different modeling perspectives have been systematically investigated focusing either on given notations (e.g. OMT) or on domain reference models (e.g. SAP). In contrast, many successful informal methods for business analysis and requirements engineering (e.g. JAD) emphasize team negotiation, goal orientation and flexibility of modeling notations. This paper addresses the question how much formal and computerized support can be provided in such settings without destroying their creative tenor. Our solution comprises four components:
(1) A modular conceptual modeling formalism organizes individual perspectives and their interrelationships. (2) Perspective schemata are linked to a conceptual meta meta model of shared domain terms, thus giving the architecture a semantic meaning and enabling adaptability and extensibility of the network of perspectives. (3) Inconsistency management across perspectives is handled in a goal-oriented manner, by defining the analysis goals as meta rules which are automatically adapted to perspective schemata. (4) Continuous incremental maintenance of inconsistency information is provided by exploiting recent view maintenance techniques from deductive databases.
The approach has been fully implemented as an extension to the ConceptBase meta database management system and has been experimentally applied in the context of business analysis and data warehouse design.

1 Introduction

As observed in [Poh94], modeling processes proceed along three dimensions: representational transformation, domain knowledge acquisition, and stakeholder agreement. Existing methodologies tend to emphasize one of these dimensions over the others: the modeling *notations*, the available *knowledge* within a specific domain, or the *people* involved in the analysis project. All three method types have a long history, with little interaction between them.

The management of inconsistent partial models is an inevitable part of requirements engineering (RE) [Bal91,FF91,Eas96]. Multiple stakeholders with conflicting opinions, contradicting requirements and alternative perspectives cause these inconsistencies.

All methodologies support multiple partial models to represent the set of requirements. They differ substantially in the preferred coupling of the partial models. This requires cross-model analysis to guarantee consistency between the partial models. The extent, justification and customizability of the performed analysis constitute a main difference between the reviewed methodologies and illustrate the specific problems with the team- and goal-oriented methods.

Notation-oriented methods manifest their assistance in the set of modeling notations they offer. Their philosophy can be characterized by the slogan *In the language lies the power*. Examples of notation-oriented methods are structured analysis approaches, as, e.g., Modern Structured Analysis [You89], and object-oriented techniques, as, e.g., UML [FS97]. They attach great importance to the consistency of the developed models. Conflicts between stakeholders, inconsistencies induced by a different terminology or simple name clashes have to be resolved 'outside' the model. The analysis goals are defined directly on the constructs of the notations, i.e. on the contents of the corresponding (maybe hypothetical) meta models.

Since the mid-80s, researchers have attempted to formalize semi-formal notations via a transformation to well-understood specification formalisms like logic [Gre84], graph grammars and algebraic specifications. They specify a fixed semantics the user must accept and cannot modify. A recent and very comprehensive example is a formal semantics for SSADM (Structured Systems Analysis and Design Method) [DCC92] based on algebraic specification [BFG$^+$93] by [Hus94].

A different strategy is employed by the **domain-oriented analysis methods**. For a specific application domain, e.g., public administration or furniture industry, they offer a predefined set of reference models. Reference models describe typical data, processes and functions, together with a set of consistency tests which evaluate relationships between the models. Reference models represent the knowledge collected in multiple analysis projects within a particular domain: *In the knowledge lies the power*. The reuse of reference models can considerably reduce the analysis effort. However, it can be inflexible since the user can tailor the notations, the constraints or contents only to the degree foreseen by the developers of the reference models.

The SAP Business Blueprints are reference models from the business domain [SAP97]. The Aris Toolset [IDS96] offers a platform for working with reference models. It offers hard-coded constraint checks within and across the models. Analysis goals exist only implicitly. They are reflected by the implementation of the reference models, i.e. by the contents and the structure of the models.

Goal- and team-oriented approaches specifically address the objective to capture requirements from different information sources and to make arising conflicts productive: *In the people lies the power*. Prominent examples include IBM's JAD (Joint Application Design) [Aug91], SSM (Soft Systems Methodology) [Che89], and PFR (Analysis of Presence and Future Requirements) [Abe95] focus on the *early* and *direct* participation of all stakeholders, the rapid generation of *joint results*, the *tolerance* of conflicting perspectives, a *goal-oriented process*, and *informal, graphical notations*. Experiences in the application of JAD give evidence for a 20% to 60% increased productivity compared with semiformal and formal methods [GJ87,Cra94]. It is typical for these methods that the execution is supported by highly skilled group facilitators which animate the participants, guide the analysis process and keep an eye on the compliance with the specified analysis goals. Conflicts and inconsistencies are tolerated for the benefit of a fast and creative acquisition process. Moreover conflicts are employed as a tool for the analysis process. For each topic in the domain they collect perspectives from different stakeholders to provoke conflicts and use them to guide further discussions and interviews.

Teamwork remains very informal to enhance creativity. Neither notations nor analysis goals are predefined by the methods but specified by the participants according to the actual problem to be solved. To accomodate the change of goals during project execution, the customization of analysis goals and notations is possible even during a running project. At present, no supporting tools are available beyond simple groupware tools. The main reasons for this dilemma are the high degree of customizability the tools must offer and the lack of formalizations available.

In the next section we give a detailed overview of our approach. In Sect. 3 we explain the axiomatization of a modular conceptual modeling language as well as the transformation of analysis goals. Both are employed at set-up time of the requirements engineering repository for a specific project. The inconsistency management component described in Sect. 4 enables a tolerant modelling environment at run-time. A detailed application example of the approach is presented in Sect. 5. The paper ends with a comparison to related work in Sect. 6 and a summary and outlook in Sect. 7.

2 Overview of the Approach

The informal team-based information acquisition is not subject to any formalization (though it could at least be recorded in multimedia). The potential for formalization and computer-based tools lies in the other part of the methods: the *cross-perspective analysis* which is performed by moderators and analysts to extract knowledge and further questions from the collected information. The team produces many perspectives in a very short time containing lots of conflicts and inconsistencies. The situation for the analysts becomes even harder since the notations and the analysis goals can change from one project to another. The manual comparison of perspectives becomes a big problem and is both time-consuming and error-prone.

The basis of our formalization are the analysis goals and the notations as specified by the stakeholders at the beginning of method execution. We forge links to the notation- and the domain-oriented methods by formally transforming the domain-oriented analysis goals into integrity constraints over notational meta models. The result is a set of syntactic and domain-oriented inter-relationships between the notations, just as it is the case in the notation- and the domain-oriented methods. But in our approach they are automatically generated from

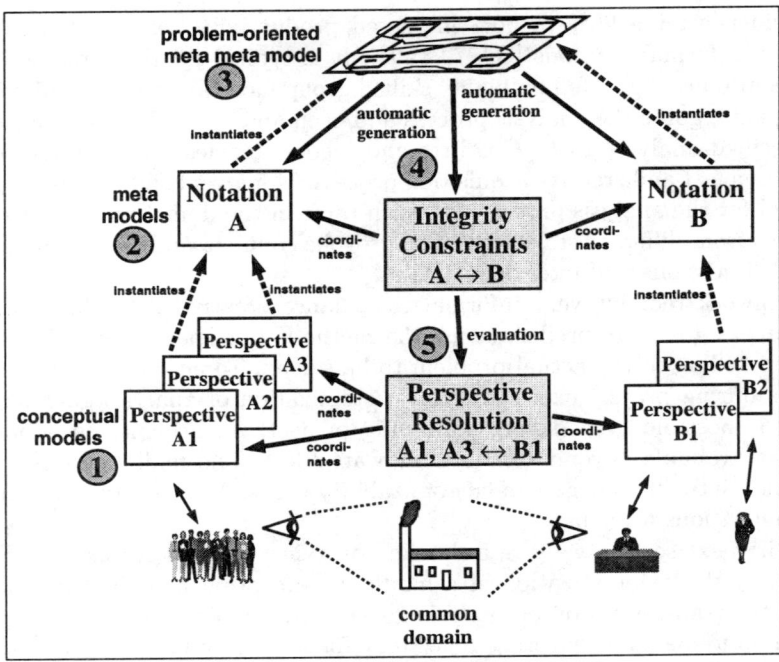

Fig. 1. Overview of the approach

user-defined declarative, notation-independent specifications of analysis goals. Figure 1 presents the components of our approach.

(1): Separation of Multiple Perspectives. The conceptual models represent individual perspectives of stakeholders. The figure shows three perspectives (A1,A2, A3) expressed in Notation A and two perspectives (B1,B2) expressed in Notation B. Our separation mechanism offers independent modeling contexts (modules) and enables the representation of inconsistent conceptual models.

(2): Extensible Meta Modeling. The notations used to express the perspectives are defined on the second level, the meta level. The example comprises two notations, Notation A and Notation B. Since the notations are subject to modification, the modeling formalism must support the creation and modification of meta models. These meta models also reside in separate modules.

(3): Specifying Common Domain Terms and Analysis Goals. A shared meta meta model inter-relates all perspective notations. It specifies the domain structure and the analysis goals. This model is created by teamwork at the beginning of the analysis project and documents the common language of all participating stakeholders. The perspective notations are views on this model, i.e. a notation covers a specific fragment of the common domain terms.

This assignment of notations to domain fragments gives the architecture a semantic meaning. The semantics of the domain structure is defined by the analysis goals - formulas which formalize the correct or intended behaviour as well as expected problems of the domain components. These goals define the scope of the cross-perspective check performed on the bottom level between concrete conceptual models.

(4): Transformation of Analysis Goals. To close the gap between the domain-oriented analysis goals and the perspectives expressed in notations and to enable a distributed modeling activity and consistency check, the analysis goals of the meta meta model are automatically transformed to integrity constraints on the notation meta models. The relationships between different notations reside in so-called resolution modules which are connected to the corresponding notation modules via `coordinates` links. In the figure we have a resolution module for the two notations mentioned before.

(5): Continuous Inconsistency Documentation. To avoid interrupting the creative modeling activity in the presence of inter-perspective inconsistencies, the cross-perspective analysis takes place in separate resolution modules. The figure presents a resolution module (the shaded module on the bottom level) to check the perspectives `A1,A3` and `B1`. This is also the place where the conflicts are documented and continuously monitored.

3 Components Involved in System Set-Up

The repository has to be tailored towards the specific needs of each requirements engineering project. The required effort depends on the differences between the analysis goals of the new and the already performed projects. The following subsections introduce the main components involved in such a system set-up, namely, the modularization of a knowledge base to enable multiple perspectives of a common domain, and the transformation of analysis goals to enable an efficient and distributed inconsistency check.

3.1 M-Telos: Separation of Multiple Perspectives

The conceptual modeling language Telos [MBJK90] was designed for managing (meta) information about information systems. It integrates aspects from database design, knowledge representation and conceptual modeling. The object-oriented Telos data model supports the abstraction principles classification/instantiation, specialization/generalization and aggregation. A basic concept of Telos is the representation of every single piece of information as an object with its own identity. The unlimited instantiation hierarchy enables classes to be themselves instances of other classes, so-called meta classes. Meta classes may again be instances of meta meta classes, and so on.

A version of Telos called O-Telos was formalised in [Jeu92] and implemented in ConceptBase [JGJ+95], a deductive object manager for meta databases. This axiomatization enables the interpretation of an Telos object base as a special case of a deductive database with stratified negation and perfect model semantics [Min87].

M-Telos extends O-Telos by introducing so-called **modules** as a separation mechanism. A module provides an independent modeling context where users can create an individual analysis perspective in the form of a conceptual model. The intended application scenario of modules in concurrent conceptual modeling processes induces the need for **communication** between modules [NKF94]. The module concept supports cooperation among group members by the possibility to define local modules.

It is often the case that one modeling task depends on another one and reuses a part of its results. To support this situation, two modules can communicate by setting up an **import-relationship**. The importing module obtains access to the contents of the imported module. To protect a specific part of the module contents, the concept allows the division of the accessible contents of a module into a private and a public part.

We need not only a modeling context but also a context for the resolution of multiple perspectives. We use dedicated modules for this monitoring task, the so-called **resolution modules**. As our experiences indicate [NJJ+96], such resolution modules need a special way to access the monitored modules. Therefore the module concept offers a **coordination relationship** between modules which enable a resolution module to access all accessible objects of the monitored modules.

The formal semantics of a M-Telos object base is given by a mapping to a deductive database containing predefined objects, integrity constraints and deductive rules. This set of objects, constraints and rules constitute the **axiomatization** of M-Telos. The complete set of axioms is presented in [Nis96].

A main goal of the axiomatization of M-Telos was to preserve the **simplicity** of the O-Telos formalization given in [Jeu92]. We formulated 76 axioms, of which 32 were slightly modified axioms from the O-Telos formalization. 31 of the new axioms are new predefined objects, seven define new rules and six describe new constraints.

Based on the axiomatization some important properties of a M-Telos object base can be proven formally. It can be shown that every module satisfies the *referential integrity*. This property guarantees that for every object accessible within a module also all referenced objects are accessible within that module. The phenomenon of a hanging link in a module can therefore not appear in M-Telos.

The modules in a M-Telos object base always form a specific structure. It can be proven that modules always form a tree with a unique root, the module containing the initial system objects. This guarantees that it's contents is accessible in every single module.

3.2 Transformation of Global Analysis Goals

The goal- and team-oriented methods are designed to employ conflicts in a creative manner. They employ highly overlapping perspectives and acquire almost all information from different stakeholders. Due to this redundancy, a large number of relationships exist between perspectives. The cross-perspective analysis employs the *analysis goals* specified in the problem-oriented meta meta model to check these relationships.

The analysis goals are formulated as so called **meta formulas**: They are specified on meta meta level but make statements about objects that reside two abstraction levels below - on the conceptual model level (cf. Fig. 1). This is necessary since the perspectives we actually want to analyse reside two levels below the meta meta model.

Although it is possible to use the analysis goals as they are we will transform them to integrity constraints on the notations' meta models. At this point we have to make clear our terminology: an *analysis goal* is a formula that is specified within the meta meta model and is thus a meta formula. An *integrity constraint* is specified within the notation meta models and is automatically generated from an analysis goal.

The analysis goals represent the agreement among the stakeholders about the goals, or more specific, the questions and problems, the analysis project is dedicated to. Accordingly, our architecture manages the analysis goals within the central module. But the analysis and modeling process does not run in a centralized way, it is distributed and involves many agents. A central control instance will then be a system bottleneck. On the other hand, a complete distribution without any central control instance like in [NKF94] would not cover the global relationships. To be efficient in such a setting and at the same time be able to manage the global connection we follow the approach of [ACM95] which is a compromise of the two extremes mentioned before: The environments for the perspective development are distributed and work autonomously but there still exists a central instance which has knowledge about their possible inter-relationships. Applied to our case: from the global meta meta model we generate integrity constraints which can be evaluated locally within the modules of the meta level. The global module needs not be accessed during inconsistency monitoring time.

We explain the mechanism in two steps: First we describe the technique of partial evaluation which is used to transform an analysis goal into integrity constraints. Since not all analysis goals need to be transformed to all modules we guide the partial evaluation by generating a transformation plan, i.e. the assignment of analysis goals to modules.

Partial Evaluation of Analysis Goals. We employ the technique of partial evaluation to transform a meta formula into a set of integrity constraints. In [Jeu92] the application of this technique to the O-Telos object model is presented. We can directly adapt the results to M-Telos. We will therefore only sketch the technique of partial evaluation.

The basic idea is to evaluate as many literals of the meta formula as possible when the system architecture is set up. The meta models of the notations on meta level are already known at this time. When a literal $(x\ in\ c)$[1] of the meta formula where c denotes an object of the meta meta model is evaluated, the variable x is substituted by an existing object of the meta level. For each solution of the literal a new formula is generated where the evaluated literal is substituted by $TRUE$ and each occurances of x by the respective solution. If this procedure is successfully repeated until all such literals are evaluated the resulting formulas denote integrity constraints on the meta level.

The resulting formulas contain no more objects of the meta meta model but only objects of the meta model of a notation. It is therefore only valid for that particular notation. If not all literals of the above type can be evaluated, this meta formula is not partially evaluable within that particular module. The implementation of a partial evaluator for Telos is presented in [BCJ+94].

Optimization of Evaluation Plans. Unnecessary partial evaluations of analysis goals may arise if modules are connected via *coordinates* relationships: If there exists a *coordinates* link from module A to module B then everything accessible in B is also accessible in A. Any analysis goal that could be transformed for B therefore can also be transformed for A. Since the transformed constraint becomes accessible in A anyway, a separate transformation for A is not necessary. To avoid such inefficiency we compute for every analysis goal the minimal set of modules it must be transformed to.

Our algorithm operates on a graph structure where the modules form the nodes while the *coordinates* relationships form the links. This enabled us to adapt graph theory algorithms to solve our problem. We have proven ([Nis96]) that for every analysis goal the algorithm computes the minimal set of destination modules such that the analysis goals's accessibility in all (potential destination) modules is guaranteed.

This concept of completeness is defined with respect to the given module structure on the meta level. But there exists a second view on completeness with respect to the analysis goals of the meta meta model: The transformation is complete if all analysis goals of the meta meta model have been transformed.

This kind of completeness does not always hold. If there is no notation for a specific fragment of the meta meta model then the analysis goals specified for this fragment could not be transformed to integrity constraints. The result is that some formal statements represented within the meta meta model could not be tested during the analysis process. In some cases this kind of incompleteness is not a problem or even desired. But in all cases it is useful for the users to get information about analysis goals that can not be transformed.

An automatic completion of the module structure on the meta level is not always possible. A tool could constitute additional resolution modules but cannot automatically establish new notations if a fragment of the meta meta model

---

[1] The literal $(x\ in\ c)$ denotes an instantiation relationship between the object x and the class c.

is not covered yet. We developed an algorithm computing additional resolution modules such that an analysis goal becomes transformable (see [NJ97] for details). The result is in general not minimal. One minimal set can be computed by an algorithm which follows the computation of a minimal set of functional dependencies in relational database schema design [EN94]: A module is eliminated if its relationships are covered by the reminding modules in the set. We present such an algorithm in [NJ97].

4 Continuous Inconsistency Documentation

In an concurrent modelling activity it is sometimes more profitable not to repair detected inconsistencies immediately but to keep them as *open problems*. Model designers can continue working without spending time in resolving detected errors. The list of unresolved inconsistencies can be handeled in special meetings at certain milestones. In the following we describe our approach in tolerating inconsistencies within a deductive object base.

We call an object base **primary inconsistent** w.r.t. an integrity constraint if the object base violates this constraint. The tolerance of inconsistencies leads to inconsistent objects within a M-Telos object base. But a totally anarchistic state of the object base is not desired. The inconsistent objects must be managed in the sense that the object base knows about the inconsistent objects it contains [FF91,RF94]. We will call objects of the object base that cause an inconsistency **provisionally inserted**. Since we not only have insertions that cause inconsistencies but also deletions, we also have **provisionally deleted** objects.

Once we tolerate provisional objects we get problems with the traditional detection of inconsistencies: It may happen that the current object base satisfies an integrity constraint only because there exist provisional objects [Lei90]. In such a case we call the object base **secondary inconsistent** w.r.t. an integrity constraint. The tolerance of inconsistencies thus comprises two tasks: the detection and the management of provisional objects.

Inconsistencies may occur within a single conceptual model and during the comparison of different models. The ViewPoints approach [NKF94] distinguishes between an in-ViewPoint and an inter-ViewPoint check and employs different techniques to handle them. In our framework we do not need to recognize such a difference and can apply the same mechanisms for both kinds of consistency checks. The check of a single model as well as the check of multiple models takes place within a single module - the cross-perspective check is performed in a resolution module where all models of the coordinated modules are accessible. All the mechanisms we present in this section therefore apply to both the single perspective check and the cross-perspective check.

4.1 Detection of Inconsistencies

Like other approaches that deal with inconsistency detection [Sim86,Bal91,FP93] we use rules instead of closed formulas: For an integrity constraint φ we assume an **inconsistency view** $\varphi' \Rightarrow incons_\varphi$ where $incons_\varphi$ is a new predicate symbol and φ' is a closed formula. $incons_\varphi$ is deducible if and only if φ fails, i.e. φ' is the negation of φ.

We call an object that is inserted (deleted) by the current transaction **primary provisionally inserted** (deleted) w.r.t. an inconsistency view $incons_\varphi$ if it takes part in a new computation of $incons_\varphi$. For the formal definition of this property we employ an extension of and-or-trees known from the deductive database area [GL90,ML91]. To do this we have to translate the inconsistency view into an equivalent set of Datalog¬ clauses [LT84]. In the most simple case, all and-nodes which are leaves of a new derivation of $incons_\varphi$ and were inserted by the current transaction are then primary provisionally inserted. Due to the use of negation in the body of deductive rules the general case is more complex: We have to change between two object base states in order to evaluate the inconsistency view before and after the transaction. Details of this procedure can be found in [Bau96].

We use a quite similar technique to define secondary provisional objects. Instead of using inconsistency views we now employ **consistency views**: The consistency view of an integrity constraint φ is a rule $\varphi \Rightarrow cons_\varphi$ where $cons_\varphi$ is a new predicate symbol. $cons_\varphi$ is then deducible if and only if the constraint φ is satisfied by the object base.

We again use the and-or-tree for the formal definition of a secondary inconsistency. An object base is secondary inconsistent w.r.t. the integrity constraint φ if the consistency view $cons_\varphi$ is deducible from the object base, but is not deducible from the object base without any provisional objects. In this sense all inserted (deleted) objects of the current transaction that take part in a new derivation of the consistency view $cons_\varphi$ while no derivation without provisional objects exists, are **secondary provisionally inserted** (deleted) objects. Since this definition introduces new provisional objects on the basis of already existing provisional objects we have to compute the least fixpoint of this set.

We distinguish between two detection modes for an integrity constraint: **eager** and **on-demand**. In the eager detection mode the system will check after each transaction for new and for (maybe accidentally) repaired inconsistencies. This mode offers a continuous conflict monitoring (e.g. within a resolution module) which is of course time-consuming and slows down the system. This mode is preferable in a critical development phase (e.g. shortly before an important project review) and when developing critical components (e.g. the control system of an atomic power plant). The eager detection mode is traditionally applied in database area, e.g., [Bor85,Lei90], and some of the logic-based approaches, e.g., [GH91]. In [Bal91] the eager mode is also used for software engineering. All the above given definitions are based on an eager detection in the sense that they all were formulated w.r.t. a current transaction.

In the on-demand mode the user controls the timing of the inconsistency check. Here it is not possible to use the current transaction as a filter because no such transaction exists; all objects that take part in the derivation of the inconsistency view will be declared as primary provisionally inserted objects.

The detection of provisionally deleted objects is not possible without the concept of a 'current transaction'. The same holds for secondary provisional objects. The on-demand mode is preferable in situations where a fast working style is required, as, e.g., in a brainstorming session. Since the consistency of the database w.r.t. a specific integrity constraint will not be checked after a transaction this mode runs quite fast. On the other hand the users get no idea about the quality of their model. This mode is often used in requirements engineering environments, as, e.g., IPSEN [Lef93] and CONMAN [KS88]. Also in the ViewPoints approach [NKF94,EN96] the user invokes the check of an integrity constraint.

detection	primary	secondary
eager	view maintenance	view maintenance + meta interpreter
on_demand	meta interpreter	meta interpreter

Fig. 2. Detection techniques used in different modes

We employ the and-or-tree for the theoretical definition of primary and secondary provisional objects, but not for the implementation of the inconsistency detection. Instead we use efficient incremental view maintenance in combination with a meta interpreter. View maintenance is a machanism that detects all new derivations of a deductive rule or view caused by a transaction. We changed the mechanism developed in [SJ96] such that it returns the whole derivation path.

In eager detection mode, the view maintenance mechanism reports primary inconsistencies. For secondary inconsistencies we must complete the reported derivation trees to include objects that already exist in the object base using the meta interpreter. In on-demand mode, view maintenance is not applicable. We use the meta interpreter to generate the derivation trees where we can detect primary and secondary inconsistencies. Figure 2 summarizes the inconsistency detection mechanisms used in different modes.

4.2 Management of Inconsistencies

Provisionally inserted objects become part of an object base although they violate one or more integrity constraints. For provisionally deleted objects we use a specific feature of Telos: each object has an additional component indicating its *belief time*. The belief time is assigned by the system at transaction time (insertion or deletion). The belief time is a time interval starting at the moment the object was inserted and ending at the moment it is deleted from the object base. Thus, deleted objects are not removed from the object base - instead the object becomes a historical object. Provisionally deleted objects are therefore still accessible. To access historical objects the user must explicitly state that a certain query should be evaluated using the state of the object base at a specific moment.

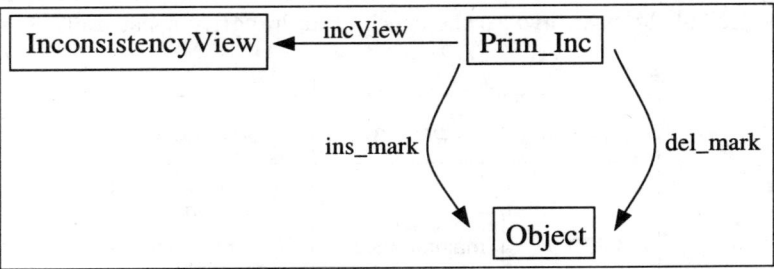

Fig. 3. Marking primary inconsistencies

To avoid a completely anarchical situation, all provisional objects are marked within the object base. The predefined (class) objects indicating a primary provisional object are shown in Fig. 3. The object InconsistencyView is a class containing all inconsistency views as instances. Every primary inconsistency, i.e. every validation of an integrity constraint resp. every derivation of the inconsistency view, is identified by a unique instance of Prim_Inc. The instance refers to the actual inconsistency view via the attribute incView and to the provisional inserted and deleted objects by the attributes ins_mark and del_mark, resp.

Secondary provisional objects are marked in a similar way. The class structure is given in Fig. 4. In addition to the inserted and deleted objects, we also mark the provisional objects which cause this secondary inconsistency (by attribute depends_on). If all these objects would loose their provisional status and become 'normal' objects, the secondary inconsistency would be repaired.

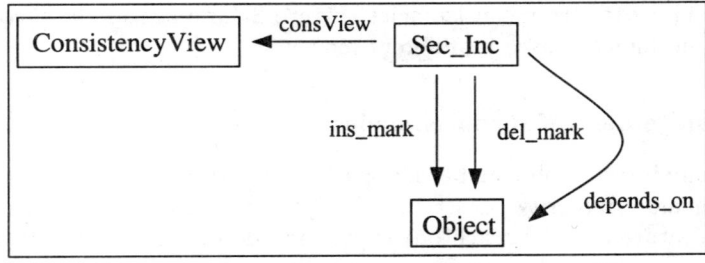

Fig. 4. Marking secondary inconsistencies

The management of inconsistencies in the eager detection mode does in addition include the detection of accidentally repaired inconsistencies. We therefore store for every provisional object a part of the derivation tree it takes part in as the justification for its provisional status. The justification tree consists of all literals (not their rules) on the path from the marked object to the root and the direct children of positive nodes. If one of these literals is no longer deducible from the object base, the derivation is destroyed and the justification for the provisional status is no longer valid and the object becomes a 'normal' member of the object base. This technique is similar to reason maintenance systems (RMS) [Doy79] which manage justifications of deduced information.

Everytime an object looses its provisional status we also check the secondary inconsistencies. For every secondary inconsistency we store all the provisional objects that cause this inconsistency. In case the provisional status of an object is annulled we just have to follow these dependencies, delete them and check if this was the last dependency. In this case we also annul all secondary inconsistencies of that integrity constraint because we found a derivation without any provisional objects.

Violation ?		Consequences
Incons.View	Cons.View	
strong	strong	At this combination a transaction must not introduce a primary or a secondary inconsistency. The integrity constraint must be satisfied by the object base.
strong	weak	At this combination a transaction must not introduce a primary inconsistency - but it can introduce a secondary inconsistency. The object base must satisfy or qualified satisfy the integrity constraint.
weak	strong	This combination allows primary inconsistencies to be introduced but no secondary. The object base must satisfy or violate the integrity constraint.
weak	weak	This combination does not make any restrictions concerning the violation of the integrity constraint: primary and secondary inconsistencies are both allowed. The object base may violate the integrity constraint.

Fig. 5. The four consistency levels

4.3 User Control

The user can control the tolerance of inconsistencies in different ways. We already mentioned the possibility to specify the detection mode of integrity constraints. A user can also declare if an integrity constraint may be violated or not. We use the term *strong* for a constraint that must not be violated and *weak* for one that may be violated. We even go one step further and allow the user to distinguish between primary and secondary inconsistencies. For each view we can specifiy the detection Mode and the possibility to violate it. The declaration of an inconsistency view as strong means that no primary inconsistencies of the corresponding integrity constraint may exist; for a consistency view this leads to the prohibition of secondary inconsistencies.

The introduction of primary and secondary inconsistencies implies a three valued status of an integrity constraint: *satisfaction* if no primary and secondary violations exist, *qualified satisfaction* if it is secondary violated but not primary, and *violation* if it is primary violated. Figure 5 summarizes the four different consistency levels we then can specify for an object base w.r.t. an integrity constraint.

5 Industrial Application: Supporting the PFR Analysis Method

The German consulting firm and software house USU applied our approach to support their requirements engineering methodology PFR (Analysis of Presence and Future Requirements) [Abe95] and employed the resulting tool in several commercial projects. In the first of these projects, we helped in the use of ConceptBase, in subsequent projects the USU analysts used the system directly. We first give an informal overview of the methodology, then describe the development of the meta meta model used for formalization, and finally give a few examples of defined analysis goals. More details on the experiences can be found in [NJJ+96].

PFR is mainly employed in the early phases of projects developing information systems supporting business processes. The method has three steps:

- In a two-day workshop, stakeholders agree on the scope of the analysis project: the current problems which should be solved and in correspondence to this, the domain structure and the analysis goals. The group also makes a rough analysis of the current business processes in terms of information exchange among organizational units, identifies weak spots and drafts a redesigned business process.
- The perspectives identified as critical to success are then captured in detail by interviews, workflow and document analysis. The acquisition process is accompanied by a *cross-perspective analysis* of the captured information for consistency, completeness, and local stakeholder agreement. The results of the comparisons guide subsequent interviews to clarify conflicts and complete the models.
- In a second workshop the goal is to draw together individual perspectives to achieve global *stakeholder agreement*. The step is accompanied and followed by the development of a comprehensive requirements document of typically several hundred pages.

USU's experience in applying this method to a large number of projects has shown that an analysis by hand based on the informal visual notation of the perspectives is time-consuming, haphazard, faulty, and often incomplete. A supporting tool should therefore

1. represent the information from all perspectives in a formal but natural way (which may be different from customer to customer or from project to project) such that they can be easily communicated to stakeholders,
2. represent perspectives even if they are violating the formal properties of the used notation or contradicting the contents of other perspectives, such that the analysis can take place in a separate step,
3. enable the comparison of diagrams represented according to different (semi-) formal notations, and maintain the detected conflicts during repair actions, since old conflicts may disappear and new problems may surface.

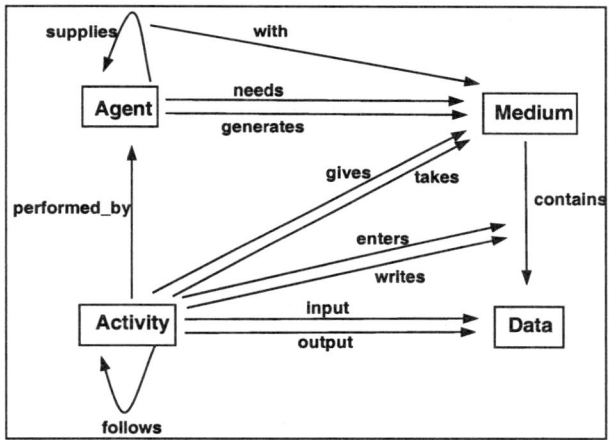

Fig. 6. Example: The PFR meta meta model

5.1 Designing the PFR Meta Meta Model

The first workshop leads to a problem-oriented meta meta model defining shared domain terms and analysis goals. Figure 6 presents a model that is used as a default in PFR analysis projects. It is modified to fit to the actual problems and analysis goals if necessary. The current status of the processes is analysed from three perspectives: the *information-exchange* within the first workshop, the *activity-sequence* and the *document-structure* within the detailed acquisition process in the second step.

The meta meta model in Fig. 6 explains the basic concepts of these perspectives and their interrelationships. The information-exchange perspective is represented by an **Agent** who **supplies** other agents **with** a **Medium**, the activity-sequence by the **Activity** that is **performed_by** an **Agent** and produces **Data** as input or output, and the document-structure by a **Medium** that **contains Data**.

The meta meta model contains a precise description of the terms that are employed during a PFR analysis. Its structure focuses on the expected problems in the specific domain. The distinction between **Medium** and **Data**, for example, is essential to talk about the unnecessary exchange of documents, i.e. documents which contain data that is not used by any activity.

Figure 7 presents a part of the PFR environment as an example of the two top levels of our architecture. The top level module contains the PFR meta meta model together with an analysis goal stating that "Every exchanged Medium must contain Data". This goal formalizes the basic requirement that an efficient business process should not include exchange of documents that do not contain useful data. The formal definition of this goal will be given in Sect. 5.2.

Below the PFR meta meta model reside the notation meta models to formulate the information-exchange and the document-structure perspectives. The resolution module connected to both notation modules contains transformed versions of the applicable analysis goal. It specifies an integrity constraint on both perspective notations. The exact formal definition of this integrity constraint will also be given in Sect. 5.2.

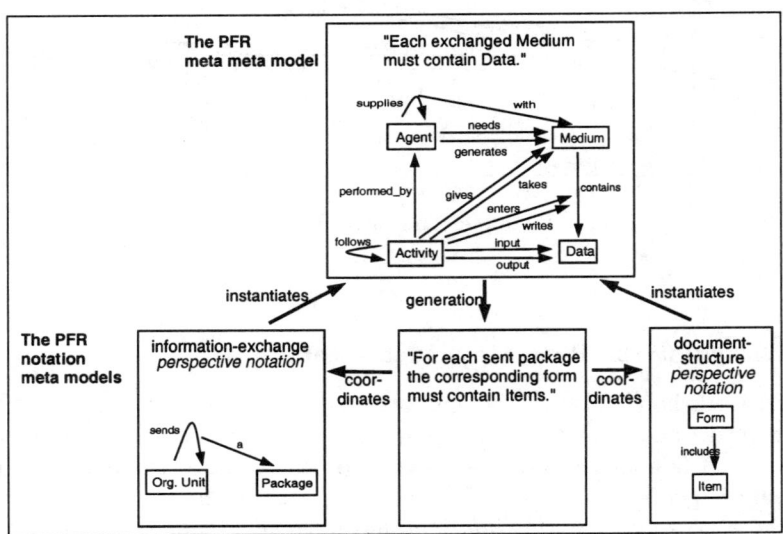

Fig. 7. Example: The PFR resolution architecture

5.2 Analysis Goals for PFR Perspectives

Perspectives are related semantically by analysis goals which define consistency of knowledge *within* an individual perspective as well as the consistency *between* different perspectives. The USU application projects identified more than 70 analysis goals describing the consistency of the captured information, which could largely be reused across all application projects.

About a dozen additional analysis goals served to analyse the properties of the finally reconciled business process model. This includes goals like "Show the trace of form X305.", to detect the reason for the long handling time of the form X305. All together, USU produced over 80 analysis goals.

The development of these goals was begun while developing the meta meta model structure and continued throughout the first two application projects. For short analysis goals it was relatively easy to understand their meaning by looking at their specification. But after defining some more complex ones we observed that an additional textual description is necessary. USU therefore set up a 'use handbook' containing the goal specification, the technical process of calling it using ConceptBase, a textual explanation of the indended meaning, and a set of possible interpretations of the violations. This was quite helpful in follow-up projects where also untrained consultants were able to analyse the perspectives just by following the instructions in this handbook.

In the following, we present examples of analysis goals together with interpretations of their violations. The examples are organized according to the principle character of the goal, namely the analysis of a single perspective, the analysis of interrelationships among perspectives, and the analysis of the whole business process. In case one and three we specify the analysis goals in natural language, but we will use the second case to give an example of a meta formula and to illustrate the partial evaluation.

Analysis of a single perspective. Consider the activity sequence perspective. USU defined an analysis goal capturing the constraint that data can only be used by an activity (indicated by the `input` relation) after it was created (via the `output` relation). The analysis goal specifies that data must be produced before it is used as as `input`.

Violations of that goal can be interpreted as

1. a mistake, if the interviewed employee indicated a wrong sequence.
2. a mistake of the interviewer who modeled an `output` relation to `Data` instead of an `input` or a wrong direction of the `follows` link.
3. a conflict, where two `data` objects are used as homonyms.
4. a conflict between the activity sequences of two agents.
5. a not expressible phenomenon, where the conflicting second `output` is a correction of the `data` resulting from the initial `output`

Analysis of interrelationships among multiple perspectives. The following meta formula is the formalization of the analysis goal given in natural language in Fig. 7. In this formula we denote with #o the object identifier of an object with name o. The expression $o!a$ refers to the object identifier of the attribute a of object o.

$$(m' \text{ in } \#Medium) \wedge (d' \text{ in } \#Data) \wedge (s' \text{ in } \#Agent!supplies) \wedge$$
$$(e' \text{ in } \#Medium!contains) \wedge (w' \text{ in } \#Agent!supplies!with) \wedge (med \text{ in } m') \wedge$$
$$(supp \text{ in } s') \wedge (with \text{ in } w') \wedge (with \text{ from } supp) \wedge (with \text{ to } med)$$
$$\Rightarrow \exists \, data, cont \, (data \text{ in } d') \wedge (cont \text{ in } e')$$
$$\wedge (cont \text{ from } med) \wedge (cont \text{ to } data)$$

In the transformation step the variables m', d', s', e', w' are replaced by objects of the two notations for the information-exchange and document-structure perspectives. For example, we can evaluate the literal $(m' \text{ in } \#Medium)$ to $(\#Package \text{ in } \#Medium)$. This solution for variable m' leads to the substitution of literal $(med \text{ in } m')$ by $(med \text{ in } \#Package)$. Performing all such substitutions as well as the elimination of $TRUE$ whenever possible, leads to the following integrity constraint:

$$(med \text{ in } \#Package) \wedge (supp \text{ in } \#OrgUnit!sends) \wedge$$
$$(with \text{ in } \#OrgUnit!sends!a) \wedge (with \text{ from } supp) \wedge (with \text{ to } med)$$
$$\Rightarrow \exists \, data, cont \, (data \text{ in } \#Item) \wedge (cont \text{ in } \#Form!includes)$$
$$\wedge (cont \text{ from } med) \wedge (cont \text{ to } data)$$

The violations of that goal can be interpreted as follows:

1. a mistake: the modeller forgot to model the items of that form.
2. a synonym: the authors of the two or more perspectives used different names for the same form.

Business process analysis. Much of the Business Process Re-engineering literature contends that the document flow within a company offers potential for optimization. USU therefor defined an analysis goal which searches within the media flow between agents for agents who get a document that contains only data that is already supplied to them by other media.

The violations can be interpreted as follows:

1. The supply of the deduced medium is unnecessary and the whole data is also available from other media. Either this is an intended situation and the agent should choose among the different media, or it is not intended and the delivery of that medium is subject to further optimization studies.
2. The agent performs a comparison check of the same data located on different media.
3. The agent must perform the same activity on the same data carried by different media. So far, this fact cannot be expressed by our M2-model.

5.3 Lessons Learned

USU's experiences show that conceptual metamodeling technology can provide a valuable complement to informal teamwork methods of requirements engineering. In particular, formal representations and cross-perspective analysis can help identify a wide variety of conflicts and, perhaps more important, monitor them continuously during the RE process.

However, it is equally clear thet these statements must be qualified. The definition of fixed relationships between meta models is not robust enough to handle the variations in form of modeling notations, how the notations are used by different consultants and companies, or the bottlenecks in the modeling process.

Meta meta models do not only provide this robustness to a large degree, but they also allow the analyst to focus meta modeling on domain-oriented as well as on notation-oriented aspects.

A major gap in the approach, both from the technological perspective and from the methodological perspective, is that conflict analysis is only driven from the top, the shared meta meta model. The complementary grounding of negotiations, shared scenarios of reality rather than shared abstractions, was often observed in application projects but could not yet be directly captured in the ConceptBase models. We hypothesize that scenarios may be a way to go beyond conflict identification and monitoring towards active support for conflict resolution [WPJH98]. The basic architecture includes this level but significant research will be required to work out its formal and technical interaction with the approach presented here.

6 Related Work

Separation mechanisms have been developed for different purposes in requirements engineering and for modeling environments. The *Requirements Apprentice* [RW91] uses a context mechanism called *Cliché* to represent predefined domain descriptions. Since different domain descriptions may be inconsistent to each other, this separation is necessary. They are organised in a specialization hierarchy and can be used as a starting point in requirements engineering. ARIES [JH91] employs a similar concept called *Folder*. A Folder captures partial domain information and is used for the development of a requirements specification. The engineer creates a new Folder and maybe a relationship to one of the predefined domain descriptions. He then extends this description according to the actual problem domain.

The modularization presented in this paper is compatible with module concepts developed for software architecture languages (as, e.g., [Nag90]). A module is a collection of information (conceptual models and program statements, resp.) and provides information hiding by encapsulating its content. The communication is supported by import relationships between modules which extend the set of accessible information or resources. To control the communication the contents is divided into a public and a private part. To handle a large number of modules they provide the local definition of modules as a structuring principle. We adapted this for M-Telos and exactly formalized the principles of usability specified for software module hierarchies for deductive databases.

Borgida [Bor85] developed a method for managing exceptions to constraints in object-oriented databases. He works with a special kind of integrity constraints: they only affect a specific class and a specific attribute of that class. If a constraint is violated an object is created that documents this violation. The user then must give an excuse for that violation. If the reason of the violation should become a permanent exception it can be specified as an exceptional case. To avoid a permanent violation of the constraint it will be rewritten such that the exception does no longer violate the constraint, but the constraint is still able to detect all other violations. In contrast to our approach the rewriting keeps the constraint applicable, i.e. the object base must still satisfy it. But the rewriting step leads to a high management overhead and is possible only for very simple constraints. The pressure to specify an excuse for a constraint violation is an interesting feature that might be useful in some stages of a cooperation activity like requirements engineering.

Balzer [Bal91] developed a declarative approach for tolerating and managing inconsistencies in relational databases. He uses special relations called Pollution Marker to mark inconsistent information. For each integrity constraint a specific Pollution Marker relation is generated. The integrity constraint is rewritten as a deductive rule which automatically fills this relation. The rules correspond to the inconsistency and consistency views we employed for our approach. Inconsistent information is marked only indirectly because it still resides in the base relations from which the Pollution Marker is deduced. We directly marked the inconsistent information in the object base.

Tolerating inconsistencies is accepted as fundamental by the ViewPoint approach [NKF94,EN96]. They argue that consistency checking may be appropriate only at specific stages in the development process. The detection of an inconsistency may not require immediate resolution. Their process model therefore explicitly distinguishes between rule application, returning that a rule holds or not, and the inconsistency handling activity. Rules are always bilateral: they reside in a source ViewPoint and make a statement about the contents of another not yet defined ViewPoint. In our approach the participants define for which perspectives a cross-perspectives analysis will be performed by defining resolution modules and their relations (on the bottom level). In contrast to the ViewPoint approach we can analyse an arbitrary number of perspectives in one shot. They only perform on-demand consistency checking and don't offer the possibility to monitor inconsistencies using an eager check mode.

Existing perspective resolution approaches are limited to a fixed set of analysis goals and in many cases concentrate on syntactical relationships. Leite and Freeman employ in [LF91] a purely syntactic perspective comparison. The contents of perspectives are represented by a set of production rules. They compare the rule bases of two perspectives by identifying the most probable rule pairs as well as the rules with no pairs. On basis of the evaluated mapping they detect wrong, missing and inconsistent information. They do not take information about the domain into account. The analysis rules are predefined in the Static Analyzer and cannot be customized by the user.

The viewpoint analysis of Kotonya and Sommerville [KS96] comprises two stages: the correctness and completeness of the viewpoint documentation and the conflict analysis. The completeness of a viewpoint documentation is checked according to the predefined viewpoint structure. This structure defines the required components and attributes of a viewpoint. A problem-oriented definition of the structure by the user is not supported. The conflict analysis is performed by the requirements engineer with the help of the provided toolset.

7 Conclusions and Further Work

For some years software specification and design methods have been formalized by a transformation to well-understood formalisms like logic, graph grammars or algebraic specifications to enable a computer-based analysis. It is characteristic of these approaches to assign the methods a fixed semantics the user must accept when using such a system. Beyond that it is assumed that the various partial conceptual models form views on a consistent entire model.

In some other parts of practice just the opposite trend can be observed. Informal teamwork methods leave the details of notations to a great extent to the user and consciously employ conflicts and inconsistencies as an analysis tool, instead of avoiding them. These methods (examples are JAD, SSM and PFR) enjoy increasing popularity exactly because they give negotiation and mutual learning priority over a fixed axiomatization or restriction by reference models. To enhance analysis quality and efficiency formalization and computer support is also desireable for these methods, but they must offer features different to the approaches mentioned above.

In this paper we developed a comprehensive solution for a computer-based support of team- and goal-oriented analysis methods. We extended the formal conceptual modeling language Telos by a separation mechanism called modules, which enables the representation of multiple, conflicting perspectives.

We developed the model-based perspective resolution where the knowledge about the structure of the domain and the analysis goals are specified in a meta meta model. The use of M-Telos as representation formalism keeps even the meta meta model customizable. By declaring the notations as partial views on this model we define a connection between the semantic domain description and the syntactic perspective schemata. We used this connection for the transformation of domain-oriented analysis goals into notation-based integrity constraints. Since in many cases the simple evaluation of cross-perspective relationships is not enough we developed a technique for continuous maintenance of inconsistency information based on deductive database technology.

Our approach is completely implemented in ConceptBase [JGJ+95], a deductive object base manager which uses M-Telos as object model. Based on the USU experiences, we are currently adapting the approach for the analysis of cooperative engineering processes within and across companies working in the chemical and medical technology sectors [JJL98,JK98].

The four components of our approach can also be used in stand-alone mode together with existing modeling environments or viewpoint mechanisms. The simple axiomatization of the module concept enables its adaption to existing, even non-Telos repositories (as, e.g., the Microsoft Repository [BHS+97]) to represent multiple development perspectives. The combination of the goal-oriented inconsistency management concept with notation-centered CASE tools lead to a more guided modeling process with customizable, domain-oriented integrity constraints. This also works for distributed environments like the ViewPoints approach. Since the constraints are checked locally as before, the central goal definition implies no decrease of system performance.

Data warehousing [Inm96] is concerned with the extraction, integration, aggregation and customization of distributed, heterogenuous operational data. Building, using and managing a data warehouse requires the features we developed in this paper. Data come from multiple sources and may be inconsistent with each other, thus a separation mechanism is needed. To be able to interpret the data right, the existence of conflicts must be monitored and the infected data must be marked.

Acknowledgment: This work was supported in part by the Deutsche Forschungsgemeinschaft under Collaborative Research Center IMPROVE, by the German Ministry of Research under its project AdCo, and by the European Commission under ESPRIT Long Term Research contracts CREWS and DWQ. We would like to thank Manfred A. Jeusfeld and Martin Staudt for their contributions to this work. Thanks are also due to our students Lutz Bauer, Farshad Lashgari, Thomas List, Rene Soiron and Christoph Quix for implementing the system.

References

[Abe95]   P. Abel. Description of the USU-PFR analysis method. Technical report, USU GmbH, Möglingen, 1995.

[ACM95]   S. Abitebuol, S. Cluet, and T. Milo. A database interface for file updates. In M.J. Carey and D.A. Schneider, editors, *Proc. of the 1995 ACM SIGMOD Intl. Conf. on Management of Data*, pages 386–397, May 1995.

[Aug91]   J.H. August. *Joint Application Design: The Group Session Approach to System Design*. Yourdon Press, Englewood Cliffs, 1991.

[Bal91]   R. Balzer. Tolerating inconsistency. In *Proc. of the 13th Intl. Conf. on Software Engineering (ICSE-13)*, pages 158–165, Austin, Texas, 1991.

[Bau96]   L. Bauer. Inconsistency managemnent in multi-user modeling environments. Master's thesis, RWTH Aachen (in German), 1996.

[BCJ+94]   A. Brogi, S. Contiero, M. Jeusfeld, R. Soiron, J. Lloyd, and M. Milkowska. Applications of Gödel. In K.R. Apt, M. Jarke, W. Nutt, E. Pedreschi, and D. de Schreye, editors, *Gödel and Parallel Prolog, ESPRIT BRA 6810 (Compulog 2), Deliv. 6.2.1*, August 1994.

[BFG+93]   M. Broy, C. Facchi, F. Grosu, R. Hettler, H. Hu"smann, D. Nazareth, F. Regensburger, O. Slotosch, and K. Stolen. The requirement and design specification language spectrum: An informal introduction. Technical Report TUM-I9311+I9312, Technische Universität München, 1993.

[BHS+97]   P.A. Bernstein, K. Harry, P. Sanders, D. Shutt, and J. Zander. The microsoft repository. In *Proc. of the 23rd Intl. Conf. on Very Large Data Bases (VLDB)*, pages 3–12, Athens, Greece, August 1997.

[Bor85] A. Borgida. Language features for flexible handling of exceptions in information systems. *ACM Trans. on Database Systems*, 10(4):565–603, December 1985.

[Che89] P.B. Checkland. Soft systems methodology. In J. Rosenhead, editor, *Rational Analysis for a Problematic World*, pages 71–100. John Wiley & Sons, Chichester, 1989.

[Cra94] A. Crawford. *Advancing Business Concepts in a JAD Workshop Setting*. Prentice-Hall, Englewood Cliffs, NJ, 1994.

[DCC92] E. Downs, P. Clare, and I. Coe. *Structured Systems Analysis and Design Method*. Prentice-Hall, 2 edition, 1992.

[Doy79] J. Doyle. A truth maintenance system. *Artificial Intelligence*, 12:231–272, 1979.

[Eas96] S.M. Easterbrook. Learning from inconsistency. In *Proc. of the 8th Intl. Workshop on Software Specification and Design*, Schloss Velen, Germany, March 1996.

[EN94] R. Elmasri and S.B. Navathe. *Fundamentals of Database Systems*. The Benjamin/Cummings Publishing Company, 1994.

[EN96] S.M. Easterbrook and B.A. Nuseibeh. Using viewpoints for inconsistency management. *Software Engineering Journal*, 11(1):31–43, January 1996.

[FF91] M.S. Feather and S. Fickas. Coping with requirements freedoms. In R. Balzer and J. Mylopoulos, editors, *Proc. of the Intl. Workshop on the Development of Intelligent Information Systems*, pages 42–46, Niagara-on-the-Lake, Ontario, Canada, April 1991.

[FP93] P. Fraternali and S. Paraboschi. A review of repairing techniques for integrity maintenance. In *Proc. of the 1st Intl. Workshop on Rules in Database Systems*, pages 333–346, Edinburgh, Scottland, 1993.

[FS97] M. Fowler and K. Scott. *UML Destilled: Applying the Standard Object Modeling Language*. Addison-Wesley, 1997.

[GH91] D. Gabbay and A. Hunter. Making inconsistency respectable: A logical framework for inconsistency in reasoning, part i - a position paper. In Ph. Jorrand and J. Kelemann, editors, *Int. Workshop on Fundamentals of Artificial Intelligence Research (FAIR'91)*, pages 19–32. LNAI 535, Springer-Verlag, 1991.

[GJ87] C.F. Gibson and B.B. Jackson. *The Information Imperative: Managing the Impact of Information Technology on Business and People*. Lexington Books D.C. Heath, Lexington, Mass., 1987.

[GL90] U. Griefahn and S. Lüttringhaus. Top-down integrity constraint checking for deductive databases. In D. H. Warren and P. Szerdei, editors, *Proceedings of the 7th International Conference on Logic Programming (ICLP '90)*, pages 130–146. MIT Press, June 1990.

[Gre84] S. Greenspan. *Requirements Modeling: A Knowledge Representation Approach to Requirements Definition*. PhD thesis, Department of Computer Science, University of Toronto, 1984.

[Hus94] H. Hussmann. Formal foundations of ssadm: An approach integrating the formal and pragmatic world of requirement engineering. Habilitationsschrift, Technische Universität München, June 1994.

[IDS96] IDS Prof. Scheer GmbH, Saarbrücken. *ARIS-Toolset Manual V3.1*, 1996.

[Inm96] W.H. Inmon. *Building the Data Warehouse*. QED Publishing Group, 1996.

[Jeu92] M.A. Jeusfeld. *Update Control in Deductive Object Bases*. PhD thesis, University of Passau (in German), 1992.

[JGJ+95] M. Jarke, R. Gallersdörfer, M.A. Jeusfeld, M. Staudt, and S. Eherer. ConceptBase - a deductive object base for meta data management. *Journal of Intelligent Information Systems, Special Issue on Deductive and Object-Oriented Databases*, 4(2):167–192, March 1995.

[JH91] W.L. Johnson and D.R. Harris. Sharing and reuse of requirements knowledge. In *Proc. of the 6th Annual KBSE Conference, Syracuse*, September 1991.

[JJL98] M. Jarke, M.A. Jeusfeld, and T. List. Goal-oriented information flow management in chemical engineering processes. In M. Nagl and W. Marquardt, editors, *Integration von Entwicklungssystemen in Ingenieuranwendungen*. Springer-Verlag, to appear (in German), 1998.

[JK98] M. Jarke and S. Kethers. Experiences in initiating a regional engineering cooperation network: Problem analysis and modeling techniques. Wirtschaftsinformatik, to appear (in German), 1998.

[KS88] G.E. Kaiser and R.W. Schwanke. Living with inconsistency in large systems. In *Proc. of the Intl. Workshop on Software Version and Configuration Control*, pages 98–118, Stuttgart, January 1988. B.G. Teubner.

[KS96] G. Kotonya and I. Sommerville. Requirements engineering with viewpoints. *Software Engineering Journal, Special Issue on Viewpoints in Requirements Engineering*, 11(1):5–18, January 1996.

[Lef93] M. Lefering. An incremental integration tool between requirements engineering and programming-in-the-large. In *Proc. of the 1st Intl. Symposium on Requirements Engineering*, pages 82–89, 1993.

[Lei90] P. Leikauf. *Consistency Ensurance by Management of Inconsistencies*. Diss. ETH Nr. 9208. ETH Zürich, (in German), 1990.

[LF91] J.C.S.P. Leite and P.A. Freeman. Requirements validation through viewpoint resolution. *IEEE Transactions on Software Engineering*, 17(12):1253–1269, December 1991.

[LT84] J.W. Lloyd and R.W. Topor. Making Prolog more expressive. *Journal of Logic Programming*, 1(3):225–240, 1984.

[MBJK90] J. Mylopoulos, A. Borgida, M. Jarke, and M. Koubarakis. Telos: Representing knowledge about information systems. *ACM Transactions on Information Systems*, 8(4):325–362, October 1990.

[Min87] J. Minker, editor. *Foundations of Deductive Databases and Logic Programming*. Morgan Kaufmann Publishers, Inc., 1987.

[ML91] G. Moerkotte and P.C. Lockemann. Reactive consistency control in deductive databases. *ACM Transactions on Database Systems*, 16(4):670–702, 1991.

[Nag90] M. Nagl. *Programming-In-The-Large*. Springer-Verlag, 1990.

[Nis96] H.W. Nissen. *Separation and Resolution of Multiple Perspectives in Conceptual Modeling*. PhD thesis, RWTH Aachen, Germany, (in German), 1996.

[NJ97] H.W. Nissen and M. Jarke. Goal-oriented inconsistency management in customizable modeling environments. Technical Report 97-12, RWTH Aachen, Aachener Informatik-Berichte, 1997.

[NJJ+96] H.W. Nissen, M.A. Jeusfeld, M. Jarke, G.V. Zemanek, and H. Huber. Managing multiple requirements perspectives with metamodels. *IEEE Software*, pages 37–47, March 1996.

[NKF94] B. Nuseibeh, J. Kramer, and A. Finkelstein. A framework for expressing the relationships between multiple views in requirements specification. *IEEE Transactions on Software Engineering*, 20(10):760–773, October 1994.

[Poh94]   K. Pohl. The three dimensions of requirements engineering: A framework and its application. *Information Systems*, 19(3), 1994.
[RF94]   W. Robinson and S. Fickas. Supporting multi-perspective requirements engineering. In *Proc. of the IEEE Intl. Conf. on Requirements Engineering*, pages 206–215, Los Alamitos, California, April 1994. IEEE Computer Society Press.
[RW91]   H.B. Reubenstein and R.C. Waters. The requirements apprentice: Automated assistance for requirements acquisition. *IEEE Transactions on Software Engineering*, 17(3):226–240, March 1991.
[SAP97]   SAP. Business blueprint for success. Technical Report SAp Info D&T No. 53, SAP AG, March 1997.
[Sim86]   E. Simon. *Conception et Realisation d'un sous Systeme d'Integrite dans un SGBD Relationnel*. PhD thesis, Universite de Paris VI, 1986.
[SJ96]   M. Staudt and M. Jarke. Incremental maintenance of externally materialized views. In *Proc. of the 22nd Intl. Conf. on Very Large Data Bases (VLDB'96)*, pages 75–86, Bombay, India, September 1996.
[WPJH98]   K. Weidenhaupt, K. Pohl, M. Jarke, and P. Haumer. Scenarios in systems development: Current practice. *IEEE Software*, pages 34–45, March 1998.
[You89]   E. Yourdon. *Modern Structured Analysis*. Prentice Hall, Englewood Cliffs, New Jersey, 1989.

Author Index

Astesiano, Egidio, 95

Berzins, Valdis, 121
Bjørner, Dines, 1
Broy, Manfred, 43

Colón, Michael A., 273

Dũng, Đỗ Tiến, 133

Finkbeiner, Bernd, 273

George, Chris, 133
Ghezzi, Carlo, 155
Gruner, Stefan, 235

Heisel, Maritta, 179
Huber, Franz, 43

Jarke, Matthias, 331
Jähnichen, Stefan, 179

Kamsties, Erik, 203

Luckham, David C., 293

Luqi, 257

Manna, Zohar, 273
Meldal, Sigurd, 293

Nagl, Manfred, 235
Nissen, Hans W., 331

Paech, Barbara, 43

Reed, Joy, 223
Reggio, Gianna, 95
Rombach, H. Dieter, 203
Rumpe, Bernhard, 43

Schürr, Andy, 235
Sipma, Henny B., 273
Spies, Katharina, 43

Uribe, Tomás E., 273

Vigna, Giovanni, 155

Wieringa, Roel, 69

Lecture Notes in Computer Science

For information about Vols. 1–1447

please contact your bookseller or Springer-Verlag

Vol. 1448: M. Farach-Colton (Ed.), Combinatorial Pattern Matching. Proceedings, 1998. VIII, 251 pages. 1998.

Vol. 1449: W.-L. Hsu, M.-Y. Kao (Eds.), Computing and Combinatorics. Proceedings, 1998. XII, 372 pages. 1998.

Vol. 1450: L. Brim, F. Gruska, J. Zlatuška (Eds.), Mathematical Foundations of Computer Science 1998. Proceedings, 1998. XVII, 846 pages. 1998.

Vol. 1451: A. Amin, D. Dori, P. Pudil, H. Freeman (Eds.), Advances in Pattern Recognition. Proceedings, 1998. XXI, 1048 pages. 1998.

Vol. 1452: B.P. Goettl, H.M. Halff, C.L. Redfield, V.J. Shute (Eds.), Intelligent Tutoring Systems. Proceedings, 1998. XIX, 629 pages. 1998.

Vol. 1453: M.-L. Mugnier, M. Chein (Eds.), Conceptual Structures: Theory, Tools and Applications. Proceedings, 1998. XIII, 439 pages. (Subseries LNAI).

Vol. 1454: I. Smith (Ed.), Artificial Intelligence in Structural Engineering. XI, 497 pages. 1998. (Subseries LNAI).

Vol. 1455: A. Hunter, S. Parsons (Eds.), Applications of Uncertainty Formalisms. VIII, 474 pages. 1998. (Subseries LNAI).

Vol. 1456: A. Drogoul, M. Tambe, T. Fukuda (Eds.), Collective Robotics. Proceedings, 1998. VII, 161 pages. 1998. (Subseries LNAI).

Vol. 1457: A. Ferreira, J. Rolim, H. Simon, S.-H. Teng (Eds.), Solving Irregularly Structured Problems in Prallel. Proceedings, 1998. X, 408 pages. 1998.

Vol. 1458: V.O. Mittal, H.A. Yanco, J. Aronis, R-. Simpson (Eds.), Assistive Technology in Artificial Intelligence. X, 273 pages. 1998. (Subseries LNAI).

Vol. 1459: D.G. Feitelson, L. Rudolph (Eds.), Job Scheduling Strategies for Parallel Processing. Proceedings, 1998. VII, 257 pages. 1998.

Vol. 1460: G. Quirchmayr, E. Schweighofer, T.J.M. Bench-Capon (Eds.), Database and Expert Systems Applications. Proceedings, 1998. XVI, 905 pages. 1998.

Vol. 1461: G. Bilardi, G.F. Italiano, A. Pietracaprina, G. Pucci (Eds.), Algorithms – ESA'98. Proceedings, 1998. XII, 516 pages. 1998.

Vol. 1462: H. Krawczyk (Ed.), Advances in Cryptology - CRYPTO '98. Proceedings, 1998. XII, 519 pages. 1998.

Vol. 1463: N.E. Fuchs (Ed.), Logic Program Synthesis and Transformation. Proceedings, 1997. X, 343 pages. 1998.

Vol. 1464: H.H.S. Ip, A.W.M. Smeulders (Eds.), Multimedia Information Analysis and Retrieval. Proceedings, 1998. VIII, 264 pages. 1998.

Vol. 1465: R. Hirschfeld (Ed.), Financial Cryptography. Proceedings, 1998. VIII, 311 pages. 1998.

Vol. 1466: D. Sangiorgi, R. de Simone (Eds.), CONCUR'98: Concurrency Theory. Proceedings, 1998. XI, 657 pages. 1998.

Vol. 1467: C. Clack, K. Hammond, T. Davie (Eds.), Implementation of Functional Languages. Proceedings, 1997. X, 375 pages. 1998.

Vol. 1468: P. Husbands, J.-A. Meyer (Eds.), Evolutionary Robotics. Proceedings, 1998. VIII, 247 pages. 1998.

Vol. 1469: R. Puigjaner, N.N. Savino, B. Serra (Eds.), Computer Performance Evaluation. Proceedings, 1998. XIII, 376 pages. 1998.

Vol. 1470: D. Pritchard, J. Reeve (Eds.), Euro-Par'98: Parallel Processing. Proceedings, 1998. XXII, 1157 pages. 1998.

Vol. 1471: J. Dix, L. Moniz Pereira, T.C. Przymusinski (Eds.), Logic Programming and Knowledge Representation. Proceedings, 1997. IX, 246 pages. 1998. (Subseries LNAI).

Vol. 1472: B. Freitag, H. Decker, M. Kifer, A. Voronkov (Eds.), Transactions and Change in Logic Databases. Proceedings, 1996, 1997. X, 396 pages. 1998.

Vol. 1473: X. Leroy, A. Ohori (Eds.), Types in Compilation. Proceedings, 1998. VIII, 299 pages. 1998.

Vol. 1474: F. Mueller, A. Bestavros (Eds.), Languages, Compilers, and Tools for Embedded Systems. Proceedings, 1998. XIV, 261 pages. 1998.

Vol. 1475: W. Litwin, T. Morzy, G. Vossen (Eds.), Advances in Databases and Information Systems. Proceedings, 1998. XIV, 369 pages. 1998.

Vol. 1476: J. Calmet, J. Plaza (Eds.), Artificial Intelligence and Symbolic Computation. Proceedings, 1998. XI, 309 pages. 1998. (Subseries LNAI).

Vol. 1477: K. Rothermel, F. Hohl (Eds.), Mobile Agents. Proceedings, 1998. VIII, 285 pages. 1998.

Vol. 1478: M. Sipper, D. Mange, A. Pérez-Uribe (Eds.), Evolvable Systems: From Biology to Hardware. Proceedings, 1998. IX, 382 pages. 1998.

Vol. 1479: J. Grundy, M. Newey (Eds.), Theorem Proving in Higher Order Logics. Proceedings, 1998. VIII, 497 pages. 1998.

Vol. 1480: F. Giunchiglia (Ed.), Artificial Intelligence: Methodology, Systems, and Applications. Proceedings, 1998. IX, 502 pages. 1998. (Subseries LNAI).

Vol. 1481: E.V. Munson, C. Nicholas, D. Wood (Eds.), Principles of Digital Document Processing. Proceedings, 1998. VII, 152 pages. 1998.

Vol. 1482: R.W. Hartenstein, A. Keevallik (Eds.), Field-Programmable Logic and Applications. Proceedings, 1998. XI, 533 pages. 1998.

Vol. 1483: T. Plagemann, V. Goebel (Eds.), Interactive Distributed Multimedia Systems and Telecommunication Services. Proceedings, 1998. XV, 326 pages. 1998.

Vol. 1484: H. Coelho (Ed.), Progress in Artificial Intelligence – IBERAMIA 98. Proceedings, 1998. XIII, 421 pages. 1998. (Subseries LNAI).

Vol. 1485: J.-J. Quisquater, Y. Deswarte, C. Meadows, D. Gollmann (Eds.), Computer Security – ESORICS 98. Proceedings, 1998. X, 377 pages. 1998.

Vol. 1486: A.P. Ravn, H. Rischel (Eds.), Formal Techniques in Real-Time and Fault-Tolerant Systems. Proceedings, 1998. VIII, 339 pages. 1998.

Vol. 1487: V. Gruhn (Ed.), Software Process Technology. Proceedings, 1998. VIII, 157 pages. 1998.

Vol. 1488: B. Smyth, P. Cunningham (Eds.), Advances in Case-Based Reasoning. Proceedings, 1998. XI, 482 pages. 1998. (Subseries LNAI).

Vol. 1489: J. Dix, L. Fariñas del Cerro, U. Furbach (Eds.), Logics in Artificial Intelligence. Proceedings, 1998. X, 391 pages. 1998. (Subseries LNAI).

Vol. 1490: C. Palamidessi, H. Glaser, K. Meinke (Eds.), Principles of Declarative Programming. Proceedings, 1998. XI, 497 pages. 1998.

Vol. 1491: W. Reisig, G. Rozenberg (Eds.), Lectures on Petri Nets I: Basic Models. XII, 683 pages. 1998.

Vol. 1492: W. Reisig, G. Rozenberg (Eds.), Lectures on Petri Nets II: Applications. XII, 479 pages. 1998.

Vol. 1493: J.P. Bowen, A. Fett, M.G. Hinchey (Eds.), ZUM '98: The Z Formal Specification Notation. Proceedings, 1998. XV, 417 pages. 1998.

Vol. 1494: G. Rozenberg, F. Vaandrager (Eds.), Lectures on Embedded Systems. Proceedings, 1996. VIII, 423 pages. 1998.

Vol. 1495: T. Andreasen, H. Christiansen, H.L. Larsen (Eds.), Flexible Query Answering Systems. IX, 393 pages. 1998. (Subseries LNAI).

Vol. 1496: W.M. Wells, A. Colchester, S. Delp (Eds.), Medical Image Computing and Computer-Assisted Intervention – MICCAI'98. Proceedings, 1998. XXII, 1256 pages. 1998.

Vol. 1497: V. Alexandrov, J. Dongarra (Eds.), Recent Advances in Parallel Virtual Machine and Message Passing Interface. Proceedings, 1998. XII, 412 pages. 1998.

Vol. 1498: A.E. Eiben, T. Bäck, M. Schoenauer, H.-P. Schwefel (Eds.), Parallel Problem Solving from Nature – PPSN V. Proceedings, 1998. XXIII, 1041 pages. 1998.

Vol. 1499: S. Kutten (Ed.), Distributed Computing. Proceedings, 1998. XII, 419 pages. 1998.

Vol. 1501: M.M. Richter, C.H. Smith, R. Wiehagen, T. Zeugmann (Eds.), Algorithmic Learning Theory. Proceedings, 1998. XI, 439 pages. 1998. (Subseries LNAI).

Vol. 1502: G. Antoniou, J. Slaney (Eds.), Advanced Topics in Artificial Intelligence. Proceedings, 1998. XI, 333 pages. 1998. (Subseries LNAI).

Vol. 1503: G. Levi (Ed.), Static Analysis. Proceedings, 1998. IX, 383 pages. 1998.

Vol. 1504: O. Herzog, A. Günter (Eds.), KI-98: Advances in Artificial Intelligence. Proceedings, 1998. XI, 355 pages. 1998. (Subseries LNAI).

Vol. 1506: R. Koch, L. Van Gool (Eds.), 3D Structure from Multiple Images of Large-Scale Environments. Proceedings, 1998. VIII, 347 pages. 1998.

Vol. 1507: T.W. Ling, S. Ram, M.L. Lee (Eds.), Conceptual Modeling – ER '98. Proceedings, 1998. XVI, 482 pages. 1998.

Vol. 1508: S. Jajodia, M.T. Özsu, A. Dogac (Eds.), Advances in Multimedia Information Systems. Proceedings, 1998. VIII, 207 pages. 1998.

Vol. 1510: J.M. Zytkow, M. Quafafou (Eds.), Principles of Data Mining and Knowledge Discovery. Proceedings, 1998. XI, 482 pages. 1998. (Subseries LNAI).

Vol. 1511: D. O'Hallaron (Ed.), Languages, Compilers, and Run-Time Systems for Scalable Computers. Proceedings, 1998. IX, 412 pages. 1998.

Vol. 1512: E. Giménez, C. Paulin-Mohring (Eds.), Types for Proofs and Programs. Proceedings, 1996. VIII, 373 pages. 1998.

Vol. 1513: C. Nikolaou, C. Stephanidis (Eds.), Research and Advanced Technology for Digital Libraries. Proceedings, 1998. XV, 912 pages. 1998.

Vol. 1514: K. Ohta,, D. Pei (Eds.), Advances in Cryptology – ASIACRYPT'98. Proceedings, 1998. XII, 436 pages. 1998.

Vol. 1515: F. Moreira de Oliveira (Ed.), Advances in Artificial Intelligence. Proceedings, 1998. X, 259 pages. 1998. (Subseries LNAI).

Vol. 1516: W. Ehrenberger (Ed.), Computer Safety, Reliability and Security. Proceedings, 1998. XVI, 392 pages. 1998.

Vol. 1517: J. Hromkovič, O. Sýkora (Eds.), Graph-Theoretic Concepts in Computer Science. Proceedings, 1998. X, 385 pages. 1998.

Vol. 1518: M. Luby, J. Rolim, M. Serna (Eds.), Randomization and Approximation Techniques in Computer Science. Proceedings, 1998. IX, 385 pages. 1998.

Vol. 1520: M. Maher, J.-F. Puget (Eds.), Principles and Practice of Constraint Programming - CP98. Proceedings, 1998. XI, 482 pages. 1998.

Vol. 1521: B. Rovan (Ed.), SOFSEM'98: Theory and Practice of Informatics. Proceedings, 1998. XI, 453 pages. 1998.

Vol. 1522: G. Gopalakrishnan, P. Windley (Eds.), Formal Methods in Computer-Aided Design. Proceedings, 1998. IX, 529 pages. 1998.

Vol. 1524: G.B. Orr, K.-R. Müller (Eds.), Neural Networks: Tricks of the Trade. VI, 432 pages. 1998.

Vol. 1526: M. Broy, B. Rumpe (Eds.), Requirements Targeting Software and Systems Engineering. Proceedings, 1997. VIII, 357 pages. 1998.

Vol. 1529: D. Farwell, L. Gerber, E. Hovy (Eds.), Machine Translation and the Information Soup. Proceedings, 1998. XIX, 532 pages. 1998. (Subseries LNAI).

Vol. 1531: H.-Y. Lee, H. Motoda (Eds.), PRICAI'98: Topics in Artificial Intelligence. XIX, 646 pages. 1998. (Subseries LNAI).

Vol. 1096: T. Schael, Workflow Management Systems for Process Organisations. Second Edition. XII, 229 pages. 1998.